Beginning Java and Flex

Migrating Java, Spring, Hibernate, and Maven Developers to Adobe Flex

Filippo di Pisa

Apress®

Beginning Java™ and Flex: Migrating Java, Spring, Hibernate, and Maven Developers to Adobe Flex

ISBN-13 (pbk): 978-1-4302-2385-6

ISBN-13 (electronic): 978-1-4302-2386-3

Printed and bound in the United States of America 9 8 7 6 5 4 4 3 2 1

President and Publisher: Paul Manning
Lead Editor: Tom Welsh
Technical Reviewer: Bradford Taylor
Editorial Board: Clay Andres, Steve Anglin, Mark Beckner, Ewan Buckingham, Gary Cornell,
    Jonathan Gennick, Jonathan Hassell, Michelle Lowman, Matthew Moodie, Duncan Parkes,
    Jeffrey Pepper, Frank Pohlmann, Douglas Pundick, Ben Renow-Clarke, Dominic Shakeshaft,
    Matt Wade, Tom Welsh
Project Manager: Debra Kelly
Copy Editor: Sharon Terdeman
Compositor: Tricia Bronkella
Indexer: Ann Rogers and Ron Strauss
Artist: April Milne
Cover Designer: Anna Ishchenko

Distributed to the book trade worldwide by Springer-Verlag New York, Inc., 233 Spring Street, 6th Floor, New York, NY 10013. Phone 1-800-SPRINGER, fax 201-348-4505, e-mail orders-ny@springer-sbm.com, or visit http://www.springeronline.com.

For information on translations, please e-mail info@apress.com, or visit http://www.apress.com.

Apress and friends of ED books may be purchased in bulk for academic, corporate, or promotional use. eBook versions and licenses are also available for most titles. For more information, reference our Special Bulk Sales–eBook Licensing web page at http://www.apress.com/info/bulksales.

The source code for this book is available to readers at http://www.apress.com. A "live" version of the source code is maintained by the author at https://filippodipisa.svn.cvsdude.com/apress_flexjava/archive/. (Username: apressapress, Password: FlexAndJava).

I dedicate this book to my father, Pino, my mother, Raffaella, my sister, Beatrice, and my wife, Soledad, the most important people in my life.

Contents at a Glance

Contents

About the Author

■ **Filippo di Pisa** fell in love with IT in 1983, when his auntie Maria Rosa gave him one of the first home computers on the market—the Texas Instruments TI-99/4A—for Christmas. After passing through the Sinclair Spectrum and Commodore era at the age of 24, he started his first IT company assembling PCs. Then he rode the new economy bubble launching various dot-coms—always software driven. Partly for business reasons, but largely because of a passion for programming and software engineering, he learned many high-productivity technologies such as Java, Spring, Hibernate, Acegi Security, ActionScript, Flex, ColdFusion, Fusebox, JavaScript, and Perl. Filippo is now a London-based consultant working for a number of household names in the UK market. Since growing up in Bologna (Italy), he has lived in Milan, Madrid, and Barcelona. He married Soledad in Ibiza on June 27, 2009.

About the Technical Reviewer

■ **Bradford Taylor** is an Architect for the Dallas-based business and technology consulting firm Credera. He has more than 13 years of experience in Java Enterprise Application Development and has been developing Flex/Spring applications for the past 4 years. Most recently he has been helping develop the Open Source E-Commerce framework Broadleaf Commerce.

Bradford has been involved in a variety of projects, including e-commerce, company portals and Flex applications. While at Credera, he has worked on The Container Store's implementation of Broadleaf Commerce. He has also helped Pursuant re-architect its Unifyer application, wrote the latest implementation of Truthcasting, worked with Blockbuster on enhancements to its e-commerce platform, and made enhancements to its Silverlight Movie browsing application.

Before his work at Credera, Bradford consulted at Neiman Marcus to create user applications to work with its customer data mart. He started his career at Nextel, where he worked on the company portal and developed Nextel's internet application for phone resellers. He has worked with banks, the Department of Defense, major retailers, and small companies to help develop both Java and Flash/Flex applications to meet their business needs.

Acknowledgments

I dedicate this book to my father, Pino, my mother, Raffaella, and my sister, Beatrice, who have stood by me through my whole crazy life.

I have many people to thank for their support on this book, but the one person I would really like to acknowledge is my wife, Soledad. For the past six months she has watched TV using a headset, or just reading the subtitles, so as not to disturb me in my nightly writing.

The second person without whom this book could not have been written is my colleague and friend Chris Seal. He helped me a lot, reading chapter after chapter, making suggestions from the project management point of view and improving my Italian-English. Thanks Chris!

I would also like to thank the fantastic Apress team who believed in me while I was writing this book, and provided excellent support in authoring and the technical aspect. In particular, I am really pleased to have worked with Steve Anglin, Tom Welsh, Debra Kelly, Bradford Taylor, Sharon Terdeman, and Matthew Moodie. Thanks a lot!

A special thanks also to my agent and friend Shervin Rahmani from explorerec.com who believed in me from the beginning and introduced my consulting services to some of the UK's top-name companies.

Filippo di Pisa

Introduction

Over the past few years, the now open source Adobe Flex Framework has been adopted by the Java community as the preferred framework for Java RIAs using Flash for the presentation layer. Flex helps Java developers build and maintain expressive web and desktop applications that deploy consistently on most web browsers and a growing number of mobile devices.

Beginning Java and Flex describes new, simpler, and faster ways to develop enterprise RIAs. This book is not only for Java or Flex developers but for all web developers who want to increase their productivity and the quality of their development.

In this book I will show you how to develop using the most popular Java lightweight frameworks such as Spring and Hibernate, using Flex and ActionScript 3 as the view layer. Once you have mastered this new development frontier, including concepts like Dependency Injection (DI) and Object Relationship Management (ORM), you will very likely want to use them for all your projects. Flex and Java are becoming very popular for both business and interactive applications, and they can open doors to the different branches of software development such as gaming, finance, advertising, and desktop applications of all kinds.

Who This Book Is For

If you are a developer who wants to use Java and Flex together, then this book is for you! This is especially so if you are any of the following.

- An ActionScript/Flash developer–You really should read this book because it will show you how best to use Java in your applications. Learning Java is a great way of immersing yourself in the latest software engineering patterns and frameworks.

- A Java developer–If you are a Java developer and know about Enterprise JavaBeans (EJBs), I really suggest you should think about using POJOs and Java frameworks such as Spring and Hibernate. By reading this book you will also pick up Flex, which puts the power of Flash into your presentation layer. Learning Flex will bring you into the world of Adobe and Flash, which promises to become increasingly important. With CS5, the next release of Flash, Adobe promises that we will be able to write ActionScript applications and compile them to native Objective-C ready to run on the iPhone!

- A Web developer–If you are using languages such as PHP or Cold Fusion, please consider switching to Java lightweight frameworks. I guarantee that once you have mastered them your productivity will soar, and–thanks to Java–the quality of your code will get better too. For any web developer, learning Flex is a must even if you are already an Ajax or JavaFX guru. And along with Flex and ActionScript 3 you will also pick up knowledge of Flash, which at the time of this writing is everywhere.

The Book

This book has been designed to help you in three ways.

1. First, it gives you an easily understood overview of the different technologies that we are going to use.
2. Then it shows you how to set up your development environment.
3. With all the prerequisites taken care of, you learn how to use each framework in turn, starting with Spring and moving on to Hibernate, then BlazeDS, then Flex, and finally putting everything together using Maven.

Here is a brief summary of what each chapter deals with.

Chapter 1 introduces you to the technologies that we are going to use, including Java, Flex, Spring, and Hibernate. It also sums up the benefits of object-oriented programming over procedural or scripting languages, and the strengths of a lightweight programming approach.

Chapter 2 introduces the sample application that we are going to use in this book and its architecture.

Chapter 3 shows you how to set up all the development tools you will need. While reasonably straightforward, this could turn out to be a painful, annoying, and time-consuming process unless you do it right. It can take a lot of time and effort to configure a complex development environment, but it really makes a difference once you have it up and running smoothly.

Chapter 4 covers the most important aspects of the Spring framework. You will learn the key concepts of DI and Inversion of Control (IoC) and how to configure Spring and inject beans into the Spring IoC container using both XML configuration and Java annotations.

Chapter 5 demonstrates how to create a Java EE data-driven application using both JDBC and ORM frameworks. I will show you the Data Access Object (DAO) pattern architecture and the difference between using "plain old JDBC" and Spring JDBC to connect to a database. Then I will explain the value of using Hibernate and Spring instead of the Spring JDBC and introduce transactions, which play an important role in Java EE development.

Chapter 6 shows you how to secure a Java application using the Spring Security framework (formerly Acegi Security). You will see how Spring Security delegates all requests to filters added by default into the Spring Security filter chain stack. Then I will show you how to add a custom authentication filter into the filter chain stack, replacing the default one. Finally, I will set out the different authentication processes using databases, LDAP repositories, and static values.

Chapter 7 gives you a complete overview of the Flex framework and the Flex Builder IDE. I will explain how to create and compile a Flex project using the Flex Builder Eclipse plug-in. Then you will learn how to listen for and dispatch Flex events, create custom components, use external CSS files, data binding, control Flash MovieClips, and more. This chapter takes you through all the concepts that I think are fundamental for starting to develop using Flex.

Chapter 8 shows you the most important ways to structure data on the Flex client and to access data on a remote server. First, I will show you how to bind ActionScript data collection to ActionScript DataGrid components and how to create a real-time search into the collection using filters. Next, I will create a Java application that provides a list of users through servlets. The Flex client will retrieve the XML using the HTTPService component. Finally, I will show you how to use the Flex RemoteObject component.

Chapter 9 introduces the BlazeDS server. You will learn how to retrieve and send data from a Flex application to a Java application and how to exchange real-time messages among different clients using the BlazeDS server.

Chapter 10 puts it all together–Spring, Hibernate, BlazeDS, and Flex. We will create a Flex-Spring-Hibernate project using the Flex-Spring-Hibernate Maven archetype. The archetype creates the entire project directory structure containing all the Spring, Hibernate, and BlazeDS configuration and properties files. It also adds all the packages usually needed for this kind of application using the Model View Controller (MVC) and DAO patterns. In this chapter, I cover all the most important aspects of Flex-Spring-Hibernate-Maven development. You can reuse the same archetype to start your own project, and you'll see how your developer productivity will quickly increase.

Java and Flex let you create amazing applications using object-oriented languages and the latest software engineering techniques, making you not just a better developer but also a better software engineer.

■ ■ ■

CHAPTER 1

Developing with Java and Flex

Two of the most difficult decisions for a project manager, CIO, or developer are which platform to target and which language to use. Books have been dedicated to the relative merits of one language over another and the options are much more complex than you might think. While a developer may have a preference, based on his own experiences or selfish desires, the project may be best served by different choices.

And there are many available. The IT/developer world is constantly changing. During the last 15 years, many languages have found and lost favor, while seemingly "dead" languages such as Ruby have experienced a resurgence. (In Ruby's case, this is due to the arrival of the Rails framework). I expect this trend to continue and that the life of a developer will be one of constant evolution.

To survive in today's market, developers need to learn more than one language. However, they also need to be able to choose which is best for a particular endeavor, which can sometimes be just as difficult. In the next sections, I'm going to discuss the choices I made for this book.

Why Java?

I am not a Java fanatic, and I don't want to create a polemic saying that Java is better than C# or vice versa. My view is that every language has its place and has a market, especially since so much effort involves working with existing applications and code.

A nontechnical manager I worked with used to advise using "the best tool for the job." The best example from my past is when I had to create a Windows application that worked with iTunes via COM objects. I felt that C# would be the fastest, so C# is what I used.

I do believe that enterprise Web applications are better served by using Java. This is partly due to the hosting platforms Java runs on and the lack of dependencies on operating environments like .NET.

Developers should enjoy programming in Java and are often surprised at how fast they can obtain results. Studies have consistently shown that switching to the Java platform increases programmer efficiency. Java is a simple and elegant language that has a well-designed and intuitive set of APIs. Programmers write cleaner code with a lower bug count when compared with other languages, which in turn reduces development time.

Java is certainly more difficult to learn than scripting languages such as PHP, ColdFusion, and the like. Still, once you have mastered Java, you will find there is no comparison for writing stable, scalable enterprise applications.

PHP and ColdFusion are excellent languages, and possibly even too successful. The problem with these two languages, so common in Web environments, is not that they are not powerful enough but that they make it too easy to code poorly and still get usable results. They forgive a lot of mistakes. This has meant that too many developers write bad code, just because they can get away with it. Too often, though, while they do get usable results, their code is not stable or scalable.

Of course, there is plenty of badly written Java code, too. However, in Java, before you are actually able to do anything, you must at least know the basics of object-oriented programming, data types, serialization, unit testing, and so forth.

So while there is bad code in Java, you don't tend to get really bad code that works— unlike what you see in many ColdFusion or PHP applications.

I've been developing for many years (some would say too many!) and I am constantly striving to use the best technologies available. In my opinion, at the moment the best technologies are Java and lightweight programming (which I'll discuss later in the chapter).

Why ActionScript?

A lot of developers think of ActionScript (AS) simply as a scripting language for Flash animation and for attaching scripts on the timeline.

Well, it's not!

At least ActionScript 3 (AS3), which arrived with Flash Player 9, isn't and should in no way be confused with earlier versions of ActionScript. It is a completely new language and a whole new virtual machine, with an ability to build Web applications and games that are like nothing else in the marketplace.

With Adobe AS3, you can do so much more than with Ajax and JavaScript. It is more efficient, and elegant, and without the bizarre restrictions of what works and what doesn't. Furthermore, AS3 is cross-platform, which is crucial in today's diverse environment (Mac OS, Windows and Linux), and cross-browser without too much hassle. AS3 supports regular expressions, binary sockets, remote data access, X-Y-Z axis manipulation, 3D drawing, 3D effects, audio mixing, peer-to-peer (P2P) communication and more. AS3 is compiled in a totally different bytecode from its predecessor. Flash Player 9 and Flash Player 10 both contain two virtual machines for backward compatibility with all AS releases.

Adobe Flex, a software development kit for creating applications based on Flash, has added a new dimension. It allows you to develop amazing user interfaces (UI) and rich Internet applications (RIA) in an elegant way while using Java design patterns and server-side capabilities.

Why Java and ActionScript Together?

If you are already an AS developer, you may be asking yourself why you should bother to learn Java, especially as Flex and AS allow you to use any number of server-side technologies and Web services.

On the other hand if you are a Java developer, you may be thinking—AS and Flex are still scripting languages, and Ajax with Spring MVC Swing or other Java frameworks work, so why bother? (MVC is a complete design pattern that I'll cover in Chapter 5.)

The fact is, even aside from Java's stability, elegance, and performance, the frameworks that Java has at its disposal greatly improve the software engineering productivity cycle. And Flex and Java together allow the developer to build very complex and well-presented applications in very quick time frame.

Furthermore, server frameworks like BlazeDS allow you to connect to back-end distributed data and push data in real time to Adobe Flex and Adobe AIR applications. The results can be staggering. This means you can work with Java objects directly within your Flex application and vice versa.

You can use the power of Java for server-side business logic, and the AS3 API to create a fantastic UI, games, video streaming applications, and much more. Moreover, Flex and AS are not JavaScript competitors; you need to use both to obtain the best results for your RIA applications.

Flex provides different APIs and libraries to use JavaScript, Ajax, and certain browser features. The only negative that I see in both Flex/AS3 and Java is the steep learning curve for scripters. And that is exactly why I have written this book!

Programming Using Lightweight Frameworks

A framework is a basic conceptual structure used to address complex issues. In software programming, the term commonly denotes code that is generic in function but can be overridden by user code using specific functionality. Frameworks can be similar to software libraries and they share many common characteristics, such as being reusable abstractions of code wrapped in an API. One difference with libraries is that the flow of control is dictated by the framework and not the caller.

In the past few years, there have been a lot of frameworks built in the Java community using plain old Java objects (POJO). A POJO is "plain" in the sense that it is not a JavaBean, an Enterprise JavaBean, or anything of that sort; it's just an ordinary object.

■ **Note** An Enterprise JavaBean is not a single class but a representative of an entire component model. The core principle shared by all lightweight enterprise Java frameworks is the use of plain old Java objects (POJOs) for the data access and business logic.

Lightweight technologies have evolved due in large part to a "developer rebellion" against the heavyweight and cumbersome EJB 2.1 (and earlier). Lightweight frameworks have the stated aim of making developers more productive and their applications less error-prone. This is achieved by removing the rigid EJB 2.1 infrastructure classes and interfaces and the "over the top" XML deployment descriptors. (Lightweight, by the way, means light load, not soft or weak.) Lightweight frameworks promote better and cleaner applications through better architecture. They are easier to reuse, which saves time and money.

Hibernate, for example, is a lightweight ORM (Object-relational Mapping) framework that can be great for implementing business and persistence logic. It allows interaction between the database and Java. For example, you can generate your database schema directly from your Java classes, and vice versa.

In this book I have chosen to use the most popular and stable Java and AS frameworks for creating business and media web applications, namely:

- Spring (a lightweight container)

- Hibernate (the most popular ORM)

Benefits of Lightweight Frameworks

When you have to develop an enterprise application, you must decide on the best language and the correct development methodology. There are 2 main approaches to developing an application—procedural and object-oriented (OO). The procedural approach organizes the code by manipulating data with functions. This style of programming dominated software development for years, implemented by very popular languages such as C, Pascal and others.

The object-oriented method organizes code around objects that have relationships and collaborations with other objects, making the application easier to understand, maintain, extend, and test than with a procedural design.

Despite the benefits of object-oriented design, most Web applications, including Java EE applications, are written in procedural style. Web languages such as PHP and Cold Fusion haven't supported OO design until the latest releases, and Java EE itself encourages developers to write procedural code because of EJB, a standard architecture for writing distributed business applications.

EJB is a heavyweight framework that provides a large number of useful services like declarative transactions, security management, and so forth. It was adopted enthusiastically by most Java developers, who had to abandon their OO skills to configure lots of XML, and write procedural Java code to build EJB components. For several years, EJB was the de facto standard— until the rise of POJO lightweight frameworks.

The goal of POJO is to support writing Java applications using standard OO design and patterns. EJB encouraged developers to write procedural code, thus losing the advantage of many of the best practices used for normal Java development. Other Web languages tried to follow the EJB architecture by concentrating development on a component base. Now both Java and other Web languages are moving back to OO design. However POJO alone is not sufficient in enterprise applications development, where you need security management, persistence objects, and all the other services implemented by the EJB framework.

The solution is to use POJO lightweight frameworks that are not as intrusive as EJB and significantly increase developer productivity. POJO lightweight frameworks provide services without requiring that the application classes implement any special interfaces. With lightweight frameworks you can write EE applications using an OO design, and later in this book I'll show you how to manage these libraries just by configuring an XML file.

Lightweight framework programming can save you lots of time, in particular through avoiding the need for lots of code and complex OO design patterns. However, before using Java and Flex lightweight programming, you need to have good OO design skills otherwise you will get into trouble. If your OO design skills are in need of refreshing, you may want to take a look at Java objects and Java design patterns before proceeding.

The lightweight frameworks that I use and describe in this book are Spring, Hibernate for Java, and Flex for AS and Flash. Using all of these together, you'll see how you can write fast and elegant code to produce amazing RIA applications.

In Table 1-1, I have summarized the differences between standard EJB, Web languages, and POJO approaches.

Table 1-1. *Differences in various progamming approaches*

Operation	Web Languages	EJB	POJO
Business logic	Procedural style	Procedural style	Object-oriented design
Database access	Odbc, Jdbc, Sql	JDBC/Entity beans	Persistence framework
Returning data to the view	Components	DTOs	Business objects
Application assembly	Most of the times architected by the developer	Explicit JNDI lookups	Dependency injection
Transaction management	-	EJB container	Spring framework
Security management	-	EJB container	Spring security

Introduction to Spring

Spring is a lightweight framework based on the Dependency Injection (DI) pattern. It is lightweight because Spring uses POJO, which makes it very powerful and very easy to extend or implement.

Spring's primary use is as a framework for enabling the use of Inversion of Control (IOC). It is also a powerful Java Enterprise application framework that provides a large number of features and services. Spring is initially a bit difficult to understand, but once mastered, you will see a great improvement in your productivity. For enterprise applications, Spring is an excellent tool because it is a complete, well-written, well-documented, scalable, and open source—with a lot of community support.

With Spring, you are able to inject all your classes directly into the container using an XML file. This means that the Spring container instantiates all classes and injects into others as defined by XML. You no longer have any dependency lookup problems.

Think of Spring as a container that assembles all your classes together and any part can easily be swapped out. Each part is just a plain Java object.

Without DI, you would have to create a layer that assembles everything, and probably you would also have to change the code for any environment because of the code embedded relationship between the different classes.

```
public class UserService (){

    private UserDao userDao;

    public UserService(){
        userDao = new UserDao();
    }
}
```

With DI, you solve this problem because you have to create a parameterized version of the same code, allowing it to accept injected classes

```
public class UserService (){

    private UserDao userDao;

    public UserService(UserDao userDao){
        userDao = userDao;
    }
}
```

But Spring is not just an IOC framework (though everything is based on the IOC framework). Spring provides services and resources for database connection pools, database transaction, security, messaging, caching, and much more. To manage the security of all your application with groups, roles, and permissions, for example, you only have to inject some classes into the Spring security framework.

Spring supports all major data access technologies such as JDBC, Hibernate, JPA, and Ibatis. For example, to query a database you don't have to create the code to manage the connection, process the result set, and release the connection itself. All these processes are handled by Spring.

The typical architecture of a Spring application comprises a presentation layer that uses a service layer to communicate to the data access layer, which can deal with database, mail servers, or any other data containers, as shown in Figure 1-1.

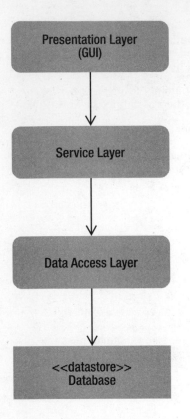

Figure 1-1. Architecture of a Spring application

The presentation layer contains all views and components that are concerned with the presentation of the application to the user. Typically, the view is implemented with JSP or a similar technology; in this book we'll use Flex.

The service layer represents the business logic of the application. All operations pass through the service layer. You can have different service layers for different services, such as UserServices, MailServices, and so on. In the upcoming chapters, you will learn how to expose the Java Spring service layer to Flex/AS, and to allow the presentation layer to use it.

The data access layer provides all methods to save, send, and retrieve data. Usually the data access layer works with the database, mail servers, .xml, or the file system.

As mentioned previously, Spring is based on a IoC container where all objects(beans) are instantiated. To help you understand this concept better, I'm going to use a basic IOC Flex container I wrote to inject different .xml files to different service layers. My application needed to provide different content to the view, such as video, images, and text, and everything is based on different XML files. At the time, I had to create the application as quickly as possible, and I had other applications to create, so the more code I could reuse and the faster I could deliver the project, the better I would be.

My goal was to create a container where I could inject the .xml files and relate them to the different content factories of the application. I copied precisely the Spring .xml syntax to make it readable by the Spring developer. Below is the application .xml file to show you how I injected the .xml files to the different content factories.

```
<beans>
  <bean id="XMLArticlesList" claz="com.publicis.iocframework.core.XMLLoader"↵
path="articlesList.XML" />
```

XMLLoader is a core class of my IOC framework that loads XML from a given path.

```
<bean id="articlesService"
claz="com.publicis.articles.business.ArticlesServiceImpl">
  <constructorarg value="articlesDao" ref="articlesDao" />
</bean>
```

ArticlesServiceImpl is the application service layer, and you have to pass into the default constructor the object type articlesDao.

```
<bean id="articlesDao" claz="com.publicis.articles.dao.XML.ArticleDaoXML">
    <constructorarg value="XMLArticlesList" />
</bean>
```

ArticlesDaoXML is the data access layer and you have to pass into the constructor an object XML type.

As you can see, I am able to inject classes and manage their dependencies directly from an XML file without recompiling and changing my code. Moreover, I can reuse the XmlLoader core class to load into the IOC container any XML file and reuse it for a different application. For example, I could pass the XmlArticlesList object to another object simply by adding a new XML tag like this:

```
<bean id="mediaDao" claz="com.publicis.articles.dao.XML.mediaDaoXML">
    <constructorarg value="XMLArticlesList" />
```

Dependency injection frameworks exist for a number of platforms and languages, such as AS, Flex, Java, C++, PHP, ColdFusion, Microsoft, .NET, Ruby, Python and Perl. Below is a table with the most popular IOC frameworks for AS, Flex, and Java.

Table 1-2. Dependency injection frameworks

Language/platform	DI Framework
AS	Spring ActionScript (formerly Prana Framework)
AS	di-as3
AS	Syringe
Flex	Flicc
Flex	Mate
Flex	Swiz

Java	Google Guice
Java	JBoss microcontainer
Java	Spring framework
Java	Java 5 / EJB 3
Java	Spring ME

Introduction to Hibernate

Hibernate is another very popular lightweight POJO Java framework. Before I discuss Hibernate, let me introduce you to object-relational mapping (ORM) frameworks.

Many software applications use relational databases to store data, including such products as Oracle, MySql, Microsoft SQL Server, PostgreSql, and others. Various frameworks, such as JDBC or ORM, are used to retrieve data from such databases. An ORM framework provides a service to map the relational model to the OO model. Hibernate is an ORM framework that has become a natural choice for working with POJO (though it supports EJB 3.0 as well).

In practice, Hibernate maps your database tables to classes. A standard ORM also provides persistence objects, which means it will persist data for you so that you don't have to write tedious SQL statements using JDBC. For example, to insert or update data into the database, you can use the method save(entity), which saves you a lot of time compared with writing the full SQL INSERT or UPDATE.

The table mapped in the OO model is called an entity and all entities are persistent in a Hibernate session. You will learn how to inject this session into the Spring container and also how to use Spring Hibernate Templates to make your life easier. After mastering these techniques, you'll see how easy it is to work with databases and OO, and if you have worked with SQL, JDBC and other technologies before, I think you will be pleasantly surprised.

Hibernate also provides Hibernate Query Language (HQL), in which you can write code that's similar to SQL to retrieve data from a persisted object. For example, imagine that you have mapped the database table users to the entity User, and you want to select a user by his id. To do so, you can write an HQL query like this:

```
int id = 2;
String hql='from User u where u.id = :id ';
Query query = session.createQuery(hql);
query.setInt(id);
User user = (User)query.uniqueResult();
```

Hibernate works with a large number of databases such as Oracle, MySQL, MS SQL server, Sybase, IBM DB2, and others. You just have to tell Hibernate the database dialect you want to use, to ensure that Hibernate uses the correct and fully optimized SQL for that database. In the next chapter, you will learn how to set the dialect for MySQL and the other databases.

To round off this Hibernate introduction, let me use a UML diagram, shown in Figure 1-2, to illustrate a simple physical relational database mapped to OO classes.

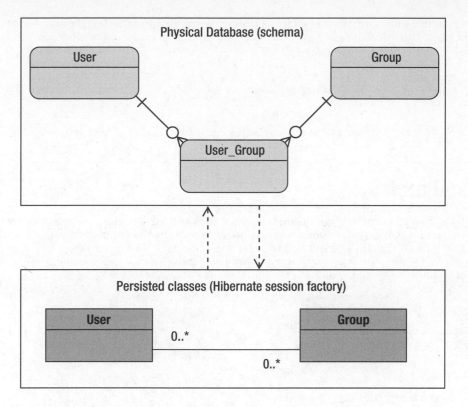

Figure 1-2. Database tables mapped to object-oriented classes.

The Benefits of Hibernate

After reading the previous sections, you probably already recognize the many advantages that ORM frameworks and persistence objects offer. We talked about the method `save` that allows you to insert/update data into the database, avoiding the tedious INSERT or UPDATE SQL statements. Hibernate saves you typing in the tedious SQL, though it allows you to use SQL when necessary.

Another benefit of Hibernate is that it never updates the database if the object state hasn't changed. In hand-coded JDBC, it is very common to have to write code to avoid this very problem. When a user presses the submit button on a form, even without making any changes, JDBC doesn't know so it updates the database anyway.

Hibernate also provides a very efficient caching system. You can cache persistent objects and enable cluster cache to memory or the local disk.

With Hibernate, you can work with different database types just by changing the property `dialect`. This means you can use your application with a different database by just changing one line of code. Sometimes, however, you will still need to write SQL to retrieve data using complex queries. These are hard to formulate with just the Hibernate filters, so Hibernate offers you a choice. Either you can work with Hibernate's query language (HQL), which allows you to query your persisted objects with a language similar to SQL, or you can revert to standard SQL usage, which forces Hibernate to use normal SQL.

A key advantage of Hibernate from my point of view is its integration with Spring. In fact, Spring provides a Hibernate Template that simplifies the use of Hibernate. The Hibernate Template provides convenience methods that enable the developer to write less code, as you can see from the following:.

```
public void remove(User user) {
        getHibernateTemplate().delete(user);
}
```

Hibernate also provides hooks so Spring can manage sessions and transactions in a transparent and elegant way.

Introduction to BlazeDS

Now we're ready to look at another important piece for connecting Spring services to the user interface—BlazeDS, a technology for remotely connecting to Java objects and for sending messages between clients. As Adobe points out, BlazeDS allows you to connect to back-end distributed data and push data in real time to Adobe Flex and Adobe AIR rich Internet applications (RIA). You can think of Blaze as a bridge between Adobe Flex (the presentation layer) and Java Spring Services (the business logic layer), as shown in Figure 1-3. Figure 1-4 outlines the BlazeDS server architecture.

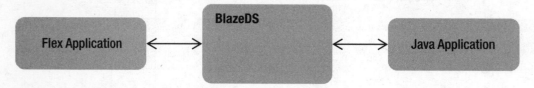

Figure 1-3. BlazeDS acts as a bridge between Flex and Java.

If you are an AS developer, you may have developed many applications using XML or SOAP. Adopting BlazeDS means your application will load data up to 10 times faster than with those text-based formats, as it employs an AMF (Action Message Format) data transfer format. (AMF is based on SOAP. If you're from an AS and Flash background, you should be familiar with AMF; if you're from a Java background, you just need to know AMF is much faster than standard SOAP in this environment).

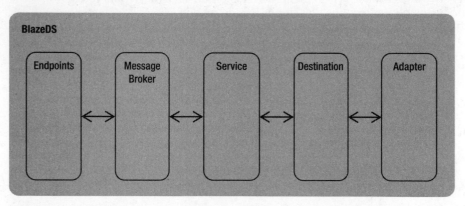

Figure 1-4. The architecture of a BlazeDS server.

BlazeDS implements real time messaging and you can have multiple clients connected to the same server. BlazeDS pushes data over HTTP so there is no problem with firewall configuration. The BlazeDS technology is free under an open source license, which means that you can extend it or use it with different client technologies.

BlazeDS vs. Adobe LiveCycle Data Services

If you are already involved with Flex development, you may be aware that many users are confused about the differences between Flex Data Services, Adobe LiveCycle Data Services ES, Adobe LiveCycle Data Services DS, and BlazeDS. In this book, I will cover only BlazeDS, as it is open source, and it is powerful with strong performance. However, I want to clear up the confusion and give you an understanding of the big picture or maybe big puzzle that is Adobe Data Services.

Part of the confusion is relatively easy to solve—Flex Data Services was renamed to Adobe LiveCycle Data Services, commonly referred as LiveCycle DS. In LiveCycle ES, the ES means Enterprise Suite, and this is an SOA-based platform that provides many built-in services like sending and receiving emails, calling web services, executing SQL, uploading files via FTP, and so forth. You can add new services using Java POJOs, and on the top of the base platform, there are solution components like Adobe LiveCycle Forms ES, Adobe LiveCycle PDF Generator ES, Adobe LiveCycle Digital Signatures ES, and more. One of the solution components is Adobe LiveCycle DS, which is basically a subset of Adobe Life Cycle Data Services ES.

There is a free version of Adobe LiveCycle DS called DS Express, which is restricted to a single application and a single CPU, so it can't be used for production work. Finally, there is BlazeDS, which is open source and provides a subset of functionalities of LiveCycle DS. Table 1-3 shows the substantial differences between LiveCycle DS and BlazeDS. (Source `http://sujitreddyg.wordpress.com/2008/01/31/BlazeDS-and-lcds-feature-difference/`). For more details on the features, please visit `http://www.adobe.com/products/livecycle/dataservices/features.html`.

Table 1-3. Differences between LiveCycle DS and BlazeDS.

Features	LiveCycleDS	BlazeDS
Data management Services		
Client-Server synchronization	x	
Conflict resolution	x	
Data paging	x	
SQL adapter	x	
Hibernate adapter	x	
Document Services		
LiveCycle remoting	x	
RIA-to-PDF conversion	x	

Enterprise-Class Flex application services		
Data access/remoting	x	x
Proxy service	x	x
Automated testing support	x	
Software clustering	x	x
Web tier compiler	x	
Enterprise Integration		
WSRP generation	x	
Ajax data services	x	x
Flex-Ajax bridge	x	x
Runtime configuration	x	x
Open adapter architecture	x	x
JMS adapter	x	x
Server-side component integration	x	x
ColdFusion integration	x	
Offline Application Support		
Offline data cache	x	
Local message queuing	x	
Real - Time Data		
Publish and Subscribe messaging	x	x
Real -time data quality of service	x	
RTMP tunneling	x	

Introduction to Flex

In the previous sections, we talked about Java POJO and lightweight frameworks programming, and also the bridge between the Java business logic to the presentation layer. We will present our data or media using Flex. Adobe defines Flex as a highly productive, free, open source framework for building and maintaining expressive web applications that deploy consistently on all major browsers, desktops, and operating systems. However, as with all marketing talk, I bet that still leaves you somewhat perplexed. Maybe if you are an ActionScriptor, you think Flex is just a set of components for bad developers!

On the other hand, if you are a Java developer, maybe you think Flex is merely a scripting language like JavaScript that you can use to build a Flash micro site.

The more correct answer in my view is that Flex is a framework that sits on top of AS3. It allows you to develop Flash driven-business and media applications. Flex was built for software developers with object-oriented skills to enable them to write stable Flash applications. Flex is very similar to Java Swing (a framework for creating graphical user interfaces (GUIs) for applications and applets in Java). A plus for Flex is that it runs in Adobe Flash Player, meaning that you can deploy your application to all major browsers, desktops, and operating systems. Another plus is that Flex is AS, so you can develop GUIs, games, and amazing animations. Flex also has remote objects, so you can use your remote objects, such as Java objects, with your AS objects.

Flex can be a little frustrating at first, but give it time. Not all of its advantages are immediately apparent, but the more you use it, the more you will come to see the benefits. Chances are, you will end up using the Flex compiler even for a simple microsite. Why? Simply because you will see that is easier to debug, write code, compile, and it is also standard OO.

And remember—Flex is not MXML! The only real problem I see with Flex is an overuse of MXML, which is bad coding and often done by those without an appreciation of OO programming. *(MXML is an XML-based markup language originally from Macromedia. It was created for building the user interface, not the client business logic.)*

Relying too heavily on MXML causes applications to be unstable, whether due to bad architecture or bad code, and they are ultimately difficult to maintain. It's a far better practice to use AS for the business logic and keep MXML just for the view and some UI components.

■ **Note** The mindset you need to employ is that Flex is used for Rich Internet Applications, not Rich Web Applications. There isn't a clear line between RIAs and RWAs, but Flex is definitely on the RIA side of things in that you are building applications that are desktop-like but use the Internet for deployment ease and connectivity to services. This is in contrast to AJAX, which is more toward the RWA end of the spectrum in that it increases functionality and usage efficiency of web pages.

Flex vs. Ajax

Ajax stands for Asynchronous JavaScript and XML. It means that you can combine HTML, JavaScript, and XML to create client Web applications that can interact with a server asynchronously. In practical terms, it means your web page can load and send data to the server without needing to reload the page.

If you are coming from a Java POJO lightweight programming background, you may be wondering why you should have to learn a Flash-driven language when you already have thousands of productive Java frameworks. As I suggested earlier for the ActionScriptor, just give it a little time or one full project and you'll reap the benefits. I have developed a lot using JavaScript and Ajax, and while JavaScript is improving day by day, it is still a scripting language. It supports just simple linear animations and it is not a strongly typed OO language.

Flex also supports vector graphics natively while Ajax has only limited support. Flex includes cross-browser support, and much more. For example, debugging Flex is much easier than debugging JavaScript and if you fix something in one browser, you know it will be fixed in all browsers.

You can be much more productive with Flex, and produce code that is more elegant and maintainable. If you are coming from an OO environment, you will find Flex very easy to learn. If you are coming from scripting language background, Flex is likely to be harder than Ajax to learn, but you will ultimately be working in a much better environment. You will have a proper OO software design and reap all the benefits that this offers.

Flex, Flash Cs3, and ActionScript

Flex and Flash speak the same underlying technology and that is AS3. Flex was created with the aim of improving the RIA application development environment while providing a brand new set of components and a layout manager inspired by the Java Swing framework. Flex brings with it new server side connectivity classes and much more robust Flash remoting and V2 Components. The first version of Flex was more than just for RIA and UI development and a lot of Flash developers viewed Flex with suspicion.

With the second release Macromedia released the Flash Component Kit, a Flash component that allows to export Flash objects for Flex. Thanks to this component more Flash developers adopted Flex because the integration between Flash and Flex became simple. For example, with the Flash Component kit, it is very easy to export a Flash CS3 MovieClip as a Flex object.

With the Flex framework, you can create AS or Flex projects. The difference is that a Flex project includes the Flex.swc library with all the Flex components. Before you start an AS project, you should create a library or a project where the goal is just animation or graphics. Otherwise, it is better to first create a Flex project to be able to use the Flex layout managers and components, making the application/microsite much more scalable and manageable.

■ **Note** Flex doesn't mean MXML, and Flash doesn't mean AS, both are a layer on top of AS3.

In my view, Flash CS3 is going to evolve into a designer tool and is not for the serious developer. Flex3 is a robust application/microsite development tool, it is easy to integrate with BlazeDS, supports a real debugger, and unit stress testing, and thanks to HTTPService and other useful classes, the server-side connectivity is much cleaner and more robust, and it's a lot faster to load a simple file, such as an XML file.

It is also easier to create custom components and there are fantastic functionalities like states and view stack. I've been using Flash CS3 IDE for many years now and I don't see any value to continue to use it for coding. I use it just for design and static animation projects or movie clips.

Some developers have told me that with CS3 you can easily skin components and that it is better for building microsites. Flex not only provides the ability to use standard CSS style sheets, but thanks to a great Flash CS3 component called "Flex Skin Design Extension for Flash," you have the same functionality and can take advantage of everything else that Flex offers. To download the component, you will have to register with the Adobe web site, at

```
https://www.adobe.com/cfusion/entitlement/index.cfm?e=flex_skins
```

Once the component is installed, it opens Flash CS3 and you will see a new set of templates called Flex Skin Project (Template>Flex Skin) . I prefer to use the CSS style sheets but concede that sometimes it is faster and easier for a designer to use this good component.

ActionScript vs. MXML

MXML is an XML-based user interface markup language. MXML is translated to an AS3 class that is 100-percent compatible. It is the correct format to instantiate MXML classes via a new constructor. For example, you use the <mx:Button> tag to create an instance of the Button control using the following MXML statement:

```
<mx:Button id="myButton" label="I'm a button!"/>
```

That is exactly the same for the following AS code:

```
var myButton : Button = new Button();
myButton.label = "I'm a button!"
```

I prefer to use MXML just for the Views of the application because it is more readable for the designers and is easier to use with the layout managers and style sheets.

However, excessive use of MXML can cause code-decoupling and make code difficult to read and implement.

Introduction to UML

In previous sections I spoke about Java POJO lightweight frameworks programming, Flex, AS, and BlazeDS the bridge between Java and Flex. You should now have a rough idea of all the technologies that you will need to develop a new generation of RIAs.

Before presenting the sample applications and talking about the languages themselves, I want to introduce the Unified Modeling Language (UML) for planning and architecting the applications. UML is a standardized, general-purpose modeling language that combines the best techniques from data modeling, such as work flows, and entity relationship diagrams using various graphical techniques.

Most of the time, the decision to start a project without UML results from the mistaken belief that this will save time. But speaking from experience and a straw poll of project managers, the project will always take longer and go over budget without planning. It isn't just the development time but also testing, bug fixing, and ultimately deployment that is affected.

UML helps you to visualize the entire application before you enter the development phase and it should always be used, even with just a single developer. With UML you are able to define all processes, for both OO design and application requirements.

Using UML, you can design your approach before you get involved with the code, and if you are leading a team, you can easily organize the development—dividing the application in different parts and producing deliverables and check points. This will help you run your teams more effectively and have a better handle on the overall project. You are easily able to pinpoint the parts of code that you can reuse, and create reusable libraries for future projects. And you can visualize all the software requirements and check that all the pieces of the puzzle are there.

Basic Diagrams

At the center of UML there are many diagrams. In this book I'll cover just the most important ones:

- Use case
- Sequence
- Class
- Activity

Bear in mind that the diagrams are merely graphical windows into the model, which consists of all the elements composing your system.

Use case diagrams are very important in describing what a system does. With such diagrams, you can show an external party all cases where an actor is involved. You can relate one or more actors or many use cases.

A use case is a summary of the scenarios that comprise a single task or goal. For example, you can show an actor doing something in your application. In Figure 1-5, an actor (user) performs a login.

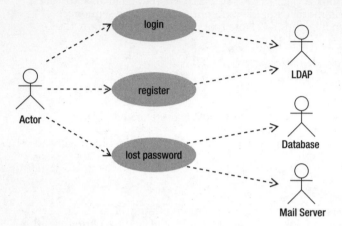

Figure 1-5. A user logs in.

Figure 1-6 shows a scenario where an actor makes reservations in a restaurant, orders dinner, and, finally, pays the bill.

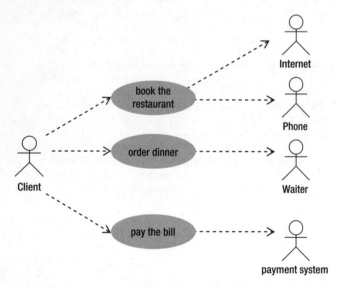

Figure 1-6. A restaurant diner pays the bill.

I use these use case diagrams to document all requirements and communicate with the client. I also use them with any other developer involved in the project to make the requirements clear. It is a very useful way to individuate the different classes and libraries.

Sequence diagrams describe all the operations and messages between the different objects involved in the scenario, organized by time. You can put more detail into your use case diagrams to more fully explain what is happening. For example, let's look at the previous use case where we had an actor/user who was logging in. Now we want to describe in more detail the different messages and sequences occurring between these two objects, as shown in Figure 1-7. Note that in a sequence diagram, the objects are listed from the left to the right.

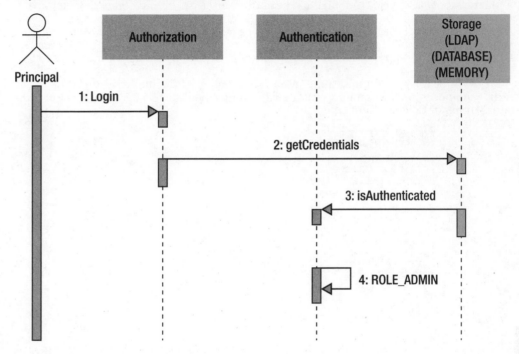

Figure 1-7. More details about what happens when a user logs in.

Activity diagrams are useful for describing processes. The most important elements of these diagrams are activities, actions, and decisions. An activity is a process being modeled; that is, something is being done. The activity is composed of actions that are all the steps of that activity. If we were to create an activity diagram related to the user logging in, for example, one activity would be to authenticate the user, and this would include a number of different actions, such as checkIfUserExists and getCredentials.

Activity diagrams have their roots in flowcharts so are quite familiar. Even a non-technical person should be able to follow one.

Class diagrams let you translate into code all of the objects, messages, processes and actions that you have described with the use case, sequence, and activities diagrams in order to start the development cycle. A class diagram describes classes and the relationships between them. Unlike the other diagrams, class diagrams are static and display just the interaction between classes, not processes or time. For example, I can use a class diagram to describe the relationships between users and groups, but not to describe the login process and actions.

A class diagram can show different kinds of relationships, like association, aggregation , composition, and generalization. Association is a basic relationship without any rules. A class can be associated to anotherone like a User class is associated to a Group class. Aggregation is a stronger version of the Associantion relationships, and indicates that a class owns another class. For example a class User owns his bank account. The composition relationship is even stronger than the aggregation one; they behave in the same way but the difference is that an the object that composes another object is part of the object composed, and if it is delete will be delete also the object related. Finally the relationship generalization indicates generalization throught interfaces or inheritance extending other classes. When you are going to implement generalization and inheritance try to see if the class "is a type" or "has a type" og the other class. A class Admin is a type of User, so we can or implement the interface User to the class Admin, or extend the class User with the class Admin. I prefer to use interfaces.

Each relationship can have a multiplicity, which means the number of the possible classes associated to another. For example a group may have many users, and translated into UML, this means that the class user has a relationship with multiplicity 1..*. Multiplicity can be a single number or a range of numbers.

Figure 1-8 shows three classes, Administrator, Author, and ContentEditor, implementing the interface User that composes the class group. Translated into simple English, this means that a user can be Administrator, Author or ContentEditor type.

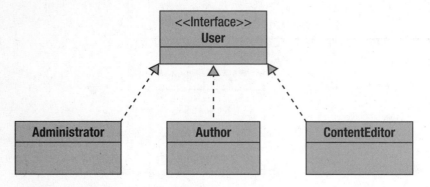

Figure 1-8. *Implementing the User interface.*

The class diagram is very important and enables you to split development of an application into different modules involving different people. Even if you are a solo developer, I suggest you use class diagrams, as they help you to organize all classes better. There are many tools that generate the stub code from the class diagram for languages such as AS and Java, so there are big benefits. Some tools keep the code synchronized with the diagrams, which means if a change occurs in the code, the diagram will change in consequence, which makes it easier to keep project managers and non-technical managers up-to-date.

If you are reluctant to spend the time to create a class diagram—if you think your OO design skills are strong enough—at least create the use case, activity, and sequence diagrams to map out the big picture. Without them you will get stuck at some point in the development cycle and spend more time bug fixing and finding solutions to finish the project than if you had used UML from the beginning.

Summary

This first chapter introduces you to the technologies that we are going to use in this book, including Java, Flex, Spring, and Hibernate, as well as the benefits of object-oriented programming over procedural or scripting languages, and of a lightweight programming approach.

In the next chapter, I will present the application that we are going to use as a demonstration and continue to use through subsequent chapters. This application will exercise all of technologies that are covered in this book. We will work through the sample application like a project, step by step, so it is easy to follow.

CHAPTER 2

Presenting the Sample Application

To explain all the technologies covered in this book, I am going to create a Flash database-driven application that uses the Adobe Flex, Spring, and Hibernate technologies and, as the Boy Scouts say, it is better to be prepared for the journey ahead.

The application will use two types of data sources: a normal database and a directory server that uses the Lightweight Directory Access Protocol (LDAP). By using two different data sources, we will be able to see how the application scales. Object-oriented (OO) design and patterns will allow us to adhere to the architecture and inject a different data provider without modifying any existing objects. To exercise the technologies involved in a very practical way, our application will create a User and Account Manager.

The goal of the application will be to allow users to manage their account details, and to allow administrators to manage groups and users. I know this is not a dazzling project, but it is a good place to start. And even without the need for animations or effects, you will see that it is still quite interesting from a software engineering perspective. We will move on to projects such as games and media-related software when we get further along; for now we will stick to a standard business application.

For simplicity's sake this application will have only two levels of permissions:

- Permission one, for users

- Permission two, for administrators

Technically speaking, we will assign two ROLES to the application itself called ROLE_USERS and ROLE_ADMIN, and we will assign these ROLES to the groups of users. For example, if a user belongs to the group Admin—associated with ROLE_ADMIN—he will be able to view and manage all users. If not, he can edit only his own details.

As I said in the previous chapter, the first step you should take in the development of a new application or project is to draw up a Unified Modeling Language (UML) diagram that outlines the workings of your application. Without UML, you risk getting bogged down in code and spending a lot of time making changes due to bugs and refactoring.

Before starting with the code, we will create all the UML. We need to understand all requirements of the application and to see how best to organize our objects and technologies. UML will also help us understand the development timings and the volume of work we'll need to do.

Architecture

To start, I want you to visualize the big picture of the User Manager, in terms of a UML Use Case diagram. In this diagram we will write down all the main use cases for the application. As you can see in Figure 2-1, there are many.

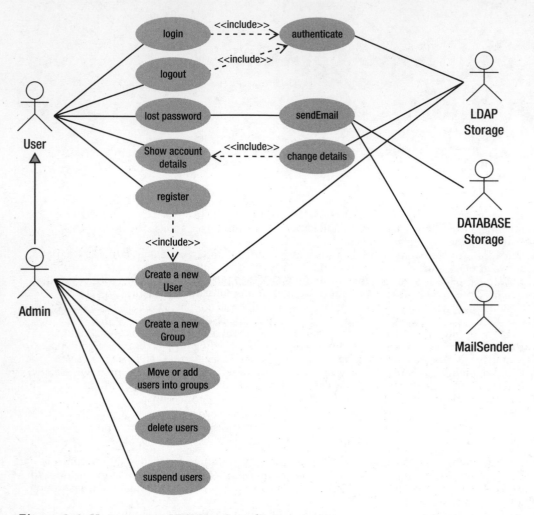

Figure 2-1. *User manager UML Use Case diagram*

In Figure 2-1 you can see five different actors, many cases, and some data managers. The human actors are the Users and the Admin, each with different roles. The users will be able to create a new account, log in, log out, recover a password, and update or change their details.

The Admin user can perform all user operations, plus create new users and groups, move users into groups, and delete or suspend users. The Admin is also a user, and in OO design you can say that the Admin object extends the User object, as shown in Figure 2-2.

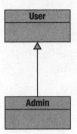

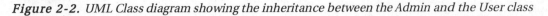

Figure 2-2. UML Class diagram showing the inheritance between the Admin and the User class

■ **Note** In Use Case diagrams the <<include>> relationship means that the use case is reusable.

That's the scenario in a nutshell—what our application is going to do. Now we have to decide how our application is going to do its job. In other words, we have to separate all messages between the different use cases.

For example, in Figure 2-1, we can see that actor Admin is able to add new Users, but we don't yet know the details of what we need to aim for. We will have to create a separate sequence diagram for each use case. Here's an example.

Figure 2-3 shows a sequence diagram that describes the lost password use case.

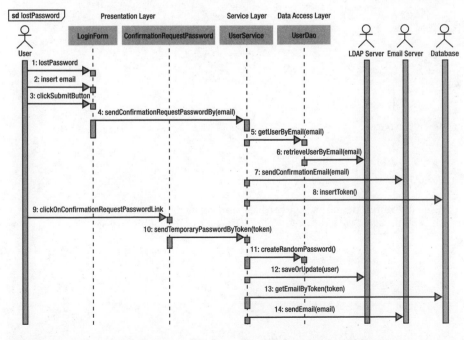

Figure 2-3. Sequence diagram that describes the lost password use case

As you can see, the user who has lost her password needs to insert her e-mail request and click the submit button. On submission, the form sends a message to the service layer called `userService,` which attempts to identify the user from the e-mail request inserted by the data access layer—userDao— into the directory server. If the user exists, the system will send a confirmation e-mail to that user to check if it was a legitimate request by the user. The system will then insert a token into the database that will match once the user clicks on the received link in the e-mail. The user must click on that link to receive a new temporary password.

Now you can complete sequence diagrams for all the use cases, and then you should create the class and activity diagrams.

If you are thinking that all these diagrams are just a waste of time, consider how much time you spend explaining what you are doing to all your stakeholders. For the layman, a picture really is worth a thousand words, and it makes people like business project managers happy to have something to put in their reports. Even more important is all the time, effort, and hair-pulling you'll save yourself.

For me, use case diagrams are the most important, closely followed by sequence and class diagrams. I generally create activity diagrams only if there are complex algorithms or processes to architect. In contrast, I don't even start to develop without a use case diagram, not even for a simple project. Use cases really help me to define all the client's requirements.

As you can see from the sequence diagram in Figure 2-3, our application will consist of a presentation layer, a service layer, and a data access layer. The presentation layer will be built using Flex; the service layer will be Java Spring; and the data access layer can be Hibernate, LDAP, or the like.

Figure 2-4 shows a typical model–view–controller (MVC) architectural pattern that allows you to divide the model (your data) from the controller (your business logic) and the view (the presentation layer).

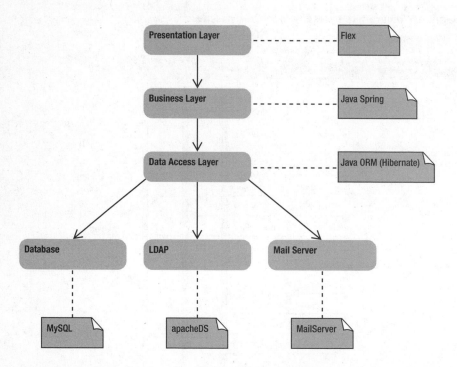

Figure 2-4. UML diagram showing the MVC architecture

The Presentation Layer

The presentation layer includes all the views and components needed for presenting data to the user. All screens, forms, animations, and pages are the province of the presentation layer. You could use various technologies such as Flex/ActionScript (AS), Javascript, Ajax, Java Swing, JSP, and more. For our user-manager sample application, I've chosen Flex/AS for the reasons previously discussed.

As you can see in Figure 2-4, the presentation layer communicates with the service layer, and that means all your application views will use methods provided by the service layer to manage data and server business logic.

As we discussed in the previous chapter, Flex (our presentation layer) talks to Java (our service and data access layer) through BlazeDS, the Java-based remoting message server. (See the introduction to BlazeDS in Chapter 1.)

The Service Layer

The service layer contains all the methods and operations that comprise the business logic of the application. Typically, the service layer provides business logic and data. For example, when the presentation layer retrieves data, it will do so through the service layer.

Figure 2-5 shows how the presentation layer accountForm creates a user, passes the user through the service layer (userService), and then saves the user into the database.

As you examine this diagram, you'll see the methods save(user) and saveOrUpdate(user) in both the service layer and data access layer. The advantage of this approach is that the service layer save method also encapsulates the method sendConfirmationEmail, without revealing the existence of the two DAOs, as shown at the following code:

```
public class UserServiceImpl implements UserService {

    private MailDao mailDao;

    private UserDao userDao;

    public void save(User user) {
        userDao.saveOrUpdate(user);
        mailDao.sendConfirmationEmail(user);
    }

}
```

In the service layer, you can encase different DAOs or other objects without needing to reveal their existence to the outside world.

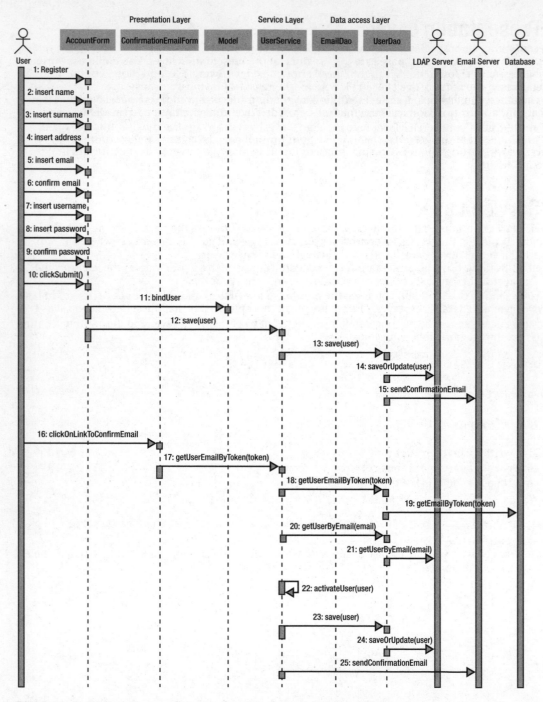

Figure 2-5. UML sequence diagram showing the account-creation process

The Data Access Layer

The data access layer provides all the operations you need to access the data. You can implement the data access layer as a database, file system, LDAP server, and more. The advantage of defining this layer is that you can shift from a database to the file system and vice versa, without any impact on the functionalities of the application.

For instance, our example uses an LDAP server to store all users, but there is no reason why we couldn't easily switch to a database server, which is just another implementation of the data access layer. For example if your service layer uses the userDao.save(user) to save the user into the LDAP server, you could create another data access layer that implements the same userDao interface and then injects it to the ServiceLayer instead of LDAP.

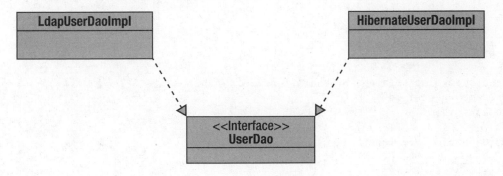
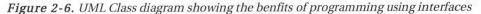

Figure 2-6. *UML Class diagram showing the benfits of programming using interfaces*

Figure 2-6 shows the class diagram of the interface userDao implemented by both LDAP and Hibernate DAOs.

Below is the XML configuration code to inject the Hibernate DAO instead of the LDAP DAO, showing how easy it is to switch from the LDAP data access layer to the Hibernate layer.

```
<bean id="userService" class="org.apress.usermanager.business.UserServiceImpl">
    <property name="mailDao" value="mailDao"/>
    <property name="userDao" ref="userDao"/>
</bean>

<bean id="userDao" class="org.apress.usermanager.dao.LDAP.UserDaoLDAPImpl">
    <property name="LDAPSession" ref="LDAPSession"/>
</bean>

<bean id="userDao"
class="org.apress.usermanager.dao.Hibernate.UserDaoHibernateImpl">
    <property name="sessionFactory" ref="sessionFactory"/>
</bean>
```

A great benefit of the DAO layer is that debugging becomes much easier because you are dividing a complex process into small classes.

The Domain Model

The domain model identifies all your application entities and their relationships. It can model your database schema or other resource objects (called entities) with reference relations. To understand this better, think of an entity as an object that maps your database table.

For example if you have a database with two tables—for users and groups—you can map them into your Java code with two entities called User and Group. Each entity will have just getter and setter methods matching each column of the database table.

Here is an example of the users table mapped to the Java class User.

Listing 2-1. Mapping the database users table to the Java entity class User

```java
@Entity
@Table(name = "users")
public class User {

    @Id @GeneratedValue(strategy = GenerationType.AUTO)
    @Column(name = "user_id")
    private Long id;

    @Column(unique = true,length = 50)
    @Basic(optional = false)
    private String username;

    @Column(length = 50)
    @Basic(optional = false)
    private String forename;

    @Column(length = 50)
    @Basic(optional = false)
    private String surname;

    @Column(length = 255)
    @Basic(optional = false)
    private String email;

    @Column(length = 255)
    @Basic(optional = true)
    private String password;

    public User(){}

    public String getUsername() {
        return username;
    }

    public String getForename() {
        return forename;
```

```java
    }

    public void setUsername(String username) {
        this.username = username;
    }

    public void setForename(String forename) {
        this.forename = forename;
    }

    public void setId(Long id) {
        this.id = id;
    }

    public Long getId() {
        return id;
    }

    public void setSurname(String surname) {
        this.surname = surname;
    }

    public String getSurname() {
        return surname;
    }

    public void setPassword(String password) {
        this.password = password;
    }

    public String getPassword() {
        return password;
    }


    public String getEmail() {
        return email;
    }

    public void setEmail(String email) {
        this.email = email;
    }
}
```

I will discuss the domain model in more depth in the upcoming chapters with regard to Hibernate and persistence objects.

Summary

In this chapter we have seen the sample application and its architecture, and discussed the importance of diagramming the workings of the application at the outset. Before actually going into development, we will spend some time in the next chapter on a topic that's reasonably simple, but if not covered could turn into a painful, annoying, and time-consuming process—development tools, setup, and configuration. We will explore the most popular tools used by the Java/Flex community in developing JEE Flex-driven applications, and the most popular tools used in software engineering.

CHAPTER 3

∎∎∎

Configuring Your Development Environment

Setting up the development environment for your application is an important milestone to complete before you start coding. Developing a Flex and Java Enterprise application requires setting up a number of tools in order to write, test, and debug Java, AS, and MXML code; create and test SQL queries and other database objects; share source code with other member of the team using a source control server; and share artifact and JAR libraries among different projects and teams using repositories and building tools.

In this chapter I will show you the tools we need and how to install them in order to start the Flex and Java Enterprise development.

The Source Code Editor: Eclipse IDE

Eclipse is an integrated development environment that helps you develop applications in many languages. Eclipse is open source software supported by the Eclipse foundation, a not-for-profit association similar in scope to the Apache foundation.

Eclipse was originally developed by OTI (Object Technology International) and then by IBM as part of the VisualAge projects. It then became part of the IBM strategy of making code open source to encourage adaptation of technologies designed to run on platforms more favored by IBM.

Thanks to its very robust and stable architecture, and due in part to being written in Java, Eclipse can run on multiple operating systems with ease. At the core of Eclipse is a plug-in manager that can load, install, and run a variety of plug-ins, each like a component that provides a different kind of service. There are plug-ins that test, debug, and run your code, and help you write the code in many different languages, such as AS, JavaScript, CF, PHP and many others. The default language is always Java.

In this chapter I'll explain which Eclipse plug-ins you need in order to create stable enterprise applications. Among the most important are Subclipse (the Subversion plug-in for Eclipse for version control) and Maven2 (the Maven Eclipse plug-in for software project management).

In my view, Eclipse is one of the best open source projects of the last five years. It is a robust, stable tool chock full of really useful functions. I always use Eclipse when developing Java, AS, and Flex applications or web sites, and I also tend to use it for minor projects and languages, such as HTML and JavaScript, using plug-ins that focus on the tasks I need.

If you are not yet using Eclipse, I suggest you start right now, not only because the exercises and projects in this book use Eclipse, but also because it's probably the best IDE I have used in my career so far.

Essentially Eclipse is a framework built using Java that provides different services to allow the plug-in development and the extension of Eclipse itself. For example, Adobe Flex Builder is an application that is built on Eclipse. Adobe offers two ways for working using the Flex Builder IDE—as a plug-in of an existing Eclipse installation or as a standalone application. I prefer to use Eclipse plug-ins where I can so I can keep everything in the same IDE, which makes managing related projects much easier. For example, you can use the FlexBuilder IDE standalone application only with Flex/ActionScript projects. To write Java, you'd have to use another Eclipse installation.

Within Eclipse, a collection of components focused on a specific task is called a *perspective*. For example, the Flex perspective shows the Flex components, such as the Flex navigator, while the Java perspective shows the Package Explorer, the JUnit window, and other tools used by Java. Each perspective contains several views related to the focus of the perspective itself.

Eclipse Projects

Managing projects with Eclipse is quite easy. A project is a folder that contains all the files needed by the application. You can create Java, AS, and Flex projects. If you have other plug-ins such as CF or PHP, you can also create these types of projects. In the coming chapters you will see how to create Maven projects. Maven is a tool that will be very useful as we build and manage libraries in our Java and Flex projects.

I suggest you keep the project organized by macro category using the Working Set. (The Working Set generally refers to the memory pages referenced during the process time interval or, in very simple terms, what pages are to be kept in the main memory for quick access. Be aware, however, that this is very RAM-intensive.)

For example, if you want to group together all projects for a specific client, you can create a Working Set for the client and select it when needed simply by selecting the Working Set for that client. The Package Explorer will show all the projects belonging to that client.

Here's how to create a Working Set:

1. Click on Select Working Set (Figure 3-1).

2. Click on New... (Figure 3-2).

3. Set the Working Set type (Figure 3-3).

4. Set the Working Set name, select one or more projects to add to the Working Set, and click Finish when you're done (Figure 3-4).

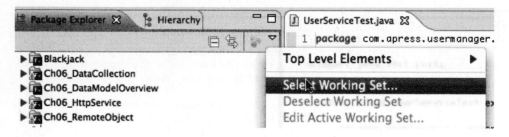

Figure 3-1. *Choose Select Working Set*

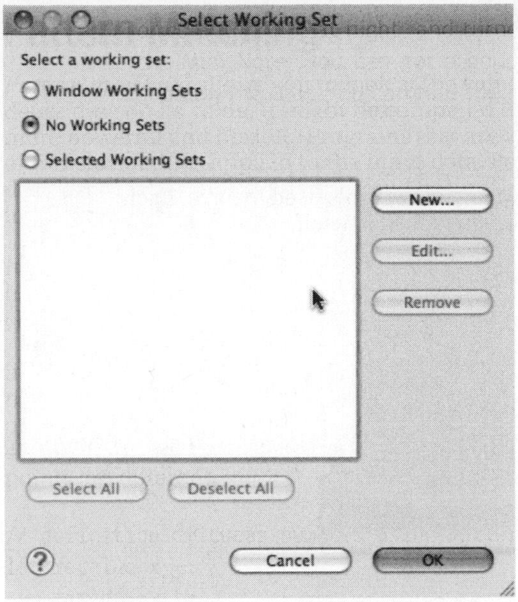

Figure 3-2. *Select new to create a new Working Set.*

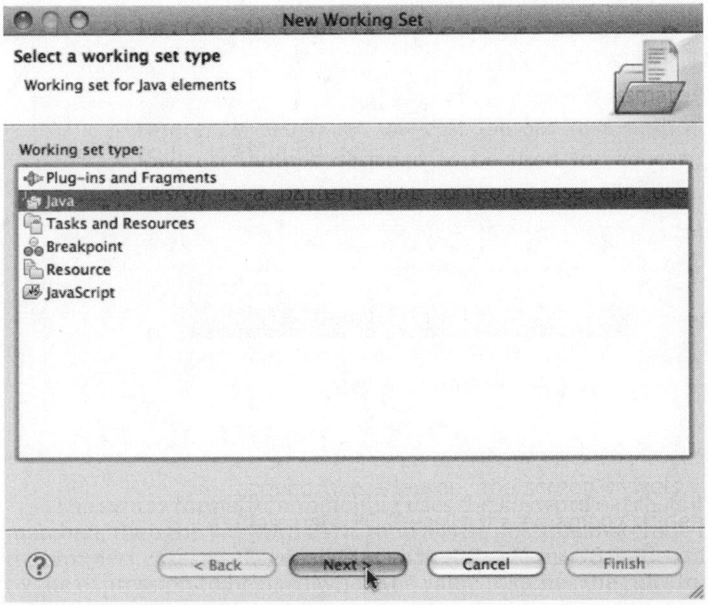

Figure 3-3. *Set the Working Set type*

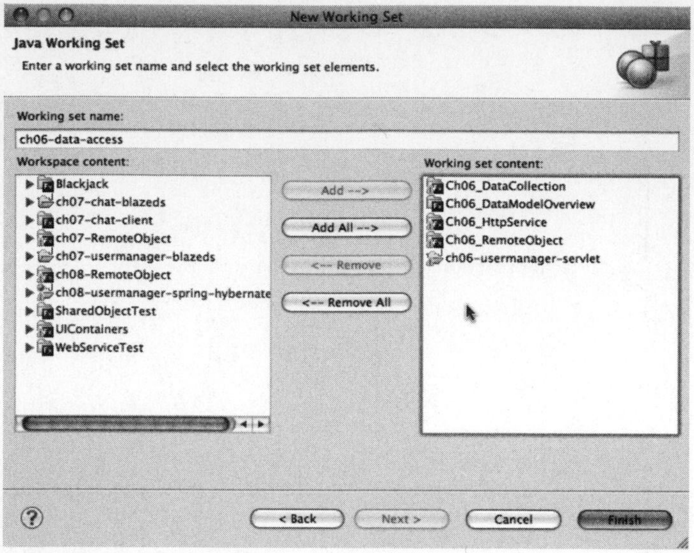

Figure 3-4. *Add projects to the Working Set*

You are then returned to the Select Working Sets dialog box where you can select your newly created Working Set (Figure 3-5), which you can see in action in Figure 3-6.

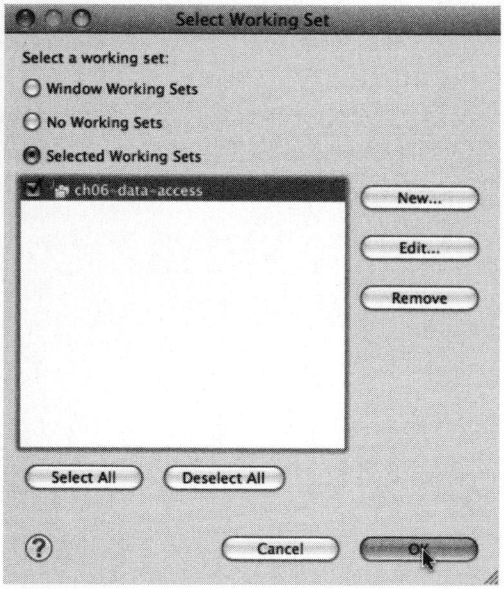

Figure 3-5. *Select the Working Set just created*

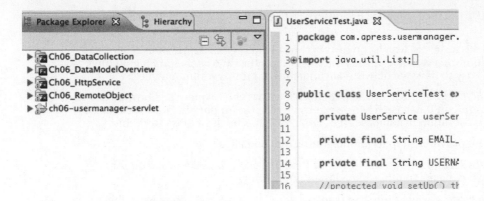

Figure 3-6. Working Set in action

When you don't need a project, close it. To do so, right-click on the root of the project and select Close Project, as shown in Figure 3-7. To open a project, right-click on the closed project and select Open Project.

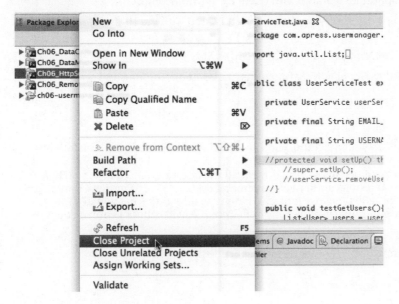

Figure 3-7. Closing a project

Eclipse Plug-ins

Plug-ins are components that can be installed using the Eclipse plug-in manager. You'll find plug-ins almost for everything at `http://marketplace.eclipse.org`. Here are the ones I find most useful:

- *Subclipse* provides support for Subversion.

- *Spring IDE* is a nice graphical user interface for browsing Spring configuration files.

- *QuickRex* is a view in which you can enter test your regular expressions. The expressions are evaluated against the test-text on the fly. Matches are highlighted and it is easy to navigate between any matches or groups within matches.

- *Eclipse SQL Explorer* is a thin SQL client that allows you to query and browse any JDBC compliant database. There is extensive support for plug-ins with specialized functions for different databases (i.e., DB2, MySQL, Oracle) and is extendible.

- *M2Eclipse* provides support for integrating Maven Eclipse.

- *VeloEclipse* is an HTML/Velocity Editor for Eclipse; it is based on veloedit for velocity parsing and outline, but adds an html editor.

- *Log4E* makes it easier to use your own logger in Java projects. You may be able to adapt your logger by defining your own templates using preferences as it is not bound to any special logging framework. There is active support for Log4j, Commons Logging and JDK 1.4 logging.

- *EclipseUtilPlugins* is a set of useful plug-ins for Eclipse.

- *Ldap Tools* provides support for working with LDAP from within Eclipse.

- *Hibernate Synchronizer* is a plug-in code generator. It is used with the Hibernate persistence framework.

- *HTML Tidy* allows you to format and check (X)HTML or XML code.

- *JSEditor* provides basic JavaScript editing functions like content outlining and syntax highlighting.

Installing Eclipse

If you already have Eclipse installed on your machine, you can skip this section; if not let's install this very popular IDE.

Go to `http://www.eclipse.org/downloads/` and download the latest version of Eclipse IDE for Java EE Developers. Choose the package relevant for your operating system (Mac, Windows, Linux), and download and unzip it in a directory called /eclipse (you can name the directory what you like but remember where it is). You can have multiple installations of Eclipse if you like, but of course you must copy them into different folders.

When you run the application (by double clicking on Eclipse.exe in Windows or Eclipse.app in Mac), you will be prompted to select your workspace, as shown in Figure 3-8.

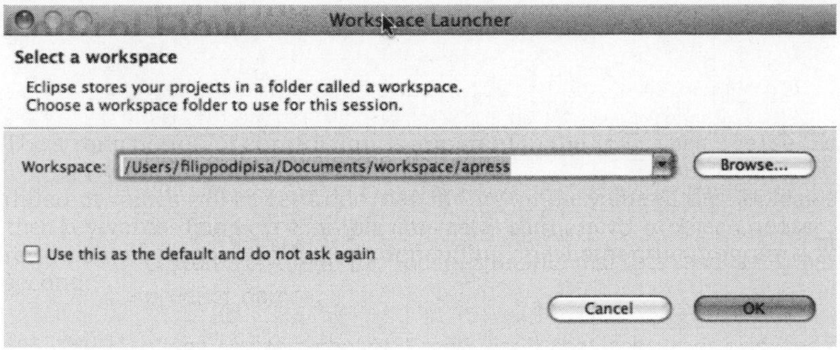

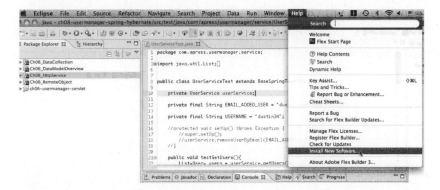

Figure 3-8. *Select a workspace dialog.*

A workspace is just a directory on your file system where your projects are located. You can have different workspaces and switch between them. When you select the workspace, you will see a welcome screen.

Most developers are surprised at the speed and performance of Eclipse and wonder how that can be, given that Java GUIs are traditionally slow with poor performance. The key to Eclipse's performance is the multiple technologies it employs. The core is Java but the GUIs use the Java-based Standard Widget Toolkit (SWT), which uses the native operating system's GUI.

Configure Eclipse for Flex and J2EE

Previous versions of Eclipse felt more like a work in progress than a finished product, and using it was painful. For example, you had to install many plug-ins and their dependencies—just to build your J2EE environment! Fortunately, the latest release of Eclipse for J2EE (called Galileo and based on Eclipse 3.5 SR1) already contains almost of the plug-ins you need for your enterprise development, so it is now ready to go out of the box and you don't have to spend a day configuring it.

However, it isn't fully complete for our needs. For our development environment, we need to install some additional plug-ins, not a difficult task. Simply select Help on the top menu bar, then click on the item Install New Software… as shown in Figure 3-9. Now click on the Available Software Sites link shown in Figure 3-10.

Figure 3-9. *Installing Eclipse plug-ins*

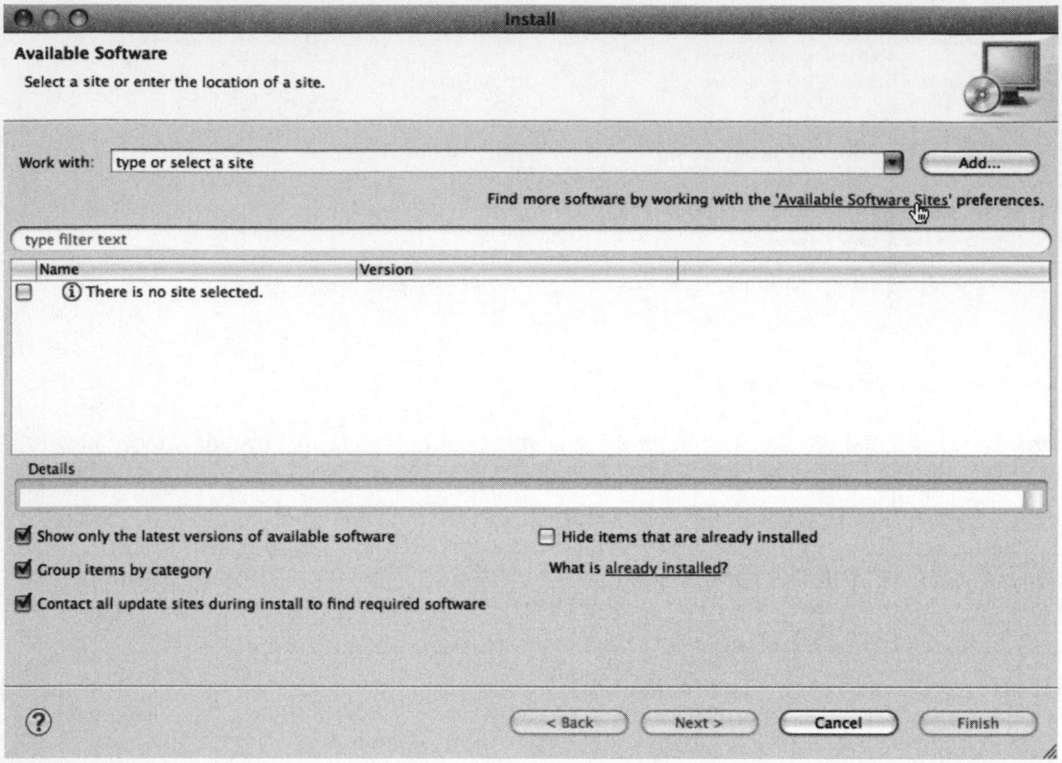

Figure 3-10. Install new plug-in dialog window

To add a plug-in, you need to enter the plug-in update URL and click on Add…. Let's install the SpringIDE plug-in, as shown in Figure 3-11. At the time of this writing, the SpringIDE plug-in update URL is `http://springide.org/updatesite`.

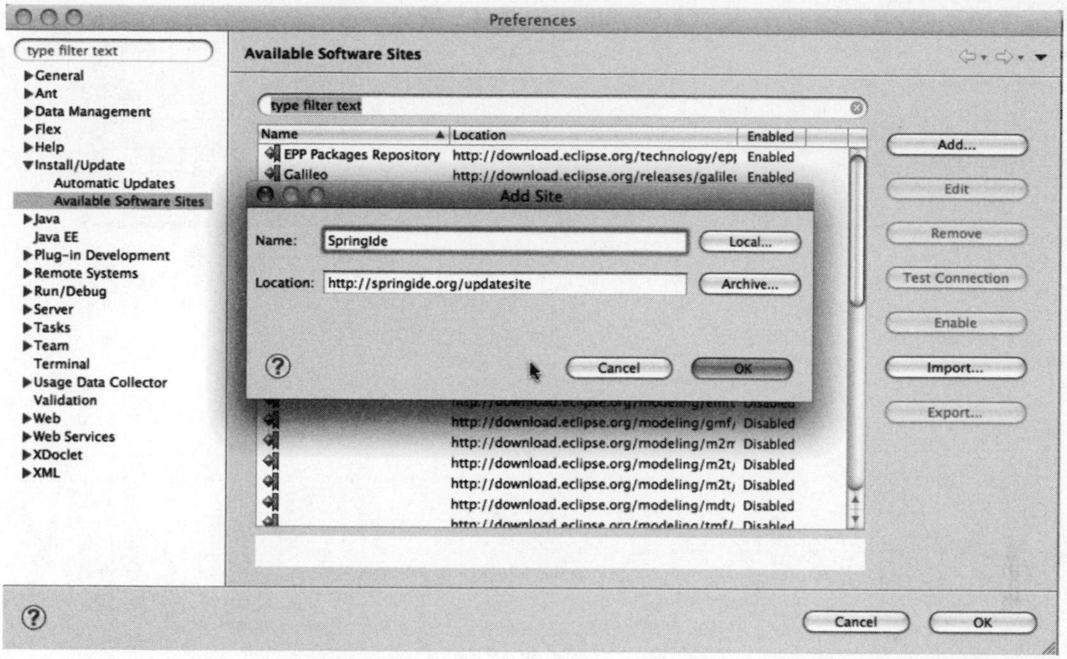

Figure 3-11. *Adding the SpringIde plug-in through the update site*

After inserting the update URL click on the OK button. To install the SpringIDE application, select the options Core, Extension(Incubation), and Extension of SpringIDE tools and click Next (Figure 3-12).

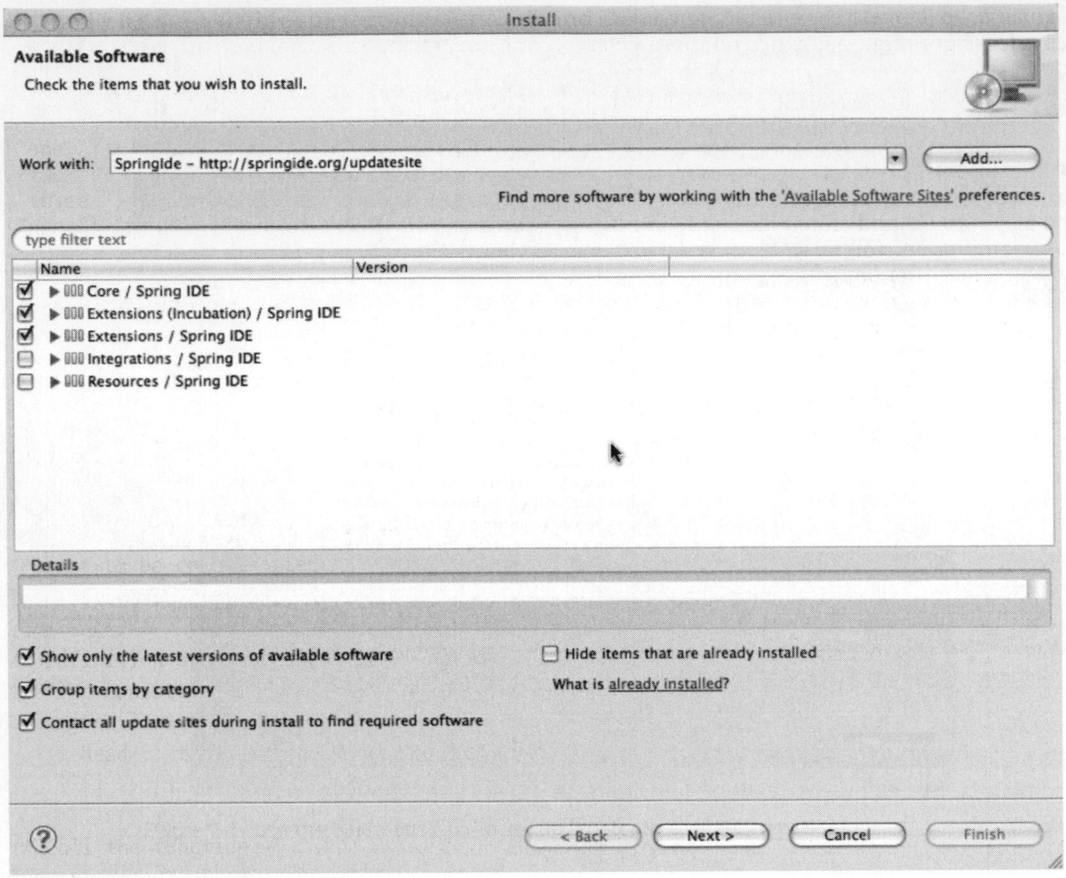

Figure 3-12. Select the SpringIde packages to install.

Then follow the instructions, accepting the license, and install. When the installation finishes, you will need to restart Eclipse. The installation procedure is the same for all plug-ins.

While you're at it, install the JBoss plug-in, a set of tools that improves Hibernate's productivity. The update site for JBoss is located at `http://download.jboss.org/jbosstools/updates/stable`.

You'll also need the plug-ins for Subversion, Flex Builder, and Maven2. These are so essential, however, that we will dedicate a section for each plug-in.

Version Control: Subversion

Subversion (SVN) is an open-source version control system that manages the life cycle of your files and directories, including version, change, history and many other aspects of application development. SVN consists of a server and a client. The server can be accessed via http or via the SVN protocol. The client can be integrated into your operating system or directly into your IDE, or it can be a standalone application.

With SVN, you can see the entire life of a file and perform operations like reverting a file to a previous release or merging it with a different version. No more backup copies spread out all over your machine.

I like to think of SVN as a kind of repository for all your projects, where different people are permitted access. Suppose you want to start a project and use SVN. The first step is to create the project within the shared repository (share project) and then download a copy of the project itself to your file system (check out). You can then start to work on that copy of the original project stored to the shared repository on another machine, and once you are happy with your amendments or enhancements, you can send all your new and edited files to the repository (commit). The SVN system will keep track of all your modifications version by version, and it will let you view the history of your revisions, revert from one revision to another one, and so on.

SVN allows many developers work on the same project at the same time. Each developer has a copy of the project on her own machine, and when she is happy with what she has done, she can commit to the repository. Problems can occur when more than one developer edits the same file and commits it to the repository. However, SVN will manage all conflicts within the file and if there isn't any conflict, it will merge the code automatically.

We will integrate SVN with our Eclipse IDE, installing the SVN plug-in called Subclipse.

The Evolution of SVN

At the turn of the century, a company called CollabNet, Inc. began working on a replacement for the Concurrent Versions System (CVS), the de facto standard for change management in the open source community. The company was specifically concerned with version control, an area where CVS had many limitations. So Collabnet decided to write its own version, based on CVS but without the bugs.

They contacted Karl Fogel, author of the book *Open Source Development with CVS* (Coriolis, 1999), and asked if he'd like to work on the new project. Coincidentally, Karl was already discussing a new version control system with another software developer, Jim Blandy, who Karl had worked with, and in fact they once had a company together called *Cyclic Software* that provided CVS support contracts. They still used CVS on a daily basis and were both frustrated with it. They had thought of a new solution and even had a name—subversion. So when the call from Collabnet came, it was an easy decision. Jim was loaned indefinitely to the project (from Red Hat Software), while CollabNet hired Karl and Ben Collins-Sussman and detailed work began in May 2000. It turned out that many people had the same concerns and frustrations and were only too happy to help.

The original design team started with some simple goals. They didn't want to redesign the application in terms of version control methodology, just improve the workings of CVS. It was decided that all CVS features would remain and the new application would preserve the development model but remove the existing flaws in both design and functionality.

Subversion was "self-hosting" on August 31, 2001, which was when the developers stopped using CVS to manage their own code and starting using Subversion for their projects instead.

Though CollabNet is still involved, Subversion is run as an open-source project that is fully compliant with the Debian Free Software guidelines (see http://www.debian.org/social_contract).

Subversion Installation

Subversion is a server and should be installed by the system administrator. If you prefer to install it yourself, you can download the latest version from http://subversion.tigris.org. At the time of this writing, you can download the server binary package at http://subversion.tigris.org/getting.html#binary-packages. Because the Subversion server installation is different for each operating system and is well-documented on the Web, I won't cover it here. However, because the server installation can be difficult, I am providing an SVN server at http://www.filippodipisa.com/apress/svn/. In order to use it, you will have to register and confirm your e-mail address.

Once the server is installed, you need only the client software to work with it. We will use both the command-line client and the Eclipse plug-in, Subclipse.

Basic SVN Project Structure

Before creating a new project, we'll discuss the standard directory structure of an SVN project, which includes three directories called trunk, branches, and tags. The trunk is the main folder of the current project. A branch is another copy of the project on the server. You can use branches to develop different versions of the application while at the same time keeping your stable version within the trunk. Once you are happy with a branch version you can merge it into the trunk; you can also merge the trunk into the branch when required. Suppose you are developing the usermanager1 version using the trunk and then you are asked to create usermanager2 with completely new functionality—but you still have to fix bugs and maintain usermanager1. Without branches, if you change the code of usermanager1, you risk breaking it or changing its functionality. Using branches, you can work on user manager1 and usermanager2 at the same time, and if you fix a bug in usermanager1 that also exists in usermanager2, you can merge the code of that bug fix from usermanager1 to usermanager2 and vice versa. Furthermore, when you are ready with the usermanager2 version, you can merge everything into the usermanager1 trunk and usermanger2 will become the trunk version.

The third folder is the tag folder, which contains all the releases of your application. When you are happy and ready to release a new version of your application, you create a new tag. Suppose you want to release a new version of your web site. You simply create a new tag of your web site and then tell the Web server to redirect to that tag. Thanks to tags, you can always roll back to the previous version if there are any problems with the new version.

Here's how to create the basic structure and commit your changes to the repository using the command line(Terminal for Mac and command prompt for Windows):

```
$ cd /tmp
$ SVN co file:///usr/local/repo
$ cd repo
$ SVN mkdir tags branches trunk
A         tags
A         branches
A         trunk
$ SVN ci -m "initial structure"
Adding         branches
Adding         tags
Adding         trunk
```

Using SVN with the Command-Line Client

As we have discussed, the Subversion server comes with the command-line SVN client.

■ **Note** Even if you are going to use a visual SVN client such as Subclipse or Tortoise, please read this section thoroughly, because there are some scenarios such as Linux servers without any GUI installed where you can use just the command-line SVN client.

To use the SVN client, open a terminal window in Mac, or a shell in Linux, or a console window in Windows. With the SVN client you can commit your changes, update your local copy with the server, check out a project from the server, and share an existing non-SVN project with the SVN server or create a new one.

Table 3-1 shows the SVN command-line client subcommands I find most useful.

Table 3-1. *Useful SVN subcommands with examples*

Command	Description
svn add Examples svn add foo.java A foo.java svn add testdir A testdir A testdir/a A testdir/b	Adds files, directories, or symbolic links to your working copy and schedules them for addition to the repository. They will be uploaded and added to the repository on your next commit. If you add something and change your mind before committing, you can unschedule the addition using SVN revert.
svn co Examples svn co http://localhost/repo/test test A test/a A test/b Checked out revision 2. $ ls test	Checks out a working copy from a repository, which means a copy of the file is downloaded from the repository to your computer.

Table 3-1. Continued

`svn cleanup`
 	
Examples:
 	
`cd test/`
 	
`svn cleanup`
	Recursively cleans up the working copy, removing locks and resuming unfinished operations. If you ever get a "working copy locked" error, run this command to remove stale locks and get your working copy into a usable state again.

`svn ci`
 	
Examples:
 	
`cd test/`
 	
`svn commit -m "my message"`
`Sending          a`
`Transmitting file data .`
`Committed revision 3.`
	Sends changes from your working copy to the repository. If you do not supply a log message with your commit by using either the --file or --message switch, SVN will launch your editor for you to compose a commit message.

`svn cp`
 	
Examples copy within your working copy:
 	
`svn copy foo.java fooBase.java`
`A          fooBase.java`
`$ svn status`
`A  +   fooBase.java`
	Copies a file in a working copy or in the repository.

`svn rm`
 	
Example:
 	
`svn delete foo.java`
`D          foo.java`
 	
`svn commit -m "my message"`
`Deleting        foo.java`
`Transmitting file data .`
`Committed revision <number revision>.`
	Removes (deletes) a file from the working copy. Deleting a file from your working copy merely schedules it to be deleted. When you commit, the file is deleted in the repository.

Table 3-1. Continued

svn export Example exporting from the repository svn export http://localhost/repo/test testwithoutsvn A testwithoutsvn/test Exported revision <revision_number> Example exporting from the working copy svn export test testwithoutsvn Export complete.	Exports a clean directory tree from the repository or from your working copy to a local directory.
svn help Example help command svn help Example help subcommand svn help ci commit (ci): Send changes from your working copy to the repository. usage: commit [PATH...]	The SVN help for command and subcommands, it will retrieve a list of all subcommands.
svn import Examples svn import -m "my message" myproject http://localhost/repo/myproject Adding myproject/foo.java … Transmitting file data .... Committed revision 21.	Imports a local directory into the Subversion server.

Table 3-1. *Continued*

`svn info`	Prints useful info about files and directories into your working copy.

```
 svn info foo.java
Path: foo.java
Name: foo.java
URL: http://myurl/foo.java
Repository Root: http://myserver.net/svn
Repository UUID: e545364f-13fe-0310-ac05-
b8676b8194c8
Revision: 3499
Node Kind: file
Schedule: normal
Last Changed Author: filippo
Last Changed Rev: 3499
Last Changed Date: 2009-02-23 11:52:54 +0000
(Mon, 23 Feb 2009)
Text Last Updated: 2009-02-23 11:04:14 +0000
(Mon, 23 Feb 2009)
Checksum: 1e7cc2bad810ce2678e4d13be93c945f
```

`svn ls`	Lists files, most useful if you want to see what files a repository has without downloading a working copy.

Example

```
svn list http://mysvnserver/repo/myproject/
foo.java
fooBase.java
…
```

`svn mkdir`	Creates a new directory under version control.

Example how to create a dir into your working copy

```
svn mkdir newdir
A         newdir
```

Example how to create a dir into the repository

```
svn mkdir -m "my message"
http://mysvnserver/repo/myproject/newdir
```

Table 3-1. *Continued*

`svn move`	Moves a file or directory in your working copy or in the repository.

```
Example how to move a file into your working copy

svn move foo.java fooRenamed.java
A           fooRenamed.java
D           foo.java

Example how to move a file in the repository

$ svn move -m "my message"
http://mysvnserver/repo/myproject/foo.java
http://mysvnserver/repo/myproject/fooRenamed.java
```

`svn revert`	Reverts any local changes to a file or directory to the latest repository version.

```
Examples

svn revert foo.java
Reverted foo.java
```

`svn status`	Displays the status of working copy files and directories. With no arguments, it shows only locally modified items (no repository access). With --show -updates, adds working revision and server out-of-date information. With --verbose, print full revision information on every item.

```
svn status myproject
 M      myproject/foo.java
A  +    myproject/fooBase.java
```

`svn update`	Picks up repository changes that have occurred since your last update.

```
$ svn update
A  myproject/foo2.java
A  myproject/foo3.java
D  myproject/fooBase.java
Updated to revision 45.
```

For each updated item a line will start with a character reporting the action taken. These characters have the following meaning:

A: Added
D: Deleted
U: Updated
C: Conflict
G: Merged

A character in the first column signifies an update to the actual file, while updates to the file's properties are shown in the second column.

■ **Note** When a project is under Subversion, just use the SVN subcommands to copy, move and delete files.

I purposely excluded the commands `merge` and `switch` from Table 3-1 as using them with from command line is often messy. If you have to use branches and merge code, I suggest using Subclipse, which provides an easy graphical interface for Subversion.

Installing Subclipse

You add the Subclipse plug-in to Eclipse much like any other plug-in, by first creating an update site in Eclipse. Follow the directions given earlier in this chapter, then insert the Subclipse update URL `http://subclipse.tigris.org/update_1.4.x`.

If the latest Subclipse version doesn't work with your installation of Subversion and Eclipse, try the following versions:

- Subclipse 1.2.x (Eclipse 3.2+) - `http://subclipse.tigris.org/update_1.2.x`

- Subclipse 1.0.x (Eclipse 3.0/3.1) - `http://subclipse.tigris.org/update_1.0.x`

Once you're back to the screen that shows the plug-in list, which should include the new one ready to be installed (Figure 3-13), select the Subclipse node, click Next, and follow the instructions.

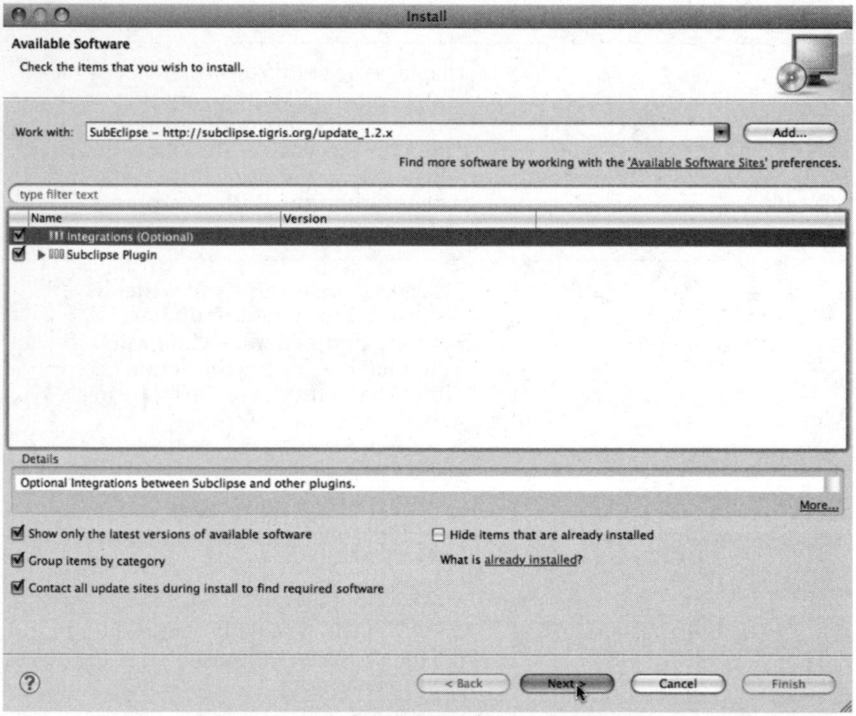

Figure 3-13. Subclipse plug-in installation

The final step is restarting Eclipse. Once that's done, the first thing you will typically want to do is open the Subclipse Repository perspective where you can create a new repository and explore your existing repositories. To change to the Subclipse Repository perspective, select Window ➤ Open Perspective ➤ Other... ➤ SVN Repository Exploring, as shown in Figures 3-14 and 3-15.

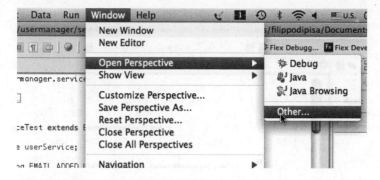

Figure 3-14. Open Perspective command

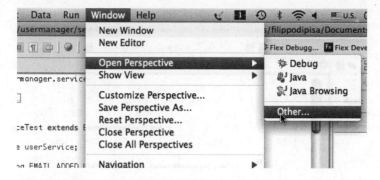

Figure 3-15. Perspectives dialog window

The Database Tools: MySQL

If you are an experienced Java developer, chances are you have some experience working with databases. If you are an animator, flash developer, or the like, however, you may not have had any database experience and worked only with xml.

In this book, we will use MySQL as the database for our applications. MySQL is a database management system that allows you to access, add, and store data. Specifically, it is a relational database management system, meaning it stores data in separate tables instead of just one table. MySQL is very fast and it is open source, which means you can run many versions of the same database on multiple servers without worrying about licensing.

MySQL supports the ANSI/ISO SQL (Structured Query Language) standard; this is the language that allows a developer to access and query the data. MySQL works on multiple platforms and I will cover the installation for both Windows and Mac. At the time of writing the latest stable version of MySQL is 5.1, which is available at: `http://dev.mysql.com/downloads/mysql/5.1.html#downloads`

Install MySQL on Windows

MySQL for Windows can be downloaded in one of three different versions. It's a good idea to choose the MSI package, which provides a wizard for installing and configuring MySQL so you can get started immediately. Once you have downloaded the executable file, run the `setup.exe` or `setup.msi` to get started. Follow the instructions and choose the Typical installation, which installs the following components:

- the MySQL server
- the MySQL command-line client
- the command-line utilities.

The final screen of the installation wizard gives you the option to launch the MySQL configuration wizard, which we will use to configure MySQL server. If you are very knowledgeable, you can navigate to the bin directory of your MySQL installation and launch the `MySQLInstanceConfig.exe` file directly. But for most, especially if you are a new or not confident user, it's best to simply choose the standard configuration.

For development purposes, you don't need to worry about the other options so leave all the defaults in place and click Next until you see the MySQL instance configuration screen (Figure 3-16). Here you can enable/disable TCP/IP networking and configure the port number that is used to connect to the MySQL server.

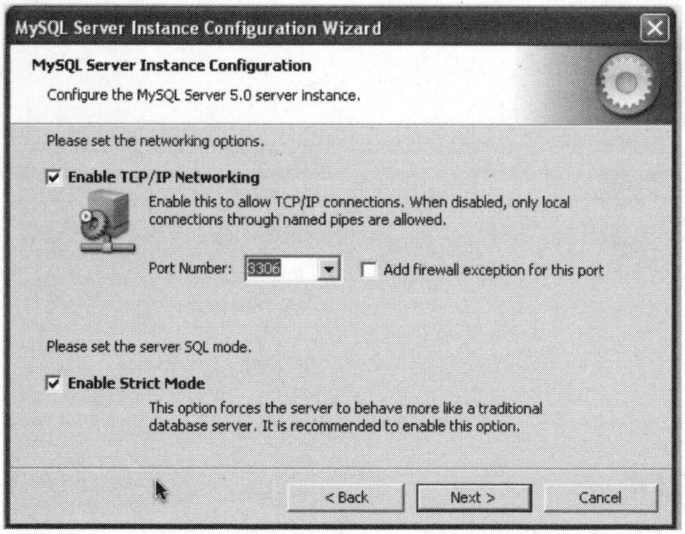

Figure 3-16. MySQL configuration dialog

TCP/IP networking is enabled by default. To disable it, uncheck the box next to the option called Enable TCP/IP Networking. Port 3306 is used by default. To change the port used to access MySQL, choose a new port number from the drop-down box or type a new port number directly into the drop-down box. If the port number you choose is in use, you are prompted to confirm your choice of port number. Before you finish configuring your MySQL server instance, it is recommended that you set a root password as shown in Figure 3-17.

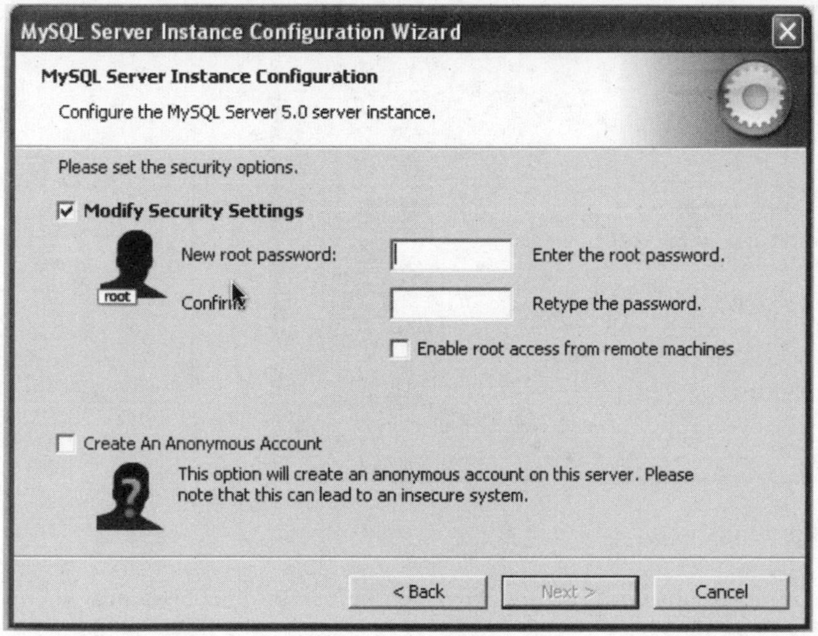

Figure 3-17. MySQL security settings, where you can set a root password

The wizard makes it easy to enable simple security, such as preventing root logins from across the network. To do this, leave the box next to "Enable root access from remote machines" blank.

You can create an anonymous user account by clicking the box next to the appropriate option, but this is not secure, so is not recommended.

The final dialog, shown in Figure 3-18, allows you to continue with the installation by clicking the Execute button, or to exit without completing configuration by clicking the Cancel button.

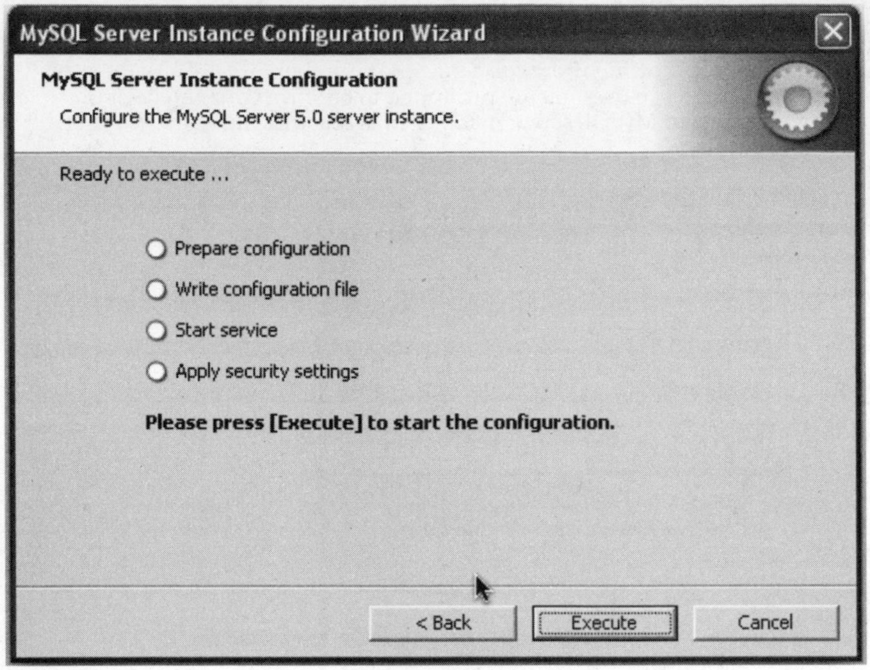

Figure 3-18. Executing MySQL configuration

When the Execute button is clicked, the Configuration Wizard performs a series of tasks and displays the progress as the tasks are performed, writing the options to the corresponding configuration file.

If you want to create a service for the MySQL server the MySQL Server Instance Configuration Wizard comes to your help, doing all the work needed to create and start the service. If you need to reconfigure an existing service, the Wizard can restart the service to apply your configuration changes. To finish and exit, simply click the Finish button.

Installing MySQL on a Mac

The latest version of Mac OS called Leopard comes with MySQL installed. To test the installation you simply open a Terminal window and write the following command

```
mysql --version
mysql  Ver 14.12 Distrib 5.0.51b, for apple-darwin8.11.1 (i686) using  EditLine
wrapper
```

The default installation uses TCP/IP on port 3306. The configuration file is located at /etc/my.conf.

Adding the MySQL GUI Tools

The MySQL GUI Tools is a set of utilities that help with MySQL management and queries. You can download it from the same location of the server. The tools come as a bundle consisting of three applications:

- MySQL Administrator
- MySQL Query Browser
- MySQL Migration Toolkit

MySQL Administrator lets you manage users and permissions, view logs, backup and restore databases, and a lot more. Figure 3-19 shows the Mac OS version of MySQL Administrator.

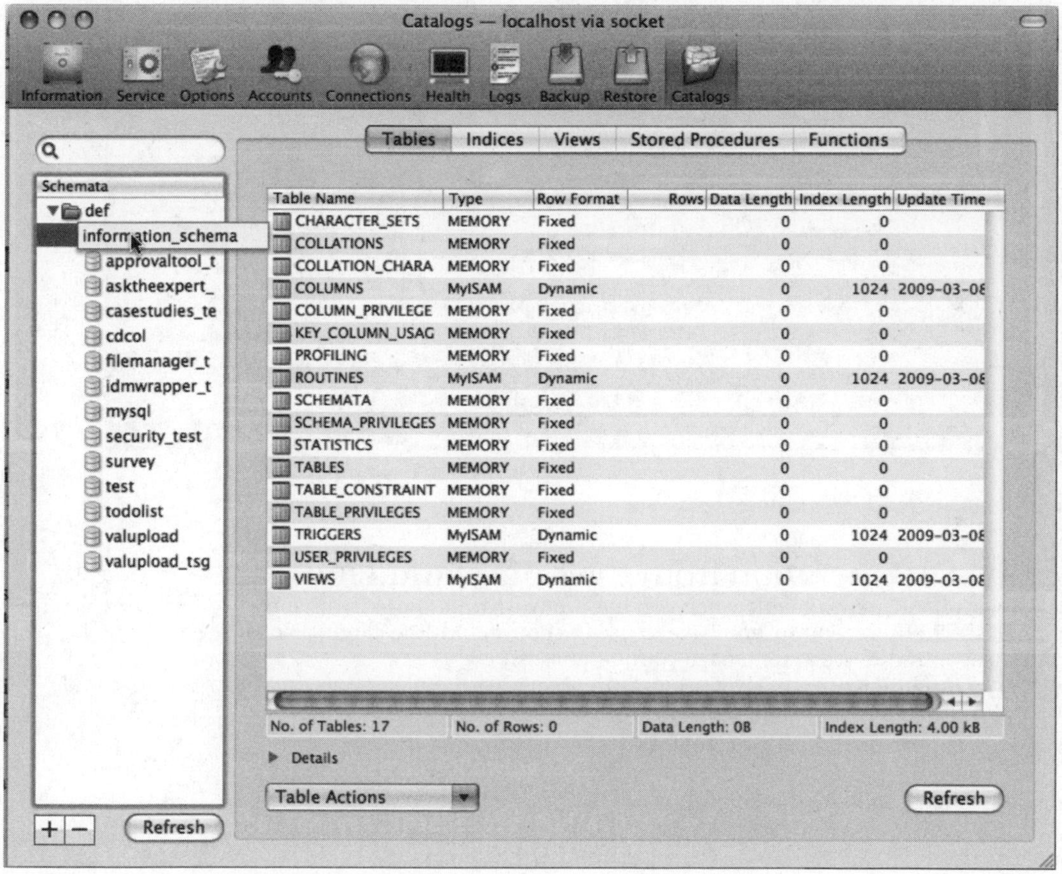

Figure 3-19. *MySQL Administrator for Mac OS*

MySQL Query Browser, shown in Figure 3-20, provides a very nice interface for running queries, creating and deleting databases, and creating, editing, and deleting tables, views, and all database objects.

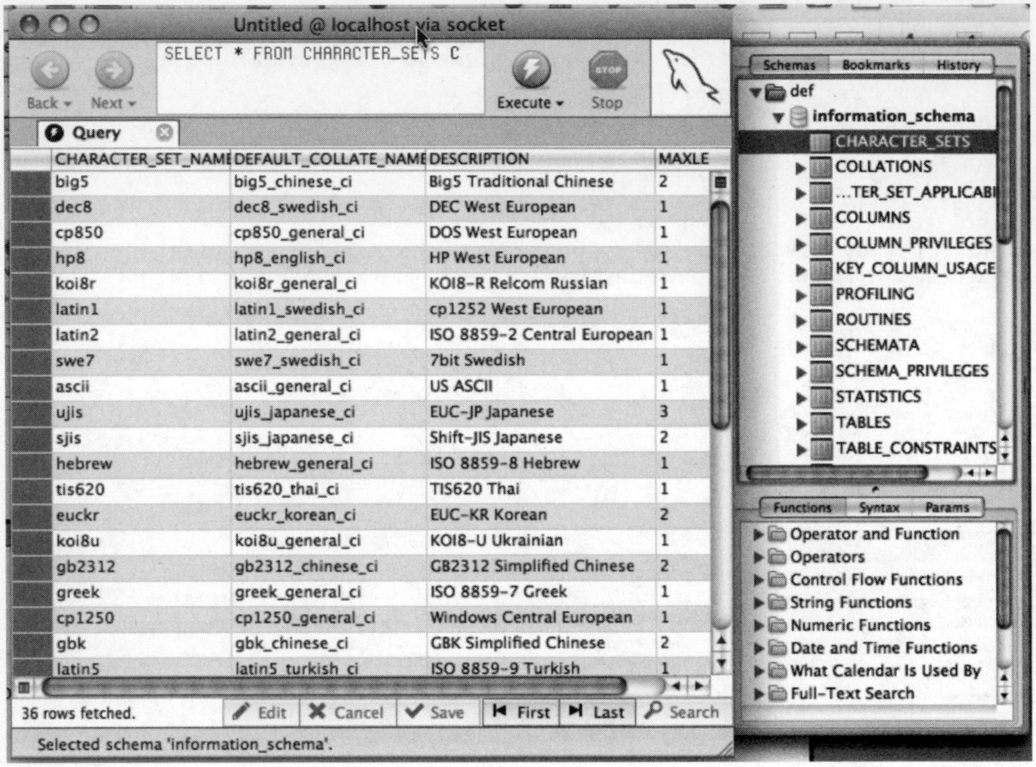

Figure 3-20. *MySQL Query Browser*

Basic MySQL Operation from the Command Line

The GUI tool is not always available when you have to work on remote Linux servers connecting via the secure shell(ssh); in this scenario, you have to use the command-line client, also known as MySQL monitor, to test your queries and manage your databases.

In order to test and learn the MySQL monitor, open a Terminal window on Mac or a Command Prompt on Windows or a Shell on Linux and write this command:

```
mysql -user root -password <yourpassword>
```

On your screen you'll see the following:

```
Welcome to the MySQL monitor.  Commands end with ; or \g.
Your MySQL connection id is 203
Server version: 5.0.51b Source distribution

Type 'help;' or '\h' for help. Type '\c' to clear the buffer.

mysql>
```

Now you have to select a database. To see the databases list, use the show databases command:

```
mysql> show databases;
+--------------------+
| Database           |
+--------------------+
| information_schema |
| approvaltool_test  |
| asktheexpert_test  |
| casestudies_test   |
| cdcol              |
| filemanager_test   |
| idmwrapper_test    |
| mysql              |
| security_test      |
| survey             |
| test               |
| todolist           |
| valupload          |
| valupload_tsg      |
+--------------------+
14 rows in set (0.00 sec)
```

To select a database, enter the use command:

```
mysql> use mysql;
Database changed
```

Now you are connected to the MySQL database that contains all information about the system. To see the list of tables your database contains, enter the command show tables:

```
mysql> show tables;
+---------------------------+
| Tables_in_mysql           |
+---------------------------+
| columns_priv              |
| db                        |
| func                      |
| help_category             |
| help_keyword              |
| help_relation             |
| help_topic                |
| host                      |
| proc                      |
| procs_priv                |
| tables_priv               |
| time_zone                 |
```

```
| time_zone_leap_second     |
| time_zone_name            |
| time_zone_transition      |
| time_zone_transition_type |
| user                      |
| user_info                 |
+---------------------------+
18 rows in set (0.10 sec)
```

To see all of a table's columns in more detail, use the describe command. For example, to see all of the host table's columns, enter:

```
describe host
```

You will see something like the following:

```
mysql> describe host;
+----------------------+---------------+------+-----+---------+-------+
| Field                | Type          | Null | Key | Default | Extra |
+----------------------+---------------+------+-----+---------+-------+
| Host                 | char(60)      | NO   | PRI |         |       |
| Db                   | char(64)      | NO   | PRI |         |       |
| Select_priv          | enum('N','Y') | NO   |     | N       |       |
| Insert_priv          | enum('N','Y') | NO   |     | N       |       |
| Update_priv          | enum('N','Y') | NO   |     | N       |       |
| Delete_priv          | enum('N','Y') | NO   |     | N       |       |
| Create_priv          | enum('N','Y') | NO   |     | N       |       |
| Drop_priv            | enum('N','Y') | NO   |     | N       |       |
| Grant_priv           | enum('N','Y') | NO   |     | N       |       |
| References_priv      | enum('N','Y') | NO   |     | N       |       |
| Index_priv           | enum('N','Y') | NO   |     | N       |       |
| Alter_priv           | enum('N','Y') | NO   |     | N       |       |
| Create_tmp_table_priv| enum('N','Y') | NO   |     | N       |       |
| Lock_tables_priv     | enum('N','Y') | NO   |     | N       |       |
| Create_view_priv     | enum('N','Y') | NO   |     | N       |       |
| Show_view_priv       | enum('N','Y') | NO   |     | N       |       |
| Create_routine_priv  | enum('N','Y') | NO   |     | N       |       |
| Alter_routine_priv   | enum('N','Y') | NO   |     | N       |       |
| Execute_priv         | enum('N','Y') | NO   |     | N       |       |
+----------------------+---------------+------+-----+---------+-------+
19 rows in set (0.00 sec)
```

With the MySQL monitor command line, you can also run and test any queries you want. For example, if you want to retrieve all data from the table host, you can write a standard SQL SELECT:

```
mysql> select * from host;
Empty set (0.07 sec)
```

Table 3-2 lists the most important commands used with the MySQL monitor command-line tool.

Table 3-2. Important MySQL monitor commands

Action	Command
Logging in	mysql -u [username] -p
Logging in to a specific database	mysql -u [username] -p [database name]
Running queries	select * from my_example_table_name;
Selecting/change database	use [database name];
Listing available databases	how databases;
Back up a database	mysqldump -c --create-options DB > file
Restore a database	mysql -p dbname < db.sql
Create a database	create database

Basic MySQL Operations Using MySQL Query Browser

MySQL Query Browser provides the same functionality as the MySQL command-line monitor, but its graphical interface makes it easier for beginners. For example, to create a database, you simply right-click and select the Create Schema item, as shown in Figure 3-21.

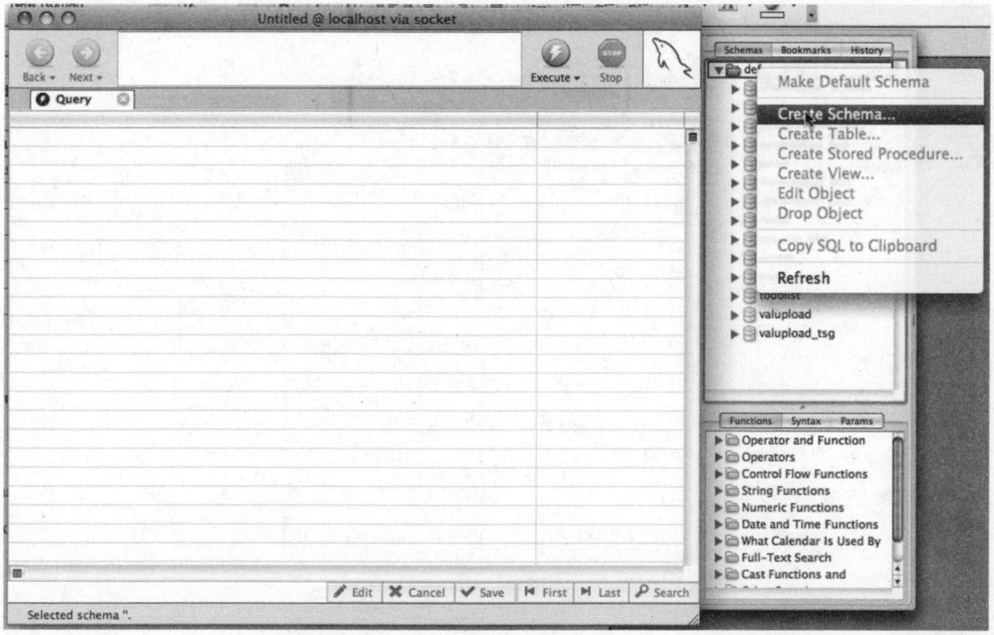

Figure 3-21. MySQL Query Browser create new database

To connect to a database, just double-click the one you're interested in. To query a table, you can drag it to the Query tab in the main window, as shown in Figure 3-22, or you can write SQL code (Figure 3-23) and click on Execute button.

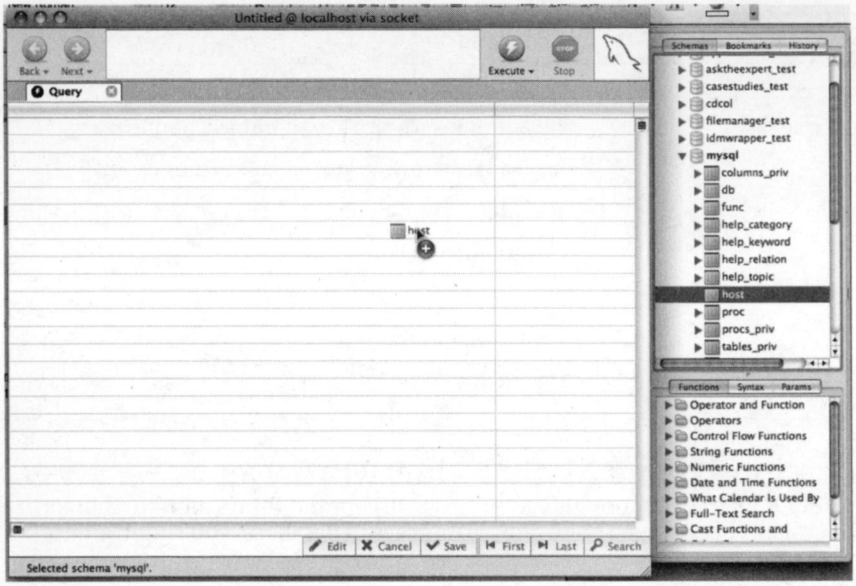

Figure 3-22. To query a table in MySQL Query Browser, drag it to the Query tab.

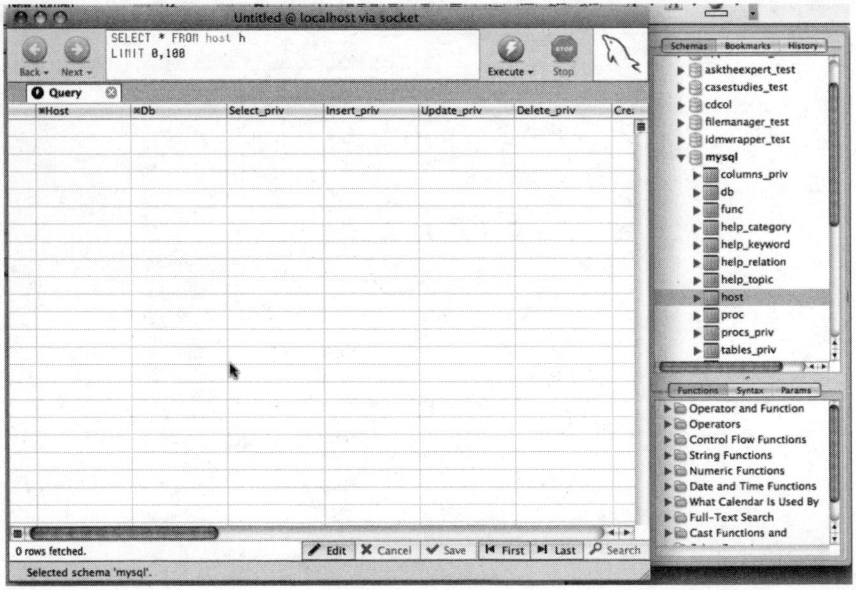

Figure 3-23. Writing SQL queries in MySQL Query Browser

To see the table details, simply expand the table node, as shown in Figure 3-24.

Figure 3-24. *Viewing table details in MySQL Query Browser*

You can also edit the table you've selected by right-clicking and selecting Edit Table (Figure 3-25), which brings up the Table Editor shown in Figure 3-26.

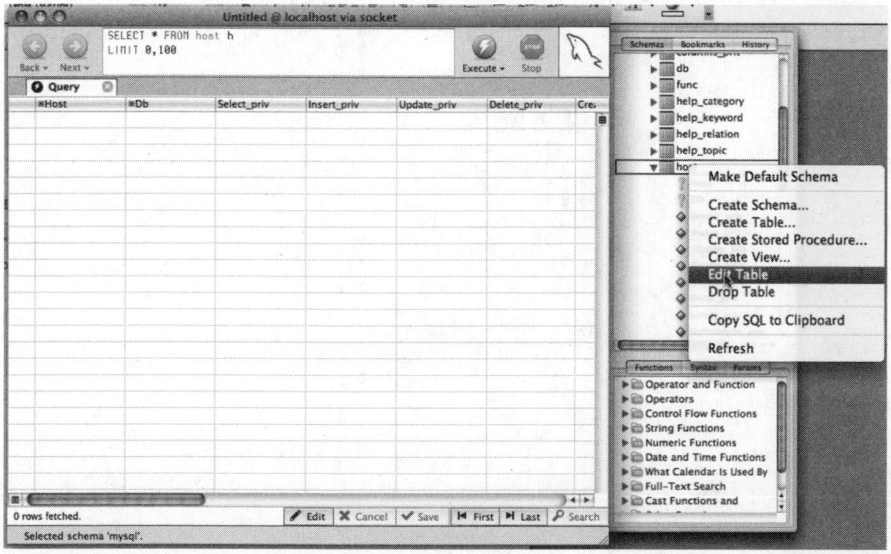

Figure 3-25. *The Edit Table command*

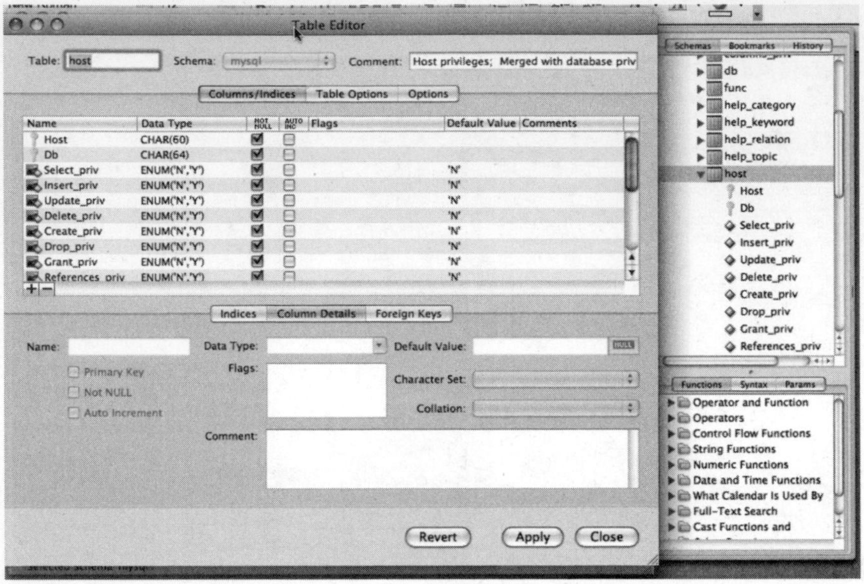

Figure 3-26. *MySQL Query Browser Table Editor*

To create a relationship between two tables, click on the foreign keys tab in Edit Table mode and select the columns of the tables that are related. For example, I have a database called `user_manager_test` with two tables—users and groups—as shown in Figure 3-27.

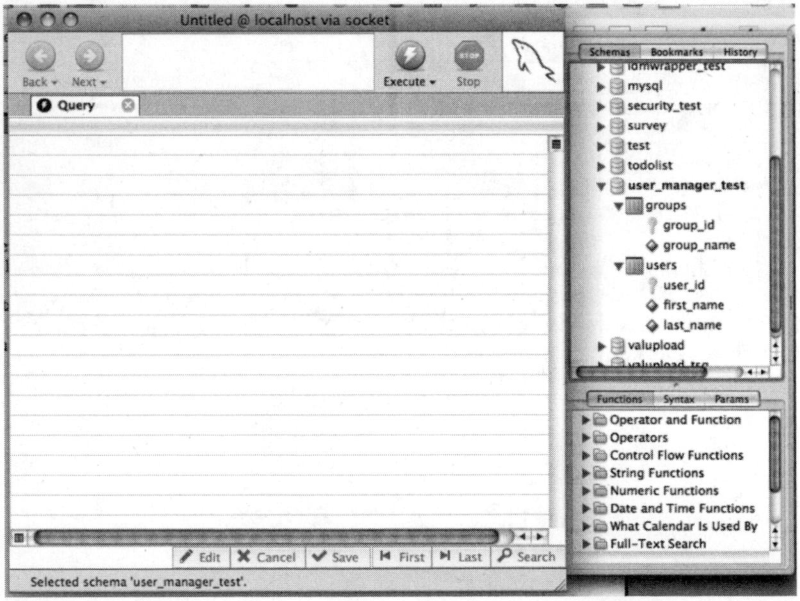

Figure 3-27. *User Manager Database expanded*

One group can have many users, so the relationship to create is one-to-many. To create the relation using MySQL query browser, edit the groups table, adding a column called `user_id`, as shown in Figure 3-28.

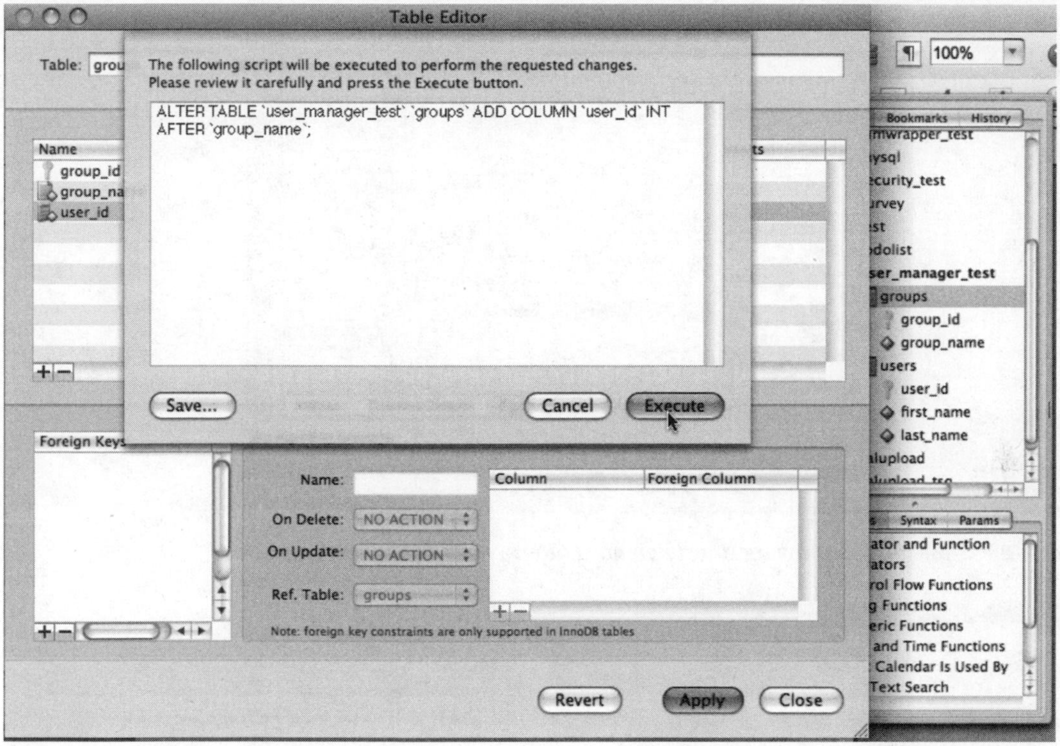

Figure 3-28. Adding a column to the groups table

When you've added the necessary information, click on Apply, then click on Execute to store your changes.

Now we have to relate the `user_id` fields from both users and groups. Click on the symbol [+] on the Foreign Keys section and select the users table in the box with the label Ref.Table (Figure 3-29). Now select the `user_id` fields for both Column and Foreign Column in the grid on the right and again, click on Apply and then Execute to store your changes (Figure 3-30).

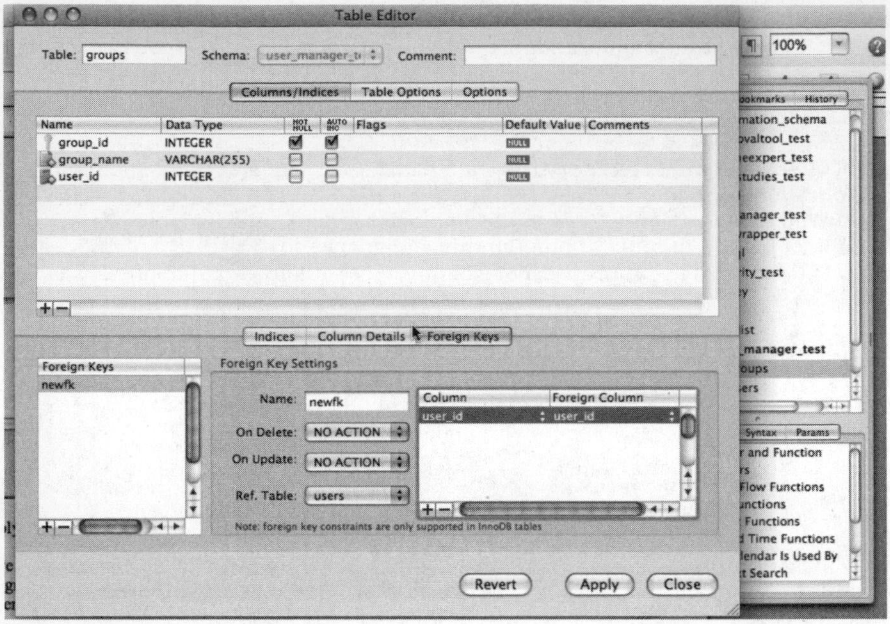

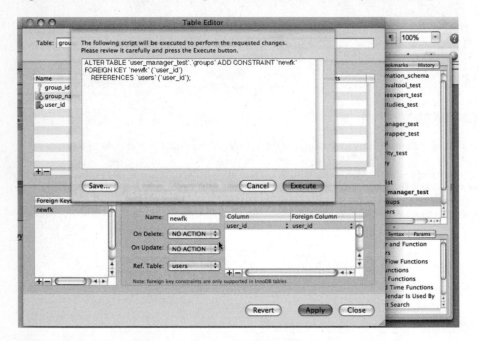

Figure 3-29. *Table editor showing how to create a one-to-many relationship.*

Figure 3-30. *Storing the newly created relationship*

MySQL Query Browser is useful for these operations, but I often find it faster to use the command-line version, so I suggest you master both.

The Java Application Container: Tomcat

The last important piece of our development environment before installing The Flex Builder and the Maven tools is the Java application container.

In the early days of the Web, one of the most popular technologies for creating dynamic pages was CGI, initially using Perl but later using a number of programming languages such as PHP and ASP. The CGI model was based on HTTP requests and response. For example you could pass parameters to a CGI page via a URL and get the result.

```
index.php?username=foo&password=secret
```

Then Java servlets emerged as a dynamic alternative to the CGI technology. Servlets are Java objects that receive requests and generate responses, but they need a container to load them into memory. The servlet container receives the HTTP request and passes it to the servlets, which then generate the result. Unfortunately, though servlets provide better performance than CGI, the technology was far too messy for manage output, such as HTML and JavaScript. The servlet technology was great for business logic, but not for presentation. To solve the problem, Sun Microsystems created Java Server Pages (JSP). JSP technology is much easier to learn as it is tag-based and can be mixed with HTML and JavaScript, so you don't need a deep knowledge of Java to get results. Basically, the JSP files are translated into servlets that are kept in memory until the server is restarted.

Tomcat was created as an application container for servlets and JSP pages, and it's among the most popular servlet containers available. The version we are going to use in this book is Tomcat 6. An easy way to understand the Tomcat container is to think of it as a framework composed of top level and connector components. For example, the context component is a connector component that tells the servlet container of the location of your application's root folder so the server can redirect all requests efficiently.

The server component is a top-level component and is an instance of the Tomcat server within the JVM (Java Virtual Machine).

Note You can create just one instance per JVM.

This isn't a book on Tomcat so I won't explain all the Tomcat components. We will use the Tomcat container to deploy all our Java-Flex applications. However, in the development phase, we will use another Java container called Jetty because it is faster and easier to configure. (I'm actually starting to use Jetty in my production servers as well, even if Tomcat is still the most popular.) Our applications will use the WAR (Web application archive) format. The WAR file contains all the application files and directories that Tomcat or Jetty will deploy. For a WAR file to work, it must contain a subdirectory called WEB-INF that needs to contain the following directories:

- Web.xml: The Web application deployment descriptor.
- Tag library descriptor files (see Tag Library Descriptors).
- Classes: A directory that contains server-side classes: servlet classes, utility classes, and JavaBeans components.

- Lib: A directory that contains JAR archives of libraries (tag libraries and any utility libraries called by server-side classes).

You can create application-specific subdirectories (package directories) in either the document root or the WEB-INF/classes directory.

Installing Tomcat

Installing Tomcat on your machine requires a JVM. Tomcat 6 is designed to run on JDK 1.5, so it is logical to use that. You can download the JVM Java installer from
`http://java.sun.com/j2se/downloads`

On Windows: You can download the Tomcat package for Windows from
`http://tomcat.apache.org/download-60.cgi`. Simply download the package and double-click to start the installation. The Tomcat installation for Windows is pretty straightforward—you just follow the wizard. Be aware that Tomcat will be installed as a Window service no matter what setting you use, and the installation will determine your Java location automatically from either the registry or the JAVA_HOME environment variable. After the installation, you can check it at
`http://localhost:8080`. You can start or stop the server easily by double-clicking on the tray icon or through the Windows Service Manager.

On Linux or Mac OS: Installing Tomcat on Linux or Mac OS is as straightforward as the Windows installation. Simply download the Tomcat 6 Binary Distribution Core (tar.gz) at
`http://tomcat.apache.org/download-60.cgi`. Create a Tomcat folder in /usr/local/. (I use /usr/local as it is standard, but Tomcat can be installed in other directories if you assign them the appropriate permissions.)

```
cd /usr/local/
```

```
sudo mkdir tomcat
```

Now go to the new Tomcat directory and unpack the tar.gz file

```
cd tomcat/
```

```
sudo tar -xvzf ~/Downloads/apache-tomcat-6.0.x.tar.gz
```

Before you can test the installation, you have to configure the tomcat-users.xml configuration file to access the Tomcat administration page. This file is located in the conf directory (tomcat/conf).

```
sudo vi conf/tomcat-users.xml
```

```
<?xml version='1.0' encoding='utf-8'?>
<tomcat-users>
  <role rolename="standard"/>
  <role rolename="manager"/>
  <user username="username" password="password" roles="standard,manager"/>
</tomcat-users>
```

```
Save the tomcat-users.xml and quit the vi editor
```

```
[esc] : wq
```

Now you can start the server by going to the bin directory and executing the shell script.

```
cd bin
```

```
sudo ./startup.sh
```

To check if it is working, you can take a look at the log at `tomcat/logs/catalina.out`:

```
cat catalina.out | less
```

Or, from your Web browser, go to `http://localhost:8080/`.

Tomcat Directories

Now that Tomcat is running, let's go over some basic concepts, such as the tomcat directories structure and content. If you go into the Tomcat root folder, you'll see many directories, like the following:

```
filippodipisa@Macintosh:/usr/local/apache-tomcat $ ls
LICENSE          RELEASE-NOTES  bin           lib          temp        work
NOTICE           RUNNING.txt    conf          logs         webapps
```

We don't need to cover them all; the most important are bin, conf, logs, and webapps. In the bin directory you'll find all the executable files to start and stop the server for the different operating systems. In the logs directory, you'll find the log files. The most important is catalina.out, the server log. The conf directory holds all tomcat configuration files, and the webapps directory is the one that will contain all your applications in both WAR and deployed formats, like this:

```
filippodipisa@Macintosh:/usr/local/apache-tomcat $ ls -l webapps/
```

```
drwxrwxrw-@  6 filippodipisa   filippodipisa        204 Jul 19  2008 examples
drwxrwxrw-@  6 filippodipisa   filippodipisa        204 Jul 19  2008 host-manager
drwxr-xr-x  13 filippodipisa   filippodipisa        442 Feb 11 19:21 idmwrapper
-rw-r--r--   1 filippodipisa   filippodipisa   31777490 Feb 11 19:21 idmwrapper.war
drwxrwxrw-@ 10 filippodipisa   filippodipisa        340 Jul 19  2008 manager
-rwxrwxrw-   1 filippodipisa   filippodipisa   10006291 Jul 28  2008 usermanager.war
-rwxrwxrw-   1 filippodipisa   filippodipisa    9501724 Jul 28  2008 usermanager
```

Tomcat Configuration Files

As noted, the Tomcat conf folder contains all the configuration files. Probably you'll never need to touch these files, but just in case you need to personalize or tune up you configuration, it is good to know what they are:

- catalina.policy – for managing security.

- catalina.properties – for setting which classes are available for all web applications or for Tomcat.

- context.xml – for configuring individual contexts. The default is using WEB-INF/web.xml files.

- logging.properties – for configuring all Tomcat logs.

- server.xml –the most important file, needed by Tomcat to set port, host, connection timeout, threads, clustering, and many other options.

- tomcat-users.xm – for managing all users who can access the main container.

- web.xml – the main descriptor for all web applications. All Web applications will contain a file called web.xml, but the Tomcat web.xml will execute before the application one.

We don't have to change the Tomcat default configuration for our purposes, and in fact you don't even have to install Tomcat as we will use the Tomcat Maven plug-in and Jetty to deploy and test our web applications. However, this chapter is meant to simulate a real environment, where you are likely to be using Tomcat.

Usually, to test I use Jetty and the Tomcat Maven plug-in. Then, before deploying on the live/testing server, I use my local Tomcat installation where I hope to replicate any problems or errors we are likely to find on the live system.

The Presentation Tools: Flex Builder

In the previous sections we covered how to set up your Eclipse IDE, the database management system, and the application container. Now you have the knowledge to start to write the application business logic and data access layers, but I still need to explain how to write and deploy the Flex presentation layer.

To create Flex applications, you need an IDE to write and debug Flex AS and MXML code. Then you need the Flex SDK framework to compile your AS/MXML classes into SWF files to be executed by the Flash Player.

Before Adobe released Flex, AS developers used the Flash IDE to compile AS classes, and different IDEs to write AS code. The most popular was FDT, a powerful Eclipse-based AS commercial editor. FDT is still around and its latest version now includes support for MXML, as well as a debugger. FTD is very good for writing code, but I still prefer Flex Builder because it is easier to configure, more standard, and quite well-documented.

If you want to use FDT, you will have to install the free version of the Adobe Flex SDK, then configure it to use the Data Visualization package in order to use the AdvancedDataGrid and other visual components available only with the professional edition of the Flex Builder. Basically, if you want to use these kinds of components with FDT, you should buy both Flex Builder and FDT licenses. In this book, we will use the Flex Builder Eclipse plug-in.

The Flex Builder is available as an Eclipse plug-in and as a standalone application built on Eclipse. I suggest installing the Eclipse plug-in so you can switch between Java and Flex without another open application. As mentioned above, the Flex Builder installs a powerful AS and MXML editor/debugger and the Flex SDK. Flex Builder 3 has new features and updates, including support for profiling and performance analysis. The profiling view displays information on performance, including memory usage and the execution time of function calls.

Installing the Flex Builder

To install the Flex plug-in, you need to download Flex Builder 3 from the Adobe website. At the time of this writing, you can download it at
`http://www.adobe.com/cfusion/entitlement/index.cfm?e=flexbuilder3`. If you like, you can try the 60-day trial version.

Once you have downloaded Flex, double-click on the executable file and follow the installation wizard. Figure 3-31 shows the first Flex Builder installation screen.

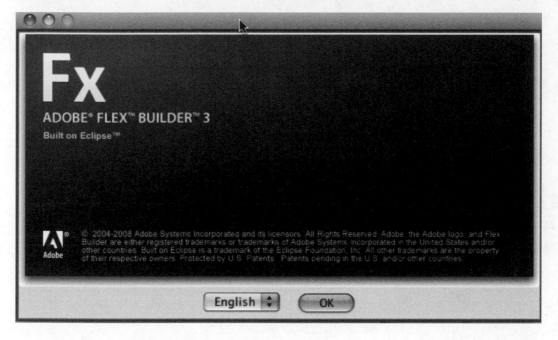

Figure 3-31. *Flex Builder installation first screen*

The installation is easy and straightforward, so we won't go through screen by screen. Follow the wizard, and just pay attention when you choose the Eclipse Folder (see Figure 3-32) in order to provide the correct path of your Eclipse installation. For example, on Mac, the Eclipse installation path could be /Applications/Eclipse/.

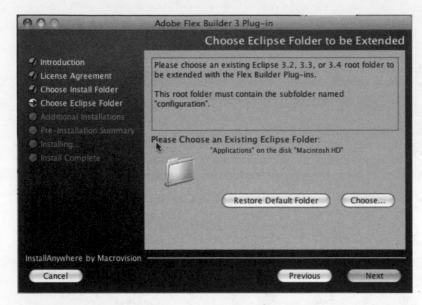

Figure 3-32. *Flex Builder installation prompting for the Eclipse folder*

Another important step is the installation of Flash Player. Note that the default is Flash Player 9 (see Figure 3-33), but if you already have Flash Player 10 installed, you should unselect the checkbox. Leave the CF Extension option unchecked, but do select JSEclipse.

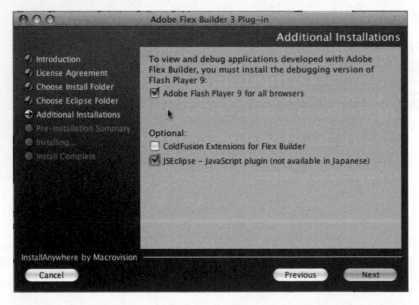

Figure 3-33. *Options for additional installations, including Flash Player*

When the installation is finished, restart Eclipse and you'll see the new Flex perspective button on the perspective bar (Figure 3-34).

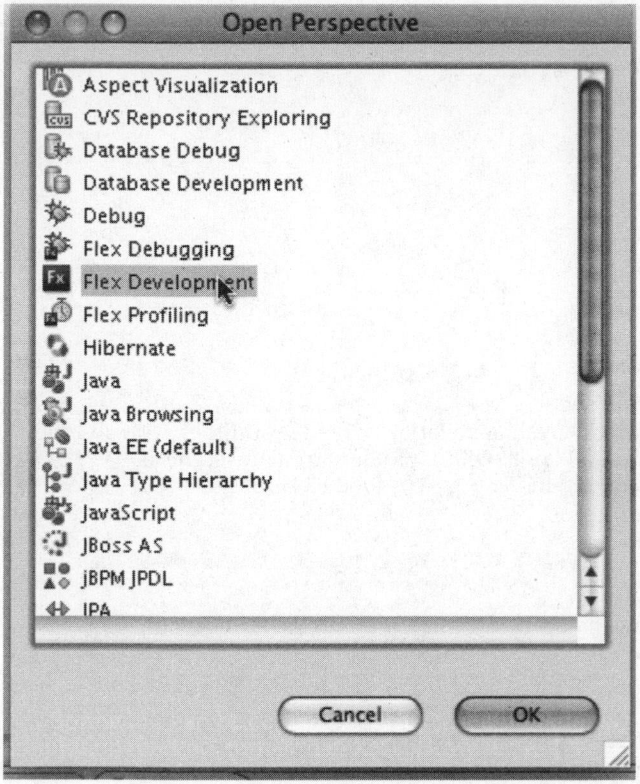

Figure 3-34. The new Flex perspective

Installing the Flex SDK 4

At the time of this writing, Flex Builder 3 comes with the Flex 3 SDK and Flash Player 9. If you want to use the Flex 4 SDK, you must install Flash Player 10 as well. Download the Flex 4 SDK at http://opensource.adobe.com/wiki/display/flexsdk/Download+Flex+4 and unzip it into your Applications folder for Mac and your Program Files folder for PC.

Next open the Eclipse Preferences (Figure 3-35) and select Flex>Installed SDKs (Figure 3-36).

Figure 3-35. *Opening Eclipse preferences*

As you can see, two default SDKs come with the fresh installation of the Flex Builder 3. To add the new SDK, click the Add button and browse for your Flex 4 SDK root folder. In my case, this is /Users/filippodipisa/Applications/Adobe Flex 3 Plug-in Eclipse 34/Adobe Flex Builder 3 Plug-in/sdks/4.0.0.4904, as shown in Figure 3-36.

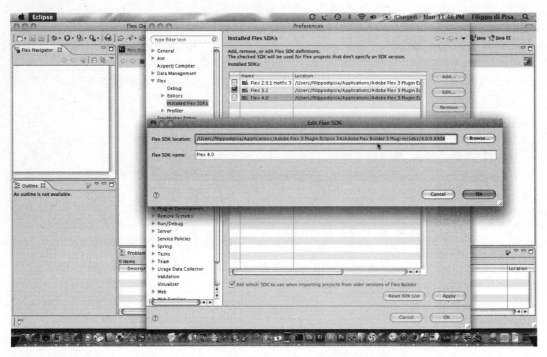

Figure 3-36. *Setting the Flex 4.0 SDK absolute path*

Now select the SDK you want to use, in our case this is version 4 (Figure 3-37).

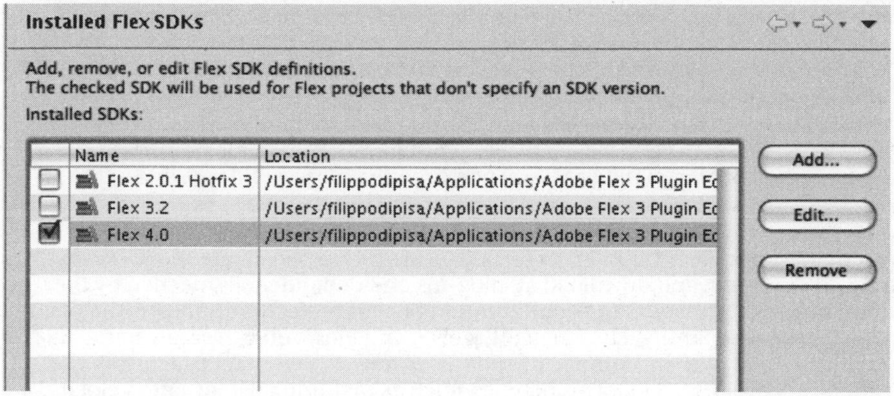

Figure 3-37. Choosing the Flex 4.0 SDK

That's it for Flex. The last important milestone for setting up our development environment is the installation and configuration of Maven.

The Build, Test and Deploy Tool: Maven

Maven is a Yiddish word that means "one who accumulates knowledge," and it is an apt description for this product.

Maven was started as a way to simplify the build process in the Jakarta Turbine project. That project actually comprised several projects that all contained their own different ANT build files, with no clear definitions of what was inside the projects and no easy way to publish project information or share JARS across several projects.

Maven has evolved to be a software project management tool that is based on the Project Object Model (POM), which provides compilation, testing, reporting, collaboration and documentation, based on a pom.xml(POM) file placed in the root of your project. The POM XML file describes all of your dependencies, plug-ins, SVN, repositories and properties of your project. Maven can save you time because it's an easy way to build and test Java-Flex projects.

Usually to build, test, and deploy a Java-Spring-Hibernate-Flex application, you would need a repository with all the libraries required from the project. An application server would need to be prepared and a tool (like ANT) set up to put everything together so you could build and test. Maven simplifies this by handling the entire build process and, at the same time, it is a complete tool for managing your Java projects.

At this time of this writing, there are two versions of Maven, and they are very different. You could actually write a book on the differences and merits of the two applications. In my view, Maven2 is a much stronger application, and all references to Maven in this book mean Maven2.

I've been developing using different build tools for both AS and Java for many years and I think Maven is the route to take as it provides all that you need to build, deploy, and test a Java project. After you use Maven for a time, you will be able to see its benefits and probably, as usually happens, you'll start to use it for all your software projects.

To start with, projects and systems that use Maven's standard, declarative build approach tend to be more transparent, more reusable, more maintainable, and easier to comprehend. For example, in order to build a Flex-Spring-Hibernate-BlazeDS application, you need a repository to contain the Spring and Hibernate Java libraries, then you need to install the BlazeDS server and configure it to work with Flex.

With Maven, you can describe all paths of your repositories and dependencies and decide which plug-ins to use for every single project. At the end of the day, Maven is a plug-in execution framework, and all the work is done by the plug-ins. There are core plug-ins that come with the product, and xml-based plug-ins are created by developers.

For instance the command `mvn clean` uses a core plug-in and the command `mvn jetty:run` requires you to specify the Jetty plug-in in your Maven project configuration XML file pom.xml.

To see the most up-to-date list of Maven plug-ins, you can browse a very useful web site at the `http://mvnrepository.com/`.

Another benefit of Maven is the ability to create archetypes. Basically, an archetype is like a template for your project that is reusable for similar projects. The archetype will create the directory structure, including all the files needed, and download all plug-ins and dependencies needed by the project, saving you a lot of time in the creation and configuration of your project. This means that if you are used to creating projects that need Spring, Hibernate, BlazeDS, and Flex, you can create an archetype with all dependencies and plug-in, compile it, and install it within your Eclipse installation.

Maven for Eclipse already comes with a lot of archetypes, such as for Spring, Hibernate, Velocity, Flex and other extremely useful ones. Later I'll show you how to create your own Maven archetype.

Installing Maven

You will need to use the Maven command-line tool and, though it's not necessary, I suggest you also download and install the Eclipse plug-in, which will give you more flexibility and save you time down the line.

Maven is open source, free to download and use, and is provided by the Apache Software Foundation. Go to `http://Maven.apache.org/download.html` to download the latest version for either Windows or the Mac. For example, at present I am using

```
filippodipisa@Macintosh:~ $ mvn -version
Maven version: 2.0.8
Java version: 1.5.0_13
OS name: "mac os x" version: "10.5.4" arch: "i386" Family: "unix"
```

I strongly recommend the following Eclipse plug-in, which can be downloaded from `http://m2Eclipse.sonatype.org/update/`

■ **Note** If you are operating in a restricted environment or behind a firewall, you might need to prepare to run Maven, as it requires write access to the home directory (~/.m2 on Unix/Mac OS X and C:\Documents and Settings\username\.m2 on Windows) and network access to download binary dependencies.

Configuring Maven

Maven configuration occurs at three levels:

- Project: most static configuration occurs in pom.xml
- Installation: this configuration is added once at the time of Maven installation

- User: this configuration is specific to a particular user

The default configuration files are located within ${user.home}/.m2/setting.xml. The location of your local repository can be changed in your user configuration. The default value is ${user.home}/.m2/repository/.

```
<settings>
  ...
  <localRepository>/path/to/local/repo/</localRepository>
  ...
</settings>
```

■ **Note** The local repository must be an absolute path.

Installing the Maven Eclipse Plug-in

The Maven Eclipse plug-in comes very useful when we have to debug our application. We'll use the plug-in also to create new Maven projects within the Eclipse IDE . It is my view that the command-line version is more complete and better to use. However, in order to debug our Flex-Java applications without having to configure our Eclipse IDE to use our external Maven installation, we need it. You can install the Maven plug-in for Eclipse by using the following update site from within Eclipse: http://m2Eclipse.sonatype.org/update/.

The most important benefits you get when installing the Maven Eclipse plug-in are:

- Automatic downloading of the required dependencies and sources from the remote Maven repositories.

- Wizards for creating new Maven projects, pom.xml, and to enable Maven support on existing projects.

- Quick search for dependencies in remote Maven repositories.

- Quick fixes in the Java editor for looking up required dependencies/JARs by the class or package name.

- Integration with other Eclipse tools, such as WTP, AJDT, Mylyn, and Subclipse.

Creating Your First Maven Project

We will start with the simplest way—the Eclipse environment. Open your Eclipse installation and select File ➤ New ➤ Maven Project.

Choose Create simple project as shown in Figure 3-38 (we skip the archetype selection for now) and the location of your project and click Next.

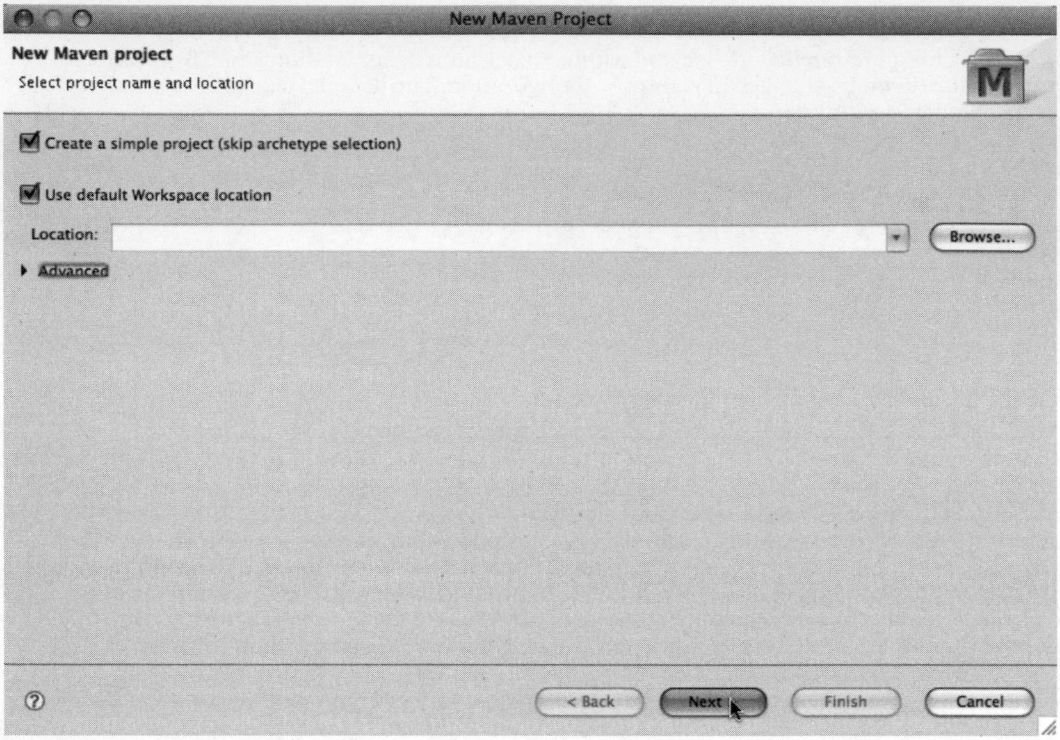

Figure 3-38. New Maven Project dialog window

Now insert a GroupId and ArtifactId for your project (see Figure 3-39). The GroupId means the path where your new project will be saved, and the ArtifactId is the name of the project itself.

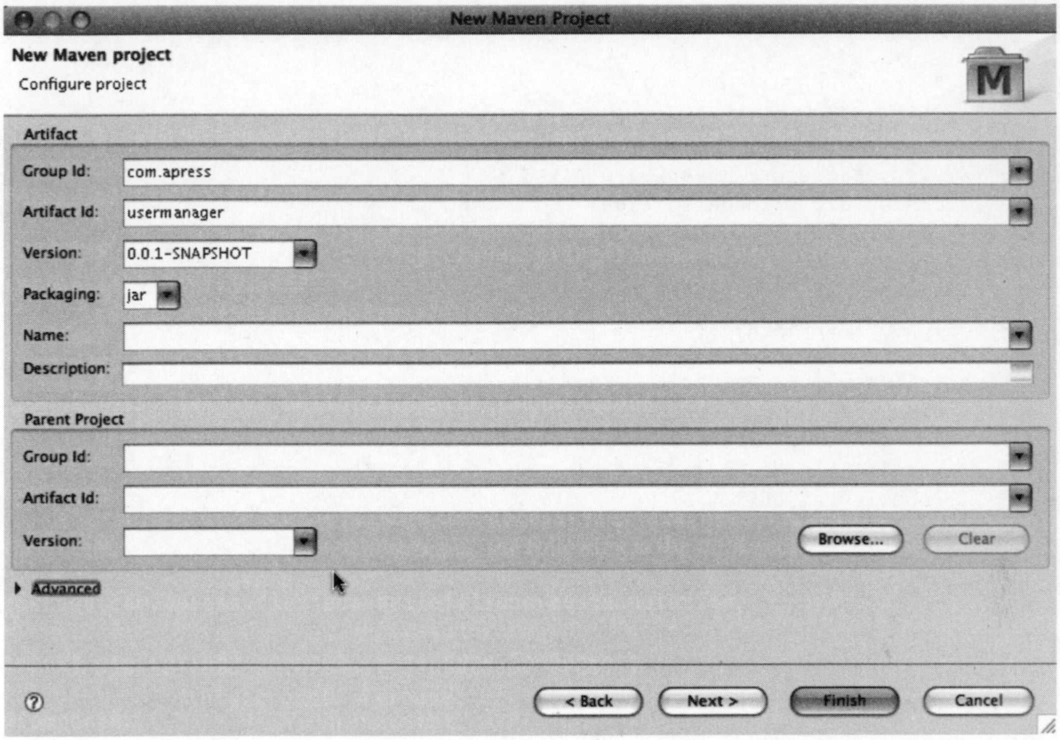

Figure 3-39. Setting your Maven project groupId and other options

Maven's application generation tool generated the following files and directories:

- MyProject
    - src/
    - pom.xml

The POM XML file will contain the basic information for the project and you'll need to add the dependencies and plug-ins for your project manually.

The POM Document

As noted earlier, it is the POM XML document that coordinates the Maven plug-in's execution and manages the dependences. So you can see how a POM XML file looks, a very basic pom file is shown in Listing 3-1.

Listing 3-1. A basic pom.xml configuration file

```
<?xml version="1.0" encoding="UTF-8"?>
<project xmlns="http://Maven.apache.org/POM/4.0.0" xmlns:xsi="http://www.w3.org/↩
2001/XMLSchema-instance" xsi:schemaLocation="http://Maven.apache.org/POM/
4.0.0 http://Maven.apache.org/Maven-v4_0_0.xsd">
        <modelVersion>4.0.0</modelVersion>
        <groupId>com.publicis.ldap</groupId>
        <artifactId>passwordmanager</artifactId>
        <version>0.0.2-SNAPSHOT</version>
        <packaging>jar</packaging>
        <name>A custom project</name>
        <url>http://www.myorganization.org</url>
        <plug-in>
                <groupId>org.apache.Maven.plug-ins</groupId>
                <artifactId>Maven-javadoc-plug-in</artifactId>
                <configuration>
                        <javadocVersion>1.5</javadocVersion>

        <excludePackageNames>com.jaxen</excludePackageNames>
                </configuration>
        </plug-in>
        <dependencies>
                <dependency>
                        <groupId>junit</groupId>
                        <artifactId>junit</artifactId>
                        <version>4.4</version>
                        <scope>test</scope>
                </dependency>
                <dependency>
                        <groupId>org.springframework</groupId>
                        <artifactId>spring</artifactId>
                        <version>2.5.2</version>
                </dependency>
                <dependency>
                        <groupId>org.springframework</groupId>
                        <artifactId>spring-test</artifactId>
                        <version>2.5.2</version>
                        <optional>true</optional>
                </dependency>
        </dependencies>
</project>
```

The POM XML configuration file is where you tell Maven which dependencies and plug-in you need for your project. The example in Listing 3-1 tells Maven to download the Spring and Junit JAR files from the public Maven repository and to include them into the project classpath. It also tells Maven to use the JavaDoc plug-in to automatically create all JavaDoc files during the build goal phase.

Building a Project with Maven

The vast majority of Maven-built projects can be created with the following commands:

```
mvn install
```

or

```
mvn clean install
```

This tells Maven to build all the modules and to install them into the local repository.

```
${user.home}/.m2/repository/
```

The local repository is created in your home directory (or alternative location you created), and it is the location where all downloaded binaries and the projects you build are stored.

For example, once downloaded, the following dependency

```
<dependency,
    <groupId>org.springframework</groupId>
    <artifactId>spring</artifactId>
    <version>2.5.2</version>
</dependency>
```

will be located at `${user.home}/.m2/repository/org/springframework/spring/2.5.2/`

If you're browsing the 2.5.2 folder, you will find all Spring JAR files.

```
$  ls .m2/repository/org/springframework/spring/2.5.2/
spring-2.5.2.jar        spring-2.5.2.jar.sha1        spring-2.5.2.pom
```

■ **Note** Some projects have multiple modules, so the library or application you are looking for could be stored in a module subdirectory.

Using Maven Plug-ins

As already noted, Maven can also be thought of as a plug-in execution framework that coordinates the execution of plug-ins in a well-defined way. Maven seems to have a plug-in for everything, and indeed includes plug-ins for compiling the source code, for running tests, for creating JARs, for creating JavaDocs, and many more.

■ **Note** One important concept to keep in mind is that everything accomplished in Maven is the result of a plug-in executing.

For example, in Java-Flex development, an application container like Tomcat or Jetty is needed to test your web application. Maven provides plug-ins for both of these containers, so you don't have to install them. As I mentioned, I prefer to Jetty as I find it faster and lighter than Tomcat. Note that the Maven Jetty plug-in is not a core plug-in; to use it you have to add the following XML to your POM XML file:

```
<plug-in>
        <groupId>org.mortbay.jetty</groupId>
        <artifactId>Maven-jetty-plug-in</artifactId>
        <version>6.1.19</version>
        <configuration>
        <contextPath>/yourContextRoot</contextPath>
        <scanIntervalSeconds>4</scanIntervalSeconds>
        <scanTargetPatterns>
                <scanTargetPattern>
                        <directory>
                                src/main/webapp/WEB-INF
                        </directory>
                        <excludes>
                                <exclude>**/*.jsp</exclude>
                        </excludes>
                        <includes>
                                <include>**/*.properties</include>
                                <include>**/*.xml</include>
                        </includes>
                </scanTargetPattern>
        </scanTargetPatterns>
        </configuration>
</plug-in>
```

The XML code tells Maven the version of the plug-in to use, the application context path, and other useful information needed by the Jetty plug-in in order to execute successfully.

To run the Jetty plug-in, simply type mvn jetty:run. This starts Jetty on port 8080 (*always be sure of what ports you are using*). Jetty will continue to run until the plug-in is explicitly stopped, either by using the command <ctrl-c> or using the command-line Maven command mvn jetty:stop.

Another Maven plug-in you'll want to install is the Maven server plug-in. I have often had to create a Flex-Java project using the ApacheDS LDAP server, but working on a team sharing a public LDAP server can be very messy. I found it was not possible to create unit test classes for testing, adding, editing, and deleting LDAP users using the shared LDAP server without conflicts or errors.

The best solution I found was to use either a local installation of the ApacheDS or the Maven ApacheDS plug-in. This local installation worked well, but the unit test used a default user and group so everyone had to set up on their local LDAP installations the same users and groups that I was using; otherwise, the test would fail. We started to share the ldiff file, a text file representing the LDAP configuration.

However, when we moved to the Maven plug-in, which creates at runtime an instance of the ApacheDS server based on a configuration file, stored into the project, everything became cleaner and easier to maintain. With this solution, everyone can build and run the project easily and without the hassle of needing a local installation of an LDAP server along with the ldiff file in order to be run the application tests.

Using Maven Dependencies

Dependency management is an important feature of Maven. It allows you to include all of your libraries automatically in your project, without having to manage them. It is easy to import dependencies; you just need to add XML tags to your POM XML file, specifying the groupid, artifactid, and the version of the dependency itself.

Maven will save you time and effort by downloading the dependency automatically from the repositories specified in your POM XML file or by your Maven configuration files ({Maven home/setting.xml}.

■ **Note** If you don't configure any repository into your pom file, Maven will use the default repositories set in the setting.xml file.

For instance, the following example code is part of a POM XML file and will download the Spring libraries needed to use the springframework APIs:

```
<dependency>
        <groupId>org.springframework</groupId>
        <artifactId>spring</artifactId>
        <version>2.5.2</version>
</dependency>
<dependency>
        <groupId>org.springframework</groupId>
        <artifactId>spring-test</artifactId>
        <version>2.5.2</version>
        <optional>true</optional>
</dependency>
```

Maven first looks for the dependencies in your local repository, then in remote repositories. If Maven doesn't find a library in either, it will return an error, asking you to install the library manually.

To avoid these errors, you simple need to identify the correct repository containing the dependency you require. Of course, you can always download the dependency/library and install it locally on your machine. To install a dependency locally, enter this Maven command:

```
mvn install:install-file -DgroupId= org.springframework -DartifactId=spring -
Dversion=↵
 2.5.2 -Dpackaging=jar -Dfile=spring-2.5.2 .jar
```

This command will install the library within your ${home}/.m2/repository/

Using Repositories

A repository in Maven is used to hold build artifacts and dependencies of differing types. Many projects will have dependencies and standard utilities that are often replicated in typical builds.

■ **Note** It is not recommended that you store your JARs in CVS or SVN.

Maven tries to promote the notion of a user local repository where JARs, or any project artifacts, can be stored and used for any number of builds. There are only two types of repositories, local and remote.

- The local repository refers to a copy on your own installation that is a cache of the remote downloads and also contains the temporary build artifacts that you have not yet released.

- Remote repositories refer to any other type of repository, accessed by a variety of protocols such as `file://` and `http://`. These repositories may include a truly remote repository set by a third party to provide their artifacts for downloading (for example, `repo1 Maven.org` houses Maven's central repository).

Local and remote repositories are structured the same way. This is so scripts can easily be run on either. In general use, the layout of the repositories is completely transparent to the Maven user.

■ **Note** Most organizations will need to set up one or more shared repositories, as not everyone can deploy to the same central Maven repository.

Setting up an internal Maven repository is simple and straightforward. While you can use any of the available transport protocols, the most popular is HTTP. You can use an existing HTTP server for this, or create a new server using Apache HTTPD, Apache Tomcat, Jetty, or any other suitable server.

To set up a simple internal repository for your organization, you can use Jetty or Tomcat. Create two folders called *internal* and *central* and open an ftp or scp port to upload the libraries. (*Don't be clever; use standard ports—21 for ftp and 22 for scp.*)

For instance your repository's HTTP URL could be
`http://yourComapny.com:8080/repo/internal`

To override the central repository with your internal repository, you need to define a repository in a settings file or in the pom file that uses the identifier *central*. Usually, this must be defined as both a regular repository and a plug-in repository to ensure access is consistent. For example:

```
<repositories>
<repository>
<id>central</id>
<name>Internal Mirror of Central Repository</name>
<url>http://localhost:8081/central/</url>
</repository>
</repositories>
<plug-inRepositories>
<plug-inRepository>
<id>central</id>
<name>Internal Mirror of Central Plug-ins Repository</name>
<url>http://localhost:8081/central/</url>
</plug-inRepository>
</plug-inRepositories>
```

However, I suggest you use an advanced repositories manager such as Artifactory. With Artifactory, you can gain full control over all the build artifacts and third-party dependencies that your organization uses and you can even share repositories throughout your interdepartmental and / or multi-team environment, no matter where your team members are. You can download Artifactory from `http://www.jfrog.org/download.php`.

Deploying Your Application

Releasing software is often a difficult and tedious exercise. When releasing Web-based projects in particular, you have to be aware of many things, including dependencies, database, view, and so forth. For example, to manually release a Flex-Java database-driven project, you will need to compile both Java and Flex, create an SVN tag, create the database, and a lot more.

Maven offers a release plug-in that provides the basic functions of a standard release process. The release plug-in takes care of a number of manual steps for you, such as updating the project POM, updating the source control management system to check and commit release-related changes, and creating tags.

The release plug-in operates in two steps: prepare and perform.

- The prepare step is run once for a release, and does all of the project and source control manipulation that results in a tagged version.

- The perform step could potentially be run multiple times to rebuild a release from a clean checkout of the tagged version, and to perform standard tasks, such as deployment to the remote repository.

To review the steps taken in the release process:

1. Check for correct version of the plug-in and POM.

2. Check if there are any local modifications.

3. Modify all POM files in the build, as they will be committed to the tag.

4. Run `mvn clean integration -test` to verify that the project will successfully build.

Here's an example of the release process. I created a JAR library called Security.jar that includes all APIs to allow an application to authenticate using an LDAP server via single sign-on or a form.

To share this library with all my company's other projects and teams, I released it on our organization's Artifactory server. The team members query the Artifactory server to see the latest version of the Security library, and they can update their POM file with the latest version or with the specific version they need.

To release the first or subsequent versions of the Security package, I take the following steps:

1. I run the command `MVN install` to make sure that the project compiles properly.

   Eventually you may want to skip all tests, and to do this you would run command `mvn install -DskipTests`.

2. I commit everything, and check that there aren't new SVN changes.

3. I run the command

```
mvn -B -Dusername=filippo -Dpassword=mypass release:prepare release:perform
```

If there are no errors, this command will compile all classes, create the SVN tag, and upload everything to the Artifactory server.

■ **Note** If you are also using Flex in your project, the first step is to compile the Flex client with the Flex compiler via Eclipse, Flex Builder, or the command line.

Creating a Maven Archetype

As I noted earlier, an archetype is like a template for your project that is reusable for similar projects, and Maven includes plenty of archetypes. For example there are archetypes to create Java Spring-Hibernate, Velocity, Flex projects and more.

■ **Note** In this book, we are going to use an archetype I created specifically for the Java-Spring-Hibernate-BlazeDS-Flex project, it uses the Flex compiler to enable easier debug and development.

Writing an archetype is quite like writing your own project and replacing the specific values with parameters. You can either create an archetype based on an existing project, using the maven command `mvn archetype:create-from-project`, or you can manually create an archetype from scratch.

To get started, run the following command:

```
mvn archetype:create -DgroupId=com.Maven.example -DartifactId=example-archetype↵
  -DarchetypeArtifactId=maven-archetype-archetype
```

There is no special build configuration required. The JAR that is built is composed only of resources, so everything else is contained under src/main/resources. Two pieces of information are required: the archetype descriptor in META-INF/maven/archetype.xml, and the template project in archetype-resources.

The archetype descriptor describes how to construct a new project from the archetype-resources provided. The example descriptor looks like the following:

```
<archetype>
        <id>example-archetype</id>
        <sources>
                <source>src/main/java/App.java</source>
        </sources>
        <testSources>
                <source>src/test/java/AppTest.java</source>
        </testSources>
</archetype>
```

Each tag defines the files that will be created when the archetype will be used. This example shows just the source and test sources, but you can also specify files for resources, testResources, and siteResources. Obviously, the groupId, artifactId, and version elements are variables that will be replaced with the values specified by the developer when running archetype:create.

To deploy an archetype, run the command mvn deploy. The archetype is now ready to be used. To do so, go to an empty directory and run the following command:

```
mvn archetype:create -DgroupId= \-DartifactId=Maven-example -DarchetypeGroupId=↵
com.maven.example -
DarchetypeArtifactId=mavenExample-archetype -DarchetypeVersion=1.0-SNAPSHOT
```

Normally, the archetypeVersion argument will not be required at this point. However, given that the archetype has not been released, if that argument is omitted, the required version would not be known (or if this was later development, a previous release would be used instead).

You now have the template project laid out in the Maven-example directory, which will look very similar to the content of the archetype-resources directory you created earlier. However, for now the content of the files will be populated with the values that were provided on the command line.

Flex Maven Archetypes

FNA is an open source project started by Adobe consulting that helps Java and Flex development with open source projects and Maven archetypes. You can see and read more about FNA at http://code.google.com/p/fna-v2/ You can find more interesting and useful Flex-Java archetypes at http://fna-v2.googlecode.com/svn/trunk/mvn_archetypes/such as:

- flex-cairngorm-stubbed-crud-archetype
- flex-cairngorm-flexunit-archetype
- flex-library-archetype

Useful Maven Commands

Table 3-3 contains several of the most useful Maven commands along with the code for your POM XML file if it is not a core plug-in, and a description of the command's purpose.

Table 3-3. *Useful Maven commands*

Command	Plug-in	Purpose
mvn eclipse:eclipse -DdownloadSources=true	```<plugin> <artifactId>maven-eclipse-plugin</artifactId> <version>2.4</version> <configuration> <additionalProjectnatures> <projectnature> org.springframework.ide. eclipse.core.springnature </projectnature>```	This will set up the Eclipse environment and download the source for the JAR files.

```
                            </additionalProjectnatures>
                            <additionalBuildcommands>
                            <buildcommand>
                            org.springframework.ide.
                              eclipse.core.springbuilder
                            </buildcommand>
                            </additionalBuildcommands>
                            <downloadSources>true
                              </downloadSources>
                            <downloadJavadocs>true
                              </downloadJavadocs>
                            <wtpversion>1.5</wtpversion>
                        </configuration>
                    </plugin>
```

`mvn install`	`core plugin`	This will build and install the artifact (JAR files) to your local repository.
`mvn clean`	`core plugin`	This will remove the target directory with the old build data.
`mvn jetty:run`	`<plugin>`	This will start your application with the Jetty server.

```
                    <groupId>org.mortbay.jetty
                      </groupId>
                    <artifactId>maven-jetty-
plugin</artifactId>
                    <version>6.1.5</version>
                    <configuration>

                    <contextPath>/idmwrapper
                      </contextPath>

                    <scanIntervalSeconds>4
                      </scanIntervalSeconds>

                    <scanTargetPatterns>

                    <scanTargetPattern>

                          <directory>

                    src/main/webapp/WEB-INF

                          </directory>
```

```
                                <excludes>

                    <exclude>**/*.jsp</exclude>

                    </excludes>

                                <includes>

                    <include>**/*.properties
                      </include>


                    <include>**/*.xml</include>

                                </includes>

                    </scanTargetPattern>
                    </scanTargetPatterns>
                      </configuration>
                </plugin>
```

Command	Plugin	Description
`mvn install cargo:start`		This will generate the WAR, starts the JBoss container, and will deploy the WAR into it.
`mvn archetype:create -DgroupId=<groupId> -DartifactId=<artifactId> -DarchetypeArtifactId=<archetypeArtifactId>`	core plugin	This will create a Maven archetype.
`mvn site`	core plugin	This will generate a site for the current project.
`mvn surefire-report:report`		This will generate a report based on the results of unit tests.
`mvn javadoc:javadoc`	`<plugin>` `<groupId>org.apache.maven.plugins </groupId>`	This will generate the Javadoc output. in target/site/apidocs.

	`<artifactId>aven-javadoc-plugin</artifactId>` `</plugin>`	
`mvn -U install`	`core plugin`	This will force Maven to update all of the snapshots in the build.
`mvn release:prepare -DdryRun=true`	`core plugin`	This will simulate a normal release preparation, without making any modifications to your project.
`mvn install:install-file -Dfile=<path-to-file> -DgroupId=<group-id> -DartifactId=<artifact-id> -Dversion=<version> -Dpackaging=<packaging>`	`core plugin`	This will install locally a library from a file.
`mvn -version`	`core plugin`	This will return the Maven version installed on your machine.
`mvn archetype:crawl`	`core plugin`	This will search for an archetype within your local setting.
`mvn archetype:generate -DarchetypeCatalog=local`	`core plugin`	This will generate an archetype from an existing project.
`mvn -B -Dusername=<username> -Dpassword=<pass> release:prepare release:perform`	`core plugin`	This will deploy artifactory.
`mvn source:jar`	`core plugin`	This will generate source.
`mvn install -DskipTests`	`core plugin`	This will build the application skipping all test classes.

Summary

Sometime it can take a lot of time and effort to configure and set up a complex development environment, but a properly set up development environment can really make a difference. I hope this chapter helps you to set up a compete J2EE Flex development environment.

In the next chapter, we will enter into the development phase, starting with Java Spring, currently one of the most popular J2EE frameworks. Now the fun begins!

CHAPTER 4

■ ■ ■

Inversion of Control

As noted in the previous chapter, Spring is a modular POJO framework that provides more than 130 packages for supporting Web and enterprise application development. At its core, Spring is a container that can manage the entire life cycle of your application objects. In this chapter, I will begin to delve into this core—the Inversion of Control (IoC) container and the Dependency Injection (DI) design pattern.

The container implements the DI pattern that allows you to keep the dependencies between different objects dynamic. For example, you can have an object that needs a reference to another object or to an external resource like a mail server. In our user manager application, the `UserServiceImpl` class has a reference to both `MailDao` and `UserDao` objects. You need to save the user to the database and send out the confirmation email.

```
public class UserServiceImpl implements UserService {

    private MailDao mailDao;

    private UserDao userDao;

    public void save(User user) {
        userDao.saveOrUpdate(user);
        mailDao.sendConfirmationEmail(user);
    }

}
```

The container manages the entire life cycle of these objects and all their references throughout the DI pattern. DI is a concrete pattern, while the Inversion of Control is a general concept that reverses the direction of the traditional lookup. The two most common type of DI, are:

- constructor injection
- setter injection

In the following example, I will use the setter injection, exposing two setter methods, to accept the properties of type `UserDao` and `MailDao`

```
public class UserServiceImpl implements UserService {

    private MailDao mailDao;

    private UserDao userDao;
```

```
    public void save(User user) {
        userDao.saveOrUpdate(user);
        mailDao.sendConfirmationEmail(user);
    }

    public setMailDao(MailDao mailDao) {
        this.mailDao = mailDao
    }

    public setUserDao ( UserDao userDao) {
        this. userDao =  userDao
    }

}
```

■ **Note** If you are familiar with design patterns in general, you are probably aware that to reduce the lookup complexity of your objects you may use a JEE Service Locator pattern. We will be exploring this pattern on the client side in upcoming chapters, using Flex within the Cairngorm framework.

Constructor injection differs from setter injection in that dependencies are injected within the constructor instead of into the setter methods:

```
public class UserServiceImpl implements UserService {

    private MailDao mailDao;

    private UserDao userDao;

    public  UserServiceImpl(){}

    public  UserServiceImpl(MailDao mailDao,UserDao userDao) {
        this.mailDao = mailDao;
        this. userDao =  userDao;
    }

    public void save(User user) {
        userDao.saveOrUpdate(user);
        mailDao.sendConfirmationEmail(user);
    }

}
```

As you can see in this example, I have used two constructors with different signatures. This is because some Java lightweight frameworks, such as Hibernate, sometimes need an empty default constructor.

The Spring IoC container supports both constructor and setter DI. It uses either an external XML configuration file or annotations to manage all the dependencies between objects. When an object is managed by the Spring container, it is called *bean*.

```xml
<?xml version="1.0" encoding="UTF-8"?>
<beans xmlns="http://www.springframework.org/schema/beans"
        xmlns:xsi="http://www.w3.org/2001/XMLSchema-instance"
        xmlns:p="http://www.springframework.org/schema/p"
      xmlns:aop="http://www.springframework.org/schema/aop" ↵
xmlns:tx="http://www.springframework.org/schema/tx"
        xsi:schemaLocation="http://www.springframework.org/schema/beans ↵
http://www.springframework.org/schema/beans/spring-beans-2.5.xsd
            http://www.springframework.org/schema/aop ↵
http://www.springframework.org/schema/aop/spring-aop-2.0.xsd
            http://www.springframework.org/schema/tx ↵
http://www.springframework.org/schema/tx/spring-tx-2.0.xsd"
        default-lazy-init="true">

    <bean id="mailDao" class="org.apress.usermanager.dao.mail.MailDaoImpl" />

    <bean id="userDao" class="org.apress.usermanager.dao.ldap.UserDaoImpl" />

    <bean id="userService"
class="org.apress.usermanager.business.UserServceImpl" >
            <property name="mailDao" ref="mailDao"/>
            <property name="userDao" ref="userDao"/>
    </bean>

</beans>
```

This example shows the Spring setter injection described by the Spring XML configuration file. In the property tag, the attribute called *name* corresponds to the setter name setMailDao, and the attribute called *ref* communicates with the container telling it the reference object to inject in (in this example, the *bean* mailDao was instantiated with another *bean* above).

■ **Note** Bean is just a naming convention; a bean is an object.

Spring Modules

The Spring architecture is divided into different modules, organized with the upper modules dependent on the lower modules, as shown in Figure 4-1. Table 4-1 describes the most important of these modules.

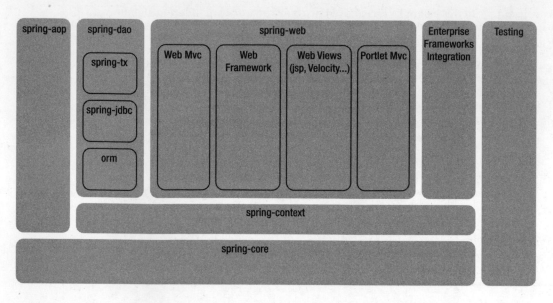

Figure 4-1. Spring modules

Underlying all modules is the Spring core, which provides the IoC container that will hold all of the Spring beans created through the XML file configurations. A Spring bean is simply a Java object injected into the Spring IoC container.

Table 4-1. The most important Spring modules

Spring Module	Description
Spring Core	The basic IoC container for the objects (beans); it will read their configuration through one or more external configuration files or with annotations.
AOP	The Spring AOP module provides Aspect Oriented Programming functionalities integrated with Spring. Spring AOP is integrated with the AspectJ framework. AOP is very useful for enterprise development—it helps in removing many scalability problems and saves time when problem solving and modularizing your application.
Context	Context extends the core module and provides an advanced implementation of the bean factory of the IoC container, called ApplicationContext. The bean factory is just the basic implementation of the IoC container that creates bean instances, which are created from the injection configuration file.

TX	This module provides transaction management services for your Java objects. Transactions are very important for enterprise development as they improve the efficiency of the connection, and thus reduce the risk of losing updates or of partial failures.
Web, Web MVC, Portlet MVC, and Web Framework	These modules are built on top of the Web module to provide the capabilities to use the standard MVC design pattern in the Web application view, as well as the services to implement other popular frameworks such as Struts. (We won't be covering these capabilities in this book; instead we will focus on the ActionScript/Flex view.)
Enterprise frameworks integration	This module makes Spring not just an IoC container but a JEE application framework as well. It includes support for popular enterprise Java frameworks such as JMS, E-MAIL, and EJB.
JDBC	This very important module provides services to access the database data. Spring JDBC is built on top of the native Java JDBC APIs, improving exception handling, query execution, and configuration, while still providing full access to the native JDBC.
ORM	This important module provides integration support for the most popular Java ORM frameworks, such as Hibernate, iBatis, and Oracle TopLink. ORM provides many benefits, especially in database driven applications.
TESTING	Creating unit and integration tests are a must for enterprise application development. Spring provides support for both, allowing you to run everything in your IDE and enabling you to reuse your configuration files between test and production environments.

Spring Maven Dependencies

Spring's modular approach lets you choose the packages needed for your applications. Table 4-1 gives you an idea of the capabilities of the major modules. We will be importing the Spring modules through Maven, the plug-in framework execution manager discussed in Chapter 3. If you have read that section about Maven, you should be up to speed and able to configure the dependency libraries needed by your application in the POM file located in the root of your application, using the XML definition as follows:

```
<dependency>
    ...
</dependency>
```

To use the Spring framework within your application through Maven, you need only to add the Spring-framework dependency in your POM file. Maven will download it from the Central Maven Repository to your local repository and application classpath.

```
<dependency>
        <groupId>org.springframework</groupId>
```

```
    <artifactId>spring</artifactId>
    <version>2.5.2</version>
</dependency>
```

This code tells Maven to download version 2.5.2 of the Spring framework package to your local repository. You can see whether the library has been added to your application by browsing the Maven dependencies tree in your Eclipse IDE (see Figure 4-2).

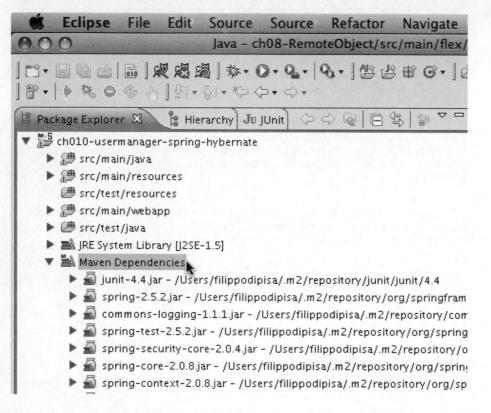

Figure 4-2. Eclipse Maven dependencies

Table 4-2 shows the important Spring Maven plug-ins for Flex-Java applications development.

Table 4-2. Spring Maven plug-ins

Artifact	POM dependency

Spring-core	```<dependency>```
	``` <groupId>org.springframework</groupId>```
	``` <artifactId>spring-core</artifactId>```
	``` <version>2.5.6</version>```
	```</dependency>```

Spring-agent	```<dependency>```
	``` <groupId>org.springframework</groupId>```
	``` <artifactId>spring-agent</artifactId>```
	``` <version>2.5.6</version>```
	```</dependency>```

spring-aop	```<dependency>```
	``` <groupId>org.springframework</groupId>```
	``` <artifactId>spring-aop</artifactId>```
	``` <version>2.5.6</version>```
	```</dependency>```

spring-aspects	```<dependency>```
	``` <groupId>org.springframework</groupId>```
	``` <artifactId>spring-aspects</artifactId>```
	``` <version>2.5.6</version>```
	```</dependency>```

spring-context	```<dependency>```
	``` <groupId>org.springframework</groupId>```
	``` <artifactId>spring-context</artifactId>```
	``` <version>2.5.6</version>```
	```</dependency>```

spring-dao	```dependency>```
	``` <groupId>org.springframework</groupId>```
	``` <artifactId>spring-dao</artifactId>```
	``` <version>2.0-m4</version>```
	```</dependency>```

spring-hibernate3	```<dependency>```
	``` <groupId>org.springframework</groupId>```
	``` <artifactId>spring-hibernate3</artifactId>```
	``` <version>2.0-m4</version>```
	```</dependency>```

| spring-jdbc | ```xml
<dependency>
        <groupId>org.springframework</groupId>
        <artifactId>spring-jdbc</artifactId>
        <version>2.5.6</version>
</dependency>
``` |
| spring-jms | ```xml
<dependency>
        <groupId>org.springframework</groupId>
        <artifactId>spring-jms</artifactId>
        <version>2.5.6</version>
</dependency>
``` |
| spring-jmx | ```xml
<dependency>
        <groupId>org.springframework</groupId>
        <artifactId>spring-jmx</artifactId>
        <version>2.0.8</version>
</dependency>
``` |
| spring-ldap | ```xml
<dependency>
        <groupId>org.springframework</groupId>
        <artifactId>spring-ldap</artifactId>
        <version>1.1.2</version>
</dependency>
``` |
| spring-mock | ```xml
<dependency>
        <groupId>org.springframework</groupId>
        <artifactId>spring-mock</artifactId>
        <version>2.0-rc3</version>
</dependency>
``` |
| spring-test | ```xml
<dependency>
        <groupId>org.springframework</groupId>
        <artifactId>spring-test</artifactId>
        <version>2.5.6</version>
</dependency>
``` |
| spring-tx | ```xml
<dependency>
        <groupId>org.springframework</groupId>
        <artifactId>spring-tx</artifactId>
        <version>2.5.6</version>
</dependency>
``` |
| spring-full | ```xml
<dependency>
        <groupId>org.springframework</groupId>
        <artifactId>spring</artifactId>
        <version>2.5.6</version>
</dependency>
``` |

Creating a Spring Project

To start a Spring project, you need to include the Spring JAR libraries in your applications classpath. To do this, you should download the Spring libraries from the Spring framework web site (without using Maven) and locate these manually in your class path. Thanks to Maven, you only need to add to your POM file (which is located in your application root) the dependency XML definition as follows:

```
<dependency>
        <groupId>org.springframework</groupId>
        <artifactId>spring</artifactId>
        <version>2.5.2</version>
</dependency>
```

Let's now create a Spring "Hello Filippo" project. We will go through this step by step and use Eclipse. (It is assumed that you have read Chapter 3 and have properly configured your development environment.) In order to create a Maven project, open your Eclipse IDE and Click, File ➤ New ➤ Other on the top bar dropdown menu (as in Figure 4-3).

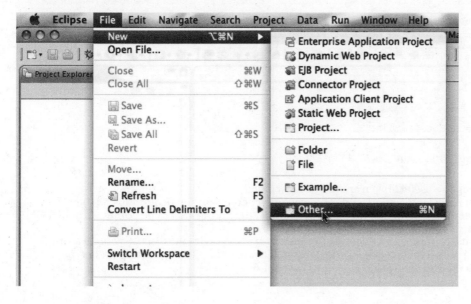

Figure 4-3. *Creating a new Maven project*

Now select "Create a Maven Project," then "Maven Project," and click the Next button, as shown in Figure 4-4.

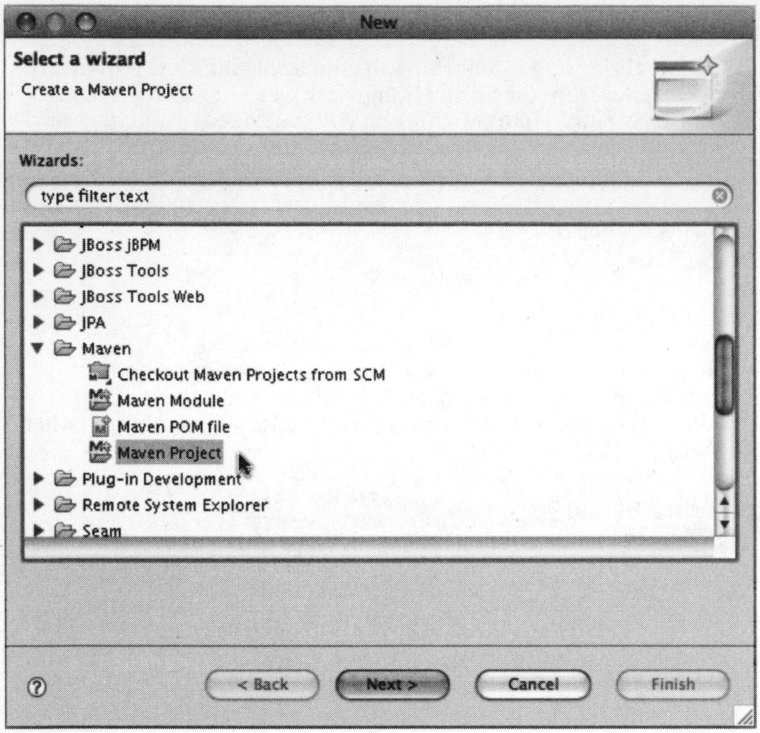

Figure 4-4. *The Maven Project wizard*

We won't be using the useful Maven archetypes discussed in Chapter 3, as for now we want to keep the project basic so it is easier to understand. The maven archetype automatically adds all the dependencies you need for a particular project. For example the Spring archetype comes with the POM already configured with all Spring dependencies.

Instead, we will use a Maven archetype that I created for the Flex-Java project. To create a simple project without using archetypes, check the box labeled "Create a simple project (skip archetype selection)" and press the Next button, as shown in Figure 4-5.

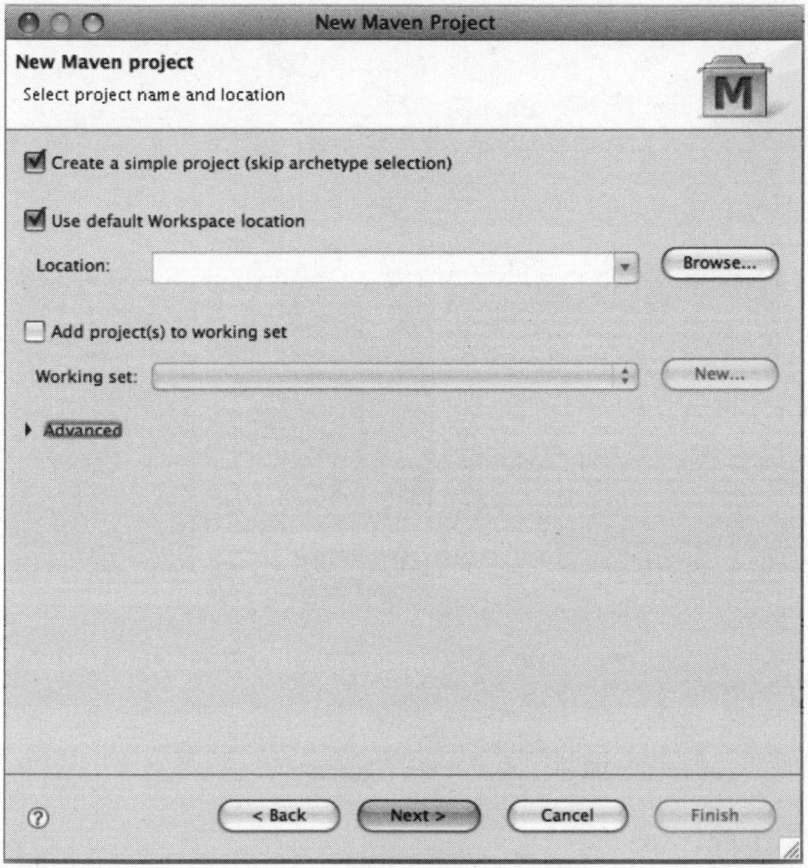

Figure 4-5. Maven project wizard showing how to skip the archetype creation

Now we come to the most complex part, so let's review some basic Maven concepts.

Groupid is the path in the Maven repository where the JAR/WAR application file will be stored once deployed or installed locally. In our example, the groupId is `com.apress.flexjava`. When you run the command `mvn install`, Maven will create the path com/apress/flexjava/ into your Maven home (usually ${HOME}/.m2/);

ArtifactId is the name of your project. In our example, this will be `hellofilippo`;

Version is the version of your project;

Packaging is the format in which you want to package your application; the most common are WAR and JAR. Because our simple example is not a Web application, we will use the JAR format;

Name is the name of your Maven project. This option is useful when another user needs to import an existing Maven project using the Eclipse Maven import project tool.

Description is the description of your project.

Parent project fields, which are useful to use POM inheritance, won't be covered in this book;

Figure 4-6 shows these values filled in on the page of the New Maven Project wizard.

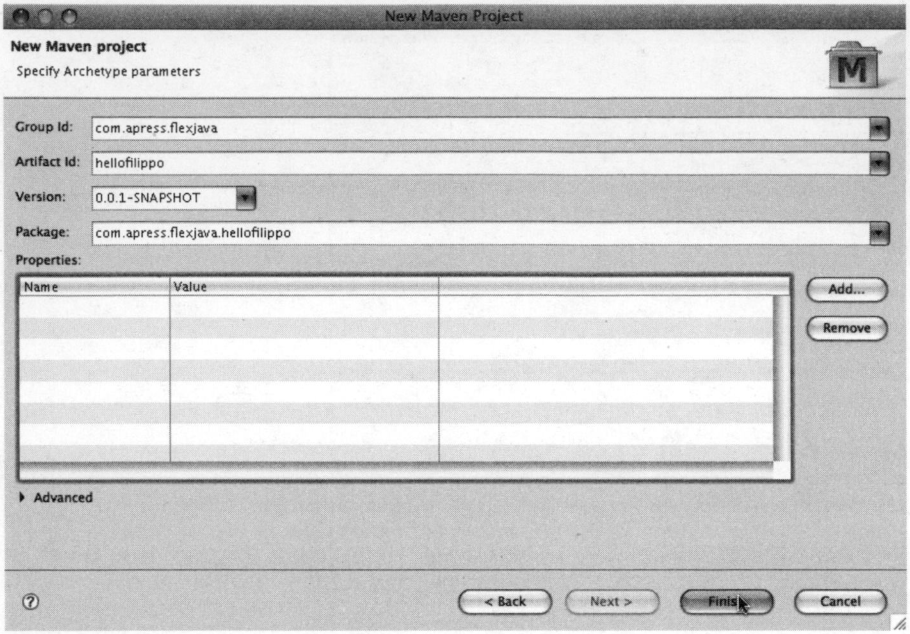

Figure 4-6. Maven project wizard configuration form

When you are happy with all values, click the Finish button. Maven will create the directory structure needed for your application and the POM file, as shown in Figure 4-7.

Figure 4-7. The directory structure of the new Maven project

If you open your POM file, you should now see the settings you added with the wizard (see Figure 4-8). To see the XML source code of your open pom.xml file, click on the tab in the lower-right corner, as shown in Figure 4-9.

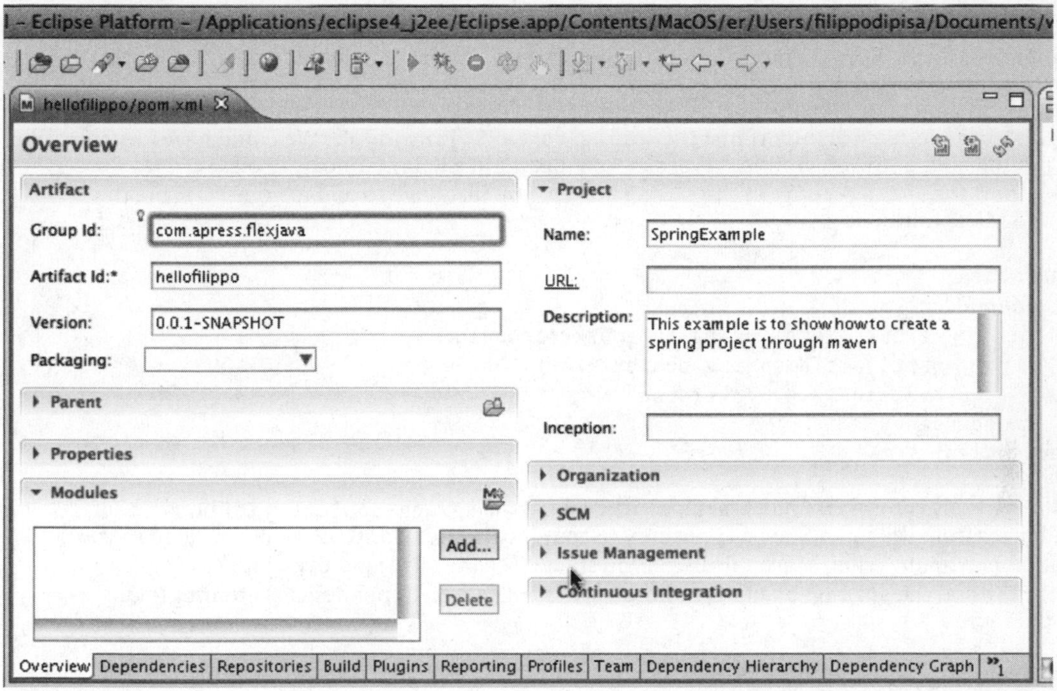

Figure 4-8. Pom.xml opened within Eclipse

Figure 4-9. Click to see the XML source code of your POM file

In source mode, you should see the following XML:

```
<project xmlns="http://maven.apache.org/POM/4.0.0" ↵
xmlns:xsi="http://www.w3.org/2001/XMLSchema-instance" ↵
xsi:schemaLocation="http://maven.apache.org/POM/4.0.0 ↵
http://maven.apache.org/maven-v4_0_0.xsd">
  <modelVersion>4.0.0</modelVersion>
  <groupId>com.apress.flexjava</groupId>
  <artifactId>hellofilippo</artifactId>
  <name>SpringExample</name>
```

```
<version>0.0.1-SNAPSHOT</version>
<description>This example is to show how to create a Spring project↩
through maven</description>
</project>
```

To start to use the Spring Framework with your project, you have to include the JAR files that contain the Spring modules you want to use in your application. In our basic example, we need only the IoC container to inject our beans into.

In this example, we will import just the `spring-context.jar` module. We could have used the full Spring module, but at the beginning it is easier to understand each module by itself.

To import the `spring-context.jar` using Maven, you just have to add to your POM file the following XML definitions:

```
<dependencies>
    <dependency>
        <groupId>org.springframework</groupId>
        <artifactId>spring-context</artifactId>
        <version>2.5.6</version>
    </dependency>
</dependencies>
```

When you save your POM file, Maven will download the `spring-context.jar` library and its dependencies from the main Maven repository to your local system, and they will be added to your application classpath. When Maven finishes, you should see the `spring-core.jar`, `spring-context.jar` and the `spring-beans.jar` libraries in your Maven dependencies libraries folder, as shown in Figure 4-10.

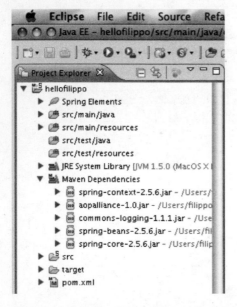

Figure 4-10. *The Spring Maven dependencies loaded in the project classpath*

The final step, before we start to write some classes and inject these into the container, is to tell the Eclipse IDE that our project is a Spring project; this option lets us use some of the IDE functionalities provided by the Spring tools Eclipse plug-ins that you should have already installed. (If you haven't installed them yet, follow the instructions in the previous chapters.)

It is simple to make Eclipse aware of your Spring project—just right-click on the project and choose the item "Add Spring Project Nature," as shown in Figure 4-11. Once you do, you will be able to use the Spring IDE tools.

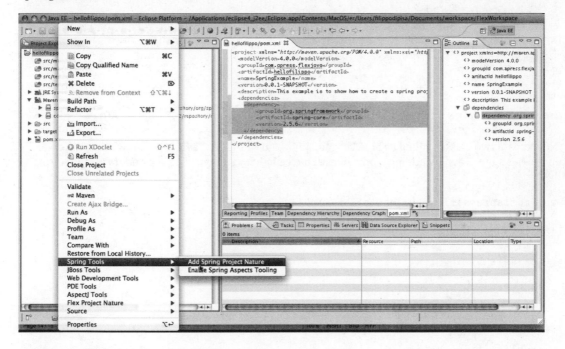

Figure 4-11. Adding the Spring Project Nature to your project

Now, finally we will start to write some code. The goal for our example application is not complicated—merely to print the string "hello filippo" to the screen. I don't know anyone apart from my mother who could be excited by this application, but the point here is to learn how to inject beans into the Spring container.

First, create one package called `com.apress.flexjava.hellofilippo` in the `src/main/java` folder (see Figure 4-12).

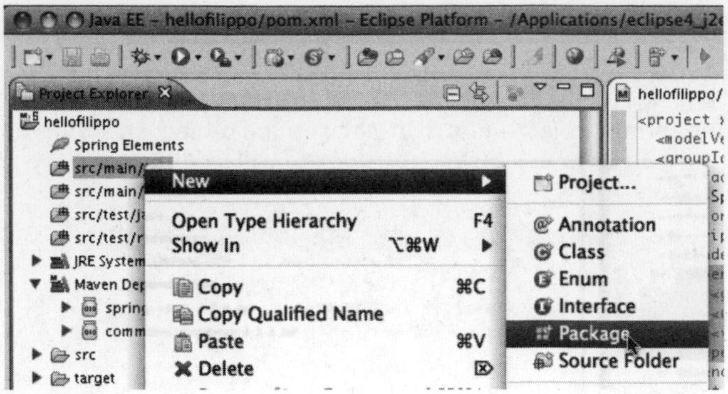

Figure 4-12. Creating a new packag

Now create two classes called `HelloFilippo.java` and `Message.java`. We start writing the code within the `Message.Java` by adding a private variable called `text` of type `String` and its public setter method.

```java
package com.apress.flexjava.hellofilippo;

public class Message {

    private String text;

    public void setText(String text) {
        this.text = text;
    }

    public String getText() {
        return this.text;
    }
}
```

To add the setter and getter methods, I suggest you use the Eclipse Generate getter and setter functionality (see Figure 4-13) as I feel it greatly improves your productivity by automatically generating the getters and setters to create (see Figure 4-14).

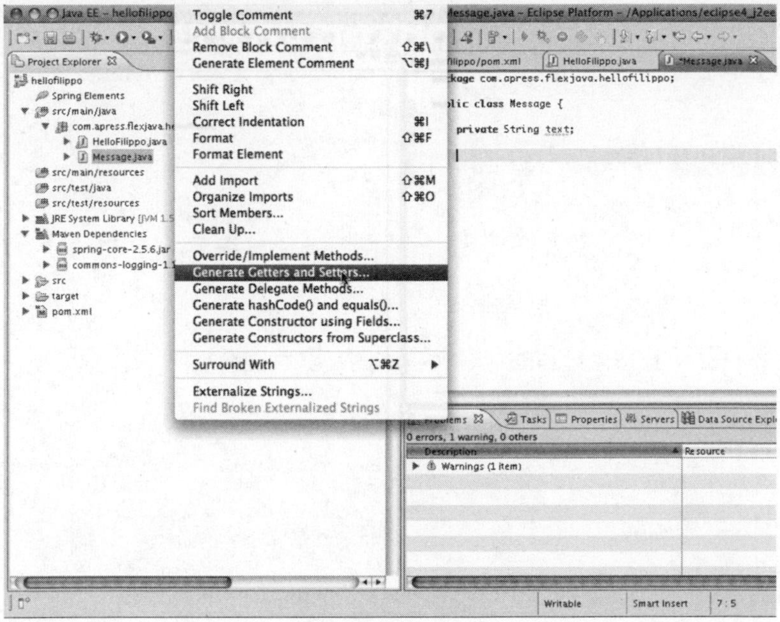

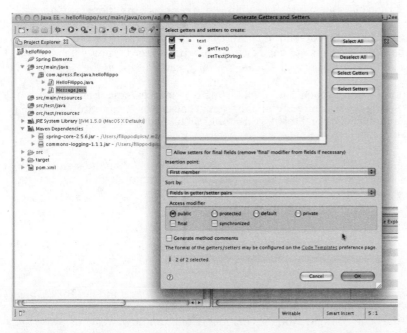

Figure 4-13. Select Generate Getters and Setters

Figure 4-14. Use Eclipse to generate getter and setter automatically

Now open the HelloFilippo class and simply add the reference to the class Message with a private var of Message type and add its public setter method. The class HelloFilippo must also provide a method to print the string to the screen. The method will be public, and it will be named hello():

```
package com.apress.flexjava.hellofilippo;

public class HelloFilippo {

        private Message message;

        public void hello() {
                System.out.println("Hello Filippo!" + message.getText());
        }

        public void setMessage(Message message) {
                this.message = message;
        }

        public String getMessage() {
                return this.message;
        }
}
```

As you can see, the HelloFilippo class has a reference to the Message class, but there is no one class that will create the needed instance of the Message class and set it into the HelloFilippo.

To do that we have to configure the Spring IoC container XML configuration file to create an instance into the container of a bean of type Message and of a bean of type HelloFilippo. The HelloFilippo bean will have a reference to the message bean. We will create this file in the src/main/resources folder.

To create the Spring configuration file, right click on the /src/main/resources/ folder and select New ➤ Other. Then choose the "Spring Bean Configuration file" item, click on the Next button, call the filename ApplicationBeans.xml, and then click on Finish. You should then see in your ApplicationBeans.xml the following code:

```
<?xml version="1.0" encoding="UTF-8"?>
<beans xmlns="http://www.springframework.org/schema/beans"
       xmlns:xsi="http://www.w3.org/2001/XMLSchema-instance"
       xsi:schemaLocation="http://www.springframework.org/schema/beans ↵
http://www.springframework.org/schema/beans/spring-beans.xsd">


</beans>
```

Now we have to add the XML definition to create the two beans of type Message and HelloFilippo in the container. To create a new bean, you need to use the XML syntax <bean id="{name_bean}" />. In the next section we will cover the bean configuration files in more details; for now, write just two beans with both id=helloFilippo and id=message.

The bean message will have a property called text with the value "How are you?" The bean helloFilippo will have a reference property to the bean with the id=message.

```
<bean id="message" class="com.apress.flexjava.hellofilippo.Message" >
     <property name="text" value="How are you?" />
</bean>

<bean id="helloFilippo" class="com.apress.flexjava.hellofilippo.HelloFilippo">
     <property name="message" ref="message" />
</bean>
```

As you can see from the preceding code, we inject into the container the two classes with their properties. In practice, the property with name="text" corresponds to the setter method setText with the class Message, and the property message corresponds to the setter method setMessage in the class HelloFilippo.

The last piece of our puzzle is to write a Main class to instantiate the IoC container with its configuration file ApplicationBean.xml; once the container has instantiated we get the bean helloFilippo that is needed for our test.

```
package com.apress.flexjava.hellofilippo;

import org.springframework.context.ApplicationContext;
import org.springframework.context.support.ClassPathXmlApplicationContext;

public class Main {

     public static void main(String[] args) {
          ApplicationContext context =
               new ClassPathXmlApplicationContext("ApplicationBeans.xml");

          HelloFilippo helloFilippo = (HelloFilippo)
context.getBean("helloFilippo");

          helloFilippo.hello();
     }

}
```

To test the code, right click on the Main.java class and select Run As ➤ Java Application (see Figure 4-15).

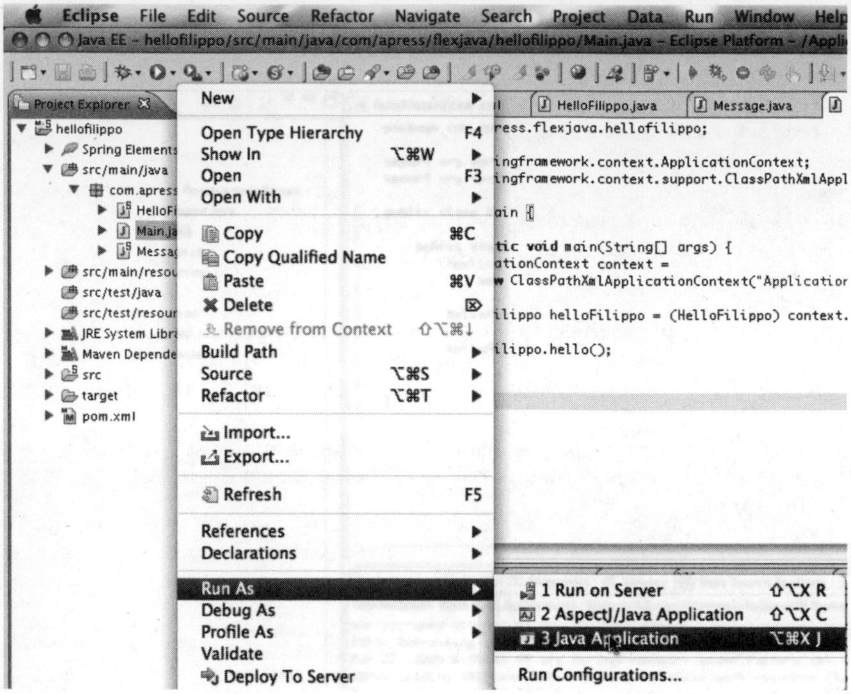

Figure 4-15. *Using Eclipse to run a Java application*

If everything is fine, you should see in the console window the message "Hello Filippo! How are you?" after all the Spring logging messages.

Configure the Spring Container

In the previous section, we saw how easy it is to create a Spring Maven project, loading the needed dependencies from the POM file and injecting classes to the IoC container using the Spring XML configuration file. Until the version 2.5 of Spring, the XML-based configuration file played an important role, but it now seems that the Spring core development team is focusing mostly on the annotations model. You can use either XML or annotations-based configuration. I actually use both, as XML is more readable, though annotations are much quicker to implement. In my view, if you want to be a Spring developer, you need to learn both methods properly. It appears that 80 percent of the market is currently using XML-based configuration, so we will start with the most common.

XML-Based Configuration

The basic Spring bean definition template is the following:

```
<?xml version="1.0" encoding="UTF-8"?>
<beans xmlns="http://www.springframework.org/schema/beans"
       xmlns:xsi="http://www.w3.org/2001/XMLSchema-instance"
```

```
      xsi:schemaLocation="http://www.springframework.org/schema/beans ↩
http://www.springframework.org/schema/beans/spring-beans-2.5.xsd">
```

```
</beans>
```

It is strongly recommended that you use the spring-beans-2.5.xsd schema, which will enable you to make use of the new Spring 2.5 features.

Writing XML Bean Definitions

Within the Spring bean definition template you can write many different bean definitions. Each bean must have a unique id and must use the Spring beans XML namespaces. Spring will manage the entire life cycle of all beans, instantiating all of them before they are used. Spring uses the singleton scope by default.

```
<bean id="message" class="com.apress.flexjava.hellofilippo.Message" >

</bean>
```

The XML above will inject a bean of type `Message` with id=“`message`”. Spring supports both constructor and dependency injection.

Constructor Dependency Injection

In our first “Hello Filippo” project, we used setter injection to set both text and message properties.

```
<bean id="message" class="com.apress.flexjava.hellofilippo.Message" >
      <property name="text" value="How are you?" />
</bean>

<bean id="helloFilippo" class="com.apress.flexjava.hellofilippo.HelloFilippo">
      <property name="message" ref="message" />
</bean>
```

However, there are times that you need to pass arguments directly to the constructor. Let's refactor our class `HelloFilippo` to use the constructor-injection.

```
package com.apress.flexjava.hellofilippo;

public class HelloFilippoForConstructorInjection {

      private Message message;

      public void hello() {
              System.out.println("Hello Filippo!" + message.getText());
      }
```

```
    public HelloFilippoForConstructorInjection(Message message){
        this.message = message;
    }

}
```

As you can see, I have created another class called `HelloFilippoForConstructorInjection` in which I deleted the setter method, and I pass the message reference object directly to the constructor. In order to use the constructor dependency injection, the new bean definition will use a new tag called constructor-arg.

```
<bean id="helloFilippoForConstructorInjection" ↵
class="com.apress.flexjava.hellofilippo.HelloFilippoForConstructorInjection">
        <constructor-arg ref="message" />
</bean>
```

Spring constructor injection accepts either beans or values. You can use the `ref` attribute to refer to another bean and the `value` attribute to directly set the attribute's value.

```
        <constructor-arg ref="message" />

        <constructor-arg value="How are you?" />
```

A common problem is when you have two or more constructors differing in just the signature attribute type. Suppose you want to inject through the constructor messages of both type Message and String.

```
package com.apress.flexjava.hellofilippo;

public class HelloFilippoForAmbiguityConstructor {

private String message;

    public void hello() {
            System.out.println("Hello Filippo!" + message);
    }

    public HelloFilippoForAmbiguityConstructor(Message message){
        this.message = message.getText();
    }

    public HelloFilippoForAmbiguityConstructor(String message){
        this.message = message;
    }

}
```

In this code, there are two identical constructors, differing in just the type of the argument. How can Spring understand which one to use? The latest version of Spring finds the type automatically, but you can specify in the XML definition the type by adding the type attribute.

```
<bean id="helloFilippoForAmbiguityConstructor" ↵
class="com.apress.flexjava.hellofilippo.HelloFilippoForAmbiguityConstructor">
      <constructor-arg ref="message" type="com.apress.flexjava.hellofilippo.Message" />
</bean>
<bean id="helloFilippoForAmbiguityConstructor2" ↵
class="com.apress.flexjava.hellofilippo.HelloFilippoForAmbiguityConstructor">
      <constructor-arg value="Nice to meet you." type="java.lang.String" />
</bean>
```

■ **Note** In the latest version of 'Spring' the above definition works without specifying type as well.

Setter Dependency Injection

The other way to inject properties is using setter injection, which we used already with the first Spring HelloFilippo project.

```
<bean id="message" class="com.apress.flexjava.hellofilippo.Message" >
      <property name="text" value="How are you?" />
</bean>

<bean id="helloFilippo" class="com.apress.flexjava.hellofilippo.HelloFilippo">
      <property name="message" ref="message" />
</bean>
```

Setter injection as constructor injection accepts both value and references. You can combine setter and construction injection. Below is an example of a class that uses setter and construction injection and its bean definition. In the constructor, there is the required property and the setter is just optional.

```
package com.apress.flexjava.hellofilippo;

public class HelloFilippoForBothSetterAndConstructiorInjection {

      private Message message;

      private String name;

      public void hello() {
            System.out.println("Hello " + name + "!" + message.getText());
      }

      public void setMessage(Message message) {
```

```
        this.message = message;
    }

    public HelloFilippoForBothSetterAndConstructiorInjection(String name){
        this.name = name;
    }

}

<bean id="helloFilippoForBothSetterAndConstructiorInjection" ↵
class="com.apress.flexjava.hellofilippo.HelloFilippoForBothSetterAndConstructiorInj
ection">
    <constructor-arg value="Chris"  />
    <property name="message" ref="message" />
</bean>
```

■ **Note** The bean name in the <ref> attribute can be a reference to any bean injected into the container, even if not defined in the XML file.

Inner Beans

For both constructor and setter injection, you can use an inner bean instead of the `ref` attribute.

For example you can inject the property `message` into the class `HelloFilippo` using an inner bean instead of reference to it.

```
<bean id="helloFilippoForInnerBean"
class="com.apress.flexjava.hellofilippo.HelloFilippo">
    <property name="message">
        <bean id="messageInnerBean" class="com.apress.flexjava.hellofilippo.Message" >
            <property name="text" value="I'm an inner bean." />
        </bean>
    </property>
</bean>
```

This can be very useful when you want to keep a bean anonymous and don't plan to use it anywhere else.

Injecting Lists and Collections

Sometimes it is useful to inject directly into a collection of other beans or values. Spring supports the injection of Properties, Map, Set, and List. In this section, we'll show some examples of how to inject a List, a Map, and a Set of messages in the class `hellofilippo`.

First, let's modify the class HelloFilippo to HelloFilippoForCollection, changing the var messages and its setter method to the List<String> type. Next, loop through the collection to reprint all messages injected.

```java
import java.util.List;

public class HelloFilippoForCollectionInjection {

        private List<String> messages;

        public void hello() {
                System.out.println("Hello Filippo!");
                for(String message : messages){
                        System.out.println(message);
                }
        }

        public void setMessages(List<String> messages) {
                this.messages = messages;
        }

}
```

Spring allows creating and adding the messages list on the fly in the configuration file:

```xml
<bean id="helloFilippoForCollectionInjection" ↵
class="com.apress.flexjava.hellofilippo.HelloFilippoForCollectionInjection">
            <property name="messages">
                    <list>
                            <value>How are you?</value>
                            <value>Fine and you?</value>
                            <value>Not so bad.</value>
                            <value>Good.</value>
                    </list>
            </property>
        </bean>
```

The result will be:

```
Hello Filippo!
How are you?
Fine and you?
Not so bad.
Good.
```

If you want to store unique objects in your collection, you have to use Set. Set differs from List in that it doesn't contain duplicate objects, and all objects are not ordered or indexed.

```java
import java.util.Set;

public class HelloFilippoForCollectionInjection {

	private Set<String> messages;

	public void hello() {
		System.out.println("Hello Filippo!");
		for(String message : messages){
			System.out.println(message);
		}
	}

	public void setMessages(Set<String> messages) {
		this.messages = messages;
	}

}
```

In your bean you will have:

```xml
<bean id="helloFilippoForCollectionInjection" ↵
class="com.apress.flexjava.hellofilippo.HelloFilippoForCollectionInjection">
		<property name="messages">
			<set>
				<value>How are you?</value>
				<value>Fine and you?</value>
				<value>Not so bad.</value>
				<value>Good.</value>
			</set>
		</property>
	</bean>
```

Map is another important collection. Map is like a table and it uses key/value pairs to store its entries, which means you can retrieve a value by its key. To show the Map injection, I have created another class called HelloFilippoForCollectionMapInjection, adding a property of type Map<String,String> that means that both key and values are of String type.

```java
import java.util.Map;

public class HelloFilippoForCollectionMapInjection {

	private Map<String,String> messages;

	public void hello() {
```

```
            System.out.println("Hello Filippo!");
            for(Map.Entry<String, String> message : messages.entrySet()){
                System.out.println(message);
            }
        }

    public void setMessages(Map<String, String> messages) {
            this.messages = messages;
        }
}
```

To inject a Map collection using the Spring configuration file is a bit different from List and Set as you have to specify both the key and the value:

```
<bean id="helloFilippoForCollectionMapInjection" ⏎
class="com.apress.flexjava.hellofilippo.HelloFilippoForCollectionMapInjection">
            <property name="messages">
                <map>
                    <entry>
                      <key>
                            <value>Chris</value>
                      </key>
                      <value>How are you?</value>
                    </entry>
                    <entry>
                            <key>
                                    <value>Filippo</value>
                            </key>
                            <value>Fine thank you.</value>
                    </entry>
                </map>
            </property>
    </bean>
```

The result will be print key=value.

```
Hello Filippo!
Chris=How are you?
Filippo=Fine thank you.
```

The last collection I find important and useful is Properties. It is similar to the Map collection except that Map can have values and keys of any type while the Properties collection supports just String types. Below are two examples of how to use the Properties collection in your Java classes and Spring configuration file.

```
import java.util.Properties;
```

```java
public class HelloFilippoForCollectionPropertiesInjection {

        private Properties messages;

        public void hello() {
                System.out.println("Hello Filippo!");
                messages.list(System.out);
        }

        public void setMessages(Properties messages) {
                this.messages = messages;
        }
}
```

```xml
<bean id="helloFilippoForCollectionPropertiesInjection" ↵
class="com.apress.flexjava.hellofilippo.HelloFilippoForCollectionPropertiesInjectio
n">
                <property name="messages">
                        <props>
                                <prop key="Chris">How are you?</prop>
                                <prop key="Filippo">Fine thank you.</prop>
                        </props>
                </property>
        </bean>
```

As always, in order to see the result, you have to amend your Main class in order to get the helloFilippoForCollectionPropertiesInjection bean from the container.

```java
HelloFilippoForCollectionPropertiesInjection
helloFilippoForCollectionPropertiesInjection =
                    (HelloFilippoForCollectionPropertiesInjection) ↵
context.getBean("helloFilippoForCollectionPropertiesInjection");

helloFilippoForCollectionPropertiesInjection.hello();
```

Here are the results. The function of the properties list is only for debugging purposes, to see the list of all properties.

```
Hello Filippo!
-- listing properties --
Chris=How are you?
Filippo=Fine thank you.
```

For all of the collections `Map, Set,` and `List`, you can use any type of object. As you can see, the Spring configuration file is pretty easy to configure and it's also scalable and very powerful.

■ **Note** You can use multiple configuration files and include references to beans in the different files.

The next section will cover topics similar to the ones we've just discussed, but will be annotation-based rather than XML.

Annotation-Based Configuration

Following the Java 5 standard, Spring 2.5 has added support for more annotations than were previously available. You can think of an annotation as a sort of metatag that defines some functionality or information. An annotation in Java starts with the symbol @and can be set anywhere, such as in class and method declarations. For example, an `@Override` annotation tells the compiler that the method must be an overridden method and to return an error if it's not.

```
public class HelloFilippoBase {

    @Override
    public void hello() {

    }
}
```

Spring IoC can be configured using just annotations, and the trend seems to be moving to the annotation method, rather than XML. However, as I mentioned earlier, I strongly suggest that you learn both methods. XML configuration is still more prevalent and it works with previous versions of Spring. This obviously means there is more existing code that uses XML, and it is very often the case that you'll have to work with existing code at some point. Moreover, annotations are spread across your code while XML is centralized in one or more files. It's a good idea to use annotation for beans that change frequently, and use XML for static beans.

Now I will show how to inject a `String` message into the class `HelloFilippoForAnnotations` using annotation-driven configuration. Before we enter into the development phase, I am going to show the most common Spring configuration annotations.

Spring Configuration Annotations

Here are the Spring configuration annotations:

@Autowired
@Required
@Resource
@PostConstruct / PreDestroy
@Component / @Repository

Basically, the @Autowired annotation removes the need for using constructor-arg or property elements in XML. @Autowire tells to Spring to auto-wire the bean property or constructor with another bean of the same type, so that if you have a method setMessage accepting an object of Message type, the object of Message type will be injected automatically without you have to specify this in your bean. Before using annotations, you have to configure your main XML configuration file to use annotations.

Let's modify the XML configuration file used so far for all the "helloFilippo" examples to allow Spring to use annotations. As shown in the following code, I use the tag <context:annotation-config /> in order to configure Spring to use annotations:

```
<?xml version="1.0" encoding="UTF-8"?>
<beans xmlns="http://www.springframework.org/schema/beans"
       xmlns:xsi="http://www.w3.org/2001/XMLSchema-instance"
       xmlns:context="http://www.springframework.org/schema/context"
       xsi:schemaLocation="http://www.springframework.org/schema/beans
       http://www.springframework.org/schema/beans/spring-beans-2.5.xsd
       http://www.springframework.org/schema/context
       http://www.springframework.org/schema/context/spring-context-2.5.xsd">
       .......
       <context:annotation-config />

</beans>
```

Without the XML element <context:annotation-config />, the compiler will return an error. Basically this element tells Spring to turn on the annotations.

Now let's create a class called HelloFilippoForAutowired with the annotation @Autowired for the method setMessage.

```
package com.apress.flexjava.hellofilippo;

import org.springframework.beans.factory.annotation.Autowired;

public class HelloFilippoForAutowired {

        private Message message;

        public void hello() {
                System.out.println("Hello Filippo!" + message.getText());
        }
        @Autowired
        public void setMessage(Message message) {
                this.message = message;
        }
}
```

The @Autowired annotation tells Spring that if the IoC contains a bean of type message, it will be injected automatically into the HelloFilippoForAutowired class. This allows you to avoid having to manually inject into your XML configuration file as in the following example:

```
<bean id="message" class="com.apress.flexjava.hellofilippo.Message" >
      <property name="text" value="How are you?" />
</bean>

<bean id="helloFilippoForAutowired"
class="com.apress.flexjava.hellofilippo.HelloFilippoForAutowired" />
```

Here's the result:

Hello Filippo! How are you?

You can use the @Autowired annotation for both properties and constructor elements. The annotation @Required tells Spring to check if DI has been performed on a property. If not, the compiler will return an error.

```
@Required
public void setMessage(Message message) {
      this.message = message;
}
```

```
@Resource
```

The @Resource annotation tells Spring to inject the bean specified within the annotation @Resource("beanName"). This is useful in cases where there are different beans of the same type and autowiring doesn't work. In our examples, we can have different beans of type messages and the annotation @Autowire could return errors.

To use the annotation @Resource, you have to add the jsr250-annotations library to your classpath, as it is a JSR-250 annotation and not a Spring-specific one. Thanks to Maven, you will need to add only the following code to your POM file:

```
<dependency>
    <groupId>javax.annotation</groupId>
    <artifactId>jsr250-api</artifactId>
    <version>1.0</version>
</dependency>
```

Next I'll create a class HelloFilippoForResource, using both @Autowire and @Resource annotations. In our XML configuration file, we will have two beans of Message type. With the @Resource annotation, we will specify which bean will be autowired in our class.

```
package com.apress.flexjava.hellofilippo;

import org.springframework.beans.factory.annotation.Autowired;
import javax.annotation.Resource;

public class HelloFilippoForResource {
```

```
private Message message;

public void hello() {
        System.out.println("Hello Filippo!" + message.getText());
}
@Autowired
@Resource(name="messageForResourceBean")
public void setMessage(Message message) {
        this.message = message;
}

}
```

Here are the beans in the configuration file:

```
<bean id="message" class="com.apress.flexjava.hellofilippo.Message" >
        <property name="text" value="How are you?" />
</bean>
<bean id="messageForResourceBean" class="com.apress.flexjava.hellofilippo.Message"
>
        <property name="text" value="Annotations are fantastic!" />
</bean>
<bean id="helloFilippoForResource"
class="com.apress.flexjava.hellofilippo.HelloFilippoForResource" />
```

As you can see in the configuration file, there are two beans of type Message, but as we specified, within the @Resource annotation parameter name, the name of the "messageForResourceBean" bean will be injected into that bean and will result in the following:

```
Hello Filippo! Annotations are fantastic!
```

Using the Annotations @PostConstruct and @PreDestroy

Both @PostConstruct and @PreDestroy are JSR-250 annotations, not Spring-specific annotations. This means you need to import the jsr250-api. Before explaining what these annotations do, I have to introduce the XML configuration bean attributes init-method and destroy-method. Sometimes you will need to execute a method immediately after instantiating the component. In our example, we want to execute the method setHardcodedMessage to set the String variable message with the value hard-coded into the class. As you can see from the example below, the method is private and cannot be used to inject anything. So the only way to populate the message property is to run that method using the init-method attribute in the XML configuration file:

```
package com.apress.flexjava.hellofilippo;

public class HelloFilippoForInitMethod {

        private String message;
```

```
    public void hello() {
            System.out.println("Hello Filippo!" + message);
    }

    private void setHardCodedMessage() {
            this.message = "This is very cool!";
    }
}

<bean id="helloFilippoForInitMethod" ↵
class="com.apress.flexjava.hellofilippo.HelloFilippoForInitMethod" ↵
init-method="setHardCodedMessage" />
```

The result will be the following:

```
Hello Filippo! This is very cool!
```

In Spring there are two ways to call a method to initialize or to destroy a component:

- using the XML attributes init-method and destroy-method as in the preceding example;
- implementing the interfaces InitializingBean and DisposableBean as in the following example;

```
package com.apress.flexjava.hellofilippo;

import org.springframework.beans.factory.DisposableBean;
import org.springframework.beans.factory.InitializingBean;

public class HelloFilippoForInitMethod implements InitializingBean, DisposableBean
{

    private String message;

    public void hello() {
            System.out.println("Hello Filippo!" + message);
    }

    private void setHardCodedMessage() {
            this.message = "This is very cool!";
    }

    public void afterPropertiesSet() throws Exception {
            setHardCodedMessage();
```

```
        }

        public void destroy() throws Exception {
        }
}

package com.apress.flexjava.hellofilippo;

import javax.annotation.PostConstruct;

public class HelloFilippoForPreConstruct {

        private String message;

        public void hello() {
                System.out.println("Hello Filippo!" + message);
        }

        @PostConstruct
        private void setHardCodedMessage() {
                this.message = "Wow! It is amazing!";
        }
}
```

When using the `@PostConstruct` annotation, you don't need to use the XML attribute `init-method` to specify the initialize method.

```
<bean id="helloFilippoForPreConstruct" ↵
class="com.apress.flexjava.hellofilippo.HelloFilippoForPreConstruct" />
```

The `@Predestroy` annotation is equivalent to the XML attribute `destroy-method`.

Using the Annotations @Component and @Repository

Finally we have arrived at the annotations that remove the need to specify almost anything in your XML configuration files. Well, almost, as you will still need to define some XML to tell Spring the packages that contain bean components, as follows:

```
<context:component-scan base-
package="com.apress.flexjava.hellofilippo.testannotations" />
```

The annotation `@Component` tells Spring that the class annotated is a bean. The default bean name will be the name of the class in lowercase and if you want, you can set your own name as an option of the annotation. To show you how to use annotation-driven configuration, let's create a new package called "testannotations" with a new `Application.xml` and a new `Main` class.

First we create in src/main/resources the new XML configuration file ApplicationForAnnotationsConfiguration.xml with the following content:

```
<?xml version="1.0" encoding="UTF-8"?>
<beans xmlns="http://www.springframework.org/schema/beans"
        xmlns:xsi="http://www.w3.org/2001/XMLSchema-instance"
        xmlns:context="http://www.springframework.org/schema/context"
        xsi:schemaLocation="http://www.springframework.org/schema/beans
                            http://www.springframework.org/schema/beans/spring-
beans-2.5.xsd
                            http://www.springframework.org/schema/context
                            http://www.springframework.org/schema/context/↵
spring-context-2.5.xsd"
                    >

        <context:component-scan base-package=↵
"com.apress.flexjava.hellofilippo.testannotations" />

</beans>
```

Next we have to create the package com.apress.flexjava.hellofilippo.testannotations and then create two classes, Message and Hello. the following is the entire code for the Message class:

```
package com.apress.flexjava.hellofilippo.testannotations;

import org.springframework.stereotype.Component;

@Component
public class MessageForAnnotationConfiguration {

        private String text = "Welcome to annotations";

        public String getText() {
                return text;
        }

}
```

And here is the entire code for the Hello class:

```
package com.apress.flexjava.hellofilippo.testannotations;

import org.springframework.beans.factory.annotation.Autowired;
import org.springframework.stereotype.Component;

@Component
public class HelloFilippoForAnnotationsConfiguration {

        private MessageForAnnotationConfiguration message;
```

```
public void hello() {
        System.out.println("Hello Filippo!" + message.getText());
}

@Autowired
public void setMessage(MessageForAnnotationConfiguration message) {
        this.message = message;
}

}
```

As you can see, both classes are annotated with @Component. The HelloFilippoForAnnotation class has the @Autowire annotation, which automatically injects the message object. Now I have to create a Main class in which to instantiate the beans and the context.

```
package com.apress.flexjava.hellofilippo.testannotations;

import org.springframework.context.ApplicationContext;
import org.springframework.context.support.ClassPathXmlApplicationContext;


public class Main {
        public static void main(String[] args) {
                ApplicationContext context =
                        new ClassPathXmlApplicationContext
                        ("ApplicationForAnnotationsConfiguration.xml");

                HelloFilippoForAnnotationsConfiguration helloFilippo =
                        (HelloFilippoForAnnotationsConfiguration) ↵
context.getBean("helloFilippoForAnnotationsConfiguration");

                helloFilippo.hello();
        }
}
```

In the Main class, I have instantiated the context loading the new Application XML configuration file, and then I get the bean helloFilippoForAnnotationsConfiguration from the IoC container. As you can see, the annotation @Component has informed Spring to inject the component with the same name of the class in lowercase. If you want to give a different name, you can specify within the @Component annotation.

```
@Component("myName")
```

However, I suggest you keep the default name. Using annotations is helpful for most scenarios, but again you will need to use XML configuration as it is more readable by everybody, centralized, and more scalable.

In the next section we are going to talk in more detail about the life cycle of a bean, so you will have the full picture.

The Bean Factory

All bean definitions are loaded into the context's bean factory. The bean factory is the container that manages the entire life cycle of any bean. A bean factory is represented by the interface `org.springframework.beans.factory.BeanFactory`, for which there are multiple implementations. In our examples, we have always used the `ClassPathXmlApplicationContext`, which is one of the multiple implementations of the bean factory.

```
ApplicationContext context =
                    new ClassPathXmlApplicationContext
                    ("ApplicationForAnnotationsConfiguration.xml");
```

Among these implementations, the ApplicationContext and the WebApplicationContext are the most important.

ApplicationContext and WebApplicationContext

ApplicationContext is a subclass of BeanFactory and adds functionalities such as the ability to load file resources in a generic fashion, to manage events, and to resolve messages supporting internationalization.

The WebApplicationContext extends the ApplicationContext by adding functionalities associated with servlets. In practice, this interface adds a getServletContext method to the generic ApplicationContext interface, and defines a well-known application attribute name that the root context must be bound to in the bootstrap process. Both ApplicationContext implementations allow you to inject properties by simply adding the file path string to the configuration file.

Properties

In JEE applications, it is common to keep properties of the different services of the application in files with the extension .properties, as shown in Figure 4-16. In our UserManager demo application, we have different property files like mail.properties, jdbc.properties, and so on. For example, usually the jdbc.properties file contains the parameters needed to connect the database to your application:

```
jdbc.driverClassName=com.mysql.jdbc.Driver
jdbc.url=jdbc\:mysql\://localhost\:3306/usermanager_test
jdbc.username=apress
jdbc.password=sserpa
hibernate.dialect=org.hibernate.dialect.MySQL5InnoDBDialect
```

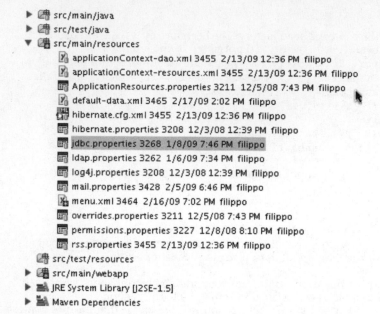

Figure 4-16. *The various properties files of an application*

In our Spring bean data source definition, we will use these properties instead of the real values. This gives makes the application easy to manage and centralizes all properties in just one directory, allowing everyone to be able to change properties without the need to put their hands in the XML configuration or classes.

```
<bean id="dataSource" class="org.apache.commons.dbcp.BasicDataSource" ↵
destroy-method="close">
    <property name="driverClassName" value="${jdbc.driverClassName}"/>
    <property name="url" value="${jdbc.url}"/>
    <property name="username" value="${jdbc.username}"/>
    <property name="password" value="${jdbc.password}"/>
    <property name="maxActive" value="100"/>
    <property name="maxWait" value="1000"/>
    <property name="poolPreparedStatements" value="true"/>
    <property name="defaultAutoCommit" value="true"/>
    <property name="testOnBorrow" value="true"/>
    <property name="validationQuery" value="select 1=1"/>
</bean>
```

All variables ${.....} in bean definitions will be substituted with values from .properties files, thanks to the work of the Spring `PropetyPlaceHolderConfigurer` object. To use the `PropetyPlaceHolderConfigurer` object, you need to add the following XML element to your configuration file:

```
        <bean id="propertyConfigurer" ↵
class="org.springframework.beans.factory.config.PropertyPlaceholderConfigurer">
        <property name="locations">
            <list>
                <value>classpath:jdbc.properties</value>
                <value>classpath:hibernate.properties</value>
                <value>classpath:mail.properties</value>
                <value>classpath:velocity.properties</value>
                <value>classpath:log4j.properties</value>
            </list>
        </property>
    </bean>
```

Figure 4-17 explains the process in a visual form.

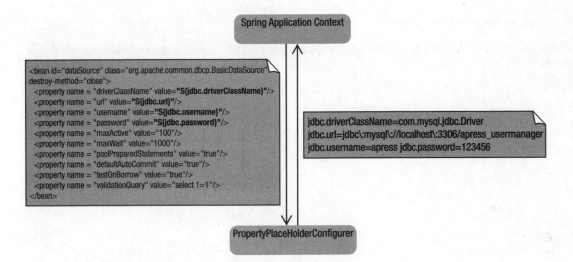

Figure 4-17. Replacing properties with actual values

You can use properties for all your needs. For example, you can use properties to set messages in the HelloFilippo example. To illustrate, let's create the `HelloFilippoForProperties` class with a message of type `String` variable.

```
package com.apress.flexjava.hellofilippo;

import org.springframework.beans.factory.annotation.Autowired;
import javax.annotation.Resource;

public class HelloFilippoForProperties {

        private Message message;
```

```java
public void hello() {
        System.out.println("Hello Filippo!" + message.getText());
}
@Autowired
@Resource(name="messageForPropertiesBean")
public void setMessage(Message message) {
        this.message = message;
}

}
```

Now let's create a *messages.properties* file in the `src/main/resources` path containing the following content:

```
message.guest=Hello Filippo! Properties are fantastic?
message.filippo = Yes they are!
```

Now we have to create the bean into our XML configuration file and load the *message.properties* file like so:

```xml
<bean id="propertyConfigurer" class="org.springframework.beans.↵
factory.config.PropertyPlaceholderConfigurer">
        <property name="locations">
            <list>
                <value>classpath:messages.properties</value>
            </list>
        </property>
    </bean>

    <bean id="messageForPropertiesBean"
class="com.apress.flexjava.hellofilippo.Message" >
                <property name="text" value="${message.guest}${message.filippo}" />
        </bean>

        <bean id="helloFilippoForProperties" ↵
class="com.apress.flexjava.hellofilippo.HelloFilippoForProperties" />
```

Finally, we have to amend our Main class to get the helloFilippoForProperties bean from the container:

```java
HelloFilippoForProperties helloFilippoForProperties =
                    (HelloFilippoForProperties) ↵
context.getBean("helloFilippoForProperties");

helloFilippoForProperties.hello();
```

And the result is:

```
Hello Filippo! Properties are fantastic? Yes they are!
```

Summary

In this chapter, I covered the most important aspects of the Spring IoC framework. We saw how to inject beans into the IoC container using both XML configuration and annotations. I explained in more detail both configurations with different practical examples. In the next chapter we will introduce the data access layer using both lightweight Java frameworks Spring and Hibernate; as you can imagine, data access is very important for enterprise application development.

CHAPTER 5

Spring JDBC and Hibernate

As I noted in Chapter 2, we will separate all our applications into 3 different main layers: the view layer, the service layer and the data access layer. We'll start by explaining how to implement the data access layer with Spring JDBC and Hibernate, using, for both, the DAO (Database Access Object) design pattern.

The DAO Design Pattern

The DAO (Data Access Object) is an object-oriented software design that provides mapping from the application calls to the persistence layer. Applications that implement the persistent storage without using the DAO design pattern, perhaps with some customized solution, may be difficult to scale or to adapt to a different environment, and this affects portability.

By using the DAO pattern, you can completely hide the data source implementation from its clients. Practically, each class that has to communicate with a data source must implement the DAO interface, which will be used by the service layer. Because the interface exposed by the DAO to clients does not change when the underlying data source implementation changes, this pattern allows the DAO to adapt to different storage schemes without affecting its clients or business components. Essentially, the DAO acts as an adapter between the component and the data source.

For example, suppose you need a class that saves, updates, and retrieves data from the database, but then you decide you don't want to use the database anymore (for whatever reason) and choose to port everything to an LDAP directory. Without the DAO pattern, it takes mammoth effort to do this. However, if you have implemented the DAO pattern, all you have to do is create a different class that works with the LDAP server—implementing the DAO interfaces so that the service layer will continue to work despite the change to the underlying data layer.

Figure 5-1 shows two classes, `LdapUserDaoImpl` and `HibernateUserDaoImpl`, both implementing the `UserDao` interface.

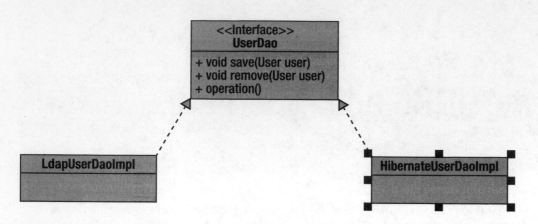

Figure 5-1. Two different implementations of the UserDao interface

The differences between the two classes will be the code inside each method. For example, the `save` method of the class `LdapUserDaoImpl` will contain different code from the `save` method implemented by the class `HibernateUserDaoImpl`, because one class must work with a database and the other class with an LDAP directory server. The following code shows the `save` method implemented by `HibernateUserDaoImpl`:

`HibernateUserDaoImpl` save method implemented

```
public void save(User user) {
     getHibernateTemplate().saveOrUpdate(user);
}
```

And here's the `save` method implemented by `LdapUserDaoImpl`:

```
public void save(User user) {
            DirContextAdapter ctx = new DirContextAdapter();
                     ctx.setAttributeValues("objectclass", new String[]
{"top",↩
 "person", "organizationalPerson", "inetOrgPerson"} );
            HashMap<String,String> map = new LdapUserAttributeMapper↩
(ldapAttributesDto).mapFromLdapUserDto(ldapUserDto);
            for(String key : map.keySet() ){
                 ctx.setAttributeValue(key, map.get(key));
            }

            ldapTemplate.bind(this.buildRdn(ldapContactDto.getUid()), ctx, null);
     }
```

Our business layer will refer to the `UserDao` interface and not to its implementation classes; by referring to the interface, it will be very easy to port our application from using a database to using LDAP storage. All we have to do is inject into our container the new class `LdapUserDaoImpl`. Easy!

The biggest difference between the Spring DAO and the DAO as originally designed is that the Spring DAO is combined with the template method pattern, making it much easier to adapt to a particular framework. In the process of interacting with a database, some steps are invariable, for example, creating the connection and starting the transaction. The original DAO implements these steps over and over again in each method of the data access object. In contrast, the Spring DAO uses the template method pattern, in which a template class is used to provide support for a specific framework. For example, the HibernateTemplate provides support for working with Hibernate for such as methods like save, update and so on.

Spring offers different DAO implementations to provide data access support for using JDBC, ORM, JNDI and LDAP. Table 5-1 summarizes the Spring data access DAO implementations.

Table 5-1. Spring data access support

Design Pattern	JDBC	HIBERNATE3	LDAP	TOPLINK
Spring DAO	JdbcDaoSupport	HibernateDaoSupport	LdapDaoSupport	TopLinkDaoSupport
Spring Template	JdbcTemplate	HibernateTemplate		TopLinkTemplate

As you can see in Table 5-1, Spring tries to use similar patterns for the different data access libraries. Usually for each data access library supported by Spring, there is a template and a DAO support class.

Introduction to Plain Old JDBC

Most Java developers have some basic experience with the JDBC. However, some readers may be coming from other languages, such as ActionScript, and may not be familiar with it, so we'll discuss it a bit.

Plain old JDBC allows connecting to a database from within Java. Basically, JDBC is a framework that provides services to the Java developer to write programs that access information stored in databases, spreadsheets, and files. A database that another program links to is called a data source. Many data sources, including products produced by Microsoft and Oracle, already use a standard called Open Database Connectivity (ODBC). Many legacy C and Perl programs use ODBC to connect to data sources. ODBC consolidated much of the commonality of various database management systems, and JDBC builds on this and increases the level of abstraction. JDBC-ODBC bridges have been created to allow Java programs to connect to ODBC-enabled database software.

This section assumes that you already have a data source established and are moderately familiar with the Structured Query Language (SQL), the command language for managing database data. Please see the SQL tutorial at www.w3schools.com/sql if you are a beginner or need some refreshing.

Before delving into the Spring JDBC, I want to show you how the traditional JDBC works, and what its problems are. Then, in next section, we can compare the old code to connect and query the database with the Spring JDBC version, and you will immediately see the benefits.

If you have read Chapter 3, your IDE should be ready to use. So let's create a database called `usermanager_test` with a table called `users` to store all of our application's users. To do that, use the MySql Query Browser, which is more visual and easier to follow than using the command line.

To create the database, right-click on the database explorer window and select the item called Create Schema, as shown in Figure 5-2.

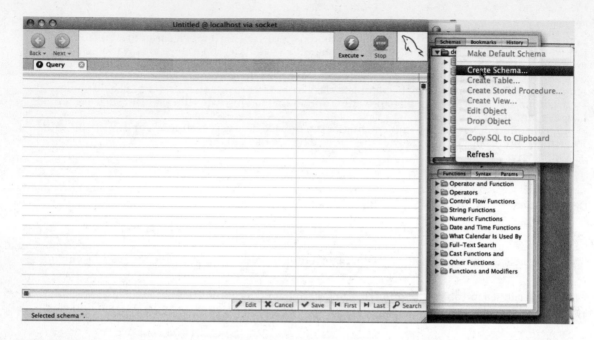

Figure 5-2. *Using MySql Query Browser to create a new database*

Once the database `usermanager_test` has been created, double-click on it and paste the following SQL code into the MySQL Query text area as in Figure 5-3, then click on the green Execute button.

```
CREATE TABLE  `usermanager_test`.`users` (
  `user_id` bigint(20) NOT NULL auto_increment,
  `forename` varchar(50) NOT NULL,
  `surname` varchar(50) NOT NULL,
  PRIMARY KEY  (`user_id`)
) ENGINE=InnoDB AUTO_INCREMENT=8 DEFAULT CHARSET=latin1
```

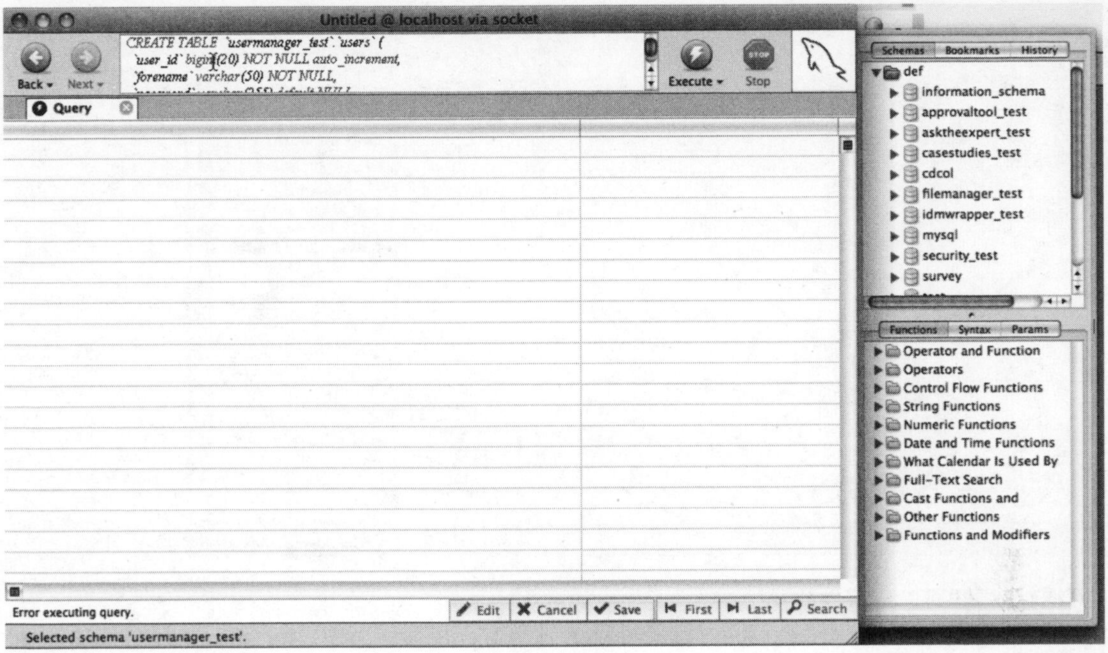

Figure 5-3. *Creating the users table in the database*

Now let's populate the table with some example data. Select the users table and paste the following code into the query text area as before. Then click on the green button to execute it.

```
INSERT INTO `users` (`forename`, `surname`) VALUES ('Michael','Davis');
INSERT INTO `users` (`forename`, `surname`) VALUES ('Paul','Roberts');
INSERT INTO `users` (`forename`, `surname`) VALUES ('Tom','Newman');
```

You have inserted three users. To test the code, try to retrieve the users by writing a standard SELECT query as in Figure 5-4.

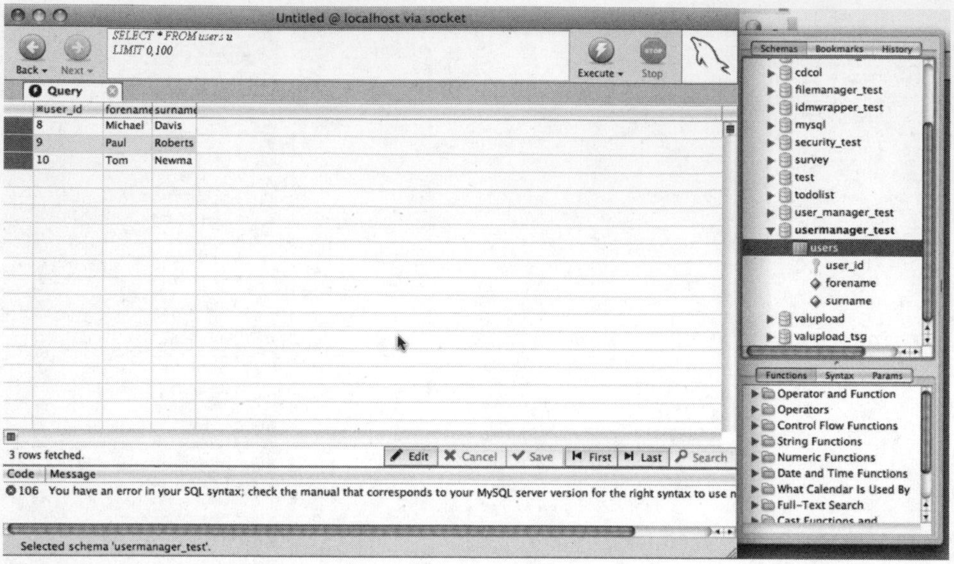

Figure 5-4. *Querying the database*

If everything is fine, let's try to write some Java code using the standard JDBC framework. To do that, create another simple Maven project called ▯usermanager▯ (just as we did in Chapter 4 for the hellofilippo application), using Eclipse as shown in Figure 5-5.

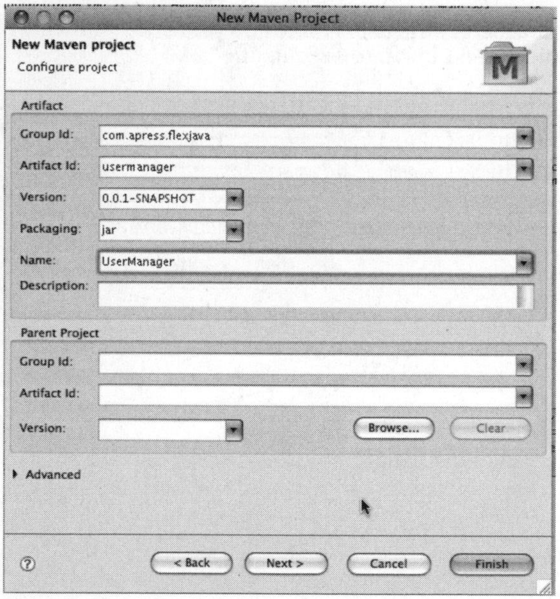

Figure 5-5. *Creating a new Maven project called usermanager*

Now let's try to retrieve all users from our database using the standard JDBC and the DAO pattern. First create a package called, `com.apress.flexjava.usermanager.model` to store all your entities. Our POM file for now won't have any dependencies. Next, create an entity called `User` with the same properties as the database table `users`.

```java
package com.apress.flexjava.usermanager.model;

public class User {

    private int userId;

    private String forename;

    private String surname;

    public User() {}

    public User(int userId, String forename, String surname){
        this.userId   = userId;
        this.forename = forename;
        this.surname = surname;
    }

    public User(String forename, String surname) {
        this.forename = forename;
        this.surname = surname;
    }

    public int getUserId() {
        return userId;
    }

    public void setUserId(int userId) {
        this.userId = userId;
    }

    public String getForename() {
        return forename;
    }

    public void setForename(String forename) {
        this.forename = forename;
    }

    public String getSurname() {
        return surname;
    }
```

```
        public void setSurname(String surname) {
                this.surname = surname;
        }
}
```

Now create another package called com.apress.flexjava.usermanager.dao, and in this package create an interface called UserDao with a method called findAll for returning a list of users.

```
package com.apress.flexjava.usermanager.dao;

import java.util.List;

import com.apress.flexjava.usermanager.model.User;

public interface UserDao {

        List<User> findAll();

}
```

Next, we have to create an implementation of the DAO interface by writing the code to connect to the database using standard JDBC. So, create another package called com.apress.flexjava.usermanager.dao.jdbc to store all implementations of the DAOs using JDBC. Here, create a class called UserDaoTraditionalJdbcImpl that implements the UserDao interface.

```
package com.apress.flexjava.usermanager.dao.jdbc;

import java.sql.Connection;
import java.sql.DriverManager;
import java.sql.PreparedStatement;
import java.sql.ResultSet;
import java.sql.SQLException;
import java.util.ArrayList;
import java.util.List;
import com.apress.flexjava.usermanager.dao.UserDao;
import com.apress.flexjava.usermanager.model.User;

public class UserDaoTraditionalJdbcImpl implements UserDao {

        private String driverClassName;
        private String url;
        private String username;
        private String password;

        public UserDaoTraditionalJdbcImpl(String driverClassName, String url,
                        String username, String password) {
                this.driverClassName = driverClassName;
```

```
        this.url = url;
        this.username = username;
        this.password = password;
    }

    public List<User> findAll() {
        List<User> usersList = new ArrayList<User>();
        String sql = "SELECT * FROM users";
        Connection conn = null;
        try {
            Class.forName(driverClassName);
            conn = DriverManager.getConnection(url, username, password);
            PreparedStatement ps = conn.prepareStatement(sql);
            ResultSet rs = ps.executeQuery();
            while (rs.next()) {
                int userId = rs.getInt("user_id");
                String forename = rs.getString("forename");
                String surname = rs.getString("surname");
                usersList.add(new User(userId, forename, surname));
            }
            rs.close();
            ps.close();
        } catch (SQLException e) {
            throw new RuntimeException(e);
        } catch (ClassNotFoundException e) {
            e.printStackTrace();
        } finally {
            if (conn != null) {
                try {
                    conn.close();
                } catch (SQLException e) {
                }
            }
        }

        return usersList;
    }

}
```

Next we have to add the MySql database dependency to the POM file otherwise when we will compile we will receive an error. Here the dependency needed:

```
<dependency>
<groupId>mysql</groupId>
<artifactId>mysql-connector-java</artifactId>
<version>5.1.6</version>
```

```
<type>jar</type>
<scope>compile</scope>
</dependency>
```

Finally, we need to create a Main class where we are going to instantiate our UserDaoTraditionalJdbcImpl,call the findAll method to retrieve all users stored into our database, and print them to the console.

Your Main class is like this:

```
package com.apress.flexjava.usermanager.business;

import java.util.List;
import com.apress.flexjava.usermanager.dao.UserDao;
import com.apress.flexjava.usermanager.dao.jdbc.UserDaoTraditionalJdbcImpl;
import com.apress.flexjava.usermanager.model.User;

public class Main {

        private static final String JDBC_DRIVE_CLASS_NAME = "com.mysql.jdbc.Driver";
        private static final String JDBC_URL = "jdbc:mysql://localhost:↵
3306/usermanager_test";
        private static final String JDBC_USERNAME = " apress ";
        private static final String JDBC_PASSWORD = " sserpa ";

        public static void main(String[] args) {
                UserDao userDao   = new
UserDaoTraditionalJdbcImpl(JDBC_DRIVE_CLASS_NAME,↵
 JDBC_URL, JDBC_USERNAME, JDBC_PASSWORD);
                List<User> users = userDao.findAll();
                for (User user : users){
                        System.out.println(user.getForename() + " " +
user.getSurname() );
                }
        }
}
```

Now you can run the application using Eclipse by right-clicking on the Main class and choosing the item ▯run as Java application▯; if everything is correct, you should see in your Eclipse console the result shown in Figure 5-6.

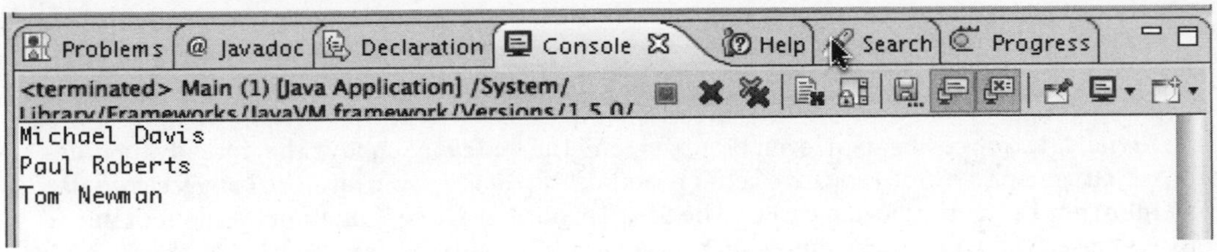

Figure 5-6. Eclipse console showing the users retrieved from the database

As you can see from the DAO implementation, using standard JDBC makes you use redundant and not scalable code, even for a simple query. When you have to execute, update, or insert database queries, the code is even more complex and dirty. To help with this problem, Spring provides the JDBC template, which essentially simplifies the use of the standard JDBC APIs. Note, however, you can use both concurrently.

Introduction to Spring JDBC

The Spring JDBC provides full access to the JDBC APIs. It simplifies the usage by providing different easy methods to execute queries and for working within the resultset. Moreover, Spring JDBC eliminates repetitive code and handles SQL errors properly.

The acquisition and release of the connection, the execution of statements, and other redundant code that I wrote in the previous example are all handled by Spring. Here is just one example to show what the code looks like using Spring JDBC instead of the traditional one.

```
public class UserDaoSpringJdbcImpl extends SimpleJdbcDaoSupport implements UserDao {
        public List<User> findAll() {
                String sql="SELECT * FROM users";
                return    getSimpleJdbcTemplate().query(sql,↵
ParameterizedBeanPropertyRowMapper.newInstance(User.class));
        }
}
```

JDBC Template

The JDBC Template is the central class in the JDBC package. It provides various overload methods to query and update a database and execute standard SQL. As with the standard JDBC, it requires a data source to work with, which can be injected from the XML configuration file as in the previous example.

The Spring JDBC framework provides a number of interfaces to handle the callback. For example, different versions of the query method allow you to query for simple types (String, long, int), maps, and domain objects.

JDBC DAO Support

The JDBC Template is thread-safe, which means you can declare a single instance in the IoC container and inject that instance into all your DAO instances. To implement this in your DAOs, you need to create a reference to the dataSource bean or, even better, extend the JdbcDaoSupport that already includes both setDataSource and setJdbTemplate setter methods. If you are using Java 1.5, I suggest you use the SimpleJdbcTemplate as indicated earlier. The SimpleJdbcTemplate is an improvement of the JdbcTemplate based on new Java 5 features such as generics. As with the JdbcTemplate, the SimpleJdbcTemplate can be instantiated or retrieve an instance extending the SimpleJdbcSupport class.

To see how this works, let's create a class called UserDaoSpringJdbcImpl in the package com.apress.flexjava.usermanager.dao.jdbc . The class must implement the interface UserDao to be able to work within our Main class without changing any code. Implementing the interface means the class will have the same method findAll() and the same UserDao data type.

The method findAll, defined in the interface UserDao, must return a List of Users, so we have to use a Spring JDBC query method to return a domain object. The query that satisfies our needs is provided by the SimpleJdbcTemplate.

The best way to use the SimpleJdbcTemplate is to extend the SimpleJdbcDaoSupport to inherit the setSimpleJdbc setter method. Then you use the query method, passing it the ParameterizeBeanPropertyMap that will automatically map the result to the User class without you having to write a custom UserMapper class. Here's the code:

```
package com.apress.flexjava.usermanager.dao.jdbc;

import java.util.List;
import org.springframework.jdbc.core.simple.ParameterizedBeanPropertyRowMapper;
import org.springframework.jdbc.core.simple.SimpleJdbcDaoSupport;
import com.apress.flexjava.usermanager.dao.UserDao;
import com.apress.flexjava.usermanager.model.User;

public class UserDaoSpringJdbcImpl extends SimpleJdbcDaoSupport implements UserDao
{
        public List<User> findAll() {
                String sql="SELECT * FROM users";
                return
getSimpleJdbcTemplate().query(sql,ParameterizedBeanPropertyRowMapper↩
.newInstance(User.class));
        }
}
```

To test and run the new application that implements the Spring JDBC libraries, you have to configure your POM XML configuration file in order to download all Spring dependencies, as shown in the following:

```
<dependencies>
        <dependency>
                <groupId>org.springframework</groupId>
                <artifactId>spring-context</artifactId>
```

```
                <version>2.5.6</version>
        </dependency>
        <dependency>
                <groupId>org.springframework</groupId>
                <artifactId>spring-jdbc</artifactId>
                <version>2.5.6</version>
        </dependency>
        <dependency>
                <groupId>mysql</groupId>
                <artifactId>mysql-connector-java</artifactId>
                <version>5.1.6</version>
                <type>jar</type>
                <scope>compile</scope>
        </dependency>
</dependencies>
```

Then you need to create a Spring bean definition file where you are going to define the beans to instantiate the datasource and the userDao beans into the Spring container.

Create a file called applicationContext.xml within /src/main/resources, selecting on the Eclipse top bar the items file ➤ new ➤ Spring Bean Definition.

Once the file has been created, you have to define the dataSource bean, as in following:

```
<bean id="dataSource" class="org.springframework.jdbc.datasource↩
.DriverManagerDataSource">
    <property name="driverClassName" value="${jdbc.driverClassName}"/>
    <property name="url" value="${jdbc.url}"/>
    <property name="username" value="${jdbc.username}"/>
    <property name="password" value="${jdbc.password}"/>
</bean>
```

Secondly, define the userDao bean where you will inject the bean dataSource that you just created using the setter injection, as shown here:

```
<bean name="userDao" class="com.apress.flexjava.usermanager.dao.jdbc↩
.UserDaoSpringJdbcImpl">
        <property name="dataSource" ref="dataSource" />
</bean>
```

If you look at the dataSource bean settings, you will notice that I used variables to set all dataSource properties. As already discussed in Chapter 4, the values within ${...} will be replaced with the values matched in the file with extension .properties. Loading everything from an external .properties file, the application will be more scalable and configurable.

For this example, I have created a file called jdbc.properties and placed it into the folder src/main/resources, which is in the classpath.

The jdbc.properties file will contain the values needed to set up the connection with the database.

```
jdbc.driverClassName=com.mysql.jdbc.Driver
jdbc.url=jdbc:mysql://localhost:3306/usermanager_test
jdbc.username=apress
```

```
jdbc.password=sserpa
```

As you saw in Chapter 4, in order to load the properties into the container, Spring provides the
`PropertyPlaceholderConfigure` class that accepts the path of one or more properties files. In order to
use an external properties file using the `PropertyPlaceholderConfigure` class, you have to add the
following bean to your applicationContext.xml configuration file, as shown here:

```xml
<bean id="propertyConfigurer" class="org.springframework.beans.factory↩
.config.PropertyPlaceholderConfigurer">
    <property name="locations">
        <list>
            <value>classpath:jdbc.properties</value>
        </list>
    </property>
</bean>
```

Here is the complete code for the applicationContext.xml Spring configuration file:

```xml
<?xml version="1.0" encoding="UTF-8"?>
<beans xmlns="http://www.springframework.org/schema/beans"
      xmlns:xsi="http://www.w3.org/2001/XMLSchema-instance"
      xmlns:p="http://www.springframework.org/schema/p"
      xmlns:context="http://www.springframework.org/schema/context"
      xmlns:aop="http://www.springframework.org/schema/aop"
      xmlns:tx="http://www.springframework.org/schema/tx"
      xmlns:jee="http://www.springframework.org/schema/jee"
      xsi:schemaLocation="
                http://www.springframework.org/schema/beans http://www↩
.springframework.org/schema/beans/spring-beans-2.5.xsd
                http://www.springframework.org/schema/context http://www↩
.springframework.org/schema/context/spring-context-2.5.xsd
                http://www.springframework.org/schema/aop http://www↩
.springframework.org/schema/aop/spring-aop-2.5.xsd
                http://www.springframework.org/schema/tx http://www↩
.springframework.org/schema/tx/spring-tx-2.5.xsd
                http://www.springframework.org/schema/jee http://www↩
.springframework.org/schema/jee/spring-jee-2.5.xsd">

    <!-- @Required processor -->
    <bean class="org.springframework.beans.factory.annotation↩
.RequiredAnnotationBeanPostProcessor"/>

    <!-- Exception translation bean post processor -->
    <bean class="org.springframework.dao.annotation↩
.PersistenceExceptionTranslationPostProcessor"/>

    <bean id="propertyConfigurer" class="org.springframework.beans.factory↩
.config.PropertyPlaceholderConfigurer">
```

```
        <property name="locations">
        <list>
        <value>classpath:jdbc.properties</value>
        </list>
        </property>
        </bean>

        <bean id="dataSource"
        class="org.springframework.jdbc.datasource
        .DriverManagerDataSource">
        <property name="driverClassName"
        value="${jdbc.driverClassName}"/>
        <property name="url" value="${jdbc.url}"/>
        <property name="username" value="${jdbc.username}"/>
        <property name="password" value="${jdbc.password}"/>
    </bean>

        <bean name="userDao" class="com.apress.flexjava.usermanager↵
.dao.jdbc.UserDaoSpringJdbcImpl">
                <property name="dataSource" ref="dataSource" />
        </bean>

        <!-- Hibernate SessionFactory -->
        <bean id="sessionFactory"
        class="org.springframework.orm.hibernate3↵
.annotation.AnnotationSessionFactoryBean">
        <property name="dataSource" ref="dataSource"/>
        <property name="configLocation"
         value="classpath:hibernate.cfg.xml"/>
         <property name="hibernateProperties">
         <value>
         hibernate.dialect=${hibernate.dialect}
         hibernate.query.substitutions=true 'Y', false 'N'
         hibernate.cache.use_second_level_cache=true
         hibernate.cache.provider_class=org.hibernate.cache.EhCacheProvider
         hibernate.hbm2ddl.auto=update
         hibernate.use_sql_comments=true
         hibernate.show_sql=true
         </value>
         </property>


        </bean>


</beans>
```

Finally, you need to create a `Main` class where you instantiate your `beanfactory` to get the `userDao` bean and call the `findAll` method to retrieve all users stored into the database and print them to the console.

Here is the complete code for the `Main` class:

```java
package com.apress.flexjava.usermanager.business;

import java.util.List;
import org.springframework.context.ApplicationContext;
import org.springframework.context.support.ClassPathXmlApplicationContext;
import com.apress.flexjava.usermanager.dao.UserDao;
import com.apress.flexjava.usermanager.model.User;

public class Main {

        public static void main(String[] args) {
                ApplicationContext context = new ClassPathXmlApplicationContext
 ("applicationContext.xml");
                UserDao userDao  = (UserDao)context.getBean("userDao");
                List<User> users = userDao.findAll();
                for (User user : users){
                        System.out.println(user.getForename() + " " +
user.getSurname() );
                }
        }
}
```

Now you can run the application using Eclipse as shown before by right-clicking on the `Main` class and choosing run as Java application; if everything is correct, you should see the information(INFO) logs of the Spring container and then the query result, as shown in Figure 5-7.

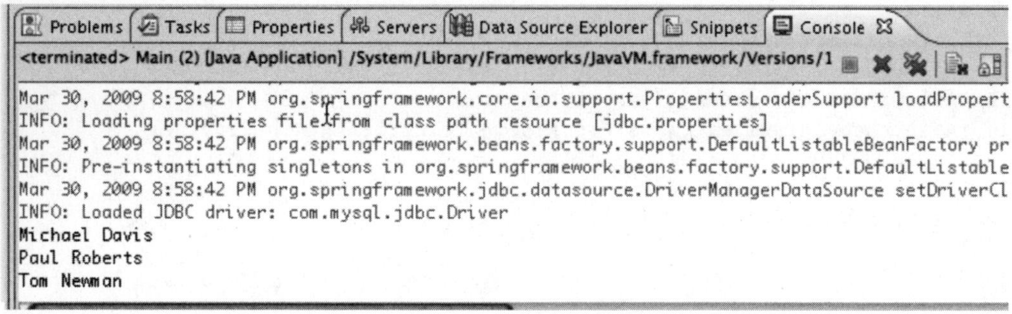

Figure 5-7. *Eclipse console showing the users retrieved from the database plus the Spring INFO logs*

You can see the differences between the class that uses the Standard JDBC and the class that uses the Spring JDBC by using the Eclipse compare tool. Select the two classes to compare, right-click on one of them to bring up the context menu, then choose Compare With ➤ Each Other (see Figure 5-8). The results of the comparison are shown in Figure 5-9. I leave it to you to judge which is better!

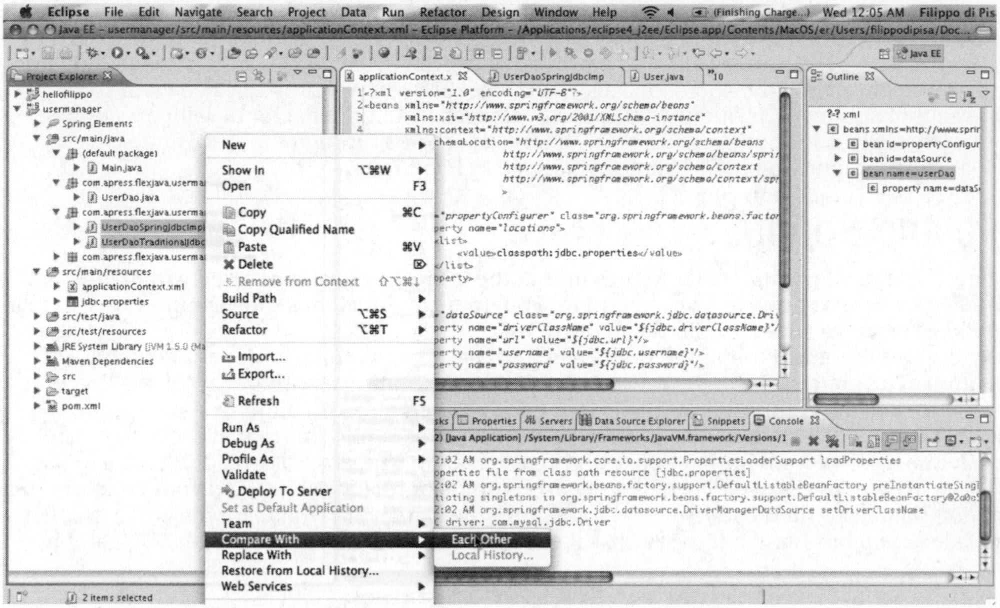

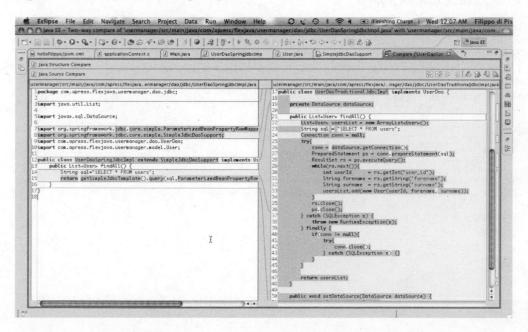

Figure 5-8. *Compare files using Eclipse*

Figure 5-9. *Comparison between traditional JDBC and the Spring JDBC implementation*

The JDBC framework is too large to be explained in just one chapter. I haven't covered SQLErrorHandling and the CallBack interfaces because in this book I am going to focus more on the ORM and Hibernate frameworks for the data access layer. However, even if you use 70 percent ORM and Hibernate and 30 percent JDBC, you should master JDBC, because you will probably need it at some point; there are a lot of applications out there that use it. Moreover, I think that for developers coming from Web languages such as PHP or ColdFusion (CF), it is easier to go through the JDBC and SQL standard than starting directly from ORM frameworks such as Hibernate.

Hibernate and Spring

Hibernate is one of the most popular ORM frameworks at the moment and can be used with many different technologies. Spring provides full support for Hibernate and includes some support classes in a way that's similar to what we have seen for the Spring JDBC.

Hibernate requires metadata to map all domain object classes and their properties to database tables and columns. The metadata can be provided as XML or annotations. In this chapter, we'll look at both though we'll focus on the annotations method as I find that it's simpler, more readable, and ultimately faster. Then we will see how to use some interesting Maven plug-ins that allow us to create the database schema directly from our Java code and vice versa. This means that you don't have to use the tedious SQL or SQL manager to create tables or add columns or relationships. And your code will run on all the different databases on the market, just by telling Hibernate which database dialect to use. For example, here I show you how easy it is to set the Hibernate dialect in order to use the MySQL database

```
hibernate.dialect=org.hibernate.dialect.MySQL5InnoDBDialect
```

and Hibernate magically transforms all your Java code into MySQL SQL code. Pretty cool! Now let's see how to add Hibernate to the Spring project.

Add Hibernate to your Spring Project

Hibernate implementation classes require access to the SessionFactory in order to work. The SessionFactory is a thread-safe and sharable object representing a single datasource. A SessionFactory requires a datasource and the mapping metadata. Spring provides a FactoryBean to simplify the configuration of a sharable SessionFactory. Figure 5-10 illustrates how the ORM works.

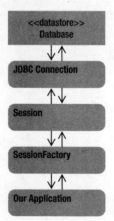

Figure 5-10. How the ORM works

The following listing configures the sessionFactory bean with all the properties needed by the sessionFactory in order to connect to the database(dataSource bean), to map the objects (we use an external file called hibernate.cfg.xml), and to work with Hibernate.

```
<bean id="sessionFactory" class="org.springframework.orm.hibernate3
.annotation.AnnotationSessionFactoryBean">
        <property name="dataSource" ref="dataSource"/>
        <property name="configLocation" value="classpath:hibernate.cfg.xml"/>
        <property name="hibernateProperties">
            <value>
                hibernate.dialect= org.hibernate.dialect.MySQL5InnoDBDialect
                hibernate.query.substitutions=true 'Y', false 'N'
                hibernate.cache.use_second_level_cache=true
                hibernate.cache.provider_class=org.hibernate.cache.EhCacheProvider
                hibernate.hbm2ddl.auto=update
                hibernate.use_sql_comments=true
                hibernate.show_sql=true
            </value>
        </property>
</bean>
```

Practically speaking, the SessionFactory contains all your database objects mapped to your Java domain objects. If you want to map a database using either annotation or XML and you forget to define the SessionFactory bean, it won't work.

To add Hibernate to your Spring project, you just need to add the Maven dependency to the POM file that you used for the previous examples, as shown here:

```
<dependency>
    <groupId>org.hibernate</groupId>
    <artifactId>hibernate</artifactId>
        <version>3.2.6.ga</version>
</dependency>
<dependency>
    <groupId>org.hibernate</groupId>
    <artifactId>hibernate-annotations</artifactId>
        <version>3.4.0.ga</version>
</dependency>
<dependency>
        <groupId>org.hibernate</groupId>
        <artifactId>hibernate-commons-annotations</artifactId>
        <version>3.3.0.ga</version>
</dependency>
```

Configure Hibernate

As I noted earlier, you can configure Hibernate within a Spring project using either XML or annotations. For either, you have to create a `sessionFactory` bean with a reference to your dataSource bean and a list of your mapping classes.

You can set the list of the mapping classes by either injecting a list into the bean or by loading it from an external file. The following example injects a list of our mapping classes. Remember that this is just an example to show you how to inject a list, because for the sample application you will use an external file where you'll configure all the mapping classes. For now, add the sessionFactory bean into the applicationContext.xml XML configuration file; later on I will show you how to organize your application better with different Spring configuration files for the different scopes. For example, I will move the sessionFactory bean to the applicationContext-dao.xml where I will define all the bean-related DAOs.

```
<bean id="sessionFactory" class="org.springframework.orm.hibernate3↩
.annotation.AnnotationSessionFactoryBean">
      <property name="dataSource" ref="dataSource"/>
              <property name="mappingClasses">
                      <list>
            <value>com.apress.flexjava.usermanager.model.User</value>
            <value></value>
                      </list>
      </property>
              <property name="hibernateProperties">
              <value>
                  hibernate.dialect=${hibernate.dialect}
                  hibernate.query.substitutions=true 'Y', false 'N'
                  hibernate.cache.use_second_level_cache=true

hibernate.cache.provider_class=org.hibernate.cache.EhCacheProvider
                  hibernate.hbm2ddl.auto=update
                  hibernate.use_sql_comments=true
                  hibernate.show_sql=true
          </value>
</bean>
```

As you will note in this example, I set the hibernate.dialect properties with a properties var that I haven't set yet in any properties file. To do that, open the jdbc.properties file located into the `src/main/resources` folder and add the following line of code:

```
hibernate.dialect=${hibernate.dialect}
```

Then open your POM file and, within the <properties> XML tags, add the following XML definition:

```
<hibernate.dialect>
      org.hibernate.dialect.MySQL5InnoDBDialect
</hibernate.dialect>
```

Now that you have set the hibernate dialect, you must provide the Maven Hibernate 3 plug-in with the connection details; otherwise, you will get an error when you run or build the application using Maven. I will add the parameters needed by the Hibernate3 Maven plug-in in the jdbc.properties file, and I will use the same JDBC connection details defined in the POM.

Here is the code that you have to add to the jdbc.properties file after the hibernate.dialect definition:

```
# Needed by Hibernate3 Maven Plugin defined in pom.xml
hibernate.connection.username=${jdbc.username}
hibernate.connection.password=${jdbc.password}
hibernate.connection.url=${jdbc.url}
hibernate.connection.driver_class=${jdbc.driverClassName}
```

The next example shows getting the list of mapping classes from an external configuration file. The following in bold is the external file where I define the mapping classes:

```
<bean id="sessionFactory" class="org.springframework.orm.hibernate3↩
.annotation.AnnotationSessionFactoryBean">
    <property name="dataSource" ref="dataSource"/>
    <property name="configLocation" value="classpath:hibernate.cfg.xml"/>
    <property name="hibernateProperties">
      <value>
        hibernate.dialect= =${hibernate.dialect}
        hibernate.query.substitutions=true 'Y', false 'N'
        hibernate.cache.use_second_level_cache=true
        hibernate.cache.provider_class=org.hibernate.cache.EhCacheProvider
        hibernate.hbm2ddl.auto=update
        hibernate.use_sql_comments=true
        hibernate.show_sql=true
      </value>
    </property>
</bean>
```

As you can see in the property named configLocation, there is a reference to an XML file called *hibernate.cfg.xml* placed into the classpath. Figure 5-11 shows the location of this file.

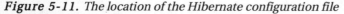

Figure 5-11. *The location of the Hibernate configuration file*

The hibernate.cfg.xml file will contain all mapping classes like the following:

```xml
<?xml version="1.0" encoding="utf-8"?>

<!DOCTYPE hibernate-configuration PUBLIC
"-//Hibernate/Hibernate Configuration DTD 3.0//EN"
"http://hibernate.sourceforge.net/hibernate-configuration-3.0.dtd">
<hibernate-configuration>
    <session-factory name="sessionFactory">
        <mapping class="com.apress.flexjava.usermanager.model.User" />
    </session-factory>
</hibernate-configuration>
```

I prefer this configuration as it is better to have all your mapped classes in a separate file, in order to keep the main configuration file clean. In the next chapter, we will see how to separate the XML configuration for the different services into different configuration files, to avoid having just one big application file. For example, we will move all our DAOs beans into a configuration file called application-dao.xml, and so on. Later on, we will focus more on annotations, as well making the XML file configurations much lighter and readable.

Now I'm going to discuss how to map your database objects to your Java domain objects using XML. Even though all our example applications will use annotations, it's still important to become familiar with this method because it is used by a lot of applications.

XML-Based Configuration

Using XML-based configuration is not efficient very because, for each entity class that you want to map, you have to create an XML file that tells Hibernate which database object is mapped to each Java domain class. Then you have to inject each file into the sessionFactory. To use the XML configuration, you have to create an instance of the Spring class `LocalSessionFactoryBean` belonging to the package `org.springframework.orm.hibernate3`.

As discussed, you must have an XML file for each mapping class. For example if you have a database with three tables like users, orders, groups, and you want to map just the tables users and groups, you will need two XML files that tell Hibernate where to find the related Java classes for each database object you want to map. For example, the table users maps to the class User, and the table groups maps to the class Group.

Within the XML file you can define all properties for the mapping type. You can have different kinds of mapping depending on your database schema. You can map relationships between tables, indexes, and more. Understanding how to map a single database table and the relationship of one-to-many and one-to-one with other tables is essential before you start to develop JEE database-driven applications.

If you are not familiar with databases, you should master these concepts before getting into the development cycle. For example, a user can be related to many groups and many orders, and a group can be related to many users, but an order can be related just to one user. Practically speaking, a user can be added to many groups and a group can have many users, and a user can have one or many orders, but the same order can't belong to many users, only to one.

What this means is that the table users has a many-to-many relationship with the table groups, and a one-to-many relationship with the table orders.

The diagram in Figure 5-12 shows the use of union tables to represent a many-to-many relationship.

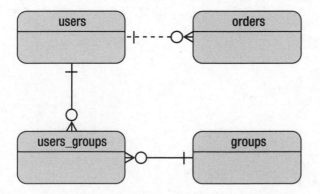

Figure 5-12. *The relationships between the tables users,orders, and groups*

You can retrieve a user and all his related groups using SQL by using the JOIN statement like this:

```
SELECT * FROM users u INNER JOIN groups g on u.user_id = g.user_id
```

Using Hibernate is much easier as Hibernate manages everything and lets you avoid the tedious SQL code; you just have to tell the ORM what kind of relationship an object has with another one. Let's see how to map a table using XML configuration.

Mapping a Database Table

In your `usermanager` example application, you should have already created a database called `usermanager_test` with a table named users containing three example users. On the Java side, you should have a domain object class User.java

To retrieve users within our Java code, we have used both the standard and the Spring JDBC approaches. Now we'll use Hibernate. To do this, we have to map the `User` Java class to the database table `users`. Then Hibernate will treat each record of the table users as a Java User object, storing the mapping in a sessionFactory.

Before adding the mapping XML files, let's create a new folder within our package to keep our project organized. I'm going to create a new source folder called Hibernate within `main/src/resources`. To create a new source folder, right-click on your project and choose New ➤ Source Folder as in Figure 5-13.

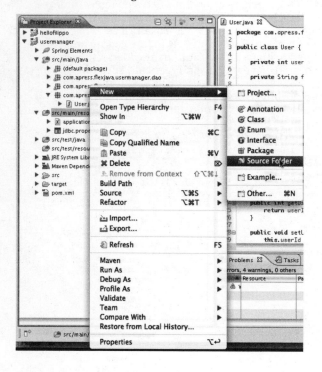

Figure 5-13. *Creating a source folder for storing resource files*

Then insert the path `src/main/resources/hibernate` into the form field labeled Folder name, and click on Finish (see Figure 5-14).

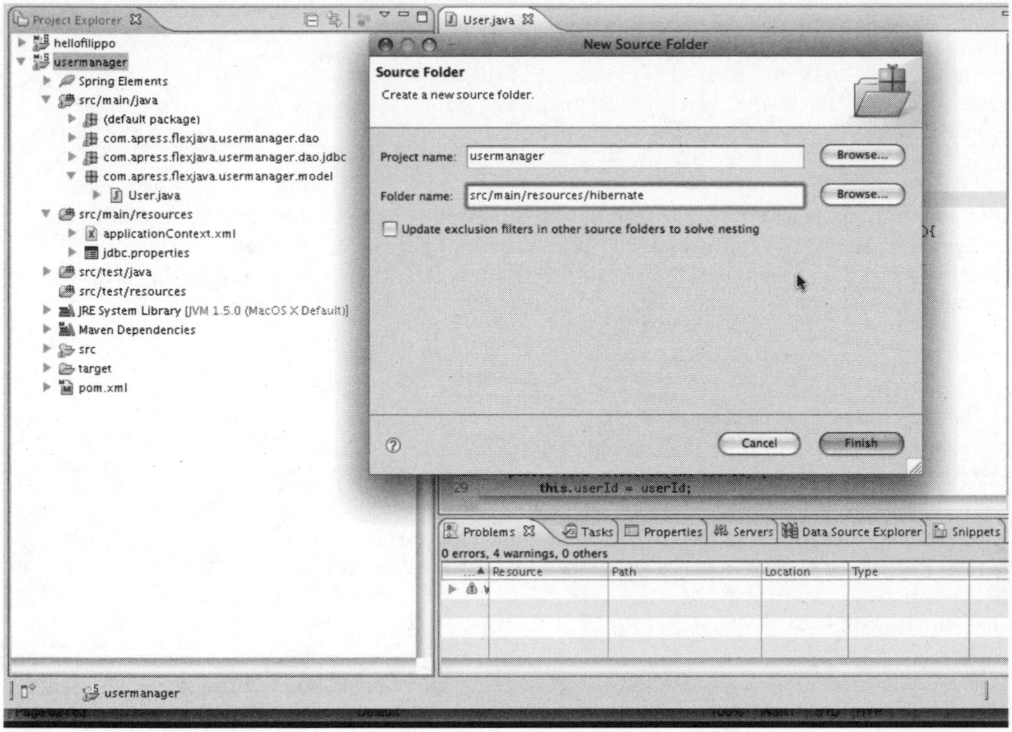

Figure 5-14. *Creating the Hibernate folder to contain the Hibernate XML configuration files*

To map the table users using XML, create a file in the new source folder
(main/src/resources/hibernate) called *User.hbm.xml* containing the following XML code:

```
<?xml version="1.0" encoding="UTF-8"?>
<hibernate-mapping package="com.apress.flexjava.usermanager.model">
    <class name="User" table="users">
        <id name="id" column="user_id" access="field" />
        <propery name="foreName" column="forename" />
        <propery name="surName" column="surname" />
    </class>
</hibernate-mapping>
```

As you can see, this first tells Hibernate to map the table users with the domain class User within the
package com.apress.flexjava.usermanager.model:

```
<hibernate-mapping package="com.apress.flexjava.usermanager.model">
    <class name="User" table="users">
```

Then it tells Hibernate to map the class properties id, forename, and surname of the domain class
User with the table columns user_id, forename, and surname of the table users.

155

```
<class name="User" table="users">
        <id name="id" column="user_id" access="field" />
        <propery name="foreName" column="forename" />
        <propery name="surName" column="surname" />
</class>
```

Once you have mapped the entity class, you have to add it to your `sessionFactory`. Usually you configure the `sessionFactory` by creating a file called `hibernate.cfg.xml` in the `src/main/resources` folder as shown in Figure 5-15. For our scenario, `hibernate.cfg.xml` will contain the following code:

```
<?xml version="1.0" encoding="utf-8"?>

<!DOCTYPE hibernate-configuration PUBLIC
"-//Hibernate/Hibernate Configuration DTD 3.0//EN"
"http://hibernate.sourceforge.net/hibernate-configuration-3.0.dtd">
<hibernate-configuration>
    <session-factory name="sessionFactory">
        <mapping class="com.apress.flexjava.usermanager.model.User" />
    </session-factory>
</hibernate-configuration>
```

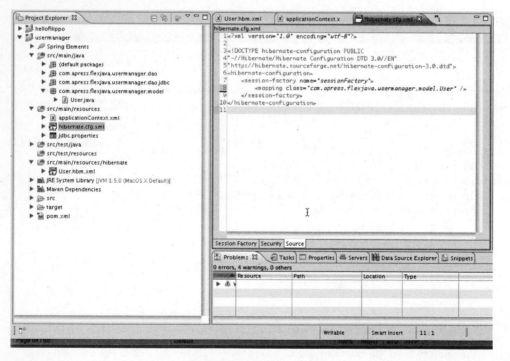

Figure 5-15. Where hibernate.cfg.xml is located

The code is easy to follow. For each object that you want to persist, you inject it into a sessionFactory using the XML definition `<mapping>`.

Before starting to write our Hibernate implementation of the userDao, I'm going to show you how to map more complex database schema, not just one table. For this, I'll use annotations for configuring, though, which are much more intuitive than the XML-based alternatives.

Annotation-Based Configuration

Persisting an entity using annotations is as easy as XML, but in my view it is a lot cleaner and you avoid the need to create an .hbm.xml file for each class you want to map. This saves you a lot of time in both maintenance and implementation. If you are not familiar with the concept of annotations, please read Chapter 4

In order to persist an entity class, you must annotate it using the `@Entity` annotation. By default, the entity maps a table using the name of the class itself. To assign the table name, you can use the `@Table` annotation to provide the name of the database table that you want to map. For example, the entity class User can be mapped to the table called users using the annotation @Table(name="users"). To map a property, use the @Column annotation. To define a unique identifier for the entity mapped, use the `@Id` annotation. You can choose different strategies with the `@Id` annotation depending on how you want to generate the unique identifier. For our example, we will let the system create an incremental unique identifier using the `@GeneratedValue(strategy = IDENTITY)` annotation importing both `import javax.persistence.GeneratedValue;` and `import static javax.persistence.GenerationType.IDENTITY`.

To use Hibernate annotation in your project, you have to add the Hibernate JAR libraries to your class path. Thanks to Maven, you have to add only the following dependency to your POM file, and Maven will download the JAR files defined in the XML and will add into your class path.

```
<dependency>
        <groupId>org.hibernate</groupId>
        <artifactId>hibernate-annotations</artifactId>
        <version>3.4.0.GA</version>
</dependency>
```

Mapping a Database Table

As explained above, to map a database table, you annotate the entity class with the @Entity annotation followed by the @Table annotation where you define the database table name. Then you annotate each property that you want to map with the @Column annotation, placing it above the setting of the private variable or above the setter method.

The following example maps the entity User to the database table called users.

```
package com.apress.flexjava.usermanager.model;

import static javax.persistence.GenerationType.IDENTITY;
import java.util.List;
import javax.persistence.Column;
import javax.persistence.GeneratedValue;
import javax.persistence.Id;
```

```java
import javax.persistence.JoinColumn;
import javax.persistence.Entity;
import javax.persistence.Table;

@Entity
@Table(name="users")
public class User {

        @Id
        @GeneratedValue(strategy = IDENTITY)
        @Column(name="user_id")
        private int userId;

        @Column(name="forename")
        private String forename;

        @Column(name="surname")
        private String surname;

        public User() {}

        public User(int userId, String forename, String surname){
                this.userId   = userId;
                this.forename = forename;
                this.surname = surname;
        }

        public User(String forename, String surname) {
                this.forename = forename;
                this.surname = surname;
        }

        public int getUserId() {
                return userId;
        }

        public void setUserId(int userId) {
                this.userId = userId;
        }

        public String getForename() {
                return forename;
        }

        public void setForename(String forename) {
                this.forename = forename;
        }
```

```java
public String getSurname() {
        return surname;
}

public void setSurname(String surname) {
        this.surname = surname;
}

}
```

Within the @Column annotation ,you can define different parameters, such as name, unique, nullable, and so forth. If you don't specify any name, Hibernate will by default use the name of the variable.

Our unique identifier strategy is to make the system generate an incremental number. To do that we use the @GeneratedValue annotation with the IDENTITY strategy, which means it will generate an incremental number.

```java
@Id
@GeneratedValue(strategy = IDENTITY)
@Column(name="user_id")
private int userId;
```

Before continuing, we need to set up our project to synchronize the changes made to our Java entities within the database schema by adding the following Hibernate-Maven plug-in to our POM file after the </dependencies> tag.

```xml
<build>
      <defaultGoal>install</defaultGoal>
      <plugins>
            <plugin>
                              <groupId>org.codehaus.mojo</groupId>
                              <artifactId>hibernate3-maven-plugin</artifactId>
                              <version>2.0-alpha-2</version>
                              <configuration>
                                    <components>
                                          <component>
                                                    <name>hbm2ddl</name>
                                                    <implementation>
                                                          annotationconfiguration
                                                    </implementation>
                                          </component>
                                    </components>
                                    <componentProperties>
                                          <drop>false</drop>
                                          <update>false</update>
                                          <jdk5>true</jdk5>
                                          <propertyfile>
```

```
                                        target/classes/jdbc.properties
                                </propertyfile>
                                <skip>${maven.test.skip}</skip>
                        </componentProperties>
                </configuration>
                <executions>
                        <execution>
                                <phase>process-test-resources</phase>
                                <goals>
                                        <goal>hbm2ddl</goal>
                                </goals>
                        </execution>
                </executions>
                <dependencies>
                        <dependency>
                                <groupId>mysql</groupId>
                                <artifactId>mysql-connector-
java</artifactId>
                                <version>5.1.6</version>
                        </dependency>
                </dependencies>
        </plugin>
    </plugins>
  </build>
```

This plug-in will be executed when we launch the command mvn install, and it will create or update any database object that we mapped into our Java persistent framework. For example, as you know, the table called orders doesn't currently exist in the database. Normally we would create the table in the database with all its columns and properties manually, using a database explorer such as MySQL Query Browser or by using SQL at the command line. However, this great Maven plug-in automatically manages the process for you. If you create, annotate, and map the entity Order with the table orders (which doesn't yet exist in the database), the Maven plug-in will check whether the table orders exists and will create it if I doesn't. Otherwise, the plug-in will check to see whether the existing table has been updated. This means that you can also add a new column directly within your Java code and it will be added automatically to your database.

Remember that when using annotations, you still have to pass the fully qualified entity name to the sessionFactory in the hibernate.cfg.xml file. The only difference between the mappings of an .hbm.xml object from an annotated one is that in the first one you pass the full path of the file with the extension .hbm.xml and in the second one you pass only the package name.

```
<hibernate-configuration>
    <session-factory name="sessionFactory">
        <mapping class="com.apress.usermanager.model.User" />
        <mapping class="com.apress.usermanager.model.Authority" />
    </session-factory>
```

Mapping a One-to-One Relationship

In the previous example, our database schema had just one table to store all the users. Now we want to add more details to the user, such as an address. If you think about this in an OO way, Address can be an object that is reusable with other objects, so we will create an Address object and relate it to the User object using a one-to-one relationship—a user can have only one address and an address can have just one user.

To map a one-to-one association using annotations, you have to annotate the property that defines the relationship with the @OneToOne annotation, as follows:

```
@OneToOne(cascade = CascadeType.ALL)
@JoinColumn(name = "address_id")
private Address address;
```

The @OneToOne annotation accepts the following attributes:

Cascade allows you to set a cascading operation using the javax.persistence.CascadeType enumeration class. In our example, we use cascade = CascadeType.ALL to update all related objects when one changes. This means that when we save the User class that contains an instance of the Address class, Hibernate updates both the persistent objects and the database;

Fetch can be set using the FetchType enumeration class; the default is the eager loading;

Optional defines whether the value can be set to null;

TargetEntity is the entity the attribute is mapped to. By default, the target entity is the field type. Otherwise, it can be set to the class of an entity that stores the association.

MappedBy indicates the entity that owns the bidirectional association.

■ **Note** A bidirectional association means that both entities involved maintain a reference to each other. In our case, the entity Address has a reference to the entity User and vice versa, so the relationship is bidirectional.

So let's create an Address class in our model package and then create a relationship for it with the User class using the one-to-one annotation.

```
package com.apress.flexjava.usermanager.model;

import static javax.persistence.GenerationType.IDENTITY;

import javax.persistence.Column;
import javax.persistence.Entity;
import javax.persistence.GeneratedValue;
import javax.persistence.Id;
import javax.persistence.Table;

@Entity
@Table(name="addresses")
```

```java
public class Address {

    @Id
    @GeneratedValue(strategy = IDENTITY)
    @Column(name = "address_id")
    private Integer addressId;

    @Column(name = "street")
    private String street;

    @Column(name = "postcode")
    private String postCode;

    @Column(name = "city")
    private String city;

    @Column(name = "country")
    private String country;

    public Integer getAddressId() {
        return addressId;
    }

    public void setAddressId(Integer addressId) {
        this.addressId = addressId;
    }

    public String getStreet() {
        return street;
    }

    public void setStreet(String street) {
        this.street = street;
    }

    public String getPostCode() {
        return postCode;
    }

    public void setPostCode(String postCode) {
        this.postCode = postCode;
    }

    public String getCity() {
        return city;
    }
```

```
    public void setCity(String city) {
        this.city = city;
    }

    public String getCountry() {
        return country;
    }

    public void setCountry(String country) {
        this.country = country;
    }


}
```

Once the Address class has been created, you can reference it in the User class as follows:

```
@OneToOne(cascade = CascadeType.ALL)
@JoinColumn(name = "address_id")
private Address address;

 public Address getAddress() {
        return address;
    }

    public void setAddress(Address address) {
        this.address = address;
    }
```

Remember to add to the class User the related annotations @OneToOne and @JoinColumn imports, as follows:

```
import javax.persistence.OneToOne;
import javax.persistence.CascadeType;
```

Then map your new Address entity into your hibernate.cfg.xml configuration file located into your src/main/resources, as always.

```
<mapping class="com.apress.flexjava.usermanager.model.Address" />
```

Because you added the Maven plug-in to your POM file earlier, launching the command mvn install to compile your application will also create the database table address and the database relationship one-to-one into the users database table.

It should be noted that the one-to-one relationship is not necessarily the best approach.

Mapping a One-to-Many or a Many-to-One Relationship

As we discussed in the previous sections, we need to store all user orders in the database. A user can have many orders but an order must be related only to one user.

The simplest way to map a one-to-many or a many-to-one relationship is to annotate the property value representing the ⬜many⬜ end of the association with the @OneToMany annotation. Usually the ⬜many⬜ end is represented by an array or collection.

In our example, we will add to the User entity a new property called orders, and annotate it with the @OneToMany annotation.

Let's do it! First you have to create a new Order entity with its annotation within the package com.apress.flexjava.usermanager.model as follows:

```
package com.apress.flexjava.usermanager.model;

import java.sql.Date;
import javax.persistence.Column;
import javax.persistence.Entity;
import javax.persistence.GeneratedValue;
import javax.persistence.Id;
import javax.persistence.Table;
import static javax.persistence.GenerationType.IDENTITY;

@Entity
@Table(name = "orders")
public class Order {

    @Id
    @GeneratedValue(strategy = IDENTITY)
    @Column(name="order_id")
    private Integer id;

        @Column(name="order_date")
         private Date orderDate;

        @Column(name="ship_date")
        private Date shipDate;

    public Integer getId() {
        return id;
    }

    public void setId(Integer id) {
        this.id = id;
    }

    public Date getOrderDate() {
        return orderDate;
    }
```

```
        public void setOrderDate(Date orderDate) {
                this.orderDate = orderDate;
        }

        public Date getShipDate() {
                return shipDate;
        }

        public void setShipDate(Date shipDate) {
                this.shipDate = shipDate;
        }
}
```

Second, you have to add a property of type List<Order>, called orders, to the User class and annotate it with the annotation @OneToMany to tell to Hibernate to maintain the relationship between the two entities, User and Order.

```
package com.apress.flexjava.usermanager.model;

import static javax.persistence.GenerationType.IDENTITY;
import java.util.List;
import javax.persistence.Column;
import javax.persistence.GeneratedValue;
import javax.persistence.Id;
import javax.persistence.JoinColumn;
import javax.persistence.OneToMany;
import javax.persistence.OneToOne;
import javax.persistence.CascadeType;

public class User {

        @Id
        @GeneratedValue(strategy = IDENTITY)
        @Column(name="user_id")
        private int userId;

        @Column(name="forename")
        private String forename;

        @Column(name="surname")
        private String surname;

        @OneToOne(cascade = CascadeType.ALL)
        @JoinColumn(name = "address_id")
        private Address address;
```

```java
@OneToMany
@JoinColumn(name="order_id")
private List<Order> orders;

public User() {}

public User(int userId, String forename, String surname){
        this.userId   = userId;
        this.forename = forename;
        this.surname = surname;
}

public User(String forename, String surname) {
        this.forename = forename;
        this.surname = surname;
}

public int getUserId() {
        return userId;
}

public void setUserId(int userId) {
        this.userId = userId;
}

public String getForename() {
        return forename;
}

public void setForename(String forename) {
        this.forename = forename;
}

public String getSurname() {
        return surname;
}

public void setSurname(String surname) {
        this.surname = surname;
}

public List<Order> getOrders() {
        return orders;
}

public void setOrders(List<Order> orders) {
        this.orders = orders;
```

```
        }

        public Address getAddress() {
                return address;
        }

        public void setAddress(Address address) {
                this.address = address;
        }
}
```

Next, map the class in your Hibernate configuration file as always, and launch the command `mvn` `install`; if everything goes well, you should see in your database the new table orders, with the relationship to the users, one, as in Figure 5-16.

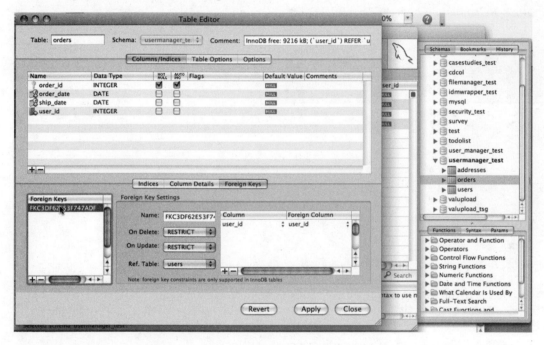

Figure 5-16. *The new table orders*

Mapping a Many-to-Many Relationship

You might also need to relate a user to one or more groups. This case is different from the previous one, as one group can belong to many users, not just to one user as with an order (see Figures 5-17 and 5-18).

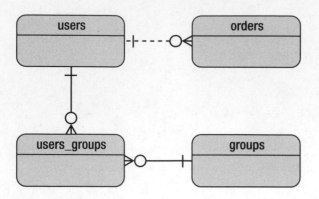

Figure 5-17. *Relationships between the tables users,orders, and groups*

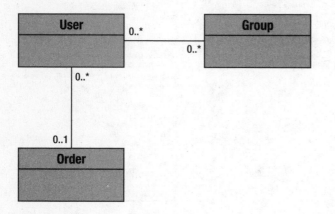

Figure 5-18. *Relationships between the entities User, Order, and Group*

As you can see in the database schema, we have used a link table to maintain the relationship. To maintain this many-to-many relationship, you can use the annotation @ManyToMany. This annotation takes the following attributes:

- Cascade allows you to set a cascading operation using the javax.persistence.CascadeType enumeration class. The default is none;

- Fetch can be set using the FetchType enumeration class. The default is Lazy;

- TargetEntity has the property type as the default; otherwise it can be set to the class of an entity that stores the association;

- MappedBy indicates the entity that owns the bidirectional association.

Now let's create the Group entity, and then we'll create the many-to-many association between the User entity and the new Group entity. The relationship will be owned by the Group class, so we have to annotate the property groups with the annotation @ManyToMany as below:

```
@ManyToMany(cascade = CascadeType.ALL)
 private List<User> users;
```

On the User class side, we add the same annotation with the attribute mappedBy to tell Hibernate that the class refers to the property users of the Group entity.

```
@ManyToMany(mappedBy="users")
 private List<Group> groups;
```

Let's see the two classes in their entirety. Here's the User class:

```
package com.apress.flexjava.usermanager.model;

import static javax.persistence.GenerationType.IDENTITY;
import java.util.List;

import javax.persistence.CascadeType;
import javax.persistence.Column;
import javax.persistence.Entity;
import javax.persistence.GeneratedValue;
import javax.persistence.Id;
import javax.persistence.JoinColumn;
import javax.persistence.ManyToMany;
import javax.persistence.OneToMany;
import javax.persistence.OneToOne;
import javax.persistence.Table;

@Entity
@Table(name = "users")
public class User {

        @Id
        @GeneratedValue(strategy = IDENTITY)
        @Column(name="user_id")
        private int userId;

        @Column(name="forename")
        private String forename;

        @Column(name="surname")
        private String surname;

        @OneToOne(cascade = CascadeType.ALL)
        @JoinColumn(name = "address_id")
```

```java
    private Address address;

    @OneToMany(cascade = CascadeType.ALL)
    @JoinColumn(name = "user_id")
    private List<Order> orders;

    @ManyToMany(mappedBy="users",
                targetEntity=Group.class,
                cascade={CascadeType.PERSIST,
                CascadeType.MERGE})
    private List<Group> groups;

    public User() {}

    public User(int userId, String forename, String surname){
        this.userId   = userId;
        this.forename = forename;
        this.surname = surname;
    }

    public User(String forename, String surname) {
        this.forename = forename;
        this.surname = surname;
    }

    public int getUserId() {
        return userId;
    }

    public void setUserId(int userId) {
        this.userId = userId;
    }

    public String getForename() {
        return forename;
    }

    public void setForename(String forename) {
        this.forename = forename;
    }

    public String getSurname() {
        return surname;
    }

    public void setSurname(String surname) {
        this.surname = surname;
```

```
        }

        public List<Order> getOrders() {
                return orders;
        }

        public void setOrders(List<Order> orders) {
                this.orders = orders;
        }

        public Address getAddress() {
                return address;
        }

        public void setAddress(Address address) {
                this.address = address;
        }

        public List<Group> getGroups() {
                return groups;
        }

        public void setGroups(List<Group> groups) {
                this.groups = groups;
        }
}
```

And here is the Group class:

```
package com.apress.flexjava.usermanager.model;

import static javax.persistence.GenerationType.IDENTITY;

import java.util.List;

import javax.persistence.CascadeType;
import javax.persistence.Column;
import javax.persistence.Entity;
import javax.persistence.GeneratedValue;
import javax.persistence.Id;
import javax.persistence.ManyToMany;
import javax.persistence.Table;
import javax.persistence.JoinTable;
import javax.persistence.JoinColumn;

@Entity
@Table(name = "groups")
```

```java
public class Group {

        @Id
        @GeneratedValue(strategy = IDENTITY)
        @Column(name="user_id")
        private Integer groupId;
        @Column(name="group_name")
        private String groupName;

        @Column(name="group_description")
        private String groupDescription;


        @ManyToMany(
                        targetEntity=Group.class,
                        cascade={CascadeType.PERSIST,
                        CascadeType.MERGE})
        @JoinTable(name="users_groups",
                        joinColumns=@JoinColumn(name="user_id"),
                        inverseJoinColumns=@JoinColumn(name="group_id"))
        private List<User> users;

        public Integer getGroupId() {
                return groupId;
        }

        public void setGroupId(Integer groupId) {
                this.groupId = groupId;
        }

        public String getGroupName() {
                return groupName;
        }

        public void setGroupName(String groupName) {
                this.groupName = groupName;
        }

        public String getGroupDescription() {
                return groupDescription;
        }

        public void setGroupDescription(String groupDescription) {
                this.groupDescription = groupDescription;
        }

        public List<User> getUsers() {
```

```
        return users;
    }

    public void setUsers(List
        this.users = users;
    }

}
```

Before running the command `mvn install`, remember to map the new `Group` entity class into your Hibernate configuration file.

After compiling, you should see a new database link table called `groups_users` and the two relationships to it within both the `users` and `groups` tables (see Figure 5-19).

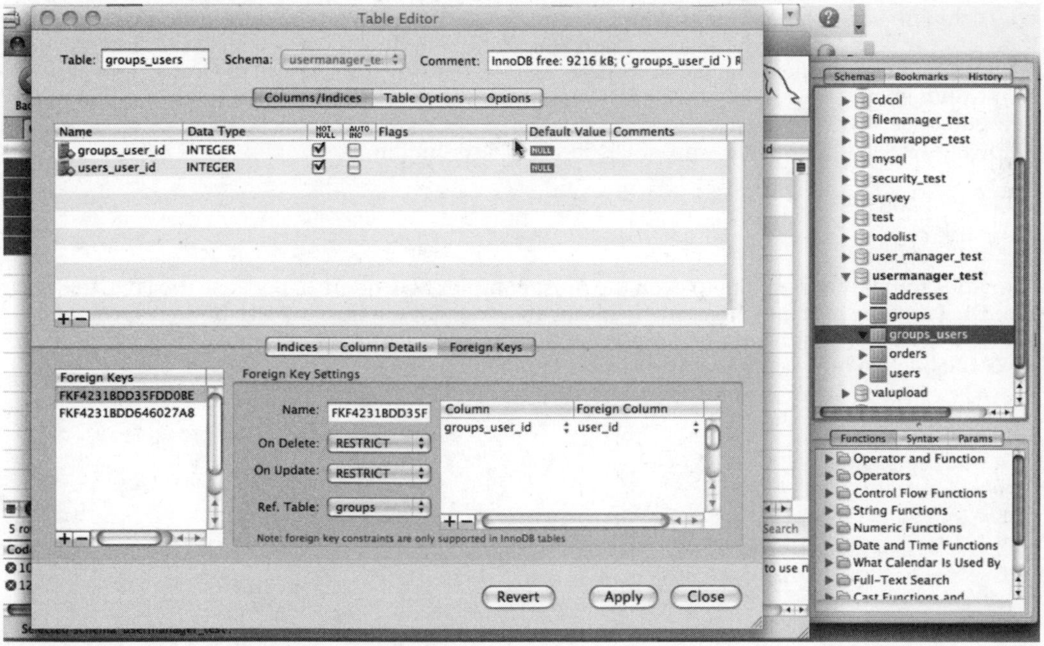

Figure 5-19. *The groups_users database link table created to maintain the many-to-many relationship between the users and the groups tables*

Using Hibernate with Spring

Spring provides support and helper classes for Hibernate architected in a similar way to the JDBC support and helper classes. As with the JDBC, there are both `HibernateTemplate` and `HibernateDaoSupport` classes that work more or less as the `JdbcTemplate` and the `JdbcDaoSupport` classes covered in the previous section.

The `HibernateDaoSupport` provides the setter method to allow the injection of the sessionFactory bean, and this will automatically create the instance of the Hibernate template you can get through the `HibernateTemplate` method.

If you want to use the `HibernateTemplate` without extending the `HibernateDaoSupport`, you should create a setter method in your class that creates an instance of the Hibernate template as in the code above. The Hibernate template offers a number of overloaded methods to query and update a persistent object and the database. But the Hibernate template is not the only way to query; indeed Hibernate also comes with the Hibernate Query Language (HQL).

Querying Using HQL

HQL is a very powerful query language with a syntax very similar to standard SQL. The difference is that with HQL you are querying persisted objects rather than database entities. For example, if you have a database table called users that is mapped to the User persisted object, to get all users using HQL you query the persisted object. Hibernate also allows you to directly use native SQL, but I strongly suggest using HQL whenever possible. If you use a standard SQL statement directly, it will restrict your choices and make it harder in the future to change to a different database, say from MySql to Oracle. In a case like that, you would need to review all of your SQL statements as they will not be completely compatible with the new database.

The following two statements show how SQL and HQL are similar:

```
SQL = "SELEC * FROM users"
HQL = "from User";
```

HQL provides functionalities to map even the most complex SQL queries. Because the HQL dialect is similar to SQL, I feel the best and most practical way to understand it is to explain how and where to use HQL dialect, and I'll also provide a table with the most used SQL queries mapped to HQL.

So let's come back to our UserManager example application to add the package `com.apress.flexjava.usermanager.dao.hibernate`, as shown in Figure 5-20.

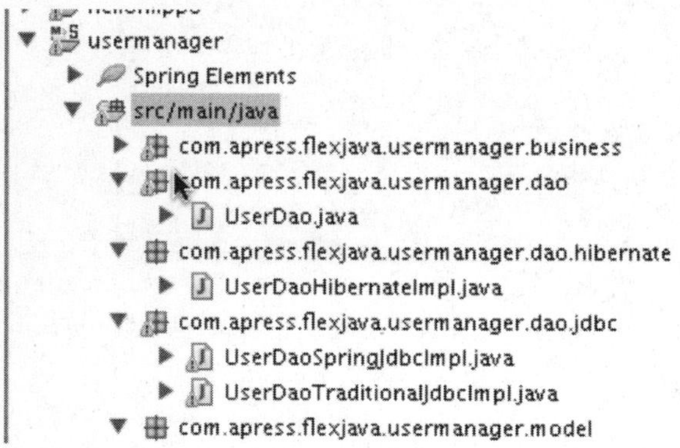

Figure 5-20. *The new com.apress.flexjava.usermanager.dao.hibernate package*

Within the new package we create a class called `UserDaoHibernate` that extends the Spring `HibernateDaoSupport` class and implements the interface `UserDao` created before.

Now let's write the findAll method as the UserDao interface requires. This is a good way to understand the value of programming using interfaces, because as you can see, we have an object of the same type (UserDao) and with the same methods as the JDBC object, but its implementation this time uses Hibernate. When you program using an interface, other classes related to the UserDao won't be aware of the difference of the underlying layer.

In this example we will use the HibernateDaoSupport class that provides us with the getSession() method to obtain the Hibernate session.

```
@SuppressWarnings("unchecked")
public List<User> findAll() {
        String HQL = "from User";
        Query query = getSession().createQuery(HQL);
        return (List<User>)query.list();
}
```

The from clause works directly with objects and you could also write the full path, but if you don't want to load all of the object's properties into memory, you must use the select clause.

```
public List<User> findAll() {
        String HQL = "select u.forename, u.surname from User u";
        Query query = getSession().createQuery(HQL);
        return (List<User>)query.list();
}
```

Now let's see how to pass a parameter in an HQL query. I also want to explain the concept of Named Queries that enable the application to store your HQL queries in your mapping files.

Passing Parameters in HQL Queries

Like SQL, Hibernate supports passing parameters in HQL queries. This means that you can retrieve a User via a passed ID attribute. For this example, we need a method to extract a User by his e-mail address, so let's add the method to the UserDao interface and then implement it into the UserDaoHibernateImpl class with the following code:

```
public User findUserByEmail(String email){
        String HQL = "from User u where u.email = :email";
        Query query = getSession().createQuery(HQL);
        query.setString("email", email);
        return (User)query.uniqueResult();
}
```

As you can see in the code above—and in Table 5-2—the Query object provides lots of methods to define the parameter name, type, and value.

Table 5-2. Query parameters

Query object	Type	Name parameter	Value parameter
query.	setString	("email",	email);

The uniqueResult() method allow the retrieval of just one object from an HQL query. If your query returns more than one result, the uniqueResult() method will return a NonUniqueResultException.

Named Queries

Named queries allow your application to store its HQL queries in a mapping file and they enable the sharing of queries. Moreover, named queries let you use SQL, which allows you to keep all your SQL in one place. However, you can use just HSQL to keep the application more portable.

To use named queries with annotations, Hibernate provides the @NamedQueries and @NamedQuery annotations. Before we see how to use named queries, let's think about why and where it would be logical to use them.

For each entity, there are always some queries you need to reuse in different DAOs or methods, so it is better to store those queries within the entity itself using annotations, thus avoiding the need to rewrite the same query in the different DAOs or methods. For example, you might need to retrieve a user using the e-mail HQL query statement in other methods beside findByEmail, so it is better to move it to the entity itself.

To do that, just open your User entity and add the following code under the @Table annotation:

```
public static final String FIND_BY_EMAIL = "User.findByEmail";

@NamedQueries({
@NamedQuery(name=User.FIND_BY_EMAIL, query="from User u where u.email = :email")
})
```

Now let's modify the UserDaoHibernateImpl findByEmail method body in order to use the new named query.

The Hibernate session provides a method to get the named query, so to adapt the code to use the new named query, you just have to rename the method createQuery(HQL) to getNamedQuery(User.FIND_BY_EMAIL), as in the following example:

```
public User findUserByEmail(String email){
        Query query = getSession().getNamedQuery(User.FIND_BY_EMAIL);
            query.setString("email", email);
            return (User)query.uniqueResult();
    }
```

Using NamedQuery, you can access the User.FIND_BY_EMAIL named query from everywhere in your code and avoid constantly rewriting code every time you need to retrieve a user by email.

HQL and Hibernate Support Matrix

Table 5-3 shows the most common SQL queries mapped to HQL.

Table 5-3. Mapping SQL and HQL

Retrieve All	
SQL	`SELECT * FROM USERS;`
HQL	`from User;`
HibernateDaoSupport	`List<User> users = getHibernateTemplate.loadAll(User.Class);`

Retrieve Unique Result	
SQL	`SELECT * FROM USERS WHERE user_id = :id ;`
HQL	`from User u where u.userId = :id;`
HibernateDaoSupport	`User user = (User) getHibernateTemplate.get(User.Class, id);`

Sorting Results	
SQL	`SELECT * FROM USERS WHERE user_age > 28 ORDER BY user_age;`
HQL	`from User u where userAge>28   order by u.userAge`
HibernateDaoSupport	

Retrieving data from joined tables	
SQL	`SELECT * FROM orders INNER JOIN products`
HQL	`from Order as o inner join o.products as p`
HibernateDaoSupport	

Table 5-3. Continued

Retrieving the latest version of a document	
SQL	`SELECT max(version) from documents`
HQL	`select max(d.version) from Document o`
HibernateDaoSupport	

Update data	
SQL	`UPDATE users set email=:email where user_id = :id`

HQL	`update User u set u.email = :email where u.userId = :id`
	
	Example:
	
	`String hql = "update User u set u.email = :email where u.userId = :id";`
	`Query query = getSession().createQuery(hql);`
	`query.setString("email","filippo@apress.com");`
	`query.setLong("id",12);`
	`int numberRowsUpdated = query.executeUpdate();`
	`System.out.println("Number rows updated " + numberRowsUpdated)`

HibernateDaoSupport	`User user = (User) getHibernateTemplate().merge(user);`

Delete data	
SQL	`DELETE FROM users  where user_id = :id`

Table 5-3. Continued

HQL	delete from User u where u.userId = :id
	Example:
	String hql = "delete from User u where u.userId = :id";
	Query query = getSession().createQuery(hql);
	query.setLong("id",12);
	int numberRowsUpdated = query.executeUpdate();
	System.out.println("Number rows deleted " + numberRowsUpdated)
HibernateDaoSupport	User user = (User) getHibernateTemplate().delete(user);

Use Native SQL

Sometimes in your projects you may need to use native SQL statements, and Hibernate provides the method createSQLQuery(String queryString)on the session interface to let you do this. You may need to use SQL, for example, when you need a particular database feature not supported by HQL or when you need to call database stored procedures.

Here's an example of using native SQL statements with Hibernate.

```
public void updateTypeById(Long id, String type){
        String sql = "UPDATE Instruction set type = :type where
instruction_id = :id";
        Query query = getSession().createSQLQuery(sql);
     query.setLong("id",id);
     query.setString("type",type);
     query.executeUpdate();
    }
```

Introduction to Transactions

Transactions are very important in enterprise applications development; they ensure the integrity of the data in all database-driven applications. Transactions are a significant part of both multi-user and single-user applications because they protect data from being accessed by other users as well as from interactions due to complex relationships with other tables. Practically speaking, a transaction is a wrapper of some database instructions that commits to write all the relevant data to the database or to roll back all the instructions if anything goes wrong. In order for this to happen, transactions should be able to be described by the following set of properties known as ACID—atomicity, consistency, isolation, and durability:

- Atomicity: The transaction updates the database only if everything goes well. If not, it leaves the database as before the transaction started (rollback);

- Consistency: A consistent transaction is one that does not break any rule of the database such as integrity constraints. Practically speaking, if for some reason the transaction violates the database's consistency rule the transaction will be rolled back and the database will be restored to the previous state;

- Isolation: The transaction will be completely invisible to other transactions until it completes successfully;

- Durability: When the transaction completes successfully, it will persist into the database and cannot be undone.

Typically, to use a transaction in your code you just have to invoke the commit () and rollback () methods, but if you have to work with more than one database, you have to use transaction management. Spring provides abstract facilities to work with different transaction manager such as JmsTransactionManager and JpaTransactionManager. PlatformTransactionManager is the interface for all other transaction managers, as shown in Figure 5-21.

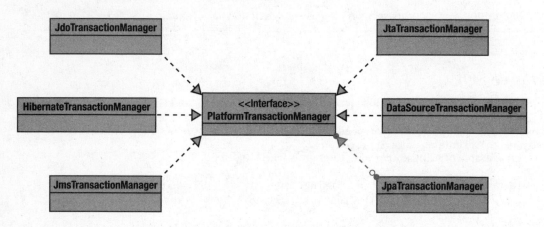

Figure 5-21. *The Spring PlatformTransactionManager interface and its different implementations*

With Hibernate you use the HibernateTransactionManager, as follows:

```
<bean id="transactionManager" class="org.springframework.orm.hibernate3↩
.HibernateTransactionManager" >
      <property name="sessionFactory" ref="sessionFactory" />
   </bean>

   <tx:annotation-driven/>
```

To use transactions properly, the best approach is using Aspect Oriented Programming (AOP). However, for developers who don't know AOP, Spring includes an annotation called @Transactional that allows you to declare methods using transactions.

To use the @Transactional annotation you need to have enabled the Spring annotations and added the XML definition `<tx:annotation-driven>` to your configuration file. Note that if you don't call your transaction manager bean with the name □transactionManager,□ you have to specify the new name in your `<tx:annotation-driven>` statement, as in the following example code:

```
<bean id="myTransactionManager" class="org.springframework.orm↵
.hibernate3.HibernateTransactionManager" >
    <property name="sessionFactory" ref="sessionFactory" />
</bean>

<tx:annotation-driven transaction-manager="myTransactionManager"/>
```

Spring includes a transaction manager for JDBC called DatasourceTransactionManager, and one for Hibernate called HibernateTransactionManager.

An easy way to understand transactions is to consider a ticket purchase, where the system must check the availability of the tickets and then decrease the stock. To highlight the difference between using transactions and not using them, I have created two UML sequences diagrams that describe the ticket-purchase process, first without using transactions and then with using them, as shown in Figures 5-22 and 5-23.

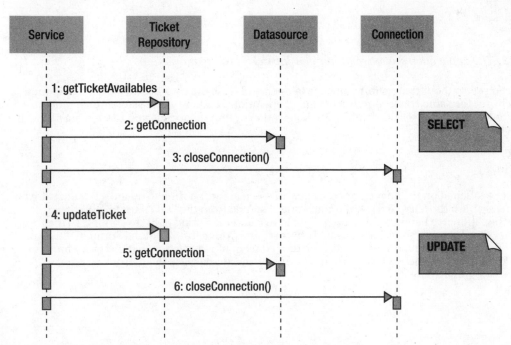

Figure 5-22. The application sequence for purchasing tickets without using transactions

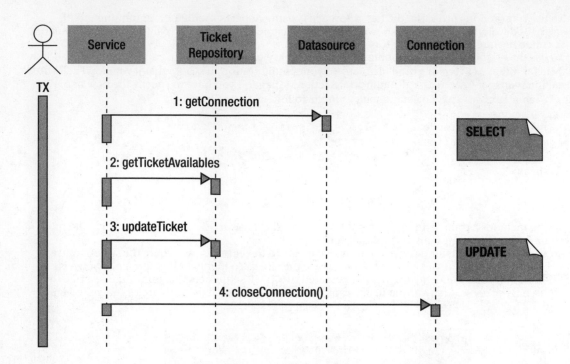

Figure 5-23. *The application sequence for purchasing tickest using transactions*

As you can see, without transaction you have to open and close the connection for each operation. With transactions, the same connection is used for all operations, making your system much more efficient. If you don't use transactions, and without isolation or proper locking, you risk having inconsistent data.

Summary

In this chapter I touched on the important concepts you need before starting to create a JEE data-driven application using both the JDBC and ORM frameworks. I started from the DAO pattern, and then I showed you the difference between using the plain old JDB and the Spring JDBC to connect to the database. After that I showed the value of using Hibernate and Spring instead of the Spring JDBC, even if sometimes it is still useful. Finally I mentioned the new concept of Transaction, which is very important for JEE development. All of these are important concepts to master because the data layer is the foundation of our application.

CHAPTER 6

■ ■ ■

Spring Security

During my career, I have had to implement so many different security packages and systems. I am a developer, though, not a security analyst, and, frankly, this bores me to death. Security, however, is a necessary evil—no one likes his beautiful application played with.

Some of the security packages and systems I used were architected from scratch while others used existing frameworks. Whenever I had to deal with security, I would try to keep it as simple as possible, for easier maintenance and because I knew others would probably be maintaining the application. But the system always had to be secure and reusable with all the interdependent sites and applications. And because security needs to be integral, it always required a lot of time and effort just to implement. When I discovered the Java Acegi security framework a while back, I was impressed, and my heart did a little flutter—perhaps I would be able to do a little less work on security. What set my pulse racing was that Acegi supported all authentication mechanisms while providing configurable storage options for users and authorities.

Some two years after Acegi Security was released, it was incorporated into the Spring framework as a built-in solution, and it became known as Spring Security. Spring Security integrates advanced security features into the framework so you can manage the entire security process during enterprise application development.

Introduction to Spring Security

The value of using Spring Security compared with other customized solutions is its portability, extensibility, and flexibility. Spring Security lets you keep the business logic separated from security, and it keeps the authentication and authorization processes decoupled, giving you the flexibility to make changes to one without affecting the other.

Practically speaking, Spring Security lets you secure an application by simply configuring an XML file, usually called security.xml. In this XML file, you can use elements declared in the Spring Security Schema, to define the URL patterns that you want to secure, as well as the type of authentication mechanism.

```
<http auto-config="true" session-fixation-protection="none" >
          <form-login login-page="/flex-client/RemoteObjectTest.html"↵
 always-use-default-target="true" default-target-url="/authorities"↵
 authentication-failure-url="/authorities"  />
          <intercept-url pattern="/messagebroker/**" access=↵
"IS_AUTHENTICATED_ANONYMOUSLY" />
          <intercept-url pattern="/flex-client/**"
access="IS_AUTHENTICATED_ANONYMOUSLY" />
          <intercept-url pattern="/authorities"
access="IS_AUTHENTICATED_ANONYMOUSLY" />
```

```
        <intercept-url pattern="/**" access=
"ROLE_ADMIN,ROLE_USERS" />
</http>

<authentication-provider>
     <jdbc-user-service data-source-ref="dataSource"/>
</authentication-provider>
```

An important step of your security plans is to decide which authentication mechanism your application is going to provide. For example an application could offer the standard login-based form, plus single sign-on and anonymous authentication. In the example above, we used standard login-based form authentication.

Spring Security supports a number of authentication models and technologies, including anonymous login, HTTP BASIC authentication headers, X.509 certificates, LDAP, and many more. HTTP BASIC Authentication, for example, processes the authentication credentials stored in the HTTP request header.

Once you have decided on the authentication type for your application, you need to think how to handle the security. In this book, we will cover Web authorization using URL patterns.

Web Authorization Using URL Patterns

Spring Security lets you define the URL patterns that need to be secured. You could, for example, decide to secure the URL path /admin and all of its subpages and files.

```
<http auto-config="true" session-fixation-protection="none" >
        <intercept-url pattern="/admin/**" access="ROLE_ADMIN" />
</http>
```

As you can see in this example, you can also associate roles with the URL pattern. All URL patterns are defined in the XML configuration file and are evaluated in the order listed. Here, the page *admin/addUser.html*, for example, can be accessed only by users having access equal to ROLE_ADMIN.

You can perform URL pattern matching for both the HTTP and HTTPS protocols. The URL pattern authentication is handled by the FilterInterceptor filter, a Spring default filter implemented into the standard Spring filter chain discussed in the next section.

The Importance of Filters

Since Spring Security 2.0 filters are initialized with the correct values and ordered by default, we don't have to manage them, as in earlier versions. Generally, filters are configured within the web.xml file and you don't have to implement anything to make them work with the Spring context security, as you used to have to do for servlets. Spring Security comes with a single proxy filter (org.springframework.web.filter.DelegatingFilterProxy) that delegates all received requests to a chain of filters managed by Spring itself. Figure 6-1 shows how this class works. You can inject the other filters into the Spring IOC container as normal beans.

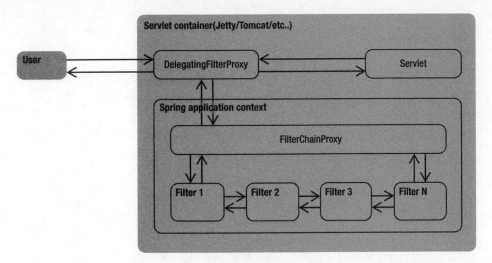

Figure 6-1. The job of the DelegatingFilterProxy and FIterChainProxy

Table 6-1 shows the most important standard Spring Security filter classes, along with the XML element and a description.

Table 6-1. Spring Security filter classes

Filter Class	Xml NameSpace Element	Description
HttpSessionContextIntegrationFilter	http	Sets the connection between the SecurityContext and HTTP requests.
LogoutFilter	http logout	Clears the SecurityHolder.
AuthenticationProcessingFilter	http form-login	Sets the Authentication into the SecurityHolder after login.
BasicProcessingFilter	http http-basic	Processes the user credentials stored into the http header.
RememberMeProcessingFilter	http remember-me	Sets a cookie to remember the user details across multiple browser sessions.
AnonymousProcessingFilter	http anonymous	Populates the context user details with an anonymous user, treating it as a normal user.
ExceptionTranslationFilter	http	If an exception is returned, the filter redirects the request to an error page.

FilterSecurityInterceptor	http	Checks if the URL pattern provided by the Web request is authorized.

With the old Acegi security, you had to define the filter list, separated with commas and pay careful attention to the order, as shown below:

```
/**=httpSessionContextIntegrationFilter,basicProcessingFilter,logoutFilter,↩
ldapTransparentSingleSignOnProcessingFilter,securityContextHolderAwareRequestFilter
,↩
exceptionTranslationFilter,filterInvocationInterceptor
```

If one of these filters was in the wrong position, the security wouldn't work. Spring Security comes with a standard filter chain ordered correctly, making security much easier. You no longer need to configure the filter list, though Spring Security does let you add custom filters to the filter stack.

```
<bean id="customizedauthenticationFilter" ↩
class="com.apress.security.CustomizedAuthenticationFilter" >
        <custom-filter position="AUTHENTICATION_PROCESSING_FILTER"/>
                ...
</bean>
```

In this example, I created a custom login filter to replace the default authentication filter.

Authentication and Authorization

Before starting to write code, it's important to consider Spring Security concepts such as principal, authentication, and authorization, all important aspects of the security process. Figure 6-2 shows the principal as well as the authentication and authorization sequences.

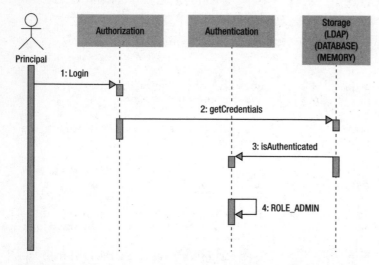

Figure 6-2. UML sequence diagram showing the Spring Security authentication process

The principal is the user or the device that needs to get access to the system. The authentication sequence starts checking the validity of the credentials handled by the principal, then the authorization process gives permission to the principal to perform different actions at different levels.

Practically speaking, the authentication process checks the user by matching the user name and password against a database or another storage server; the authorization mechanism retrieves all permission's related to the user's roles.

Spring Security lets you configure the authentication providers with the mechanism you want for storing your user's information. (Usually, it is a database or a directory server such as LDAP).

```
<authentication-provider>
        <jdbc-user-service data-source-ref="dataSource"/>
</authentication-provider>
```

Authentication Methods

In order to use a database to store your users' details, Spring Security comes with built-in queries using the following SQL:

```
SELECT username, password, enabled
FROM users
WHERE username = ?

SELECT username, authority
FROM authorities
WHERE username = ?
```

This means that if you don't specify a custom database schema, Spring Security will try to query the tables USERS and AUTHORITIES. To test the default security queries, you have to create the corresponding tables in your database as with the following MySQL code:

```
CREATE TABLE `usermanager_test`.`users` (
  `username` varchar(16) NOT NULL,
  `password` varchar(32) NOT NULL,
  `enabled` smallint(6) DEFAULT NULL,
  PRIMARY KEY (`username`)
) ENGINE=MyISAM DEFAULT CHARSET=utf8

CREATE TABLE `usermanager_test`.`authorities` (
  `username` varchar(16) NOT NULL,
  `authority` varchar(16) NOT NULL,
  KEY `usernamefk` (`username`)
) ENGINE=MyISAM DEFAULT CHARSET=latin1
```

Then you just define your authentication provider in your Spring Security XML configuration file as follows:

```
<bean id="dataSource" class="org.apache.commons.dbcp.BasicDataSource" destroy-
method="close">
    <property name="driverClassName" value="${jdbc.driverClassName}"/>
```

```
    <property name="url" value="${jdbc.url}"/>
    <property name="username" value="${jdbc.username}"/>
    <property name="password" value="${jdbc.password}"/>
    <property name="maxActive" value="100"/>
    <property name="maxWait" value="1000"/>
    <property name="poolPreparedStatements" value="true"/>
    <property name="defaultAutoCommit" value="true"/>
    <property name="testOnBorrow" value="true"/>
    <property name="validationQuery" value="select 1=1"/>
</bean>

<authentication-provider>
    <jdbc-user-service data-soure-ref="dataSource" />
</authentication-provider>
```

Easy, isn't it?

If you want to use your database schema, Spring Security lets you write your own SQL statements by just using the XML attributes users-by-username-query and authorities-by-username-query within the jdbc-users-service XML element.

```
<authentication-provider>
  <jdbc-user-service data-source-ref="dataSource"
                        users-by-username-query="SELECT * FROM
customized_users_table
 WHERE user_id = ?"
                        authorities-by-username-query="SELECT * FROM
 customized_authorities_table WHERE user_id = ?"/>
</authentication-provider>
```

If you don't want to set up a database and you have just a few static users, you can load their details into memory from a properties file or by defining them within the authentication provider tags. Here's an example that defines users within the authentication provider tags

```
<authentication-provider>
    <user-service>
      <user password="12345689" name="admin" authorities="ROLE_ADMIN,ROLE_USER" />
      <user password="79891011" name="user1" authorities="ROLE_USER" />
      <user password="11121314" name="user2" authorities="ROLE_USER" disabled="true"
/>
    </user-service>
</authentication-provider>
```

This example gets user details that were defined in a properties file:

```
<authentication-provider>
      <user-service properties="/WEB-INF/users.properties" />
</authentication-provider>
```

However, these two methods are best used only during development or while prototyping applications.

If you expect that your users will be working with multiple applications, perhaps applications that are developed using different languages and technologies, I recommend using a directory server (LDAP) to store your user details. LDAP servers are a standard, very common technology and many applications have already embedded the LDAP plug-in, allowing security integration with the standard LDAP protocol. This means you can plug an external application into your system without changing either your security or the other application's security.

I'm not going to discuss how an LDAP server works in detail, there are many excellent resources for that. However, let's look at the basics so you will be able to make some tests.

There are many LDAP servers on the market, both open source and commercial. Our example will use the open source Apache LDAP directory server, ApacheDS, which you can download from the Apache website at `http://directory.apache.org/`.

Follow the instructions to install it on your local machine. At the same URL, download and then install Apache Directory Studio (see Figure 6-3), an Eclipse-based LDAP client platform.

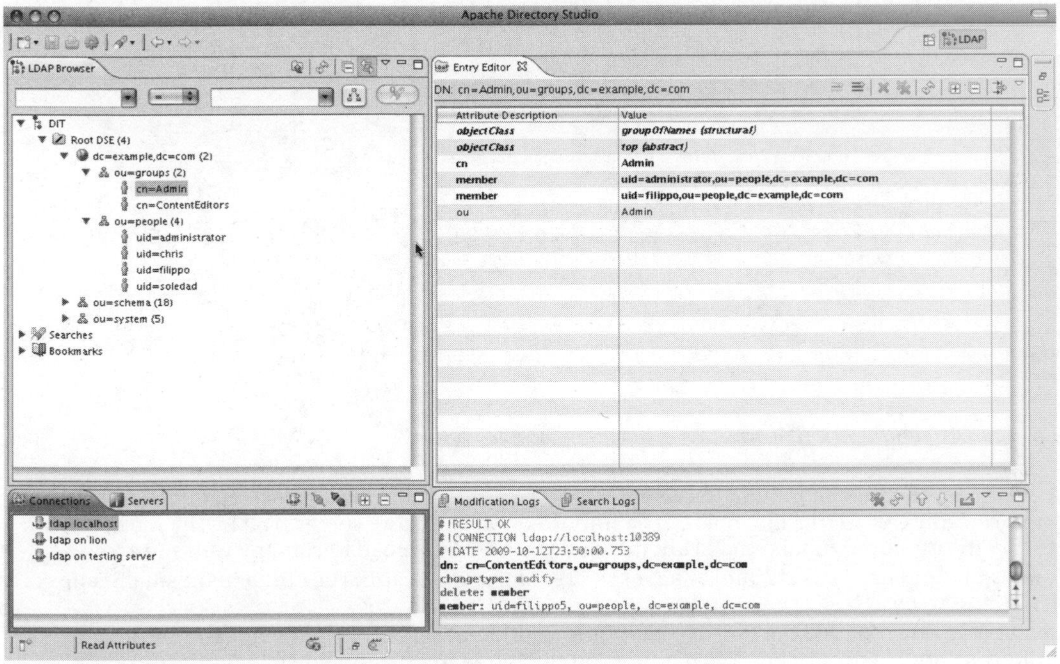

Figure 6-3. Apache Directory Studio

Usually the local installation of the ApacheDS server is on `ldap://localhost:10389`, so in your Apache Directory Studio, right click within the Connection view and select "New Connection"; in order to connect to the LDAP server you should set the previously mentioned URL as shown in Figure 6-4.

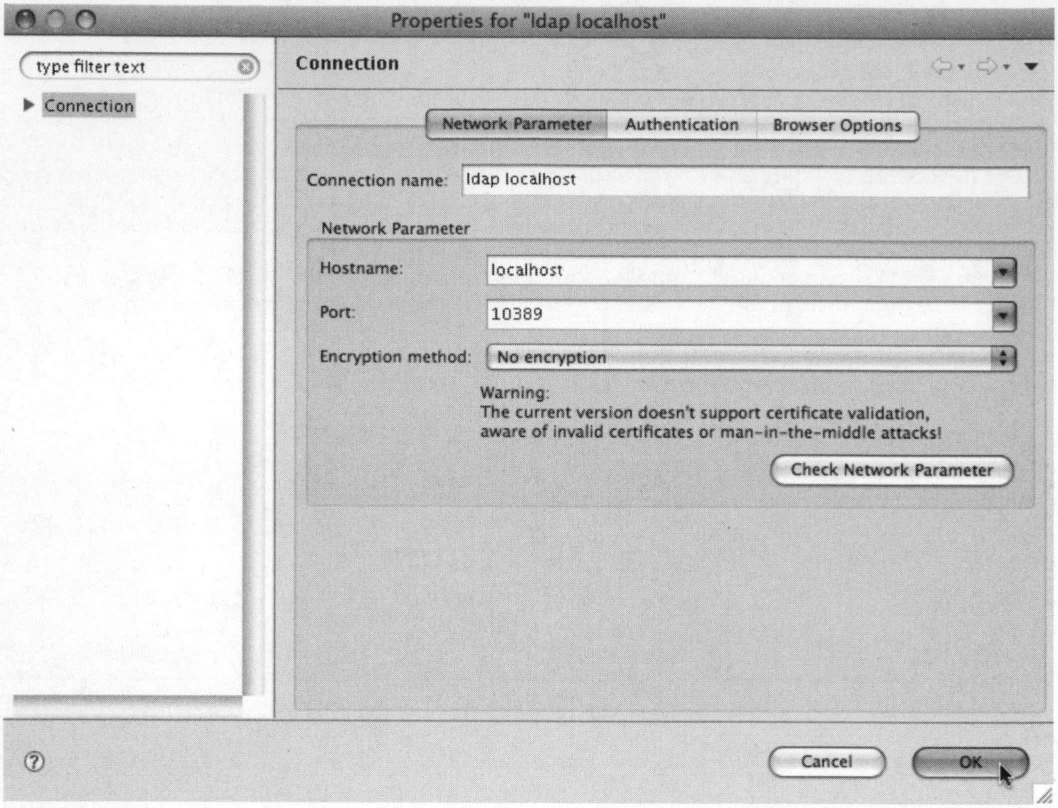

Figure 6-4. LDAP connection properties in Apache Directory Studio

Once connected, you can browse the server. To make the learning process easier, I created a user and groups example tree LDIFF file, ready to be imported to your LDAP server. The LDIFF file contains the necessary information to build the LDAP tree and you can download it from my web site at
`http://www.filippodipisa.it/books/apress/flexandjava/chapter06/ldap/usersAndGroups.ldiff`

When you've downloaded the file, import it into your LDAP server using the Apache Directory Studio import utility. To do so, click File > Import on the top menu bar as shown in Figure 6-5.

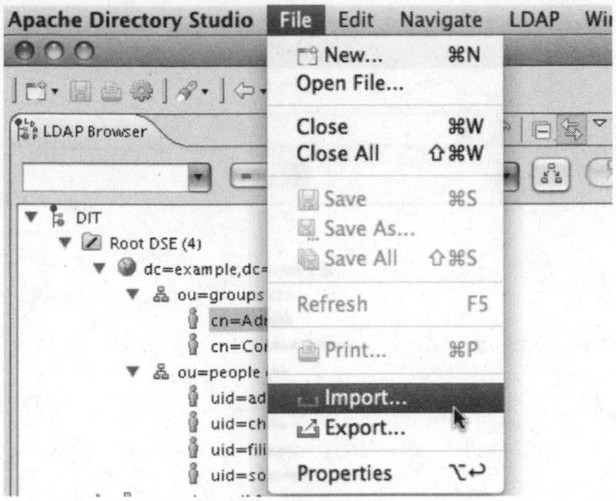

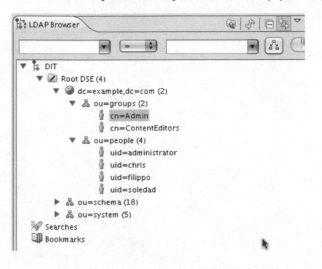

Figure 6-5. *Using the Apache Directory Studio to import the LDIFF file*

Once the import has completed successfully, you should see the LDAP tree shown in Figure 6-6.

Figure 6-6. *The LDAP tree created by importing the LDIFF file*

Assuming everything has complete successfully, your server has been set up with some users and authorities, allowing us to start to write some code to make Spring work with the LDAP server.

To use LDAP with Spring Security, you have to add to your POM file the Spring LDAP dependency (at the time of this writing, the latest version is 1.2.1) that will import into your classpath the two JAR libraries spring-ldap-1.2.1/jar and commons-lang-2.1.jar.

```
<dependency>
    <groupId>org.springframework.ldap</groupId>
```

```
    <artifactId>spring-ldap</artifactId>
    <version>1.2.1</version>
</dependency>
```

Remember to add the *security.xml* path to your `contextConfigLocation` within your *web.xml* file like any Spring security application.

```
<context-param>
    <param-name>contextConfigLocation</param-name>
    <param-value>
            classpath:/applicationContext-resources.xml
            classpath:/applicationContext-dao.xml
            classpath*:/applicationContext.xml
              /WEB-INF/applicationContext.xml
              /WEB-INF/security.xml
        </param-value>
</context-param>
```

Then you need to tell to your authentication provider to authenticate against an LDAP server as well as what method to use to search users and groups. You can define LDAP filters for groups and users using standard XML attributes within your security.xml XML file, as follows:

```
<authentication-provider>
    <ldap-user-service   server-ref="ldapServer"
                                    user-search-filter="{uid=0}"
                                    user-search-base="ou=people"
                                    group-search-filter="member={0}"
                                    group-search-base="ou=groups"/>

</authentication-provider>

<ldap-server     id="ldapServer"
                    url="ldap://localhost:10389/dc=example,dc=com"
                          manager-dn="uid=admin,ou=system"
                          manager-password="123456"/>
```

In the example above, Spring will connect to the LDAP server at `ldap://localhost:10389/dc=example,dc=com` and will search for a user within the *people* organization unit (ou) by user id.

In enterprise applications, I suggest you use LDAP authentication rather than database authentication, as it is more flexible and follows the standard Internet practice.

Decision Managers and Voters

In the Spring authentication/authorization process, a user who successfully authenticates is granted a set of authorities. Spring access decision managers then check this set of authorities to see which resources the user can have access to. These access decision managers require a group of voters that make the access control decisions. This is a very useful process for giving users the roles and permission to access different resources. Spring comes with three types of access decision managers:

`AffirmativeBased` – only one voter needed to grant the access;

ConsensusBased – more voters needed to grant the access;

UnanimousBased – all voters needed to grant the access;

If you don't configure any access decision managers, by default, Spring Security will use the Affirmativebased decision manager with the RoleVoter and the AuthenticatedVoter objects configured. The RoleVoter votes affirmative if it finds roles starting with the prefix ROLE_ within the user roles collection. The AuthenticatedVoter votes affirmative if the authentication level is higher than the required attributes IS_AUTHENTICATED_FULLY, IS_AUTHENTICATED_REMEMBERED, and IS_AUTHENTICATED_ANONYMOUSLY.

In basic terms, the RoleVoter checks the application permission level of a user, and the AuthenticatedVoter checks if the user is authenticated or not. You may have a scenario where a user is authenticated but doesn't belong to any group; in this case the user can't access any resource even if he is authenticated.

If you need a more complex security solution, you are able to customize your access decision managers easily by using the following XML elements:

For Web security:

```
<http access-decision-manager-ref="myAccessDecisionManagerBean">
   ...
</http>
```

For method security:

```
<global-method-security access-decision-manager-
ref="myAccessDecisionManagerBean">
   ...
</global-method-security>
```

Method-level security is a powerful service that Spring provides. It allows you to implement the security level on each method by assigning a role for each method.

Spring Security lets you manage security at the method level by using annotations. In order to use security annotations, you have to switch them on by adding the XML element global-method-security within your XML configuration file, as follows:

```
<global-method-security secured-annotations="enabled" />
```

Once the Spring Security annotations are on, you can use the @Secure annotation at the Java level:

```
@Secured({"ROLE_ADMIN"})
public List<User> getUsers(){

}

@Secured({"ROLE_ADMIN","ROLE_USER"})
public User getUserDetail(){

}
```

Though annotations are very useful, adding annotations to each method would cause problems in an application. This limitation can be overcome using Spring's Aspect Oriented Programming (AOP) framework, which enables you to secure many beans or services with just one declaration.

Summary

In this chapter I covered the most important Spring Security concepts. You have seen how to secure Java applications using both URL patterns and method security. I explained the important role of filters and the filter chain, and showed how Spring Security uses the DelegatingFilterProxy object to delegate all requests to the other filters added by default into the filter chain stack. Then I showed you how to add a custom authentication filter into the filter chain to replace the default one. Finally, I touched on the most important authentication processes using databases, LDAP repositories, and static values.

Application security is very important in enterprise development, and thanks to Spring Security, you don't have to be a security analyst anymore—the Spring Security framework already does most of the job. Instead, you can focus on deciding what the best user storage and authentication/authorization solution for your needs is.

In the next chapter I will introduce you to the Flex framework that we will use to develop the view layer.

CHAPTER 7

Flex (The View Layer)

Flex is a framework for building rich internet applications (RIAs) for FlashPlayer 9 and 10. Flex is a tool for developers rather than designers, and its aim is to provide the developer with classes and components to organize, handle, and present data, and to provide the functionality for creating desktop-like applications that are typically delivered via Web browser plug-ins such as Flash Player or Silverlight.

A rich Internet application is different from a typical Internet application, as it provides real-time data update, without the need for page reloading, as well as a full multimedia experience and the look and feel of a traditional desktop application. Usually the architecture of a RIA application makes use of the Model View Controller (MVC) design pattern, in which the view layer of the application interacts with the data model though the controllers. GoogleDocs are an example of a rich Internet application, while Microsoft Office and OpenOffice are desktop applications.

The FlashPlayer Overview

Flex was created to allow developers to take advantage of the visual capabilities of FlashPlayer, but to still be able to program in a more traditional way. The Flex IDE is very similar to other traditional development environments, allowing developers coming from other languages, such as C++ and Java, to be comfortable with Flex and able to use the FlashPlayer as a browser plug-in or as an independent sandbox.

It was the release of FlashPlayer 9, which introduced AS 3, regular expressions, binary sockets and XML parsing, and a radically new event model, that really enabled Flex. FlashPlayer 9 was the most significant release since the original FlashPlayer, due in part to its support for a true object-oriented language such as AS3, but also to the massive performance increase of FlashPlayer compared with the previous versions.

FlashPlayer 10 takes another quantum leap, as it introduces a new graphic engine, new 3D APIs, hardware acceleration, dynamic sound generation, dynamic streaming, access to local files, a new vector drawing API, and a new Text engine that brings print-quality publishing to the Web—all cool stuff for users that they may never have seen before. For developers, it means there is a lot cool stuff that can be accomplished without the need to introduce even more new technologies into the mix.

Flex Components

Flex provides a set of classes and components to help in creating richer user interfaces that provide a more engaging user experience, and the goal of this chapter is to introduce you to the most common of these, and show you how easy they are to use and how to extend them. However, we won't be covering all Flex components and controls, with all their properties and events. The Adobe Flex Reference is quite complete and it is pointless to rewrite it. It is more important, I think, for you to learn how to use item renderers, for example, to render a DataGrid cell as a ComboBox, or how to use view stacks, and data binding, and to manage complex data collections.

I will show you one of the most popular micro-architecture patterns that is built on top of Flex. Called Cairngorm, it allows you to use a set of design patterns to improve your application architecture and reusability. Cairngorm consists of a collection of design patterns such as the MVC, Command, and Observer patterns; these are already implemented in the micro-architecture, making the developer's life much easier.

The Flex Framework Architecture

The Flex framework has been built on top of AS classes. To make it easier to understand how the framework has been layered, the diagram in Figure 7-1 describes the Flex, Flash, and AS packages.

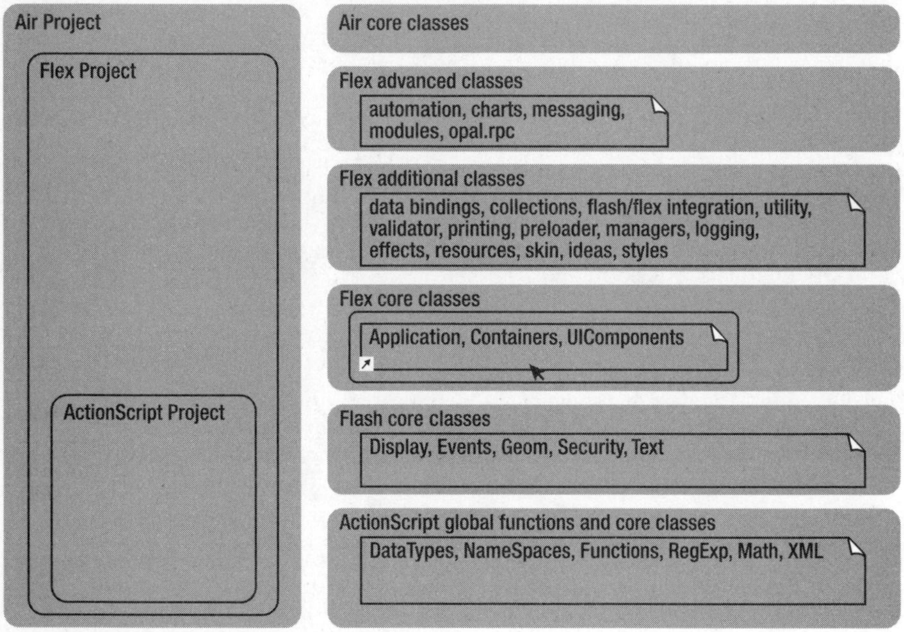

Figure 7-1. Flex, Flash, and AS packages

The AS global functions and core classes are a set of libraries that provide the functionality to develop using the new AS3, including arrays, datatypes, regular expressions, XML namespaces, and more.

The Flash core classes are included in all AS projects and are part of the AS core classes. They provide display and geometry functionality, as well as classes for bitmap filter effects, caching, and much more.

The Flex core classes provide new functionality that helps you manage your application views and states. Before Flex, all objects were placed on the stage and you manipulated scenes and MovieClips. To connect to remote data, there were technologies like Flash remoting and third-party applications like WebOrb. To manage complex data collection, there was only the Array class. The Flash IDE did provide some UI components like TextInput, DataGrid, and the like, but most of the time it was much better and faster to create a custom component extending the UI class because the Flash V2 components were not easy to skin, render, or extend.

To solve these problems, Flex offers AS3, a new, far more object -oriented language built to run on FlashPlayer 9, as well as a set of libraries to manage containers, controls, remote data, collections and much more.

Flex also introduced the concept of layout containers, a set of classes and components built to improve the display and the management of all display objects on the screen. For example, the VBox container lays out its children in a single vertical column.

Figure 7-2. Using a VBox container to lay out a TextInput, a DataGrid, and a Button component

Figure 7-2 shows how you can use the VBox container to lay out a TextInput, a DataGrid, and a Button component. Here is an example of the code:

```
var vBox : VBox = new VBox();
vBox.addChild(new TextInput());
vBox.addChild(new DataGrid());
vBox.addChild(new Button());
```

By changing the VBox container to the HBox type, all children will be laid out in a single horizontal row (see Figure 7-3).

```
var hBox : HBox = new HBox();
hBox.addChild(new TextInput());
hBox.addChild(new DataGrid());
hBox.addChild(new Button());
```

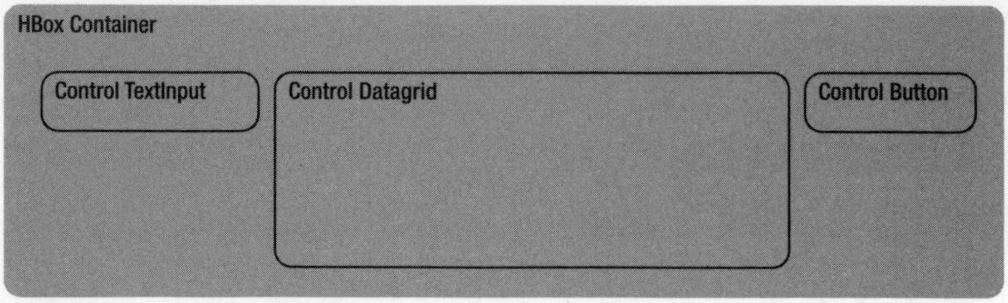

Figure 7-3. HBox type lays out all children in a horizontal row

Flex Development Overview

As I previously noted, this is not just a Flex book, and my aim is to teach you how to use AS and MXML properly and to help you understand important concepts such as the item renderer and data collection. At the end of the day, once you understand the basic concepts of layout containers, layout children, and so forth, using the Adobe Flex Builder or an online tutorial will be a quick learn, so we can focus this book on more important concepts.

Here are the basic concepts you need in order to be able to start using the Flex Builder and the Flex SDK effectively:

- Flex Builder—The IDE for developing Flex applications. Flex Builder installation was described in Chapter 3;

- Application and Layout containers—A set of components to lay out display objects;

- UI controls—User interface components like `TextInput`, `Button`, `DataGrid` and `ComboBox`;

- Data binding—Bind data between different layers and components automatically;

- AS vs. MXML usage—Write elegant, AS-based applications, reserving MXML for the views and UI components;

- Handling events—Listen and dispatch events between different layers and components;

After you have mastered these basic concepts, you will be able to choose the layout containers needed by each component or view of your application, listen and dispatch events between the different objects, and bind data.

Practically speaking, you could write a textual Black Jack game using a `VBox` layout to contain the `TextInput`, `Label`, and `Button` UI controls and events need by the application. So let's start creating our first Flex Project.

Flex Builder

Before creating your first Flex project, you need to know the basic functionalities of the Flex Builder. The important issues to understand are:

- How to create the project

- How to use the Flex Builder perspectives
- How to build an application automatically and manually
- How to run an application
- How to debug an application
- How to navigate between classes
- Short cut keys

Create a Project

There are four kinds of projects you can create using the Flex Builder:

- AS project: You can use only AS classes as shown in the diagram in Figure 7-1. Remember that in an AS project, you can't access all the Flex APIs as some libraries are not imported into the library path. Thus, if you plan to use layout containers or remote services, it's better to create a Flex project;

- Flex library project (SWC): These are very handy and they can be reused in different projects. A Flex library has an .swc extension. If you are coming from Java, you can think of an .swc file as being like an archive (.jar) file;

- Flex project: You get all the functionalities of an AS project plus all Flex libraries. Flex builder adds all Flex SWC archive libraries so you can use all sets of the Flex APIs;

- Air project: This is a desktop application based on Adobe Air—basically similar to a Flex application but with more APIs that interact directly with the operating system to let you, for example, save a file on the local machine.;

Figure 7-4 shows the different libraries imported by the Flex Builder for both Flex AS and Air projects.

```
▼ 📚 Flex 3.0.0 - /Applications/Adobe Flex Builder 3 Plug-in/sdks/3.0.0
   ▶ 📄 playerglobal.swc
   ▶ 📄 automation.swc
   ▶ 📄 automation_agent.swc
   ▶ 📄 automation_dmv.swc
   ▶ 📄 automation_flashflexkit.swc
   ▶ 📄 datavisualization.swc
   ▶ 📄 flex.swc
   ▶ 📄 framework.swc
   ▶ 📄 qtp.swc
   ▶ 📄 rpc.swc
   ▶ 📄 utilities.swc

                                       ▼ 📚 Flex 3.0.0 - /Applications/Adobe Flex Builder 3 Plug-in/sdks/
                                          ▶ 📄 playerglobal.swc
                                          ▶ 📄 flex.swc
                                          ▶ 📄 utilities.swc
```

Figure 7-4. *Libraries imported by Flex Builder for Flex AS and Air projects*

For now, let's focus on creating a Flex project. To do so, open your Flex Builder Eclipse installation and go to File ➤ New ➤ Flex Project as in Figure 7-5.

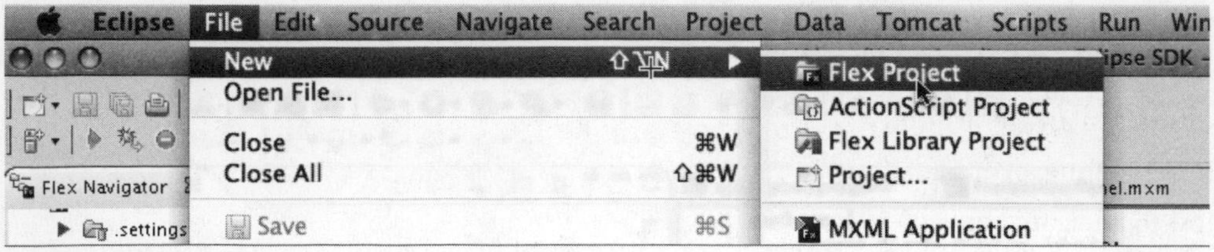

Figure 7-5. *Create a new Flex Project*

Name your project Blackjack and click on Finish (see Figure 7-6). For a basic project you don't have to set any options as you don't need Adobe Air and we are not working with any remote servers (for now anyway).

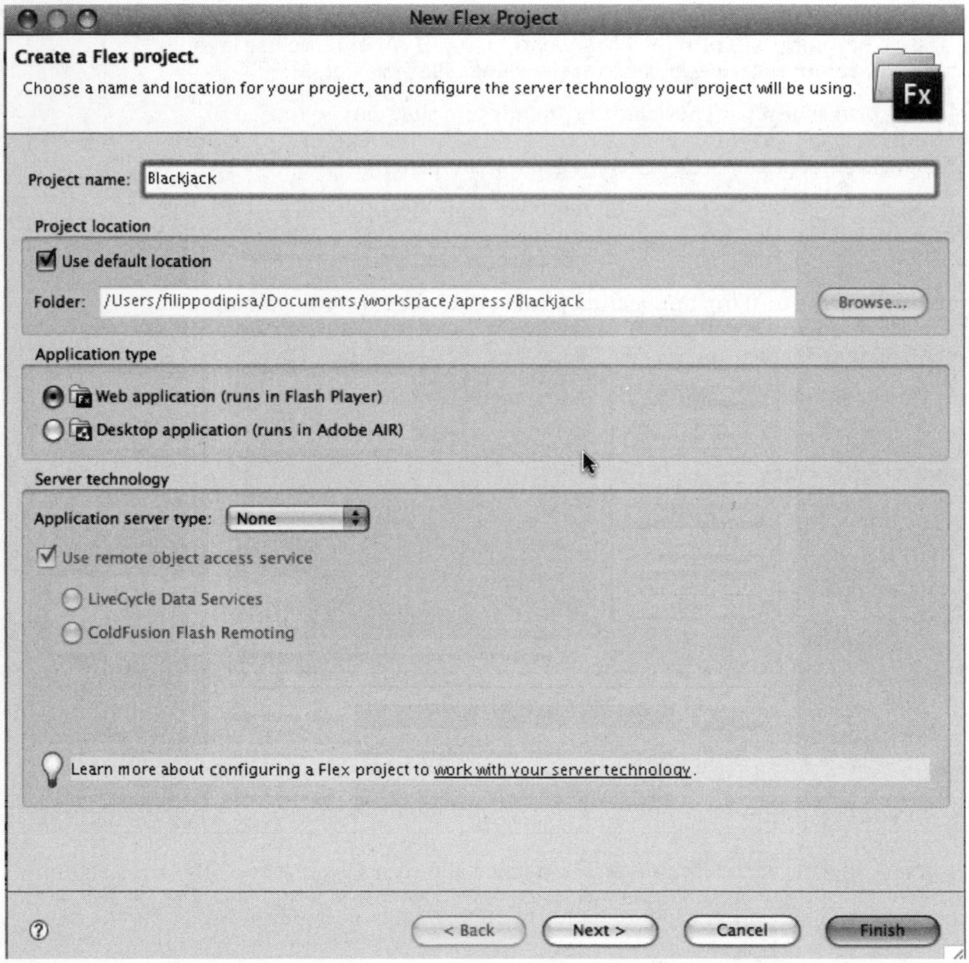

Figure 7-6. *Naming the project*

Once the project is created, Flex Builder will add the main application file using the name of the project itself, and other folders and files as follows:

- bin-debug—the target folder containing all compiled files;

- html-template—the folder containing all HTML and JavaScript templates for your project. The index.template.html is the main wrapper template containing all HTML, JavaScript code, and the main application SWF file. You can also add JavaScript to this template to interact with the application's SWF file;

- libs—the folder that contains all SWC archive libraries for the project. The folder is empty when you start a new project, until you import the libraries your project needs;

- src—the main folder that contains all source code. By default, the src folder is added to the classpath;

Figure 7-7. Reorganize the default tree

Before starting to write code, you should first reorganize the default tree created by the FlexBuilder (see Figure 7-7). Java and Maven are well-organized, and they are standard for this book so we will organize the code along those lines and keep in sync with the server. Developers can often live in bubbles where there is no thought given to the server setup, but we are better than that!

First we'll create two folders within the src folder and call them main and test (see Figure 7-8). Within the main folder, we'll create one folder called flex where we'll store all our class packages and application files, and another folder called resources to store all application assets like images and XML files.

Figure 7-8. *Creating the main and test folders*

Now we have to tell Flex Builder that our classpath has changed from the src folder to the src/main/flex/ folder. To change the default setting, just right-click on the root of the project and select properties. Then select the item labeled Flex Build Path and change the main source folder from src to src/main/flex as in Figure 7-9.

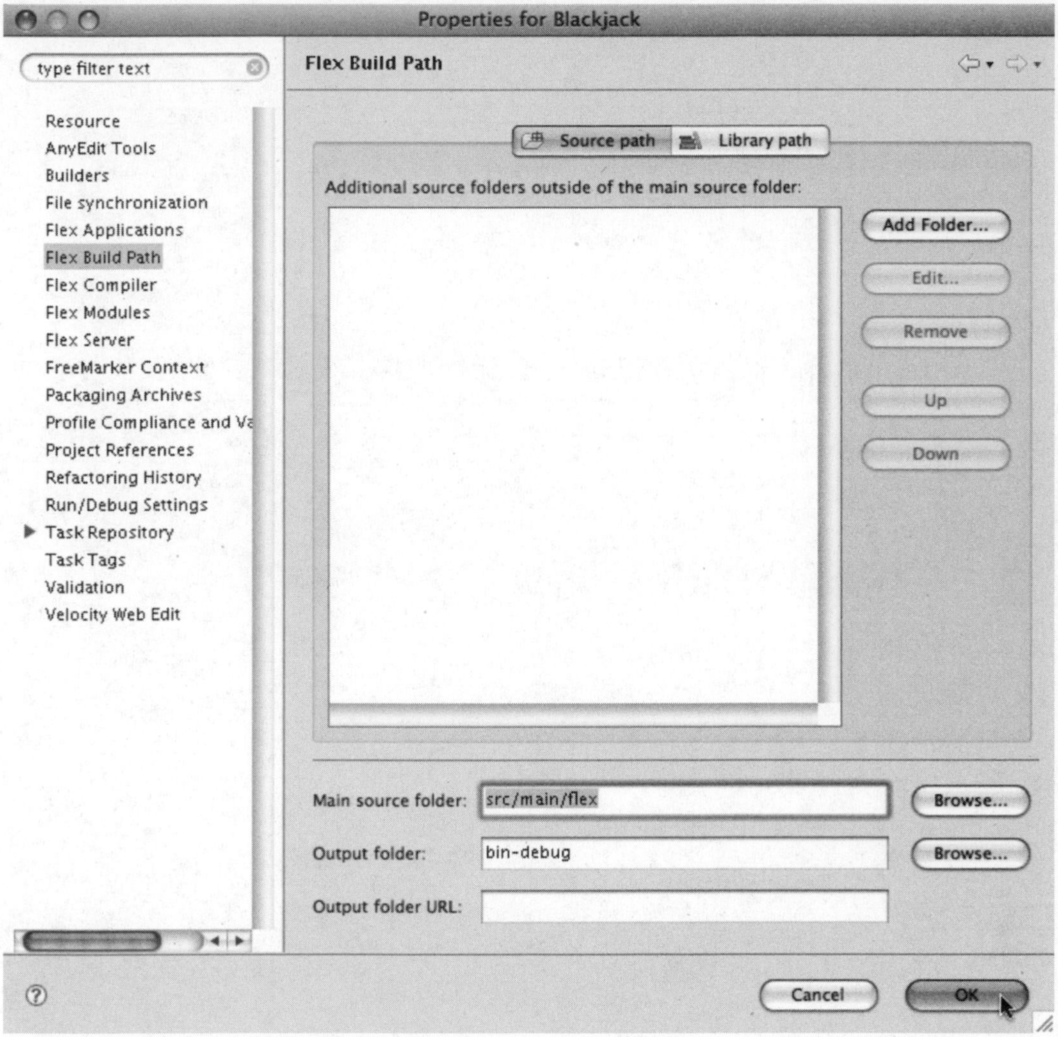

Figure 7-9. *Change the default folder setting*

Now we have to add all our resources to the classpath; click on Add Folder and enter `src/main/resources` as in Figure 7-10.

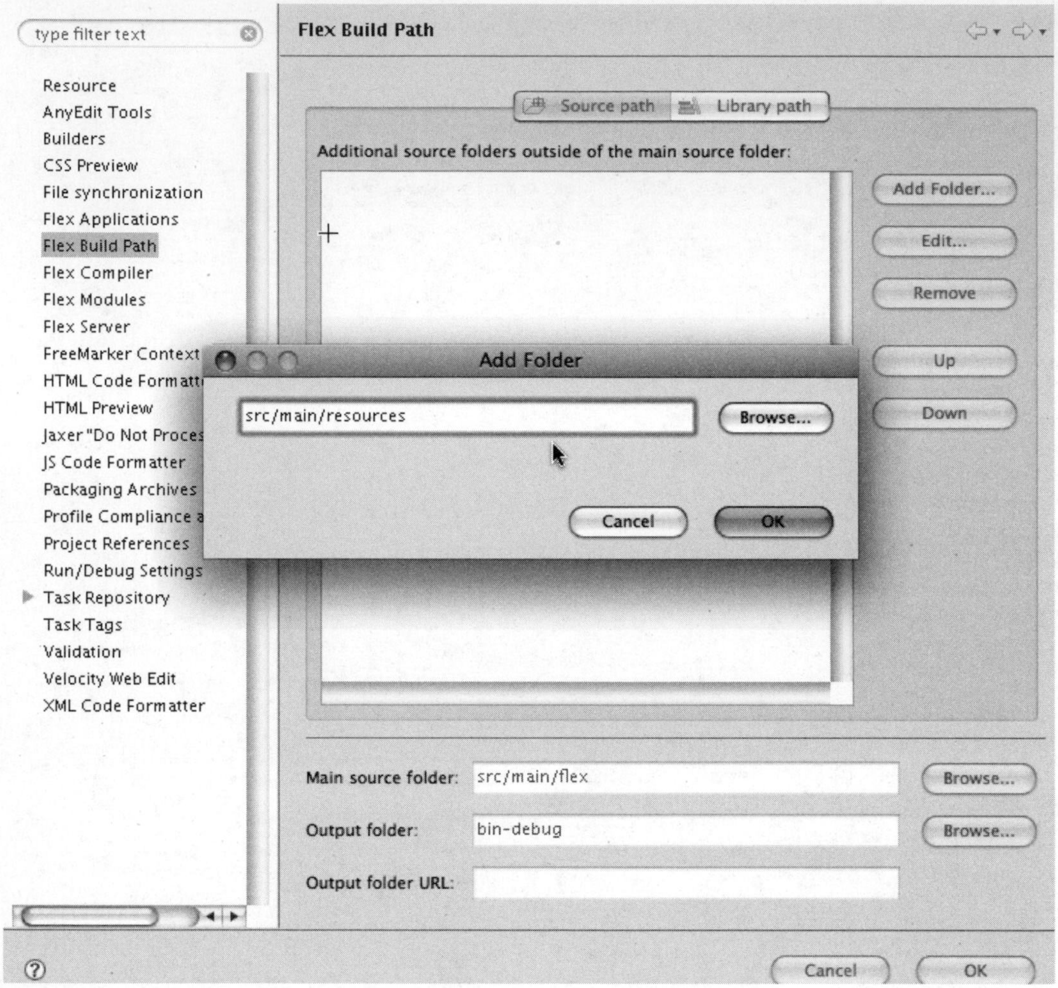

Figure 7-10. *Adding resources to the classpath*

Next we have to move the application file called `Blackjack.mxml` to the newly created `src/main/flex` folder shown in Figure 7-11.

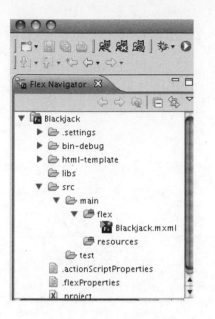

Figure 7-11. Move the Blackjack.mxml application file to src/main/flex

Flex Builder Perspectives

If you are new to Eclipse, a perspective is a set of panels and editors useful for performing specific operations. Flex Builder offers 3 main perspectives:

- Source perspective is the code editor for both AS and MXML. It includes syntax coloring and code completion;

- Design perspective is the visual editor for creating graphical user interfaces. It includes the component panel with all Flex UI components, as well as the Flex properties panel for viewing the properties of a component.

- Debug perspective is the code debugger where you can watch variables values, step through the code, and set code breakpoints to debug only a particular portion of the code.

Build an Application

Building an application is very easy and can be done automatically or manually. In automatic mode, each time you save a file, Flex Builder compiles the SWF file and generates all assets needed by the application, such as images, CSS, and HTML files. I prefer the manual approach as it is faster and it lets me decide when to build, saving system resources.

If you prefer the automatic approach, select Project ➤ Build Automatically as in Figure 7-12.

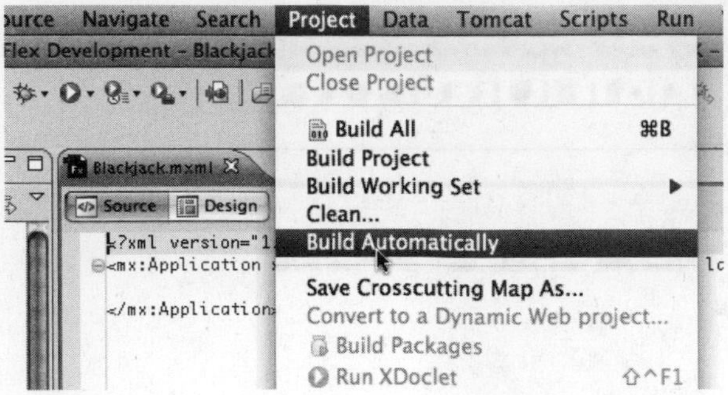

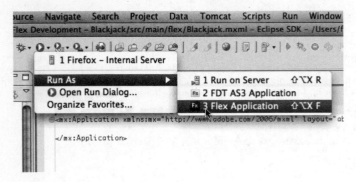

Figure 7-12. Set the Build Automatically option

■ **Note** The Flex Builder IDE is not as complete as the Java one; if you are familiar with the Eclipse Java IDE you will find less functionality.

Run an Application

To run and test an application, click the arrow next to the green arrow on the menu bar and select Run As ➤ Flex Application (see Figure 7-13).

Figure 7-13. Run and test an application

You can also select your application file, right-click, then choose Run As ➤ Flex Application (see Figure 7-14).

You can have as many application files as you need. To add an MXML Application file, right-click, on the project and select New Application.

Figure 7-14. Running a Flex Application

■ **Note** If you come from Flash development and you are used to the trace function for debugging your code, I suggest you change your habits and start to use the debugger. If you'd rather see your trace messages printed into the console window, however, you will have to run the application in debug mode.

Debug an Application

You start to debug an application in much the same way as you run it, but you either click on the arrow next to the bug icon (see Figure 7-15) and select Debug As ➤ Flex Application, or right-click on the application file and choose Debug As ➤ Flex application.

Figure 7-15. Bug icon to start the debugger

To step through the code you have to set at least one breakpoint in your code, and then you can use the play, stop, or other buttons to continue executing the code.

Navigate between Classes

Flex Builder also offers easy class navigation and the Open Resource panel. To navigate from one class to another, press CMD (Mac) or CTRL (PC) and click the object you want to introspect. For example, click the Application MXML tag and Flex Builder will open the class `Application.as` where the tag Application is based.

There's a very handy shortcut to the Open Resource panel that allows you to do a quick search for a file. Click CMD+SHIFT +R for Mac or CTRL+SHIFT+R for PC to bring up the Open Resource panel as in Figure 7-16. Begin entering the name of the file you want to open and you will see all matching items. Simply click on an item to open it.

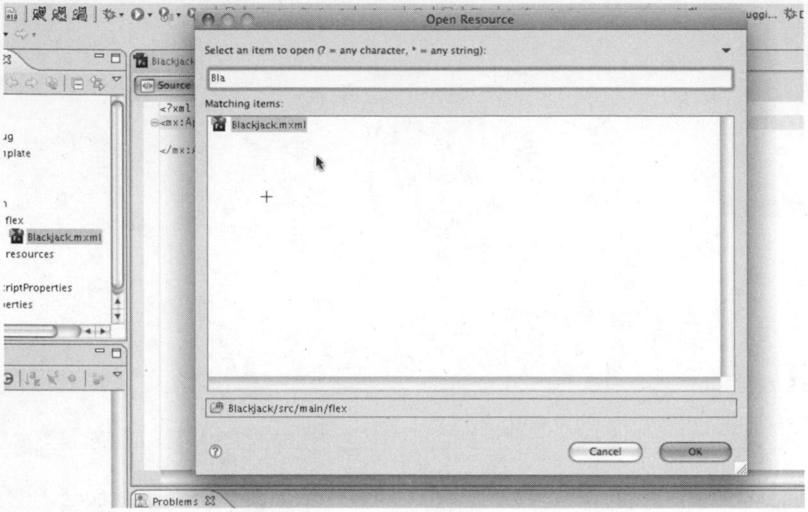

Figure 7-16. Quick search for a file

Shortcut keys

Knowing the important shortcut keys can make your development life much easier. Table 7-1 shows a number of the shortcuts you can use in Eclipse and Flex.

Table 7-1. Shortcut keys

Mac Keys	PC Keys	Function
CMD+SHIFT+R	CTRL+SHIFT+R	Open Panel Resources
CMD+F	CTRL+F	Find/Replace within the File
CMD+Click	CTRL+CLICK	Go to definition
CMD+Space	CTRL+Space	Code assist
SHIFT+F2	SHIFT+F2	Open the Language Reference
CTRL+H	CTRL+H	Open search
SHIFT+CMD+F11	CTRL+F11	Run

Now that I have introduced the basic functionalities of Flex Builder, let's see how to build user interfaces using layout containers, navigation containers, and controls, and then we will write our first Flex application.

Flex Components

Flex comes with four kinds of user interface components: application containers, layout containers, navigation containers, and controls (including text controls and data-driven controls). A single application container holds the other containers and components of an application. Layout containers position child components automatically without any need to write the code to relocate the children when an event occurs. For example, the layout container HBox places all children in a horizontal row, so that every time you add a child to the HBox container, it will move the child next to the last child in the same row. Before Flex, for the same functionality in AS, you had to calculate the position of the last child and then provide those values to the x and y coordinates of the new object.

Let's compare AS2, AS3, and MXML for creating a typical layout with two main columns and two rows nested in the second column as in Figure 7-17.

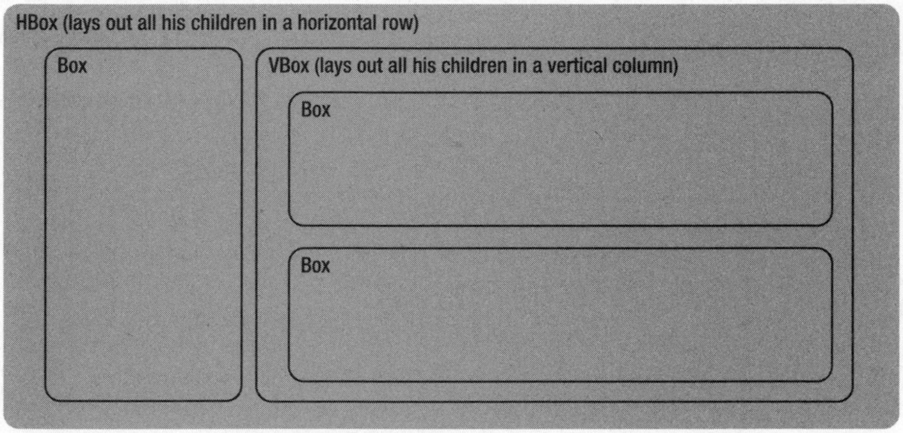

Figure 7-17. Layout for comparing AS2, AS3, and MXML

In AS 2 you would create a custom component or calculate the position of all MovieClips within the stage or within another MovieClip. In Flex using AS 3, you have to create an instance of the layout container needed and then use the function addChild to add the container to the application container or to another layout container. To illustrate the use of different containers, Figure 7-18 uses some style properties to define and color the border of each container. In this example I embedded the style code within the AS code using the function setStyle. This may not be the best way but it is easier to understand. Later on in another example I will show you how to move all style properties added using the setStyle method to an external CSS files.

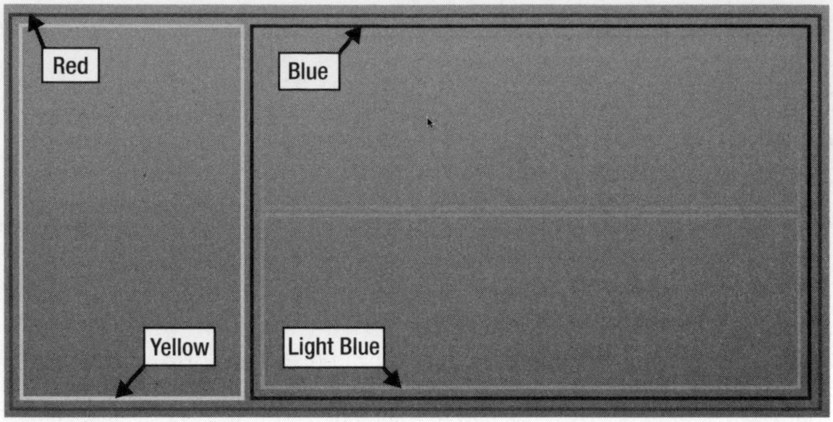

Figure 7-18. Defining container color and border

This AS code creates the layout shown in Figure 7-18.

```
<?xml version="1.0" encoding="utf-8"?>
<mx:Application xmlns:mx="http://www.adobe.com/2006/mxml"
                          layout="absolute"
                          creationComplete="init()">
    <mx:Script>
                    <![CDATA[
                    import mx.containers.Box;
                    import mx.containers.VBox;
                    import mx.containers.HBox;

                    public function init() : void {

                            //create an horizontal main container
                            var hBoxRed : HBox = new HBox();
                            hBoxRed.percentWidth=90;
                            hBoxRed.percentHeight=90;
                            //set the style for the main container
                            hBoxRed.setStyle("borderThickness",5);
                            hBoxRed.setStyle("borderStyle","solid");
                            hBoxRed.setStyle("borderColor","#F60E0E");
                            hBoxRed.setStyle("horizontalCenter",0);
                            hBoxRed.setStyle("verticalCenter",0);
                            hBoxRed.setStyle("paddingLeft",10);
                            hBoxRed.setStyle("paddingRight",10);
                            hBoxRed.setStyle("paddingBottom",10);
                            hBoxRed.setStyle("paddingTop",10);
                            //add the main container to the stage
                            this.addChild(hBoxRed);
```

```
boxYellow.percentWidth = 40;
boxYellow.percentHeight = 100;
boxYellow.setStyle("borderThickness",5);
boxYellow.setStyle("borderStyle","solid");
boxYellow.setStyle("borderColor","#F6EEOE");
//add the first child to the main container
hBoxRed.addChild(boxYellow);

//create the second child of the the main container that will↩
contain other 2 boxes
var vBoxBlue : VBox = new VBox();
vBoxBlue.percentWidth=100;
vBoxBlue.percentHeight=100;
//set the style for the container
vBoxBlue.setStyle("borderThickness",5);
vBoxBlue.setStyle("borderStyle","solid");
vBoxBlue.setStyle("borderColor","#0E14F6");
vBoxBlue.setStyle("horizontalAlign","center");
vBoxBlue.setStyle("verticalAlign","middle");
vBoxBlue.setStyle("paddingLeft",10);
vBoxBlue.setStyle("paddingRight",10);
vBoxBlue.setStyle("paddingBottom",10);
vBoxBlue.setStyle("paddingTop",10);
//add the second child to the main container
hBoxRed.addChild(vBoxBlue);

//create the first child of the BoxBlue
var boxLightBlue : Box = new Box();
boxLightBlue.percentWidth = 100;
boxLightBlue.percentHeight = 50;
boxLightBlue.setStyle("borderThickness",5);
boxLightBlue.setStyle("borderStyle","solid");
boxLightBlue.setStyle("borderColor","#05DBEE");
//add the first chidl to the BoxBlue
vBoxBlue.addChild(boxLightBlue);

//create the second child of the BoxBlue
var boxGreen: Box = new Box();
boxGreen.percentWidth = 100;
boxGreen.percentHeight = 50;
boxGreen.setStyle("borderThickness",5);
boxGreen.setStyle("borderStyle","solid");
boxGreen.setStyle("borderColor","#05EEA4");
//add the second child of the BoxBlue
vBoxBlue.addChild(boxGreen);

            }
        ]]>
      </mx:Script>
</mx:Application>
```

```
                              //add the second child of the BoxBlue
                              vBoxBlue.addChild(boxGreen);

                       }
                ]]>
        </mx:Script>
</mx:Application>
```

As you can see, I created a function `init()` and added it to the application event listener `creationComplete`, which is triggered when the application has been created. The `init()` function creates all container instances and will add them to the application container and then to the other containers that we want to nest. As noted, I used the property `setStyle` to set borders and colors for each container.

In MXML you can do the same thing, and the code will be more readable for designers and those not familiar with coding. Another advantage of using MXML for laying out objects is that you can use the Flex Builder design perspective and see your changes in real time before compiling the code. This is great for getting approval from those managers. Also, in source mode in MXML, you have access to all code help to add more styles, while in AS you don't. Here's the MXML code.

```
<?xml version="1.0" encoding="utf-8"?>
<mx:Application xmlns:mx="http://www.adobe.com/2006/mxml" layout="absolute">
        <mx:HBox   id="hBoxRed"
                          borderThickness="5"
                          borderStyle="solid"
                          borderColor="#F60E0E"
                          width="90%"
                          height="90%"
                          horizontalCenter="0"
                          verticalCenter="0"
                          horizontalAlign="center"
                          verticalAlign="middle"
                          paddingLeft="10"
                          paddingRight="10"
                          paddingBottom="10"
                          paddingTop="10">
                <mx:Box id="boxYellow"
                                  borderThickness="5"
                                  borderStyle="solid"
                                  borderColor="#F6EE0E"
                                  width="40%"
                                  height="100%">

                </mx:Box>
                <mx:VBox id="vBoxBlue"
                                  borderThickness="5"
                                  borderStyle="solid"
                                  borderColor="#0E14F6"
                                  width="100%"
```

```
                                    height="100%"
                                    horizontalAlign="center"
                                    verticalAlign="middle"
                                    paddingLeft="10"
                                    paddingRight="10"
                                    paddingBottom="10"
                                    paddingTop="10">
                <mx:Box id="boxLightBlue"
                                    borderColor="#05DBEE"
                                    borderStyle="solid"
                                    borderThickness="5"
                                    width="100%"
                                    height="50%">

                </mx:Box>
                <mx:Box id="boxGreen"
                                    borderColor="#05EEA4"
                                    borderStyle="solid"
                                    borderThickness="5"
                                    width="100%"
                                    height="50%">

                </mx:Box>
            </mx:VBox>

        </mx:HBox>
</mx:Application>
```

As you can see from the preceding code, the MXML class is shorter than the AS one. It is more familiar for people coming from HTML or other meta tag languages such as ColdFusion and JSP. However, I want to remind you to use MXML just for layout or view purposes, and to use AS for the logic of your application.

Containers

The application container allows you to add content to your application without defining any other container. Usually the application container exists to hold the main layout container of your application, and nothing else. The application container provides a default ProgressBar that you can override, to show the percentage loaded of your main SWF file.

Layout Containers

Layout containers are classes you use to position the child components in your applications. Flex provides the following layout containers:

- Canvas –the only container that doesn't automatically lay out its children; you have to use x and y coordinates or anchors to position child components;

- `Box`, `HBox`, `VBox`—the box container lays out its children in a single vertical or horizontal column using the direction property; `HBox` and `VBox` are `Box` containers with the horizontal and vertical values already set for the direction property. Practically speaking, the declaration `<mx:Box direction="vertical" />` is equal to `<mx:VBox />`;

- `Panel` and `TitleWindow`—a panel layout container creates a window with a title, a header, borders, and a content area for its children. The panel container has a layout property to automatically lay out the child components vertically, horizontally, or by setting x and y (absolute). The `TitleWindow` is a panel with more properties and methods to work as a pop-up window. In other words, a `TitleWindow` can have the close button on the right corner of the header and can be modal, which means that it gets all mouse and keyboard events until you close the window, or non-modal which means that other windows can accept events;

- `ControlBar` and `ApplicationControlBar`—the `ControlBar` container is used to put controls like buttons and others at the bottom of a `Panel` or a `TitleWindow`. The best use of a `ControlBar` is when you have to share a component with different children within a `Panel` or `TitleWindow`. For example, you could create a `ControlBar` holding the submit button of a form and reuse it with different contents loaded within the panel itself. The `ApplicationControlBar` does the same work of the `ControlBar` but you have to use the former to share components that have access to application elements such as the application navigation menu and search input text;

- `DividedBox`, `HDividedBox`, and `VDividedBox`—the `DividedBox` containers work much like the Box containers. In fact, they can automatically lay out all their children vertically and horizontally. However, you can resize the `DividedBox` container and its children by dragging the mouse on the divided bar;

- `Grid` and `Tile`—the `Grid` and `Tile` containers are very useful when you have to lay out children in multiple columns and rows, much like HTML tables. The `Grid` container works with the `GridRow` and `GridItem` components that define rows and cells. The `Tile` container lays out its children, starting new rows or columns as necessary. The main difference from the `Grid` container is that all cells of a `Tile` container have the same size.

Navigation Containers

Navigation containers are used to control the navigation between different child components. For example, think of a game that has different views, such as a Welcome screen, a High Score page, an Instructions screen, and so on. With navigation containers you can create all the different views you need for a container's children, and then control their display state. Here are the types of navigation containers:

- `Accordion`—displays its children (views) one at a time. The `Accordion` can contain many children (views) that are displayed as a series of panels. It is usually used to navigate complex forms or menus.

- ViewStack—is a collection of child containers that allows you to view the selected child. You can use the ViewStack with the LinkBar, TabBar, and ButtonBar components or by itself. The ViewStack is very useful in enterprise application development because allows you to define the collection of views you need and then bind the state of the view with the model of your application. In other words, you can create a ViewStack containing the Login Panel and the Welcome Panel. Once the Login is successful, you can set the ViewStack to the index containing the Welcome Panel, and when you log out from the application, you set the ViewStack to the index containing the Login Panel again.

- TabNavigator –works like the Accordion but organizes the contents in tabs. For example, if you have three Box containers with different contents and you want to use tabs to organize the navigation, you would use the TabNavigator container. To set the title of each Tab of the TabNavigator container, you use the property label of the Box container.

- Form—the Form layout container, combined with several child components such as FormItem and FormHeading, let you control the layout and other events of a form.

To understand how to use all the containers and their properties in more depth, I suggest using the Flex Reference within the Flex Builder Help section. Another useful web site with lots of examples of how to use the components is Flex Examples at http://blog.flexexamples.com.

Control Components

Control components are user interface objects such as Button, ComboBox, TextArea and many others that you can add to Flex containers for creating, managing and adding content to your application. All Flex components are derived from the flash.display.Sprite and mx.core.UIComponent classes and inherit methods and properties of their superclasses. Like the Flex containers, the controls can be either AS or MXML.

All Flex controls can be grouped into four main categories: standard controls, data-driven controls, text controls, and menu-based controls.

Standard Controls

The standard controls are those needed by any GUI. Indeed, most GUIs are composed of buttons, alert messages, input forms, images, and the like. Flex includes the following components:

- Alert—a modal dialog window that pops up containing a message. The default button is the OK button, however, within the show()method you can specify different options to display OK | YES | NO | CANCEL buttons;

- Button—display objects that have a text label and/or an icon on their face and can be pressed to initiate some behavior. Buttons generally are rectangular and in Flex 3 use the default skin called Halo, but you can customize the skin using styles or a custom skin;

- ButtonBar, LinkBar, TabBar, and ToggleButtonBar - these are data provider components used for objects containing data. All of them dispatch a single event called ItemClick defining the button or link that has been clicked;

- CheckBox - a very common UI control that is checked or unchecked and respectively returns the value true or false;

- ColorPicker - allows the user to choose a color from a drop-down panel containing a grid with 216 web-safe colors. You can set the attribute showTextField to show a text box indicating the color selected, and you can also set an attribute to set the text box as editable;

- DateChooser and DateField - allow the user to select dates from a calendar. The DataChooser is a graphical calendar where the user can select a date. The DateField is a composite component containing a TextInput and a Button that lets the user select a date from a calendar;

- HRule and VRule—let users create horizontal and vertical lines for dividing the contents of the containers. HRule is the equivalent of the HTML tag <HR/>;

- HSlider and VSlider –allow the user to move a slider between two end points to select a value. By default, the values range from 0 to 10 but any values can be set. HSlider creates a horizontal slider and VSlider a vertical slider.

- Image –imports images into the UI (like the <img> tag in HTML). The Image control supports different image formats including JPEG, PNG, SVG, GIF, and SWF files. You can set whether you are embedding an image in your SWF file or if you will load the image from an external source when required. Embedding images within your SWF file increases the size of your application, but once loaded the performance is better. You strategy regarding image loading will depend on the application you are developing. For example, in a game or for button icons, it is probably better to embed the images in the SWF file. However, if you are developing an image gallery, it is better to load the image as it is required. Image lets you specify the image path and even resize the image;

- LinkButton—a button with a flat, plain style to make it looks like an HTML link;

- NumericStepper—an input text field with two arrows that let you increase or decrease its value. You can set the range and the step values;

- ProgressBar—lets the user know to wait for a process in the application to complete. Flex provides two kinds of ProgressBars: determinate and indeterminate. The determinate ProgressBar is a linear progression over a time or value known. The indeterminate one is a linear progression over a time or value not known. You can set minimum and maximum values for the progression, and listen for the progress or complete events;

- RadioButton—another common control for UIs, it allows a single exclusive choice within a set of choices. Usually you use two or more radio buttons;

- VScrollBar, HScrollBar—allow you to control the displayed content in a portion of the area. Usually these controls are already included within other components, but they can also be used alone;

- SWFLoader—an extension of the Image control for loading a Flex application within another Flex application as a SWF file. It inherits all superclass Image properties so it can also be used to load and embed images or SWF files;

- VideoDisplay—used to add streaming media to Flex applications. It supports FLV formats, the standard and only supported video for FlashPlayer.

Data-Driven Controls

The data-driven controls are Flex components that allow you to display and manage the application data. Here are the data-driven controls:

- List, HorizontalList, TileList—The List control is the base class of the HorizontalList, TileList, DataGrid, Menu and Tree controls. All List controls are data-driven components, which means they take data from a objects called data providers. The main difference between the different extensions of List is the organization and layout of the data. For example List displays a vertical list of data and HorizontalList displays a horizontal list of items. The TileList control displays a list of items in vertical and horizontal rows. The TileList result can be similar to the Tile container combined with a loop to dynamically create rows and columns, though performance is much better using TileList because it instantiates objects that fit in its defined display area. List becomes very useful in combination with ItemRenderers, which allows you to render the data as you want;

- ComboBox—a very common user interface control that consists of a drop-down list from which the user can select an exclusive single value. You can set the ComboBox data by passing a collection of objects such as an ArrayCollection or an XMLListCollection to the attribute dataProvider;

- DataGrid—the most used and useful component for all data-driven applications, it consists of a grid of rows and columns that display a collection of data passed through the property dataProvider. DataGrid supports ItemRenderers for its cells, which means you can display rich media content within any cell, not just text. You can bind data and use the Data Collection APIs to filter, add, edit, and delete data;

- Tree—displays hierarchical data with an expandable tree. You can customize all icons for each branch of the tree, and because the Tree component, like the DataGrid, also works with the Data Collection APIs, you can filter, edit, add, and delete nodes and branches simply editing and binding the collection provided. By default, the icons are folders and text files.

- AdvancedDataGrid—introduced with Flex 3, this control is an extension of the DataGrid control. The main difference is that AdvancedDataGrid supports hierarchical data and grouped data, which means you can create trees with columns (see Figure 7-19).

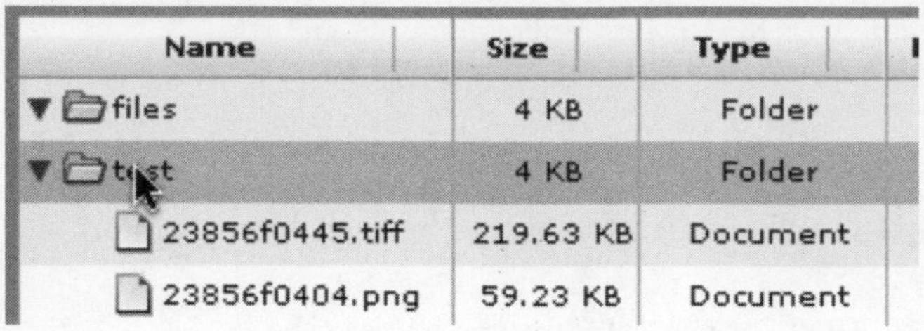

Name	Size	Type	
▼ 🗁 files	4 KB	Folder	
▼ 🗁 test	4 KB	Folder	
📄 23856f0445.tiff	219.63 KB	Document	
📄 23856f0404.png	59.23 KB	Document	

Figure 7-19. *Displaying hierarchical data in the* AdvancedDataGrid *control*

Text Controls

The Text controls are classes you use to display and input text within your application. Here are the Text controls:

- Label—shows a single line of text without any border or background. The text shown is not editable by the user, but you can bind the value with other values in your application. It supports the HTML rendering of the FlashPlayer;

- TextInput—a common UI control that consists of a text field that's optionally editable. Like the Label control, TextInput supports the HTML rendering abilities of the FlashPlayer. You can set the skin and the style, changing borders, background color and other many properties. The TextInput control also dispatches events like change and enter to allow you to do something when those events occur;

- Text—very similar to Label, with the main difference that it allows multiple lines and automatic word-wrap. Like Label, Text is totally transparent and not editable by the user. The Text control doesn't have scroll bars. It supports Flash HTML;

- TextArea—very similar to TextInput. The main difference is that it accepts multiple lines of text and has optional scroll bars. It is optionally editable and supports Flash HTML;

- RichTextEditor—a composite component containing a panel with a TextArea and a tool bar with controls that allows users to format the text. You can also add custom controls to the tool bar, or remove existing controls. RichTextEditor supports both plain text and Flash HTML.

Menu-Based Controls

The menu-based controls are classes you use to create the application's menu.

The menu-based controls are the following:

- Menu—lets you create pop-up menus on the fly. It does not have an MXML tag, and you can only use AS to create it. You provide a collection of data to it, passing the collection as an argument when you create the menu using the method Menu.createMenu(). By default, the Menu will remain visible until the user select a menu item;

- MenuBar—very similar to the Menu control, except that the MenuBar is static and always visible in your application. Practically speaking, it consists of a top-level bar containing a number of menu items that will be expanded when the user selects an item. The MenuBar has an MXML tag and you pass a collection of data through the dataProvider property;

- PopUpMenuButton—contains a secondary button that opens a Menu control. The icon and label of the main button changes when the user makes a selection from the pop-up menu. It accepts data collection through the dataProvider properties.

Using External CSS Styles

In the previous layout container examples, I styled the borders of each container to visually define their position. As you can see in the code below (which has been extracted from the previous example), I set the style properties within the MXML code. That is not good, but to I had to do to give you the big picture, to show that MXML allows you to set style properties directly within the MXML component definitions.

```
<mx:HBox   id="hBoxRed"
                borderThickness="5"
                borderStyle="solid"
                borderColor="#F60E0E"
                width="90%"
                height="90%"
                horizontalCenter="0"
                verticalCenter="0"
                horizontalAlign="center"
                verticalAlign="middle"
                paddingLeft="10"
                paddingRight="10"
                paddingBottom="10"
                paddingTop="10">
        <mx:Box id="boxYellow"
                    borderThickness="5"
                    borderStyle="solid"
                    borderColor="#F6EE0E"
                    width="40%"
                    height="100%">
```

To keep your code reusable and maintainable, the proper way to work with styles is to move all style properties outside the MXML to an external CSS file, which Flex, like HTML, supports. To use an external CSS file, first you have to create it and store it in your classpath. I generally put all my application style sheets in src/main/resources/css/. You can have multiples CSS files, depending on your needs and application architecture.

As with HTML, with CSS you can declare the style for one type of component or define a styleName and use it in any components you need. For example, the declaration

HBox {

```
        borderColor="#F60E0E"
}
```

will apply to all HBox components in your application. If you want to apply it just to a set of HBox components, you have to set the component property styleName and refer to that name in your style. For example, I can create an HBox like this:

```
<mx:HBox styleName="myHBox" />
```

and refer to it as below

```
.myHBox{
        borderColor="#F60E0E"
}
```

In this case, this style will be applied only to the components with the styleName equal to myHBox.

In order to use a remote CSS file with our layout containers' example MXML code, you have to change it as follows:

```
<?xml version="1.0" encoding="utf-8"?>
<mx:Application xmlns:mx="http://www.adobe.com/2006/mxml" layout="absolute">

        <mx:Style source="/css/containers_example.css" />

        <mx:HBox            id="hBoxRed"
                            styleName="red"
                            width="90%"
                            height="90%" >

                    <mx:Box id="boxYellow"
                                    styleName="yellow"
                                    width="40%"
                                    height="100%">

        </mx:Box>
                    <mx:VBox id="vBoxBlue"
                                    styleName="blue"
                                    width="100%"
                                    height="100%"
                                        >
                    <mx:Box id="boxLightBlue"
                                            styleName="lightBlue"
                                            width="100%"
                                            height="50%">
                </mx:Box>
                    <mx:Box id="boxGreen"
                                    styleName="green"
                                    width="100%"
```

```
                                        height="50%">
                        </mx:Box>
                        </mx:VBox>
        </mx:HBox>
</mx:Application>
```

As you can see, I removed all style properties and add the line

```
<mx:Style source="/css/containers_example.css" />
```

This tells Flex the location of the style sheet. The file `containers_example.css` will contain the following code:

```
/* css file */
.red {
        borderThickness:5;
        borderStyle:solid;
        borderColor:#F60E0E;
        horizontalCenter:0;
        verticalCenter:0;
        horizontalAlign:center;
        verticalAlign:middle;
        paddingLeft:10;
        paddingRight:10;
        paddingBottom:10;
        paddingTop:10;
}

.yellow {
        borderThickness:5;
        borderStyle:solid;
        borderColor:#F6EE0E;
}

.blue {
        borderThickness:5;
        borderStyle:solid;
        borderColor:#0E14F6;
        horizontalAlign:center;
        verticalAlign:middle;
        paddingLeft:10;
        paddingRight:10;
        paddingBottom:10;
        paddingTop:10;
}

.lightBlue {
        borderColor:#05DBEE;
```

```
        borderStyle:solid;
        borderThickness:5;
}

.green {
        borderColor:#05EEA4;
        borderStyle:solid;
        borderThickness:5;
}
```

Now you can change the style of your application by just modifying the CSS , without touching any of the logic of your application.

Changing styles can be difficult and annoying if you are not familiar with the many properties that each component offers. However, there is a very useful online tool that allows you to generate the CSS text in visual mode while interacting with the components. You can find it at
`http://examples.adobe.com/flex3/consulting/styleexplorer/Flex3StyleExplorer.html`

Use Flex with Flash IDE

When you need to create complex graphics and very personalized skins, Adobe helps with its integration of Flex into each of its design products such as Fireworks, Illustrator, and Flash. Suppose you have to skin all components and you want to use the Flash IDE rather than CSS. The first step is to download and install the Flex Skin Design Extension for Flash and the FlashComponentKit, both of which can be found at `https://www.adobe.com/cfusion/entitlement/index.cfm?e=flex_skins`

Note that in order to be able to download the Flash Component Kit you must have an adobe.com account. If you don't have one you can create it at the same URL given above.

Next, restart the Flash IDE and on the Welcome screen, click on More…. You will see a new category called Flex Skins and a new template called flex_skins, as shown in Figure 7-20. To change the entire skin, click on Flex Skins ➤ flex_skins, and you will find a MovieClip containing all Flex components as nested MovieClips (see Figure 7-21).

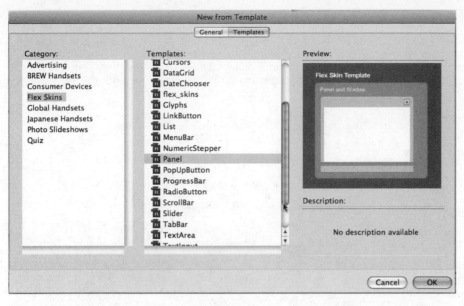

Figure 7-20. *The new Flex skin template*

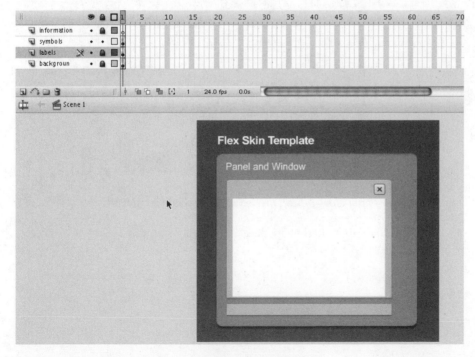

Figure 7-21. *Flex components as nested MovieClips*

For those who are familiar with Flash, it will be straightforward and easy to personalize each component, and you won't have to write any line of code. If you are not familiar with the Flash IDE, you can use the CSS to skin your application. However, to be a good Flex-Java developer, I suggest you learn more about the Flash IDE as well. In this example, we will just move the Panel close button from the right to the left in order to create the new skin (see Figure 7-22), you have to publish the Flash file, which puts two files in the output folder, one with the SWF extension and the second one with the SWC extension.

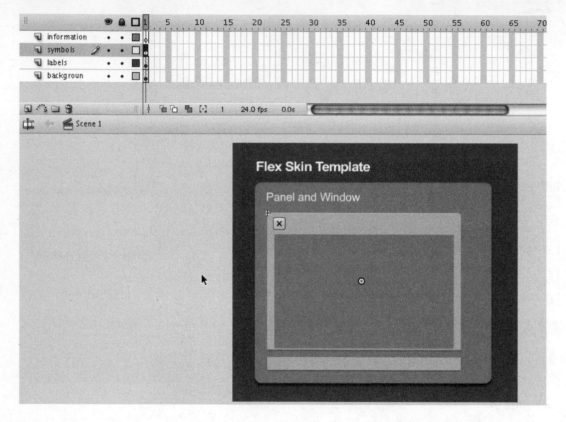

Figure 7-22. *The new skin with the Panel close button moved from the right to the left*

Now you import the new skin. To do that, on the top menu, select File ➤ Import ➤ Skin Artwork and then select the SWC file you just created (see Figure 7-23).

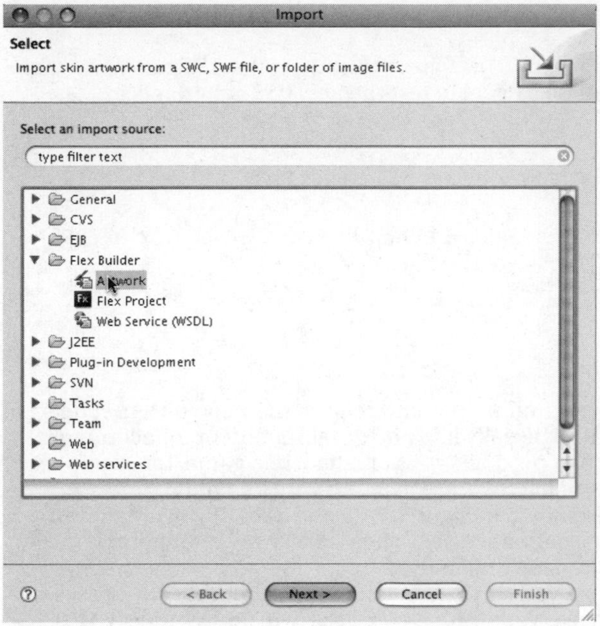

Figure 7-23. *Importing a new skin*

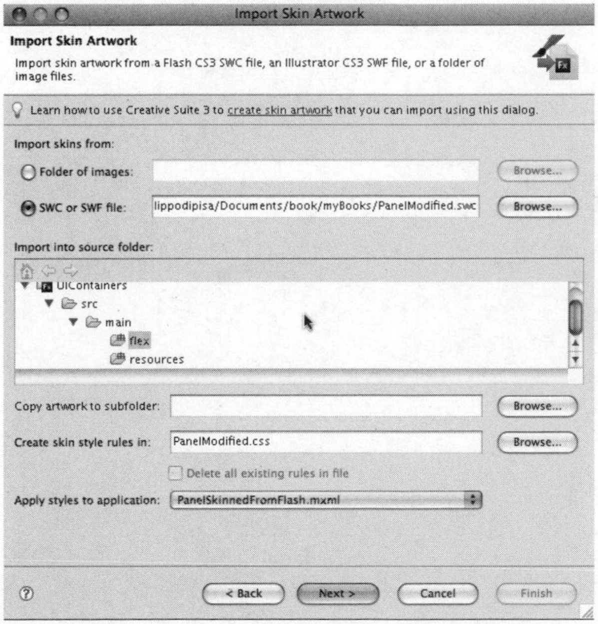

Figure 7-24. *Creating a CSS file for the new skin.*

As you can see in Figure 7-24, I told Flex Builder to create a CSS file with all the new properties for the new skin.

To test the new skin, let's create an MXML Application file where we import the CSS generated with the import skin functionality and where we instantiate a Panel to test the new CSS generated.

```
<?xml version="1.0" encoding="utf-8"?>
<mx:Application xmlns:mx="http://www.adobe.com/2006/mxml" layout="vertical">
      <mx:Style source="PanelModified.css"/>
      <mx:Panel title="title"  width="200" height="200" />

</mx:Application>
```

Create Flash Animations for Flex

Thanks to the FlexComponentKit, you can also create animations and refer to them in your AS code within Flex Builder. This functionality can be useful especially in game development or for ecommerce sites where you have to show animations of particular products or characters. In a game, for example, you could have a door that can open and close. You can create a MovieClip with two photograms representing the door open and the door closed, as shown in Figures 7-25 and 7-26. If you are new to Flash, a photogram, is an image showing part of the animation sequence. The entire animation is divided in many photograms that are placed on the Flash timeline.

When you are happy with your Flash animation, you can export it for use within the Flex classes, which allows you to change the photograms whenever you need to using the MovieClips object APIs, such as gotoAndStop(photogram number or photogram label).

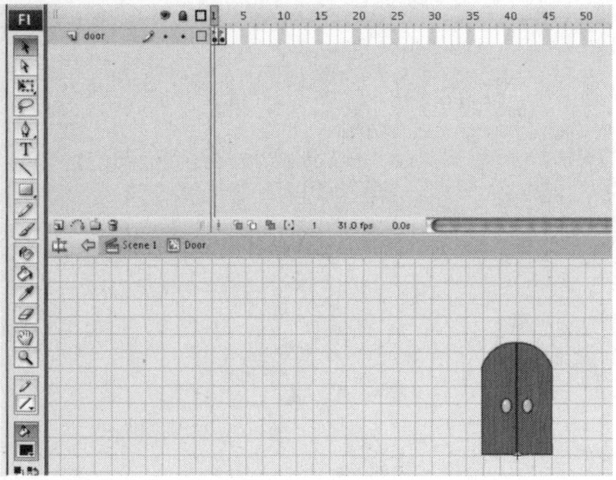

Figure 7-25. The closed door photogram

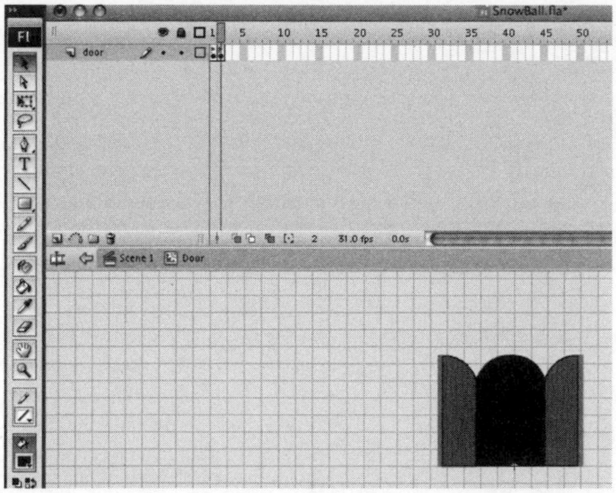

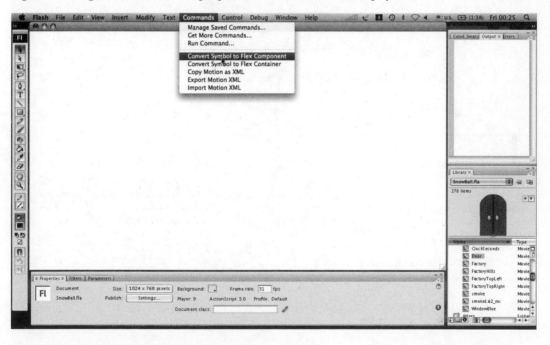

Figure 7-26. *The open door photogram*

To export a MovieClip for Flex, you have to select the MovieClip within the Flash Library and then from the Flash IDE top menu, choose Commands ➤ Convert Symbol to Flex Component as shown in Figure 7-27. Figure 7-28 shows the properties of the Door MovieClip symbol.

Figure 7-27. *Exporting a MovieClip to Flex*

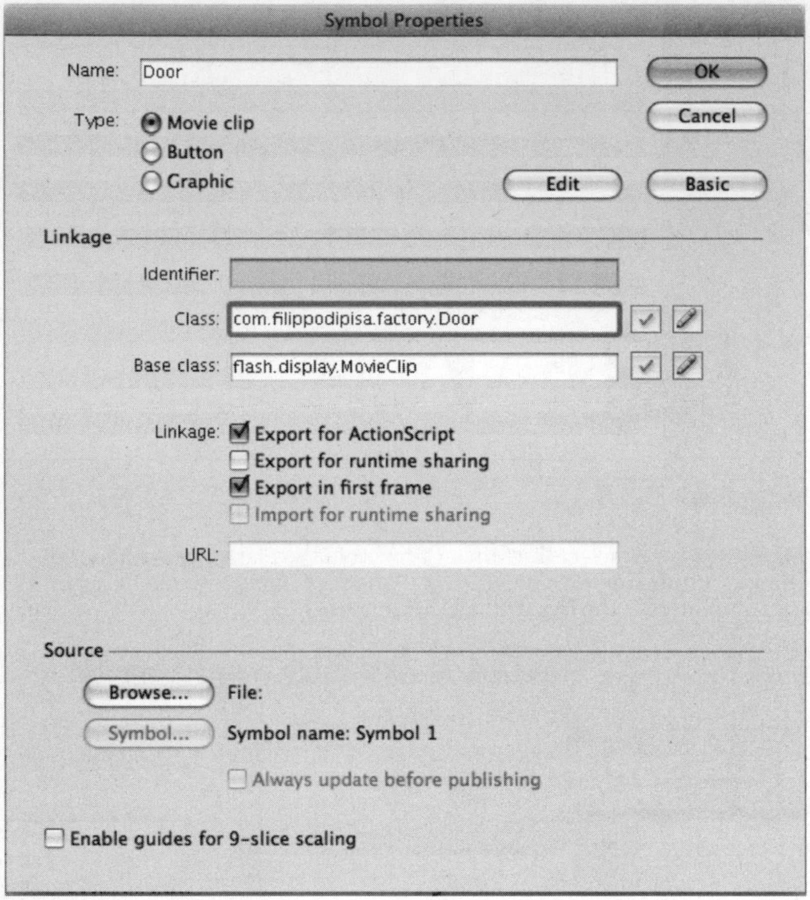

Figure 7-28. *Door properties*

Next you publish the project. The Flash compiler will create a file with the SWC extension in your output folder. The last step is to copy this file into your Flex classpath (in our case src/main/resources/movieclips/) and then you will be able to create an instance within AS, as the following code shows.

```
package com.filippodipisa.factory
{

    import flash.display.MovieClip;

    /**
     * @author filippodipisa
     */
    public class Door
```

```
        {
                public Door() : void {
                        this.gotoAndStop("close");
                }


                private function openDoor(event:Event) : void{
                        this.gotoAndStop("open");
                }

                protected function closDoor() : void {
                        this.gotoAndStop("close");
                }
        }
}
```

For example, suppose your MovieClip was called Missile. Once the SWC file is in your classpath, you can create an instance of type Missile as follows:

```
var missile : Missile = new Missile();
missile.gotoAndStop(1);
```

Remember, this is just an example, and the proper solution in game development is to work with bitmaps, not MovieClips—even if they can be useful at times.

If you have followed along and done your homework, and with the help of the Flex Reference and Flex Builder, you should be able to create and style a Flex user interface and perhaps listen and dispatch some events like click, change, and some others. In the next section, I am going to explain the Flex event model more in detail, as listening to and dispatching events are significant parts of any AS/Flex application.

Flex Events

An event is something that happens. You can listen to and create events with both AS and MXML. Almost all Flex components are based on the event model, which means they are able to dispatch and listen for events. For example, a Button dispatches many events, such as click, roll over, drag, and several others. When a component dispatches an event, it can be listened to by other components or classes.

When you click on a button, it dispatches the event click to the function you specify in the button's event listener. The function specified is called an event handler (see Figure 7-29).

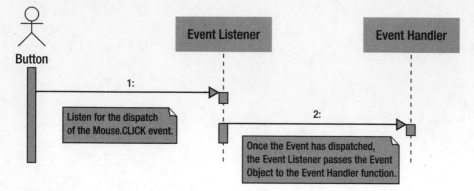

Figure 7-29. Clicking on a button

Using events with MXML is very easy. Here's an example of how to handle a click event using MXML.

```
<?xml version="1.0" encoding="utf-8"?>
<mx:Application xmlns:mx="http://www.adobe.com/2006/mxml" layout="vertical">
        <mx:Button id="myButton" label="click me!" click="doSomething(event)" />
        <mx:Script>
                <![CDATA[
                        import mx.controls.Alert;
                        private function doSomething(event : Event) : void{
                                Alert.show("The button dispatch the event of type "
+ event.type);
                        }
                ]]>
        </mx:Script>
</mx:Application>
```

As you can see from the code, all you have to do is set the event handler function within the MXML event property and pass the event to the handler. To see which events are available for each component, you can use the syntax code helper, or the Flex Builder properties in visual mode, or the Flex Builder Reference under the events section.

To open the syntax help, just press [CTRL+spacebar] within the MXML component tag as shown in Figure 7-30. The event is identified by the thunder yellow icon.

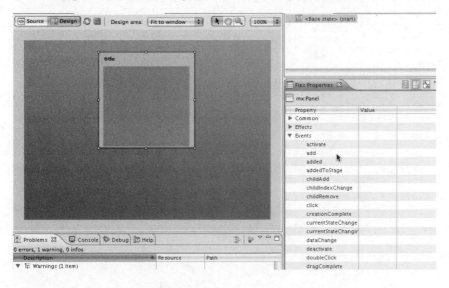

```
1  <?xml version="1.0" encoding="utf-8"?>
2  <mx:Application xmlns:mx="http://www.adobe.com/2006/mxml" layout="vertical">
3      <mx:Style source="PanelModified.css"/>
4      <mx:Panel title="title"  width="200" height="200"  />
5
6  </mx:Application>
7
```

Figure 7-30. *Finding which events are available for a component*

In visual mode, you can see all events for the component selected by using the Flex Properties panel and clicking on the button category, as shown in Figure 7-31.

Figure 7-31. *Finding available events with the Flex Properties panel*

Remember that to see information about the selected component, you can press SHIFT +F2 to open the Flex Builder Language Reference at that component's section.

As noted earlier, you can use events both in MXML and in AS because MXML is just a layer on top of AS. This means, for example, that the Button component is an AS class. Indeed, if you press the CMD key in Mac or CTRL in Window and mouse over the MXML <mx:Button /> tag, you will see it underlined, and if you click there, you open the Button AS class.

■ **Note** You can instantiate each component created with MXML or with AS within both MXML and AS. For example, if you create a class MyButton.mxml, you can use it like this:

```
<classpath:MyButton id="myButton"… />
```

or like this:

```
var myButton : MyButton = new MyButton();
```

And the reverse is also true—you can create the AS class MyButton.as and use at the same way as above.

To listen for an event in AS is a little bit different than in MXML because you have to use the addEventListener method that each component based on the event model provides. You don't have to pass the event to the handler, as we did in MXML, though, because the event listener will do it for us. Here's an example of how to listen for the click event of a button in AS:

```
<?xml version="1.0" encoding="utf-8"?>
<mx:Application xmlns:mx="http://www.adobe.com/2006/mxml"
                            layout="vertical"
                            creationComplete="init()">
    <mx:Script>
            <![CDATA[
                    import mx.controls.Button;
                    import mx.controls.Alert;

                    public function init() : void {
                            var myButton : Button = new Button();
                            myButton.label = "Click Me!";

    myButton.addEventListener(MouseEvent.CLICK,doSomething);
                            this.addChild(myButton);
                    }

                    public function doSomething(event : Event) : void {
                            Alert.show("The button dispatch the event of type "
+↵
event.type);
                    }
            ]]>
    </mx:Script>
</mx:Application>
```

The instance myButton is listening for the MouseEvent.CLICK, and when the event is dispatched it will call the function doSomething.

Events are very important for controlling your application flow. Remember that an event can be visible like the Button click event or invisible like the underlined events dispatched between classes to control the logic of your application.

■ **Note** Some events such as EnterFrame and others take a lot of memory, so it is always better to remove them when not needed.

Now let's see how to create and dispatch a Custom Events.

Custom Events

So far, you have only seen prebuilt component events, but in enterprise application development you often need custom events to control application logic. For example, you could have an event that retrieves all data from the database, or one that dispatches the x and the y coordinates of a moving wave.

To make this easier to understand, I created a funny example of a button that moves away from the mouse when you try to click it and knows the direction the button has moved away from the mouse.

So the goal of my example is to have a button that moves away on mouse rollover and dispatches an event containing the direction every time that it moves. Toward that aim, I create a CustomEvent and a CustomComponent, and use both in the application file.

The names of my classes are listed in Table 7-2.

Table 7-2. *The names of my classes for my custom component*

Type	Class Name	Class File
CustomEvent	ButtonMoveEvent	ButtonMoveEvent.as
CustomComponent	ButtonJoker	ButtonJoker.as
Application	CustomEventTest	CustomEventTest.mxml

To create the custom event ButtonMoveEvent.as , I have to extend the class flash.events.Event, as follows:

```
package
{
        import flash.events.Event;

        public class ButtonMoveEvent extends Event
        {

                public var direction : String;
```

```
        public static const BUTTON_MOVE_EVENT : String = "buttonMoveEvent";

        public function ButtonMoveEvent(type:String, direction : String){
                super(type);
                this.direction = direction;
        }

        override public function clone():Event{
                return new ButtonMoveEvent(type, direction);
        }

    }
}
```

In the custom event class, I store the direction as a public property, and provide a static constant to use within both dispatcher and listener to tell to the compiler which type of event we are dealing with.

```
dispatchEvent(new ButtonMoveEvent(ButtonMoveEvent.BUTTON_MOVE_EVENT,direction));
```

or

```
myButton.addEventListener(ButtonMoveEvent.BUTTON_MOVE_EVENT,buttonMoveHandler);
```

Now I must override the clone() method of the superclass Event to clone a copy of the event object in order to have a new instance of the event. Practically speaking, when you dispatch the ButtonMoveEvent, it will create an object containing the event type and the property direction that you want to pass to the listener.

Once the custom event class has been created, you have to create the custom component that will dispatch this event. The custom component ButtonJoker will extend the class Button because, at the end of the day, ButtonJoker is a button with extra functionality.

Listing 7-1. *ButtonJoker Custom Event Class*

```
package
{
    import flash.events.MouseEvent;

    import mx.controls.Button;

    [Event(name="buttonMoveEvent", type="ButtonMoveEvent")]

    public class ButtonJoker extends Button
    {
            private var moved  : int = 1;

            public var direction : String;
```

```
        private const LEFT : String = "left";

        private const RIGHT : String = "right";

        public function ButtonJoker(){
                this.addEventListener(MouseEvent.ROLL_OVER, moveButtonJoker);
        }

        private function moveButtonJoker(event : MouseEvent):void{
                this.x = event.stageX + ((this.width + 10) * moved);
                moved = (moved == 1)?-2:1;
                direction = (moved == 1)?LEFT:RIGHT;
                dispatchEvent(new
ButtonMoveEvent(ButtonMoveEvent.BUTTON_MOVE_EVENT,direction));
            }
        }
}
```

To make the `Button` move on rollover, you have to be sure that when you create an instance of the `ButtonJoker` object, it listens for the `MouseEvent.ROLL_OVER` event. To do this, you add the `addEventListener` within its constructor.

```
public function ButtonJoker(){
                    this.addEventListener(MouseEvent.ROLL_OVER, moveButtonJoker);
}
```

Every time that the `MouseEvent.ROLL_OVER` event is dispatched , I call a function that moves the button in the opposite direction of the previous one. For example, if the old direction was to move to the left, the new direction will be to move to the right. Every time the direction changes, I create an event of type `ButtonMoveEvent` where I store the new direction with a string indicating how the button has moved, and then I dispatch this event as shown in the listing 7-1.

When I create an instance of the `ButtonJoker` class, I will be able to listen for the `ButtonMoveEvent` event in both MXML and AS, as follows:

MXML:

```
<myComponents:ButtonJoker label="click me!"
buttonMoveEvent="buttonMoveHandler(event)" />
```

AS:

```
myButton.addEventListener(ButtonMoveEvent.BUTTON_MOVE_EVENT,buttonMoveHandler);
```

■ **Note** At the beginning of the class, I used the `event` metatag to make the `ButtonMoveEvent` event visible as an MXML attribute to the Flex Compiler.

```
[Event(name="buttonMoveEvent", type="ButtonMoveEvent")]
```

If you don't specify the event metatag, you won't be able to use it as an attribute within the MXML new component tag, and the Flex compiler will return an error in the MXML class where you want to use the event attribute; the error returns a message like "Cannot use the attribute `buttonMoveEvent` for the component type `ButtonJoker`.

The `ButtonJoker` class will extend the `Button` class to inherit all `Button` properties, events and methods. Then I add a private function called `moveButtonJoker` that will move the button and dispatch the `ButtonMoveEvent` event once the `MouseEvent.ROLL_OVER` event has dispatched (see Figure 7-32).

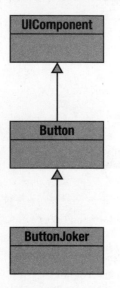

Figure 7-32. *Button and ButtonJoker class diagram*

Now that we have our `ButtonJoker` custom component and our custom event `ButtonMoveEvent`, we can create the application file where we'll test the new custom component and handle the new custom `ButtonMoveEvent`. Let's create an application file called `CustomEventTest.mxml` and then add the `ButtonJoker` component, a `TextArea`, and the event handler function for the custom Event `ButtonMoveEvent` created previously. Our goal is to write a message containing the direction of the `ButtonJoker` once it has moved. Here's the code that does all this.

```
<?xml version="1.0" encoding="utf-8"?>
<mx:Application xmlns:mx="http://www.adobe.com/2006/mxml" xmlns:myComponents="*"↩
 layout="vertical" >
     <myComponents:ButtonJoker label="click me!"↩
buttonMoveEvent="buttonMoveHandler(event)" />
     <mx:TextArea text="{message}" />
     <mx:Script>
          <![CDATA[
               import mx.controls.Button;
```

```
                [Bindable]
                private var message : String;

                public function init() : void {
                        var myButton : ButtonJoker = new ButtonJoker();
                        myButton.label = "Click Me!";

        myButton.addEventListener
        (ButtonMoveEvent.BUTTON_MOVE_EVENT,buttonMoveHandler);
                        this.addChild(myButton);
                }

                public function buttonMoveHandler(event : ButtonMoveEvent) :
void {
                        message = "The button has moved to "+ event.direction;
                }

        ]]>
    </mx:Script>
</mx:Application>
```

■ **Note** To use a custom component in your MXML, you have to add the namespace within the root tag of the MXML class. In our case, we have to add xmlns:myComponents="*".

The ButtonJoker class is very easy to understand. We create an instance of our new custom component ButtonJoker that passes the function buttonMoveHandler within the listener buttonMoveEvent. The event handler sets the variable message with the direction dispatched by the ButtonMoveEvent. The variable message is bound with the attribute text of the TextArea component, which means that every time that the variable message changes, the TextArea text property will be updated automatically.

In this example that explains how to create and dispatch a custom event, I also introduced the new concepts of custom components and data binding, both important in Flex/AS development. Let's discuss data binding in more detail.

Data Binding

Data binding is a process that keeps the values of components or data sources in sync. In other words, if you set an object as bindable it will dispatch any change to the others objects that are referring it.

In the example, we bind the variable countValue from the button component with id "count" to the TextInput component with the id "counter".

```
<?xml version="1.0" encoding="utf-8"?>
<mx:Application xmlns:mx="http://www.adobe.com/2006/mxml" layout="vertical">
```

```
        <mx:Button id="count" label="count" click="{countValue++}" />
        <mx:TextInput id="counter" text="{countValue}" editable="false" />
        <mx:Script>
                <![CDATA[
                        [Bindable]
                        private var countValue : uint = 0;
                ]]>
        </mx:Script>
</mx:Application>
```

Every time the button click event is dispatched, we increase countValue. Because we set the variable countValue as Bindable, Flex will also update automatically the value in the TexInput component. If we didn't set the Bindable metatag, the value shown in TexInput would always remain 0.

Flex provides four different solutions to bind data:

- using the [Bindable] metatag

- using <mx:Binding> metatag as follows:

```
<?xml version="1.0" encoding="utf-8"?>
<mx:Application xmlns:mx="http://www.adobe.com/2006/mxml" layout="vertical">
        <mx:Binding source="count.value.toString()" destination="counter.text" />
        <mx:NumericStepper id="count" />
        <mx:TextInput id="counter"  editable="false" />
</mx:Application>
```

The Binding metatag manages the binding between a source and a destination value.

- bind data directly to component properties as follows:

```
<?xml version="1.0" encoding="utf-8"?>
<mx:Application xmlns:mx="http://www.adobe.com/2006/mxml" layout="vertical">
        <mx:NumericStepper id="count" />
        <mx:TextInput id="counter" text="{count.value}" editable="false" />
</mx:Application>
```

Here, the value properties of the NumericStepper component is bound to the property text of the TextInput component.

- using mx.binding.utils.BindingUtils class as follows:

```
<?xml version="1.0" encoding="utf-8"?>
<mx:Application xmlns:mx="http://www.adobe.com/2006/mxml" layout="vertical"
creationComplete="init()">
        <mx:NumericStepper id="count" />
        <mx:TextInput id="counter"  editable="false" />
        <mx:Script>
                <![CDATA[
                        import mx.binding.utils.BindingUtils;

                        private function init():void{

BindingUtils.bindProperty(counter,"text",count,"value");
```

```
                    }
              ]]>
        </mx:Script>
</mx:Application>
```

BindingUtils is useful when you have to bind values within AS classes, but please don't use mixed with MXML; I only did this here for example purposes.

The best way to bind data is using the [Bindable] metatag.

In upcoming chapters I will show how to use data binding to set the state of your workflow. Practically speaking, I will show you how to use data binding to set the current view of your application, which means to open or change a screen after an event or a request has been dispatched by the user or by another process.

The second important concept introduced with the CustomEventTest example is the creation of a CustomComponent.

Creating Custom Components

Creating custom components makes an application more modular and easier to maintain. You can reuse the custom components for different parts of the application without have to rewrite the same code again and again. Another reason to create custom components is the need to personalize an existing Flex component to meet your application requirements.

■ **Note** A custom component is not just a class like the ButtonJoker shown in the previous example. It can also be a set of classes, assets, and style sheets.

All existing visual components in Flex are derived from the UIComponent AS class.

To create a new visual component, you have to extend that class. To customize an existing Flex component, you have to extend the component as we did with the Button in our ButtonJoker component.

You can create a custom component by using MXML or AS, as shown in Figure 7-33.

MXML	AS
ComboBoxEuropeStates.mxml	**ComboBoxEuropeStates.as**

`<?xml version="1.0" encoding="utf-8"?>`
`<mx:ComboBox xmlns:mx="http://www.adobe.com/2006/mxml">`
 	
`</mx:ComboBox>`
	`package com.apress.flexandjava.components.as`
	`{`
	  `import mx.controls.ComboBox;`
	  `public class ComboBoxEuropeStates extends ComboBox`
	  `{`
	
	  `}`
	
	`}`

Figure 7-33. Creating a custom component in MXML or AS

I suggest you use AS for almost all custom components. However, if your component contains other components and layout containers, you will want to use MXML as it is simpler, faster, and much easier to maintain.

MXML Custom Components

For simple and composite custom components, MXML makes life easier. For example a simple component could be a ComboBox control with a list containing all the countries of Europe.

```
<?xml version="1.0" encoding="utf-8"?>
<mx:ComboBox xmlns:mx="http://www.adobe.com/2006/mxml">
      <mx:dataProvider>
      <mx:String>Albania</mx:String>
      <mx:String>Andorra</mx:String>
      <mx:String>Armenia</mx:String>
      <mx:String>Etcetera...</mx:String>
   </mx:dataProvider>
</mx:ComboBox>
```

To create an MXML custom component, you just select the package (folder) where you want to create the component, then right-click and choose New ➤ MXML Component. Next you have to give a name to the new component. The name should be logical and descriptive to make the things easier for other developers. For example, we can call our component Countries List ComboBoxEuropeStates, which indicates it is of type ComboBox and contains the list of the Europe states.

Next you choose the component on which the new custom component will be based. We choose the ComboBox control. Once the MXML class has been created, you will see that the MXML generated automatically will be similar to the following:

```
<?xml version="1.0" encoding="utf-8"?>
<mx:ComboBox xmlns:mx="http://www.adobe.com/2006/mxml">

</mx:ComboBox>
```

The first line indicates the declaration of the XML version. The second line is the root tag of the component and contains the xmlns property to specify the Flex XML namespace. The default namespace is mx.

■ **Note** MXML components correspond to AS classes. The root tag indicates the super class of the component.

The logic of the component must be inserted within the root tag.

```
<?xml version="1.0" encoding="utf-8"?>
<mx:TextInput xmlns:mx="http://www.adobe.com/2006/mxml" change="search()">
     <mx:Script>
            <![CDATA[
                  import mx.collections.ArrayCollection;
```

```
            [Inspectable]
            public var collection : ArrayCollection;

            [Inspectable]
            public var columnSearchable : String;

        protected function search():void {
            if(this.text !='') {
                filter()
            } else {
                filterReset()
            }
        }

         private function filter():void {
            collection.filterFunction = filterRecords;
            collection.refresh();
        }

        private function filterReset():void {
            collection.filterFunction = null;
            collection.refresh();
        }

        private function filterRecords(item:Object):Boolean {
            var tags : String = item[columnSearchable];
            if( tags != null ) {
                    return tags.match(new RegExp(this.text, "i"));
            } else {
                    return false;
            }
        }

            ]]>
        </mx:Script>
</mx:TextInput>
```

AS Custom Components

Probably for the most complex components it is better to use AS for the component logic and MXML for the view as a normal application. However, you can use AS also for the view by just creating a normal AS class that extends an existing component or the UIComponent class, or a set of classes with the main class extending the UIComponent class. You can create visual and nonvisual components. An extension of the Formatter class would be an example of a nonvisual component.

■ **Note** For creating visual custom components, you extend the UIComponent class.

I already introduced AS custom components when we created `ButtonJoker`. In the `ButtonJoker` class, I extended the existing component `Button` to add more functionality, but I didn't use some important `UIComponent` methods usually used in AS-based custom components. I will do so in the next example, but first I'll show you some important methods provided by the base class `UIComponent` that we can override for our needs:

- `createChildren()`—this method is called when a call to the `addChild` method occurs. Practically speaking, when you add a custom component to the stage or to a layout container using the `addChild` method, it triggers the `createChildren()` method. This allows us to create whatever we need when the component is being added to the stage. The `ComboBox` component, for example, is composed of a `Text` and a `Button` component (the arrow), both created within the overriden `createChildren` method;

- `commitProperties()`—this method is called when a call to the `invalidateProperties` method occurs. We can therefore use `commitProperties` to control the appearance of the component on the screen. When you add the component to the screen, Flex automatically calls the `invalidateProperties` method. A problem can arise when you want change the appearance of a component by changing a property once it has already added. To change the appearance of a component at this stage, you have to add the `invalidateProperties` call within the setter of the property itself. For example, if you want the color of a button added to the screen to change when you set the property enable to false, you have to override the setter enabled method and add the `invalidateProperties` method, then override the `commitProperties` method and add the logic to change the button color;

- `measure()`—this method is called when a call to `invalidateSize` occurs; when you use the `addChild` method to add the component to the screen, Flex automatically calls the `invalidateSize` method. As in the example before, if you want to resize the button when you set a property, you have to include the `invalidateSize()` call within the setter method. Then you have to override the `UIComponent` function `measure` and add your logic to resize the component;

- `layoutChrome()`—this method is called when a call to the `invalidateDisplayList` occurs; as with the other invalidate methods, the `invalidateDisplayList` is triggered when the `addChild` method is called. The `layoutChrome` function is typically used to define the area and the objects that you want to appear in the border area of a visual component. For example, the `TitleWindow` container uses the `layoutChrome` method to set the title and the close button;

- updateDisplayList()—this method is called when a call to the invalidateDisplayList occurs; a component doesn't not appear on the screen until the updateDisplayList function is executed. For example, you can override the updateDisplayList method to change the position of all children of a component or to draw any visual elements need by the component. Practically speaking, you can draw a shape and add to the component at run time, or you can reorder all children added to a VBox container.

In the next example, we will create a calculator AS custom component that dispatches the contents of the display TextInput when it changes. To show the usage of the UIComponent updateDisplayList() method, I made the calculator component not resizable.

```
package com.apress.flexandjava.components
{
    import flash.events.Event;
    import flash.events.MouseEvent;

    import mx.containers.Panel;
    import mx.containers.Tile;
    import mx.controls.Button;
    import mx.controls.TextInput;

    [Event(name="displayChange", type="flash.events.Event")]

    public class Calculator extends Panel
    {

        private var tile : Tile;

        public var textInput : TextInput;

        private var operator : String;

        private const CALCULATOR_WIDTH : uint = 230;

        private const CALCULATOR_HEIGHT : uint = 230;

        public function Calculator() {
                super();
                setStyle ("paddingLeft", 10);
        setStyle ("paddingRight", 10);
        setStyle ("paddingTop", 10);
        setStyle ("paddingBottom", 10);
        }


            override protected function createChildren():void{
                    super.createChildren();
```

```
                textInput = new TextInput();
        textInput.percentWidth = 100;
        addChild(textInput);

                tile = new Tile();
        addChild (tile);

        for (var i:uint = 0; i < 10; i++) {
            var button:Button = new Button();
            button.label = i.toString();
            button.addEventListener(MouseEvent.CLICK, buttonClickHandler);
            tile.addChild (button);
        }

        var mathOperatorsList : Array = ["+","-","*","/"];

        for (var j:uint = 0; j < mathOperatorsList.length; j++){
            var operatorButton : Button = new Button();
                operatorButton.label = mathOperatorsList[j];
                operatorButton.addEventListener(MouseEvent.CLICK, ↵
operatorButtonClickHandler);
                tile.addChild(operatorButton);
        }

        var calculateButton : Button = new Button();
        calculateButton.label = '=';
        calculateButton.addEventListener(MouseEvent.CLICK,
calculateButtonClickHandler);
        tile.addChild(calculateButton);
          }

        private function buttonClickHandler(event : MouseEvent):void{
                textInput.text += Button(event.currentTarget).label;
                dispatchEvent(new Event("displayChange"));

        }

        private function operatorButtonClickHandler(event : MouseEvent):void{
                //implement the logic
        }

        private function calculateButtonClickHandler(event :
MouseEvent):void{
                //implement the logic
        }
```

```
        private function textInputChangeHandler(event : Event):void{
                dispatchEvent(event);
        }

    override protected function measure():void {
        super.measure();
        measuredWidth = CALCULATOR_WIDTH;
        measuredHeight = CALCULATOR_HEIGHT;
    }

    override protected function updateDisplayList(unscaledWidth:Number,
            unscaledHeight:Number):void {
        super.updateDisplayList(CALCULATOR_WIDTH, CALCULATOR_HEIGHT);
        this.setActualSize(CALCULATOR_WIDTH,CALCULATOR_HEIGHT);
    }

    }
}
```

We override the UIComponent createChildren method to create the TextInput display and all buttons once the calculator component is added to the stage. The createChildren method is triggered when we use the addChild(component instance) method or the MXML metatag <component instance> like addChild(button) is equals to <mx:Button />

```
override protected function createChildren():void{
...
}
```

Then, to make the component not resizable, we override the updateDisplayList method, forcing the width and height of the component to be set always to the default value.

```
override protected function updateDisplayList(unscaledWidth:Number,
                unscaledHeight:Number):void {
...
}
```

To end, we dispatch an event every time the display TextInput is updated.

Deploying Custom Components

The component deployment strategy depends on your needs, and you can choose different ways. You can compile a component along with your application, or you can compile it separately as an archive SWC library to use with one or more applications.

For example, the components created for the needs of a single application can be stored in the directory structure of the application itself. Usually I create an application subdirectory (package) for all my components, such as com.apress.views.components.

Then there are components that are useful for many applications. Suppose you build your own versions of a VideoPlayer or a ComboBox; both of these components would be reusable for all your applications so it is better to compile as an archive SWC library and import them into the library folder of any application that needs them.

SWC Libraries

An SWC is an archive file containing all the classes and assets needed for your components. Using SWC is much better because every time that you reuse the component you don't have to copy all AS classes, MXML, and assets across the different applications. A custom `ComboBox` component, for example, is composed of different components, images, style sheets, and more, so the best way to make it reusable is to compile everything in an archive SWC file.

When you architect your component, we should make it as extensible as possible, so that another user can extend it without touching any part of the core code.

When you compile an application that uses the custom components archived in a SWC file, you have to tell the Flex compiler where the libraries are. If you use Flex Builder, you can set the library directories that contain the SWC files by opening the properties of the project and selecting Flex Build Path (see Figure 7-34) and then setting the library directories (see Figure 7-35).

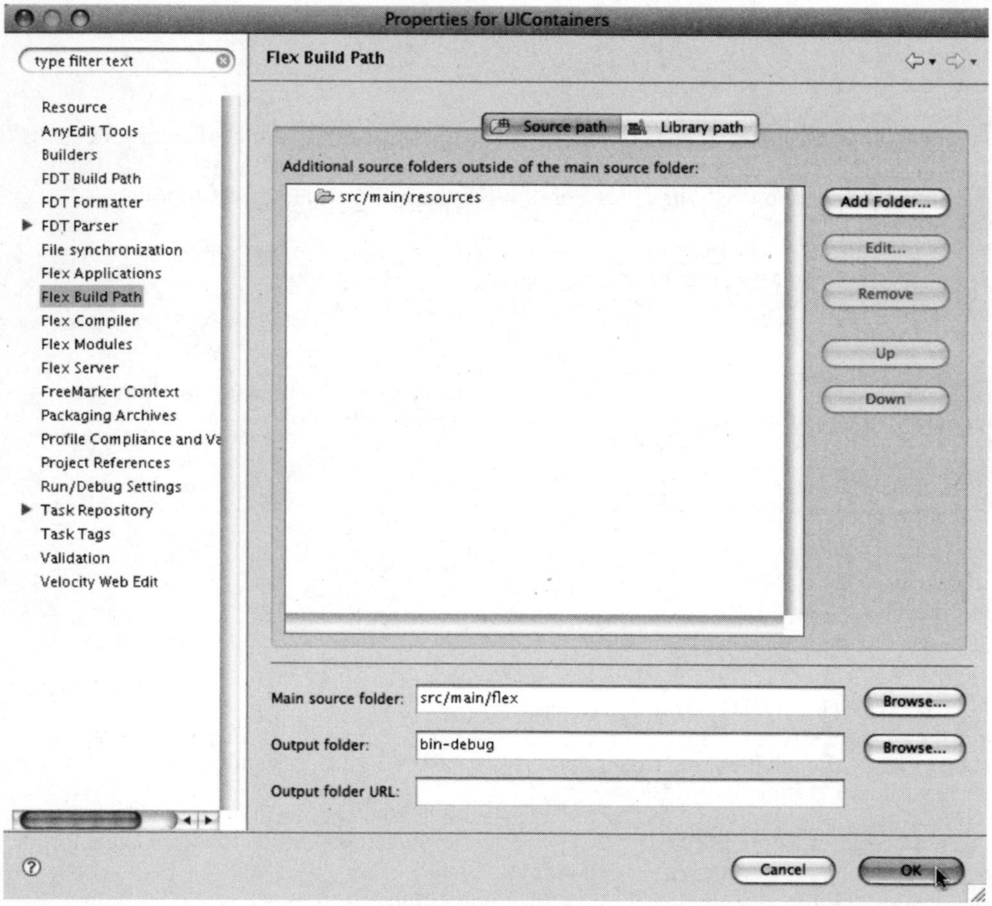

Figure 7-34. Opening the properties of the project

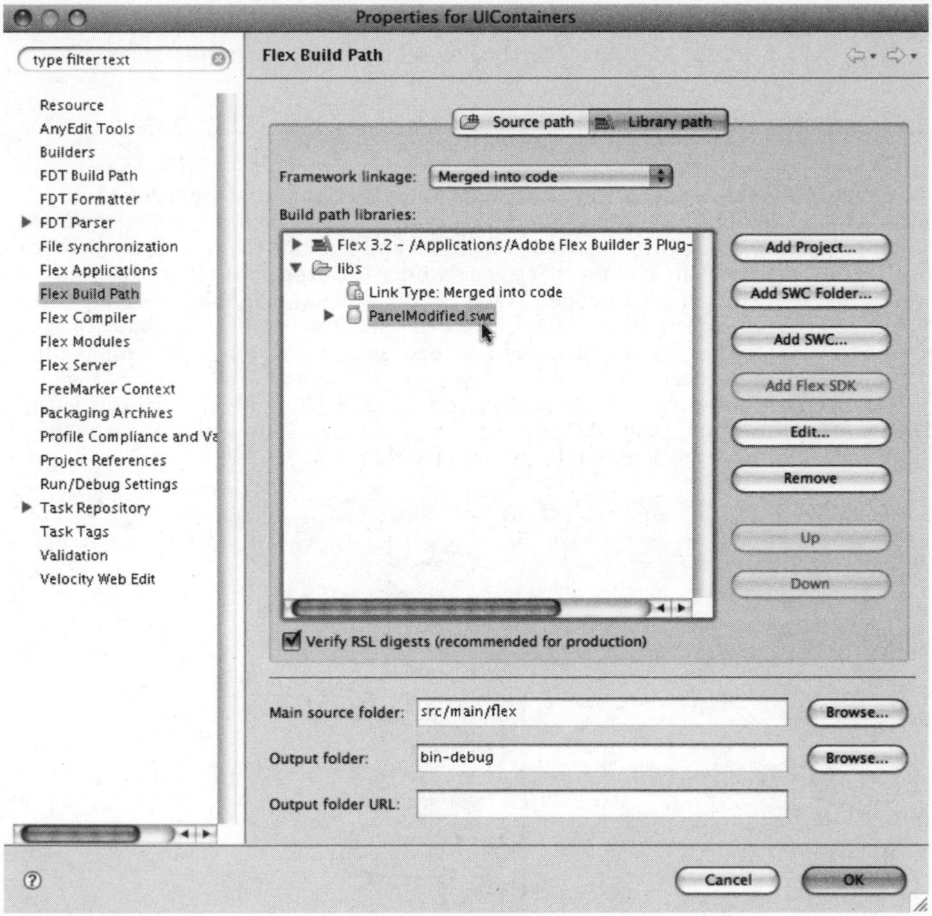

Figure 7-35. Setting the libraries directories

If you want to use the command-line compiler *mxmlc,* you have to specify the library directories using the attribute library-classpath.

```
$ mxmlc -library-path+=/libs/MyRotateEffect.swc;/myLibraries/MyButtonSwc.swc↵
 c:/myFiles/app.mxml
```

RSL libraries

If you have many applications using the same set of components and/or assets, you can create a special SWC library shared with all your applications. This special library is known as Runtime Shared Library (RSL) and it can be most useful. It is important for the performance of your enterprise applications. The RSL is downloaded on the client just once and is cached by the client. The applications that share the RSL are on the same domain and can access the assets and components stored in it. By using the RSL file, you can reduce the size of your application SWF files, giving the client better performance— but only if you have more than one application.

■ **Note** For only one application, it's better not using the RSL libraries as they could increase the size of your application.

Keep in mind, however, that RSLs are not always beneficial for applications and you need to consider the time needed for downloading both static and RSLs libraries. RSLs files are cached the first time that an application uses them. When they are needed by other applications they can be loaded by the cache and that will be much faster than loading over the network. However, the first application download will be slower than using focused, embedded SWC in your application. So the use of RSL libraries is convenient only if the same client loads more than one application sharing the same RSLs. Though this will increase the time for the first application download, subsequent downloads for all the applications sharing the RSL will be quicker.

To create an RSL file, open the properties of your project and select Flex Build Path ➤ Library Path as you did before. Then you have to expand the SWC library that you want to share and change the link type from "Merged into code" to "Runtime Shared Library" (see Figure 7-36).

Figure 7-36. *Changing the framework linkage*

The next screen (Figure 7-37) lets you verify your RSLs with a digest, in case you always want to verify the shared file.

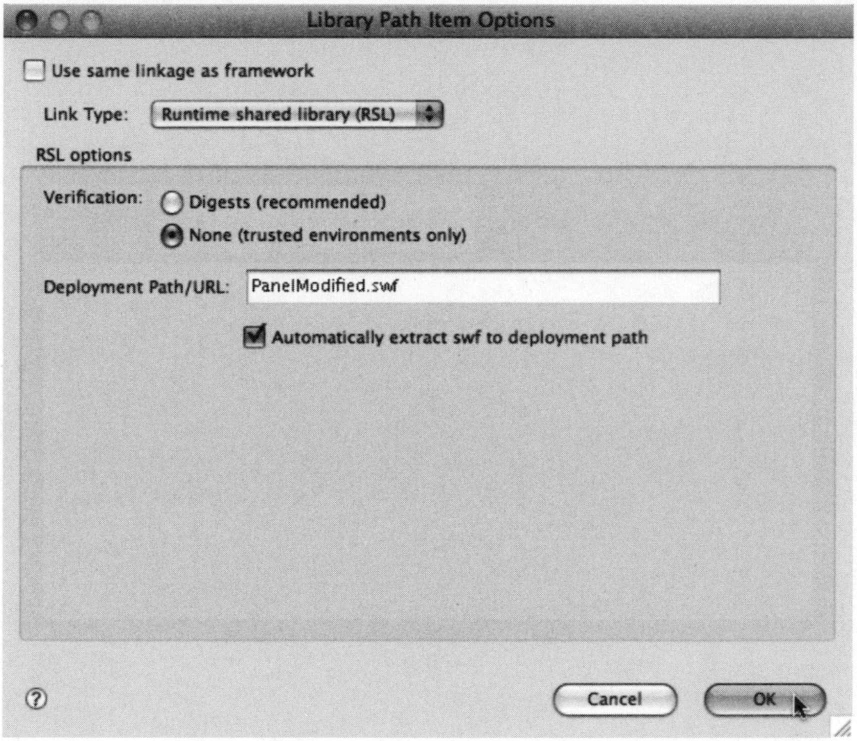

Figure 7-37. Selecting the verification option

Finally, you have to set the "Deployment Path/URL" property to specify the file that will be loaded by the application at runtime. The value can be relative or absolute like "../components/rsl.swf" or `http://www.domain.com/components/rsl.swf`.

If you choose the digest verification, you also have to set the policy-file URL to give the permission to load the file over different domains. This is needed only if you are serving the RSL from a different domain from the application's domain. If you are serving the library from the same domain, you don't need to set the policy-file-url argument.

Summary

In this Chapter I tried to give you a complete overview of Flex and Flex Builder. I started showing how to create and compile a Flex project using the Flex Builder Eclipse plug-in. Then I went through the most common Flex components and showed some examples of how to use the layout containers. Finally, I showed you how to listen for and dispatch events, create custom components, use external CSS files, data binding, control Flash MovieClips, and more, trying to cover the concepts that I think are fundamental for starting to develop using Flex. In the next chapter I will show how to manage and retrieve data within a Flex client using a database, XML, and local shared objects.

CHAPTER 8

■ ■ ■

Working with Data in Flex

No matter what kind of application you're building, you will almost certainly be working with data, and the more help you get in the form of tools and APIs, the better it is for building the application. You will often need tools to find, replace, bind, store, and access data—and the good news is that Flex provides all the tools you need.

In this chapter we'll explore the Flex data tools you'll want to use. I'll show you the process of working with data, starting from structure and representation within components using collections and data providers, and finishing with particulars of how to load data from an external source.

Flex provides a number of ways to access remote data, but it is better to first of all understand the work that Flex does for you on the client side when data is present. So we'll begin by examining some data models and using static data embedded into the Flex client so you can see how to represent and structure data within a Flex application. Then we'll move on to work with XML, SOAP, RPC and other data access solutions that work inside Flex.

An Overview of Data Models

A data model is an object that contains all properties and methods needed to store application data. The architecture of a data model is important as it is the base for your application business logic. A typical example of a data model is the User object, which consists of an ActionScript (AS) object containing all the properties required to set and get user information. The User AS entity file is called User.as. Here is an example of the AS User entity:

```
package com.apress.flexjava.usermanager.model
{
    public class User
    {
        public function User(){
        }

        public var uid          : String;

        public var username      : String;

        public var commonName    : String;

        public var lastName      : String;
```

```
        public var email        : String;

        public var password     : String;


    }
}
```

A data model can have many related objects. For example, you can have a Group object containing many users. In this case, the Group object consists of an AS class with all public properties needed to define the group. The following code shows an example of the AS Group entity containing the collection of users, which means the Group entity has a one-to-many relationship with the User entity. The Group entity AS file is called Group.as.

```
package com.apress.flexjava.usermanager.model
{
    import mx.collections.ArrayCollection;

    public class Group
    {
        public function Group(){
        }

        public var uid          : String ;

        public var commonName   : String;

        public var description  : String;

        public var users        : ArrayCollection;

    }
}
```

You can define the data model in AS or in MXML. I don't recommend using MXML for data models, but just for your information, in case it's ever useful, here is an example of the User class translated into MXML:

```
<mx:Model id="userModel">
    <user>
        <id />
        <username />
        <commonName />
        <lastName />
        <email />
        <password />
    </user>
</mx:Model>
```

In the MVC (Model-View-Controller) design pattern, the data model is the model layer. In the upcoming HTTPService section, I will show you how to make the model layer interact with the view and controller layers.

You can bind the data model to a view, or store it in a collection and bind the collection to a component. For example, you might have a registration form that, when submitted, creates a User object with the information sent by the form. Then you can bind all the User properties with the form fields to give the user another form with the confirmation data (see Figure 8-1). Here is the listing of the UserForm.mxml view:

```
<?xml version="1.0" encoding="utf-8"?>
<mx:Form xmlns:mx="http://www.adobe.com/2006/mxml" width="100%" height="100%">
    <mx:FormItem label="Common name">
        <mx:TextInput id="commonNameText"  text="{user.commonName}"/>
    </mx:FormItem>
    <mx:FormItem label="Last name">
        <mx:TextInput  id="lastNameText"  text="{user.lastName}" />
    </mx:FormItem>
    <mx:FormItem label="Email">
        <mx:TextInput  id="emailText" text="{user.email} />
    </mx:FormItem>
    <mx:FormItem label="Username">
        <mx:TextInput  id="usernameText" text="{user.username} />
    </mx:FormItem>
    <mx:FormItem label="Password">
        <mx:TextInput id="passwordText"  text="{user.password}" />
    </mx:FormItem>
        <mx:Script>
        <![CDATA[
            import com.apress.flexjava.usermanager.model.User;

            [Bindable]
            public var user : User;
        ]]>
        </mx:Script>

</mx:Form>
```

Figure 8-1. The user form created with the UserForm.mxml class

You can also create a collection of Users and bind it to a DataGrid component. Here is the listing for the UsersGrid.mxml view:

```
<?xml version="1.0" encoding="utf-8"?>
<mx:DataGrid xmlns:mx="http://www.adobe.com/2006/mxml" >
     <mx:columns>
      <mx:DataGridColumn dataField="commonName" headerText="Common Name" />
      <mx:DataGridColumn dataField="lastName" headerText="Last Name" />
      <mx:DataGridColumn dataField="email" headerText="Email" />
      <mx:DataGridColumn dataField="username" headerText="Username" />
      <mx:DataGridColumn dataField="password" headerText="Password" />
      </mx:columns>

     <mx:Script>
             <![CDATA[
                     import mx.collections.ArrayCollection;

                     [Bindable]
                     [Inspectable]


                     public function set users(usersCollection : ArrayCollection)
: void {
                            this.dataProvider = usersCollection;
                     }
             ]]>
     </mx:Script>
</mx:DataGrid>
```

And here is the Main MXML class where you can test the User collection bound to the DataGrid component. You can call the Main class DataCollectionTest.mxml:

```
<?xml version="1.0" encoding="utf-8"?>
<mx:Application xmlns:mx="http://www.adobe.com/2006/mxml"
                        xmlns:view="com.apress.flexjava.usermanager.view.*"
                        layout="horizontal"
                        creationComplete="init()"
                        horizontalAlign="center"
                        verticalAlign="middle">
     <view:UsersGrid dataProvider="{usersCollectionTest}" width="600"
height="400" />
     <mx:Script>
             <![CDATA[
                     import mx.collections.ArrayCollection;
                     import com.apress.flexjava.usermanager.model.User;

                     [Bindable]
                     public var usersCollectionTest : ArrayCollection;
```

```
        public function init() : void{
                createUsersCollectionTest();
        }

        private function createUsersCollectionTest() : void {
                usersCollectionTest = new ArrayCollection();
                for(var i:int = 0; i<10; i++){

usersCollectionTest.addItem(userFactory("commonName"+i,
                                        "lastName"+i,
                                        "email"+i,
                                        "username"+i,
                                        "password"+i));

        }
    }

        private function userFactory(commonName : String,
                                    lastName : String,
                                    email : String,
                                    username : String,
                                    password : String) : User
{

                var user : User  = new User();
                user.commonName  = commonName;
                user.lastName    = lastName;
                user.email       = email;
                user.username    = username;
                user.password    = password;
                return user;

        }

    ]]>
    </mx:Script>
</mx:Application>
```

Because we don't yet have a database or an XML list of users, in the application test code I created a loop to add 10 users to the collection:

```
private function createUsersCollectionTest() : void {
                usersCollectionTest = new ArrayCollection();
                for(var i:int = 0; i<10; i++){

usersCollectionTest.addItem(userFactory("commonName"+i,
                                        "lastName"+i,
```

```
                                                    "email"+i,
                                                    "username"+i,
                                                    "password"+i));


                              }

}
```

For the collection, I have used the new AS3 ArrayCollection, instead of a simple Array because it provides more functionality, such as the ability to sort and filter data. This can be very handy for making the grid searchable. In the next section I will cover the Flex Collection APIs, **including** an example of adding a search control to the user's DataGrid.

Structuring Data for Views

The new generation of rich Internet applications (RIAs) demands that we architect new rich user interfaces for users. These UIs must be architected to be more sophisticated so the applications don't, for instance, have to reload the page or change the screen at every user request. Data views must also be structured in such a way that users can edit, add, delete, filter, and more, all on one screen.

In previous eras, we needed to create a Web view that contained a list of users and develop the accompanying add/edit/delete/search functionality, creating many views and relating them for the user—who was loading a new page every new request. Today, all that is unnecessary. Flex lets you create an editable list of Users simply by binding a collection of User entities to the DataGrid component. You can also offer real-time sorting and filtering, giving users real-time search and sort. To do this, Flex introduced new data collection APIs that provide added functionality for presenting the underlying data. Let's take a look at these data collections now.

Data Collections

A data collection is a set of data. Each set of data can be structured in different ways, such as XML, hierarchically, or as an Array. The Flex collection model uses the following interfaces to define how a collection works:

- IList provides methods to get, set, and add data based on an index that orders the data. IList also supplies methods to get the number of items contained in the collection, remove them all, and more, but it doesn't provide sorting and filtering functionality.

- ICollectionView provides more functionality than IList, with sorting, filtering, and data cursor capabilities that allow you to show a subset of data. Furthermore, ICollectionView lets you set bookmarks in the collection for later use.

- ICursorView provides methods to enumerate a collection by pointing the cursor to a particular item. You can move the cursor backward, forward, or to a specified position in the collection.

The most common implementation of the IList and ICollectionView interfaces come with the ArrayCollection and XMLListCollection classes. Both classes can be used to access hierarchical data, and you can pass objects that require IList or ICollectionView methods and properties.

In the next example, I will bind an `ArrayCollection` with a `DataGrid` component. I'll then use the `ICollectionView` methods to sort and filter data, and because collections support notification changes, I will also allow adding a new user to the collection—and see the result in real time within the `DataGrid`.

The goal of this example is to add a search TextInput control to the user's `DataGrid`, as shown in Figure 8-2. When you change value within the `TextInput` control, the `DataGrid` content will be filtered by the value input into the search control. I'll also add two `RadioButton` controls to select which `DataGrid` column to search in.

commonName	email	lastName	password	username
commonName0	email0	lastName0	password0	username0
commonName1	email1	lastName1	password1	username1
commonName2	email2	lastName2	password2	username2
commonName3	email3	lastName3	password3	username3

Figure 8-2. The user manager sample application DataGrid

Starting with the code we used for the previous example, we just have to add a custom component that extends the TextInput control with the filter collection functionality. Basically, the new custom component will have two new properties to allow passing to the component the collection that we want to filter and the column of the `DataGrid` we want to search in. Below, the two public attributes are exposed by the component:

```
[Inspectable]
public var collection : ArrayCollection;

[Inspectable]
public var columnSearchable : String;
```

The [Inspectable] metatag defines information about an attribute of the Flex component. It means that we will be able to see the attribute within the Flex builder code hints and property inspector.

For this component I will use MXML because it is a view component. Moreover, I want to make sure you see how to use MXML to extend other components. I will call the component `CollectionTextInputFilter.mxml` and save it into the view package `com.apress.flexjava.usermanager.view`:

```
<?xml version="1.0" encoding="utf-8"?>
<mx:TextInput xmlns:mx="http://www.adobe.com/2006/mxml" change="search()">
</mx:TextInput>
```

The code above is the equivalent of

```
public class CollectionTextInputFilter extends TextInput{

}
```

The body of the CollectionTextInputFilter.mxml custom component contains the methods needed to filter the collection. First you pass to the collection the filter function filterRecords , then you refresh the collection with the data filtered:

```
<?xml version="1.0" encoding="utf-8"?>
<mx:TextInput xmlns:mx="http://www.adobe.com/2006/mxml" change="search()">
    <mx:Script>
            <![CDATA[
                import mx.collections.ArrayCollection;

                [Inspectable]
                public var collection : ArrayCollection;

                [Inspectable]
                public var columnSearchable : String;

        protected function search():void {
            if(this.text !='') {
                filter()
            } else {
                filterReset()
            }
        }

         private function filter():void {
            collection.filterFunction = filterRecords;
            collection.refresh();
        }

        private function filterReset():void {
            collection.filterFunction = null;
            collection.refresh();
        }

        private function filterRecords(item:Object):Boolean {
                var tags : String = item[columnSearchable];
                if( tags != null ) {
                    return tags.match(new RegExp(this.text, "i"));
                } else {
                    return false;
                }
            }

        ]]>
    </mx:Script>
</mx:TextInput>
```

In the main class, you instantiate the new component, binding the user's collection and the column you want to search in:

```
<view:CollectionTextInputFilter tabIndex="1"

    collection="{usersCollectionTest}"

    columnSearchable="{columnNameToSearch}" />
```

Here is the complete code of the main class (the code in bold is what was added from the previous example:

```
<?xml version="1.0" encoding="utf-8"?>
<mx:Application xmlns:mx="http://www.adobe.com/2006/mxml"
                              xmlns:view="com.apress.flexjava.usermanager.view.*"
                              layout="horizontal"
                              creationComplete="init()"
                              horizontalAlign="center"
                              verticalAlign="middle">

        <mx:VBox horizontalAlign="right">
        <mx:HBox>

                <mx:FormItem label="search">
                        <view:CollectionTextInputFilter tabIndex="1"

    collection="{usersCollectionTest}"

    columnSearchable="{columnNameToSearch}" />
                </mx:FormItem>
                <mx:RadioButtonGroup id="searchMethodGroup" ↵
 itemClick="handleSearchMethod(event)"/>
            <mx:RadioButton tabEnabled="true" tabIndex="2" label="lastName"↵
 selected="true" groupName="searchMethodGroup"/>
            <mx:RadioButton tabEnabled="true" tabIndex="3" label="email"↵
 groupName="searchMethodGroup" />


        </mx:HBox>


        <view:UsersGrid dataProvider="{usersCollectionTest}" width="600" height=↵
"400" />
        </mx:VBox>

    <mx:Script>
```

```
        <![CDATA[
                import mx.events.ItemClickEvent;
                import mx.collections.ArrayCollection;
                import com.apress.flexjava.usermanager.model.User;

            [Bindable]
            public var usersCollectionTest : ArrayCollection;

        [Bindable]
        private var columnNameToSearch : String = "lastName";

            public function init() : void{
                    createUsersCollectionTest();
            }

            private function createUsersCollectionTest() : void {
                    usersCollectionTest = new ArrayCollection();
                    for(var i:int = 0; i<10; i++){

    usersCollectionTest.addItem(userFactory("commonName"+i,
                                            "lastName"+i,
                                            "email"+i,
                                            "username"+i,
                                            "password"+i ));

                    }
            }

            private function userFactory(commonName : String,
                                        lastName : String,
                                        email : String,
                                        username : String,
                                        password : String) : User
{

                    var user : User  = new User();
                    user.commonName  = commonName;
                    user.lastName    = lastName;
                    user.email       = email;
                    user.username    = username;
                    user.password    = password;
                    return user;
            }

                            private function handleSearchMethod⏎
(event:ItemClickEvent):void {
                                    columnNameToSearch = ⏎
```

```
event.currentTarget.selectedValue as String;
                                            }


                    ]]>
        </mx:Script>
</mx:Application>
```

Now it's time to test and run the application. If everything is okay, you should see the list of users, and if you try to write lastName0 in the search box, it will filter the DataGrid in real time, as shown in Figure 8-3.

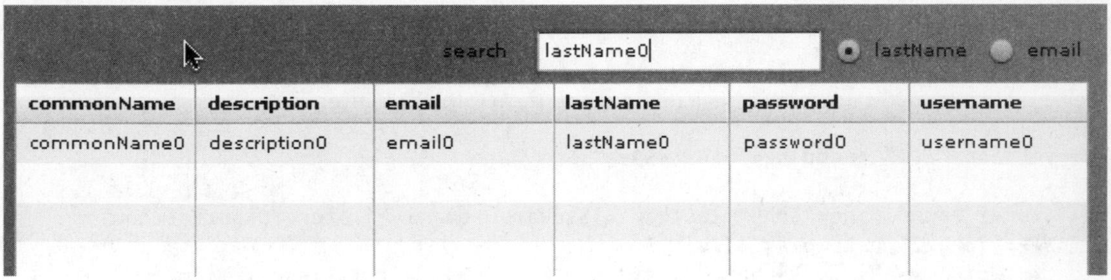

Figure 8-3. *Real-time search*

Collections are more complete than a simple array, of course, because they don't just provide new sort and filter functionality, but also dispatch events when changes are made. You can then bind those events with the data-driven Flex controls through the dataProvider property.

Access to Remote Data

In the last example we created a DataGrid containing a list of users, and we added search functionality to the collection. But a problem arises when you add new data—if you close the browser you will lose all your data.

The solution is to store the data on a server so it can be shared over the network/Internet. When you architect your application, you have to choose server-side storage, which can be a database, XML, or a directory server (LDAP). Flex provides different ways of accessing server-side data:

- HTTP GET or POST, by using the HTTPService components;

- Adobe Action Message Format (AMF), by using the RemoteObject components;

- SOAP by using the WebService components;

These three methods can be used in both AS and MXML. Let's explore these now.

HTTPService Components

HTTPService lets you work with all server-side technologies using the HTTP protocol, including CGI scripts or, even better, servlets, and it supports all HTTP commands such as GET, POST, HEAD, OPTIONS, PUT, TRACE, and DELETE. You can also use HTTPService to consume different types of responses; the common scenario is to consume an XML file, as shown in Figure 8-4.

Figure 8-4. Flex uses the HTTPService to work with remote servlets or XML

So, for example, you can create a servlet that updates an XML file containing your user list on a GET request and sends an XML response back to the client. Here is the XML user list:

```
<?xml version="1.0" encoding="ISO-8859-1"?>
<users>
        <user commonName="John" lastName="Steuard" email="j.steward@apress.com"↩
 username="john22" password="342uiy"/>
        <user commonName="Richard" lastName="Mal" email="r.mal@apress.com"↩
 username="richard3" password="54jfjei"/>
        <user commonName="Maria" lastName="Seal" email="m.seal@apress.com"
 username="maria"↩
 password="323nncx"/>
        <user commonName="Roger" lastName="Wisky" email="r.wisky@apress.com"↩
 username="roger" password="998reh"/>
</users>
```

In the AS class we use the HTTPService component to interact with the servlet, sending the user details that we want to store into the XML file and consuming the XML, then binding the result within the DataGrid component:

```
var service : HTTPService = new HTTPService();
service.url = USERS_LIST_SERVICE_URL
service.method = "GET";
service.useProxy = false;
service.resultFormat = "e4x";
service.addEventListener("fault", handleFault);
service.addEventListener("result", handleResult);
```

HTTPService is very useful for some kinds of operation, but where possible, it's better to use the RemoteObject services that I'll introduce later. For now let's create the example!

Building Our First Java and Flex Application

First we must create our Java Web application (webapp) with two servlets, one for getting the XML users list and another for adding users to the list by appending the user parameters to the URL:

- getusers servlet URL : http://localhost:8080/usermanager/getusers

- addusers servlet URL :
  http://localhost:8080/usermanager/adduser?cn=filippo&ln=dipisa&em=filippo@d
  ip.net&us=fil&ps=pass

If you are new to Java, it is time to create your first Java project using Maven. For this example, we will create just a webapp project without using Spring. To create the Maven project, on the Eclipse menu bar click File ➤ New Maven Project. In the first window, leave the default options and click on Next (see Figure 8-5).

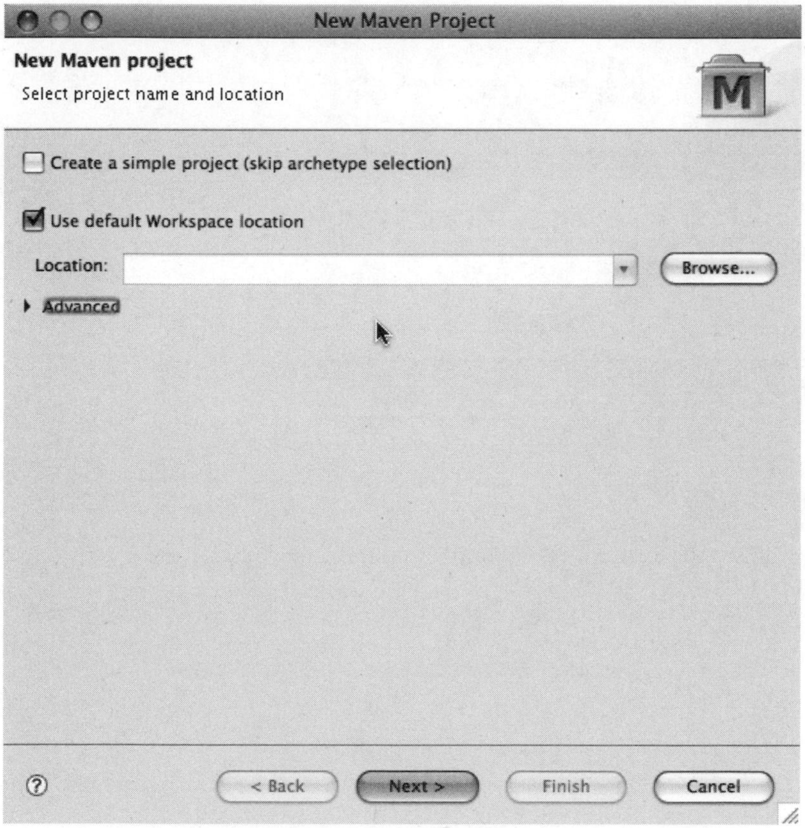

Figure 8-5. New Maven Project wizard

In the second window, enter the word "web" into the Filter box and then select the maven-archetype-webapp, as shown in Figure 8-6. Click on Next.

Figure 8-6. Choosing the Maven archetype

In the third and last window, fill in the form with the groupId and the other values for the application as shown in Figure 8-7, then click on Finish.

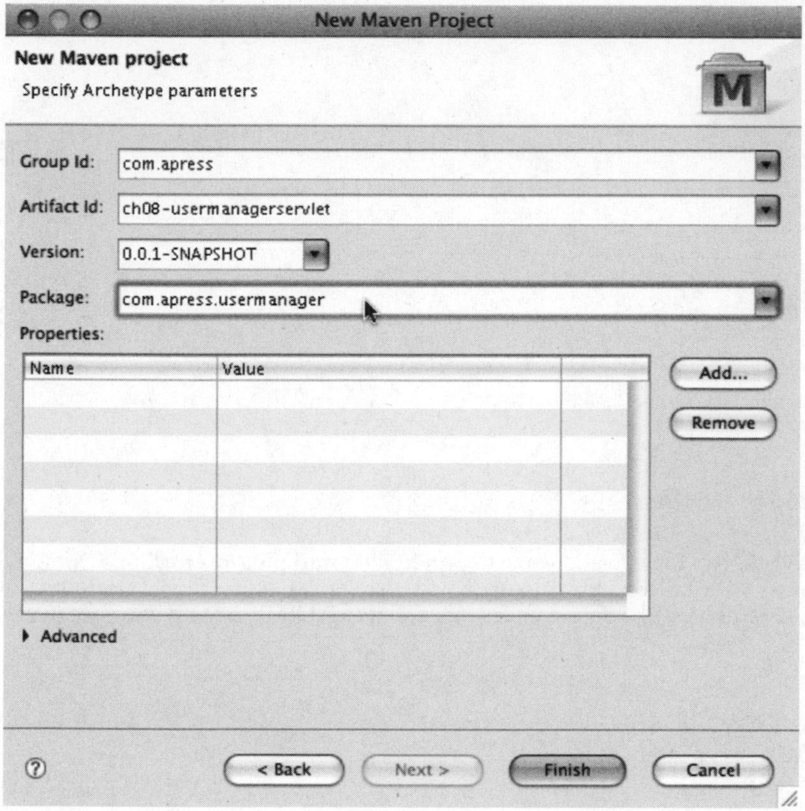

Figure 8-7. Adding the application parameters

As Figure 8-8 shows, Maven will create the project in the webapp folder with the web.xml configuration file.

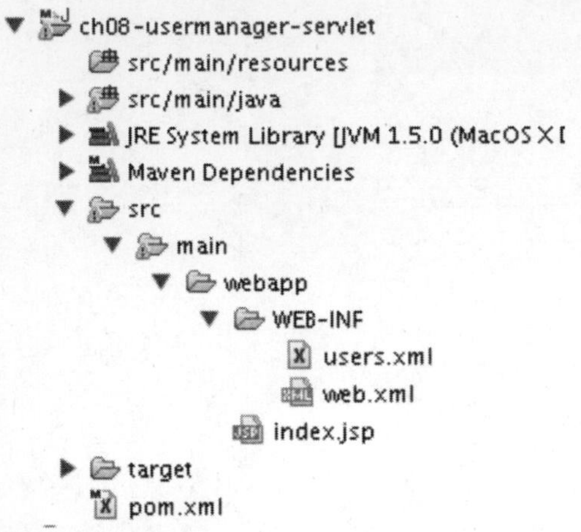

```
▼ 📇 ch08-usermanager-servlet
      📁 src/main/resources
   ▶ 📇 src/main/java
   ▶ 📚 JRE System Library [JVM 1.5.0 (MacOS X [
   ▶ 📚 Maven Dependencies
   ▼ 📂 src
      ▼ 📂 main
         ▼ 📁 webapp
            ▼ 📁 WEB-INF
                  🗙 users.xml
                  📄 web.xml
               📄 index.jsp
   ▶ 📁 target
      🗙 pom.xml
```

Figure 8-8. The tree created by the archetype

Before creating the two servlets, you have to add some dependencies and plug-ins to your POM file because you need a library to work with XML, a library to work with the servlet, and a servlet container plug-in to test the application. We will use the dependencies for servlets and XML listed below by putting them in the POM file:

```xml
<dependency>
      <groupId>javax.servlet</groupId>
      <artifactId>servlet-api</artifactId>
      <version>2.5</version>
      <scope>provided</scope>
</dependency>
<dependency>
      <groupId>xom</groupId>
      <artifactId>xom</artifactId>
      <version>1.1d2</version>
</dependency>
```

Within the <build> tags, we will define the Jetty servlet container plug-in that will let us test and run our application using Maven:

```xml
            <plugins>
                <plugin>
                    <groupId>org.mortbay.jetty</groupId>
                    <artifactId>maven-jetty-plugin</artifactId>
                    <version>6.1.19</version>
                    <configuration>
                        <contextPath>/usermanager</contextPath>
                        <scanIntervalSeconds>4</scanIntervalSeconds>
                        <scanTargetPatterns>
```

```
                                        <scanTargetPattern>
                                                <directory>
                                                        src/main/webapp/WEB-INF
                                                </directory>
                                                <excludes>

        <exclude>**/*.jsp</exclude>

                                                </excludes>
                                                <includes>

        <include>**/*.properties</include>

        <include>**/*.xml</include>

                                                </includes>
                                        </scanTargetPattern>
                                </scanTargetPatterns>
                        </configuration>
                </plugin>

        </plugins>
```

And here is the complete XML for our pom.xml file:

```
<project xmlns="http://maven.apache.org/POM/4.0.0"
        xmlns:xsi="http://www.w3.org/2001/XMLSchema-instance"
        xsi:schemaLocation="http://maven.apache.org/POM/4.0.0 http://↵
maven.apache.org/maven-v4_0_0.xsd">
        <modelVersion>4.0.0</modelVersion>
        <groupId>com.apress</groupId>
        <artifactId>ch06-usermanager-servlet</artifactId>
        <packaging>war</packaging>
        <version>0.0.1-SNAPSHOT</version>
        <name>ch06-usermanager-servlet Maven Webapp</name>
        <url>http://maven.apache.org</url>
        <dependencies>
                <dependency>
                        <groupId>junit</groupId>
                        <artifactId>junit</artifactId>
                        <version>3.8.1</version>
                         <scope>test</scope>
                </dependency>
                <dependency>
                        <groupId>javax.servlet</groupId>
                        <artifactId>servlet-api</artifactId>
                        <version>2.5</version>
                         <scope>provided</scope>
                </dependency>
```

```xml
        <dependency>
                <groupId>xom</groupId>
                <artifactId>xom</artifactId>
                <version>1.1d2</version>
        </dependency>

</dependencies>

<build>
        <finalName>ch06-usermanager-servlet</finalName>

        <plugins>
                <plugin>
                        <groupId>org.mortbay.jetty</groupId>
                        <artifactId>maven-jetty-plugin</artifactId>
                        <version>6.1.19</version>
                        <configuration>
                                <contextPath>/usermanager</contextPath>
                                <scanIntervalSeconds>4</scanIntervalSeconds>
                                <scanTargetPatterns>
                                        <scanTargetPattern>
                                                <directory>
                                                        src/main/webapp/WEB-INF
                                                </directory>
                                                <excludes>

<exclude>**/*.jsp</exclude>

                                                </excludes>
                                                <includes>

<include>**/*.properties</include>

<include>**/*.xml</include>

                                                </includes>
                                        </scanTargetPattern>
                                </scanTargetPatterns>
                        </configuration>
                </plugin>

        </plugins>

</build>
</project>
```

■ **Note** To download the plug-ins and dependencies, you must be connected to the Internet or have them in your local Maven repository.

Now you can create the servlets and map them to the web.xml file. First we'll create a package called `com.apress.usermanager.servlet` where we will create three classes as shown in Figure 8-9.

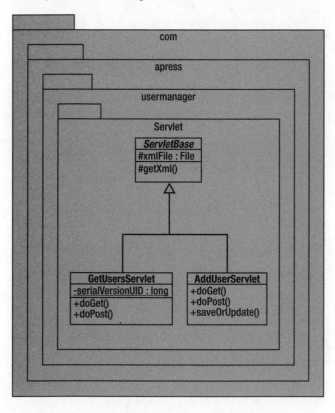

Figure 8-9. *Remote servlet UML class diagram*

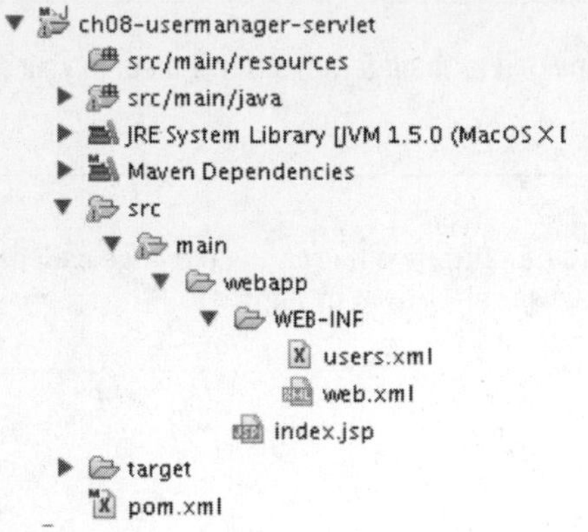

```
▼ 📱 ch08-usermanager-servlet
     📁 src/main/resources
   ▶ 📁 src/main/java
   ▶ 📗 JRE System Library [JVM 1.5.0 (MacOS X [
   ▶ 📗 Maven Dependencies
   ▼ 📂 src
       ▼ 📂 main
           ▼ 📁 webapp
               ▼ 📁 WEB-INF
                     🗙 users.xml
                     📄 web.xml
                 📄 index.jsp
   ▶ 📁 target
     🗙 pom.xml
```

Figure 8-10. The tree showing the new servlets

I created an abstract class called ServletBase within the com.apress.usermanager.servlet
package (see Figure 8-10). The ServletBase class has a protected method getXml() that returns an
nu.xom.Document document type with the content of the *user.xml* file that we created before in our
WEB-INF folder:

```java
package com.apress.usermanager.servlet;

import java.io.File;
import java.io.IOException;
import javax.servlet.http.HttpServlet;
import nu.xom.Builder;
import;
import nu.xom.ParsingException;
import nu.xom.ValidityException;

abstract class ServletBase extends HttpServlet {

        protected File xmlFile;

        protected Document getXml() throws ValidityException, ParsingException,
IOException{
                Builder builder = new Builder();
                xmlFile = new File(getServletContext().getRealPath("WEB-
INF/users.xml"));
                return builder.build(xmlFile);
        }

}
```

■ **Note** Files stored in the WEB-INF folder are not accessible from the Web. Files stored within the webapp folder are accessible from the Web.

Now we can extend `ServletBase` by creating the `GetUsersServlet` in the same package; the `GetUsersServlet` goal is to print out the XML returned from the getXml method:

```java
package com.apress.usermanager.servlet;

import java.io.IOException;
import java.io.PrintWriter;
import javax.servlet.ServletException;
import javax.servlet.http.HttpServletRequest;
import javax.servlet.http.HttpServletResponse;
import nu.xom.ParsingException;
import nu.xom.ValidityException;

public class GetUsersServlet extends ServletBase {

	private static final long serialVersionUID = 2882812753422210359L;


	public void doGet (HttpServletRequest req, HttpServletResponse res)
 throws ServletException, IOException {
		PrintWriter out = res.getWriter();

		try {
			out.println(getXml().toXML());
		} catch (ValidityException e) {
			e.printStackTrace();
		} catch (ParsingException e) {
			e.printStackTrace();
		}
		out.close();

		}


	public void doPost(HttpServletRequest req, HttpServletResponse resp)
			throws ServletException, IOException {
		super.doPost(req, resp);
	}

}
```

The `AddUserServlet` class adds an element with its attributes to the user's XML document, then physically saves the file and prints out the updated XML on the screen:

```java
package com.apress.usermanager.servlet;

import java.io.FileOutputStream;
import java.io.IOException;
import java.io.PrintWriter;
import javax.servlet.ServletException;
import javax.servlet.http.HttpServletRequest;
import javax.servlet.http.HttpServletResponse;
import nu.xom.Attribute;
import nu.xom.Document;
import nu.xom.Element;
import nu.xom.ParsingException;
import nu.xom.Serializer;
import nu.xom.ValidityException;

public class AddUserServlet extends ServletBase {


        public void doGet (HttpServletRequest req, HttpServletResponse res) throws
ServletException, IOException {
                PrintWriter out = res.getWriter();
                Document doc;
                try {
                        doc = getXml();
                        Element root = doc.getRootElement();
                        Element element = new Element("user");
                        Attribute commonName = new Attribute("commonname",↵
 req.getParameter("cn"));
                        Attribute lastName = new Attribute("lastname",
req.getParameter("ln"));
                        Attribute email = new Attribute("email",
req.getParameter("em"));
                        Attribute username = new Attribute("username",
req.getParameter("us"));
                        Attribute password = new Attribute("password",
req.getParameter("ps"));
                        element.addAttribute(commonName);
                        element.addAttribute(lastName);
                        element.addAttribute(email);
                        element.addAttribute(username);
                        element.addAttribute(password);
```

```
                        root.appendChild(element);
                        saveOrUpdate(doc);
                        out.println(doc.toXML());
                } catch (ValidityException e) {
                        e.printStackTrace();
                } catch (ParsingException e) {
                        e.printStackTrace();
                }

        }


        public void doPost(HttpServletRequest req, HttpServletResponse resp)
                        throws ServletException, IOException {
                super.doPost(req, resp);
        }

        public void saveOrUpdate (Document doc) throws IOException {
                FileOutputStream fos = new FileOutputStream(xmlFile);
                Serializer output = new Serializer(fos, "ISO-8859-1");
                output.setIndent(2);
                output.write(doc);
        }


}
```

Before running and testing the application, you need to map the servlets to the WEB-INF/web.xml file as follows:

```
<!DOCTYPE web-app PUBLIC
 "-//Sun Microsystems, Inc.//DTD Web Application 2.3//EN"
 "http://java.sun.com/dtd/web-app_2_3.dtd" >

<web-app>
        <display-name>Archetype Created Web Application</display-name>
        <servlet>
                <servlet-name>GetUserServlet</servlet-name>
                <servlet-class>
                        com.apress.usermanager.servlet.GetUsersServlet
                </servlet-class>
        </servlet>
        <servlet>
                <servlet-name>AddUserServlet</servlet-name>
                <servlet-class>
```

```
                    com.apress.usermanager.servlet.AddUserServlet
        </servlet-class>
    </servlet>

    <servlet-mapping>
        <servlet-name>GetUserServlet</servlet-name>
        <url-pattern>/getusers</url-pattern>
    </servlet-mapping>
    <servlet-mapping>
        <servlet-name>AddUserServlet</servlet-name>
        <url-pattern>/adduser</url-pattern>
    </servlet-mapping>
    <welcome-file-list>
        <welcome-file>index.jsp</welcome-file>
    </welcome-file-list>

</web-app>
```

As you can see, I mapped `GetUserServlet` as /getusers and `AddUserServlet` as /adduser. Finally, we can test the application by running the command `mvn jetty:run` from the command line within the root of our project where the pom.xml file resides:

```
$ mvn jetty:run
```

If everything goes well, you should see the following message that indicates the application is ready on port 8080:

```
2009-08-26 00:57:53.936::INFO:  Started SelectChannelConnector@0.0.0.0:8080
[INFO] Started Jetty Server
[INFO] Starting scanner at interval of 4 seconds.
```

Now open a browser, type the URL `http://localhost:8080/usermanager/getusers`, and you should see the XML from the users.xml file, as shown in Figure 8-11.

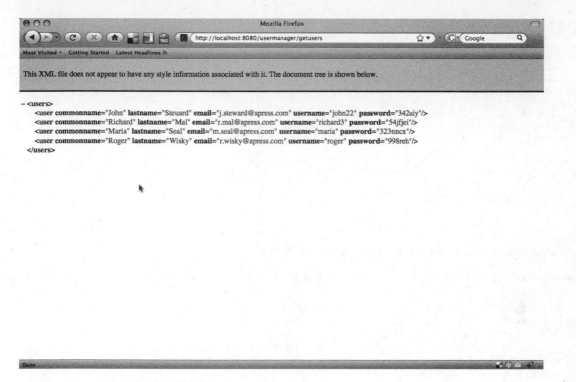

Figure 8-11. The XML generated by the getusers servlet

To see the XML updated, enter the following URL:

```
http://localhost:8080/usermanager/adduser?cn=bob&ln=seal&em=bob@apress.com&us↵
=bob32&ps=mypass
```

If you open the WEB-INF/users.xml file in Eclipse, you should see the new element just added.

Now that the server is listening on http, we can implement the HTTPService component on the Flex client. You can start from the previous DataCollection example and implement the logic in order to use the two servlets that use the HTTPService component.

In the previous example we created the data model with two entities User and Group, and the View layer with three components, one for the DataGrid, one for the UserForm and one for filtering the collection (see Figure 8-12).

commonName	email	lastName	password	username
commonName0	email0	lastName0	password0	username0
commonName1	email1	lastName1	password1	username1
commonName2	email2	lastName2	password2	username2
commonName3	email3	lastName3	password3	username3
commonName4	email4	lastName4	password4	username4
commonName5	email5	lastName5	password5	username5
commonName6	email6	lastName6	password6	username6
commonName7	email7	lastName7	password7	username7
commonName8	email8	lastName8	password8	username8
commonName9	email9	lastName9	password9	username9

search ⦿ lastName ○ email

Figure 8-12. *The DataGrid populated by retrieving users using the remote servlet*

In the `DataCollection` example, the user collection was static and created within our application test class. Now the goal is to load all users using the servlet /getusers, and then add a button to change the view and add a user through the UserForm component.

Since this is our first "major" application, please follow the next example carefully. The architecture will use a simple MVC pattern to keep the View, Model, and Controller separate, as the UML class diagram in Figure 8-13 illustrates.

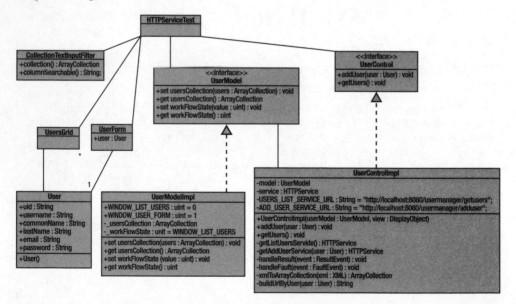

Figure 8-13. *Flex UI usermanager application*

The application model (UserModelImpl.as) will contain a workFlowState variable that will be updated every time the view changes. The workFlow will have only two views—the DataGrid containing the list of users and the Form for adding a new user. (I will provide a full listing of where this goes later.)

```
public var workFlowState : uint = WINDOW_LIST_USERS

public static const WINDOW_LIST_USERS : uint = 0;

public static const WINDOW_USER_FORM : uint = 1;
```

The workFlowState variable will be bound into a ViewStack layout container added in the Application test file; the ViewStack layout container is index-based, so it shows a View by index. In our case, index 0 is the view containing the DataGrid, and index 1 is the view containing the form.

```
<mx:ViewStack id="viewStack" selectedIndex="{model.workFlowState}">
        <mx:VBox horizontalAlign="right">
            <mx:HBox>
                    <mx:FormItem label="search">
                            <view:CollectionTextInputFilter tabIndex="1"
        collection="{model.usersCollection}"
        columnSearchable="{columnNameToSearch}" />
                    </mx:FormItem>
                    <mx:RadioButtonGroup id="searchMethodGroup"
  itemClick="handleSearchMethod(event)"/>
                    <mx:RadioButton tabEnabled="true" tabIndex="2"
label="lastName"
 selected="true" groupName="searchMethodGroup"/>
                    <mx:RadioButton tabEnabled="true" tabIndex="3"
label="email"
 groupName="searchMethodGroup" />
                </mx:HBox>
                <view:UsersGrid dataProvider="{model.usersCollection}"
 width="600" height="400" />
                <mx:HBox>
                    <mx:Button label="Add User"
click="{model.workFlowState
 = UserModelImpl.WINDOW_USER_FORM}" />
                </mx:HBox>
        </mx:VBox>
        <mx:VBox>
                <view:UserForm id="userForm" width="400" height="400" />
                <mx:HBox>
                    <mx:Button label="Back" click="{model.workFlowState
 = UserModelImpl.WINDOW_LIST_USERS}" />
                    <mx:Button label="Save" click="{control.addUser
(userForm.user);model.workFlowState = UserModelImpl.WINDOW_LIST_USERS}" />
```

```
                        </mx:HBox>
                </mx:VBox>
        </mx:ViewStack>
```

The `DataGrid` dataProvider is bound to the `usersCollection` stored in the model. We store the `usersCollection` in the model so we can update it from everywhere, and when it changes it will dispatch the change to all its observers because the model is bindable. Practically speaking, we update the `model.usersCollection` from our controller, and because the `DataGrid` dataProvider is bound with the `model.usersCollection`, the data in the grid will be updated every time the `model.usersCollection` changes.

```
private function handleResult(event:ResultEvent):void{
        model.usersCollection = xmlToArrayCollection(event.result as XML);
}
```

In the controller, we initiate the HTTPService component for both servlets, /getusers and /adduser:

```
var service : HTTPService = new HTTPService();
service.url = USERS_LIST_SERVICE_URL
service.method = "GET";
service.useProxy = false;
service.resultFormat = "e4x";
service.addEventListener("fault", handleFault);
service.addEventListener("result", handleResult);
```

The HTTPService needs to know the URL to connect to, the result format, and the two functions to handle the result or the fault events. The result will be in XML format, and to keep the code from the previous example that was using the ArrayCollection type, I built a function to convert the XML result into an ArrayCollection result:

```
private function xmlToArrayCollection(xml:XML):ArrayCollection{
        var xmlDocument:XMLDocument = new XMLDocument(xml.toString());
        var xmlDecoder:SimpleXMLDecoder = new SimpleXMLDecoder(true);
        var resultObj:Object = xmlDecoder.decodeXML(xmlDocument);
        var tmp : Object = resultObj.users.user;
        return resultObj.users.user as ArrayCollection;
}
```

Finally, the Application Test class will build the MVC model, instantiating both model and controller:

```
public function init():void{
                model = new UserModelImpl();
                control = new UserControlImpl(model);
                control.getUsers();
 }
```

When the application starts, we will call the method `control.getUsers()` that will set the HTTPService instance for the /getusers servlet and send the token to it:

```
public function getUsers() : void{
      var token : AsyncToken = getListUsersService().send( );
}
```

The servlet /getusers will return the users' XML document to the result handler, and the result will be converted into an ArrayCollection and passed to the `model.userCollection` variable. Because the `model.userCollection` variable is bound to the `DataGrid`, the `DataGrid` will be populated with the users, as shown in Figure 8-14.

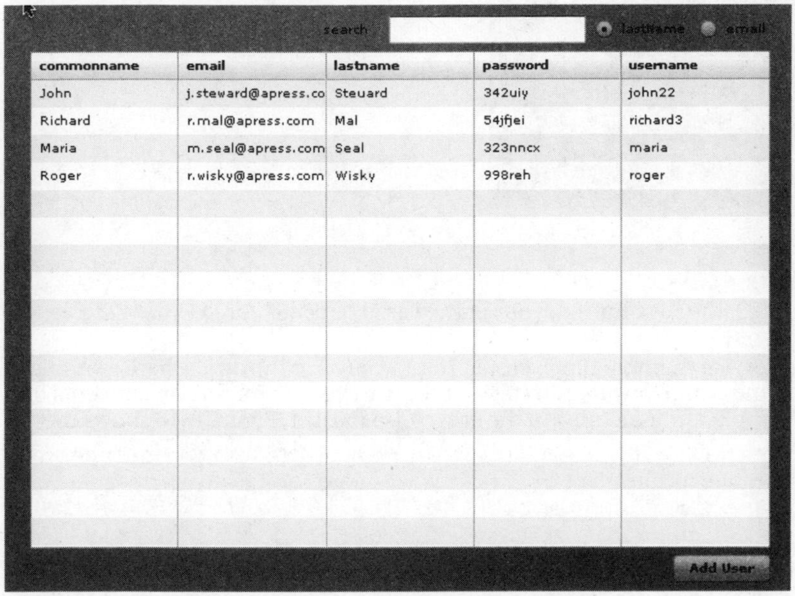

Figure 8-14. The DataGrid with the Add User button

When you click on the Add User button, you set the variable model.workFlowState to 1, and because the variable model.workFlowState is bound to the ViewStack (`<mx:ViewStack id="viewStack" selectedIndex="{model.workFlowState}">`), the ViewStack index will change from 0 to 1; because the index 1 of our ViewStack corresponds to the Form view, when you click on the Add User button you will see the Form view, as shown in Figure 8-15.

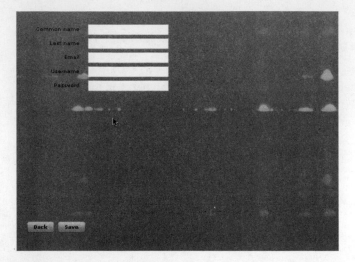

Figure 8-15. The Add User form

In the Form view, when you click the Save button, you set the variable model.workFlowState to index 0, the view that contains the DataGrid.

I could have made the HTTPService example much easier, but I wanted to introduce here a simple MVC pattern—the ViewStack and the workFlowState strategy—because they are important concepts for creating stable and maintainable applications, a must in the enterprise market. Figure 8-16 shows the example's entire tree.

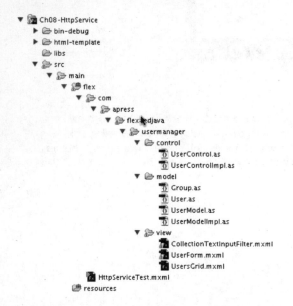

Figure 8-16. The complete application files tree expanded

As you can see here, we have created an interface and its implementation for each object. As I have already mentioned, this programming methodology is called "programming to interface." I will show just the classes added to the previous example. The classes CollectionTextInputFilter, UserForm,UsersDataGrid, User and Group have not been changed. Here is the complete code for the user implementation model—UserModelImpl.as and its interface UserModel.as:

```
package com.apress.flexjava.usermanager.model
{
        import flash.events.EventDispatcher;

        import mx.collections.ArrayCollection;

        [Bindable]
        public class UserModelImpl extends EventDispatcher implements UserModel
        {
                    private var _usersCollection: ArrayCollection;

                    private var _workFlowState : uint = WINDOW_LIST_USERS

                    public function set usersCollection (users : ArrayCollection) :
void{
                    _usersCollection = users;
            }

                public function get usersCollection() : ArrayCollection{
                return _ usersCollection;
            }

                 public function set workFlowState(value : uint) : void{
                 _workFlowState = value;
            }

        public function get workFlowState() : uint{
                return _workFlowState;
        }

        public static const WINDOW_LIST_USERS : uint = 0;

        public static const WINDOW_USER_FORM : uint = 1;


    }
}
```

And here is UserModel.as:

```
package com.apress.flexjava.usermanager.model
{
        import flash.events.IEventDispatcher;
```

```
import mx.collections.ArrayCollection;

[Bindable]
public interface UserModel extends IEventDispatcher
{
        function set usersCollection(users : ArrayCollection) : void;

 function get usersCollection() : ArrayCollection;

 function set workFlowState(value : uint) : void;

        function get workFlowState() : uint;

}
}
}
```

This is the complete code for the *controller*—the user implementation controller UserControlImpl.as and its interface UserControl.as:

```
package com.apress.flexjava.usermanager.control
{
        import com.apress.flexjava.usermanager.model.User;
        import com.apress.flexjava.usermanager.model.UserModel;

        import flash.xml.XMLDocument;

        import mx.collections.ArrayCollection;
        import mx.controls.Alert;
        import mx.rpc.AsyncToken;
        import mx.rpc.events.FaultEvent;
        import mx.rpc.events.ResultEvent;
        import mx.rpc.http.HTTPService;
        import mx.rpc.xml.SimpleXMLDecoder;

 public class UserControlImpl implements UserControl
        {

                private var model : UserModel;

                private var service    : HTTPService;

                public static const USERS_LIST_SERVICE_URL : String =
"http://localhost:8080/usermanager/getusers";
```

```
        public static const ADD_USER_SERVICE_URL : String =
"http://localhost:8080/usermanager/adduser";

        public function UserControlImpl(userModel : UserModel){
                model = userModel;
        }

        public function addUser(user:User) : void{
                var token : AsyncToken = getAddUserService(user).send( );
        }

        public function getUsers() : void{
                var token : AsyncToken = getListUsersService().send( );
    }

        private function getListUsersService() : HTTPService {
                var service : HTTPService = new HTTPService();
                service.url = USERS_LIST_SERVICE_URL
                service.method = "GET";
                service.useProxy = false;
                service.resultFormat = "e4x";
                service.addEventListener("fault", handleFault);
                service.addEventListener("result", handleResult);
                return service;
        }

        private function getAddUserService(user:User) : HTTPService {
                var service : HTTPService = new HTTPService();
                service.url = ADD_USER_SERVICE_URL + "?" +
buildUrlByUser(user);
                service.method = "GET";
                service.useProxy = false;
                service.resultFormat = "e4x";
                service.addEventListener("fault", handleFault);
                service.addEventListener("result", handleResult);
                return service;
        }

        private function buildUrlByUser(user:User):String{
                var url : String = "cn=" + user.commonName +
                                                "&ln=" + user.lastName +
                                                "&em=" + user.email +
                                                "&us=" + user.username +
                                                "&ps=" + user.password;
                return url;

        }
```

```
        private function handleResult(event:ResultEvent):void{
                model.usersCollection = xmlToArrayCollection(event.result as
XML);
        }

        private function handleFault(event:FaultEvent):void{
                Alert.show(event.fault.message);
        }

        private function xmlToArrayCollection(xml:XML):ArrayCollection{
                                        var xmlDocument:XMLDocument =↩
new XMLDocument(xml.toString());
                                        var xmlDecoder:SimpleXMLDecoder =↩
new SimpleXMLDecoder(true);
                                        var resultObj:Object =↩
xmlDecoder.decodeXML(xmlDocument);
                                        var tmp : Object = resultObj.users.user;
                                        return resultObj.users.user as
ArrayCollection;
        }
    }
}
```

And here is UserControl.as

```
package com.apress.flexjava.usermanager.control
{
        import com.apress.flexjava.usermanager.model.User;

        public interface UserControl
        {
                function addUser(user:User) : void;

                function getUsers() : void;
        }
}
```

Finally, here is the complete code of the Flex application file called HTTPServiceTest.mxml, which lets you test the new MVC application:

```
<?xml version="1.0" encoding="utf-8"?>
<mx:Application xmlns:mx="http://www.adobe.com/2006/mxml"
                        xmlns:view="com.apress.flexjava.usermanager.view.*"
                        layout="horizontal"
                        creationComplete="init()"
                        horizontalAlign="center"
                        verticalAlign="middle">
```

```
        <mx:ViewStack id="viewStack" selectedIndex="{model.workFlowState}">
            <mx:VBox horizontalAlign="right">
                <mx:HBox>
                    <mx:FormItem label="search">
                        <view:CollectionTextInputFilter tabIndex="1"

        collection="{model.usersCollection}"

        columnSearchable="{columnNameToSearch}" />
                    </mx:FormItem>
                    <mx:RadioButtonGroup id="searchMethodGroup"↩
  itemClick="handleSearchMethod(event)"/>
                <mx:RadioButton tabEnabled="true" tabIndex="2" label="lastName"↩
selected="true" groupName="searchMethodGroup"/>
                    <mx:RadioButton tabEnabled="true" tabIndex="3" label="email"↩
groupName="searchMethodGroup" />
                </mx:HBox>
                <view:UsersGrid dataProvider="{model.usersCollection}"
width="600"↩
 height="400" />
                <mx:HBox>
                    <mx:Button label="Add User"
click="{model.workFlowState =↩
 UserModelImpl.WINDOW_USER_FORM}" />
                </mx:HBox>
            </mx:VBox>
            <mx:VBox>
                <view:UserForm id="userForm" width="400" height="400" />
                <mx:HBox>
                    <mx:Button label="Back" click="{model.workFlowState
=↩
 UserModelImpl.WINDOW_LIST_USERS}" />
                    <mx:Button label="Save" click="{control.addUser↩
(userForm.user);model.workFlowState = UserModelImpl.WINDOW_LIST_USERS}" />
                </mx:HBox>
            </mx:VBox>
        </mx:ViewStack>
    <mx:Script>
            <![CDATA[
                import
com.apress.flexjava.usermanager.control.UserControlImpl;
                import com.apress.flexjava.usermanager.control.UserControl;
                import com.apress.flexjava.usermanager.model.UserModel;
                import mx.events.ItemClickEvent;
                import mx.collections.ArrayCollection;
                import com.apress.flexjava.usermanager.model.User;
                import com.apress.flexjava.usermanager.model.UserModelImpl;
```

```
                    [Bindable]
                    private var columnNameToSearch : String = "lastName";

                    [Bindable]
             private var model : UserModel;

             [Bindable]
             private var control : UserControl;

             public function init():void{
                 model = new UserModelImpl();
                 control = new UserControlImpl(model);
                 control.getUsers();
             }

                     private function handleSearchMethod(event:ItemClickEvent):void {
                     columnNameToSearch = event.currentTarget.selectedValue as
String;
                 }
             ]]>
         </mx:Script>
</mx:Application>
```

■ **Note** As I mentioned, I "program to interface," and for that approach I use an interface for each implemented class. It is common in AS to identify an interface with a capital I at the beginning of the name. For example `IUserModel.as` and `UserModel.as` should be the implementation. In Java, you add "Impl" at the end of the implemented class. I prefer the Java way, not because I'm a Java addict, but it seems cleaner, and it's good to keep the same style for both the server and the client.

In this section, I introduced many new concepts that are the basis of our Flex-Java development. In the next section I will show you how to use the RemoteObject instead of the HTTPService component.

RemoteObject Component

RemoteObject lets you access your server-side objects in a native way, which means you can access the Java object while maintaining its data type in AS and vice versa.

To use the RemoteObject, you need a data service server such as Adobe BlazeDS; this allows you to map a server-side object to your client-side object, and it automatically serializes them. For example, if you want to pass the AS User object to a Java method that takes the User as an argument and inserts it into a database or into an XML file, you just have to tell the compiler the mapping path between the AS and the Java User entity.

To Map an AS object to a server-side object, you can use the [RemoteClass] metatag, giving it the server-side object class path that you want to map. In the code listed below, you map the Java User entity (User.java), which is stored in the com.apress.usermanager.model Java package, with the AS User entity (User.as) stored in the AS com.apress.flexjava.usermanager.model package.

```
package com.apress.flexjava.usermanager.model
{
        [RemoteClass(alias="com.apress.usermanager.model.User")]
        public class User
        {
                public function User(){
                }

                public var uid          : String ;

                public var username     : String;

                public var commonName   : String;

                public var lastName     : String;

                public var email        : String;

                public var password     : String;


        }
}
```

The object on the server can interact in its native datatype for both requests and responses. RemoteObject saves a lot of development time because you don't have to expose the logic of the application as XML as you do when using the HTTPService component. Even if RemoteObject still uses HTTP to exchange data, communication is faster than using HTTPService because the data has serialized itself into a binary representation. This means that the object processing time is reduced, and the client memory use and the transfer rate are also less.

In the previous example, we dealt with server-side objects through a Java servlet consumed by the HTTPService component, appending all user properties on the URL. The next example shows how to get the same results using the RemoteObject component.

■ **Note** In this chapter I will show you just the difference between the two UserControlImpl classes using the HTTPService and the RemoteObject components. To see how to actually use this class, I refer you to chapters 9 and 10 where I will show how to configure the remote server to allow the use of the RemoteObject component.

```
package com.apress.flexjava.usermanager.control
{
```

```
import com.apress.flexjava.usermanager.model.User;
import com.apress.flexjava.usermanager.model.UserModel;

import mx.collections.ArrayCollection;
import mx.controls.Alert;
import mx.rpc.events.FaultEvent;
import mx.rpc.events.ResultEvent;
import mx.rpc.remoting.RemoteObject;

public class UserControlImpl implements UserControl
{
        private var model : UserModel;

        private var service   : RemoteObject;

        public static const USER_SERVICE : String = "userService";

        public function UserControlImpl(userModel : UserModel){
                model = userModel;
                service = getUserService();
        }

        public function addUser(user:User) : void{
                service.addUser(user);
        }

        public function getUsers() : void{
                service.getUsers();
        }

        private function getUserService() : RemoteObject {
                var service : RemoteObject = new RemoteObject();
                service.addEventListener("fault", handleFault);
                service.addEventListener("result", handleResult);
                return service;
        }

         private function handleResult(event:ResultEvent):void{
                model.usersCollection = event.result as ArrayCollection;
        }

        private function handleFault(event:FaultEvent):void{
                Alert.show(event.fault.message);
        }

    }
}
```

As you can see, the AS changes are very simple. I just added the mapping metatag to the AS User entity class and I switched the control class to use the RemoteObject component instead of HTTPService. Then I deleted code that was no longer needed, such as the xmlToArrayCollection and the buildUrlByUser functions that the HTTPService logic required. Figure 8-17 shows the differences in using the HTTPService and RemoteObject components.

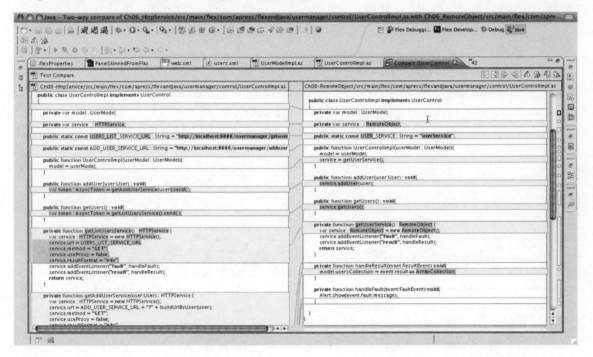

Figure 8-17. *Comparison of the HTTPService and RemoteObject controllers*

On the Java side, I don't need the servlet anymore; I can directly call the method addUser in the Java class as I did before within the servlet. The results are two servlets fewer, less code on the AS side, the advantage of working with the native User datatype on both server and client, greater speed over the wire, and a faster, more responsive client.

This doesn't mean that HTTPService is useless, but in our data-access strategy, we want to use it just for the services for which we can't use the RemoteObject components, such as for an RSS feed or a remote service. We will explore the server part of the RemoteObject example in Chapter 9 where we will call some Java methods using RemoteObject.

WebService Component

The WebService component allows us to consume Internet Web services—XML remote application interfaces that provide APIs to interact with the application itself.

The Web services XML interfaces define the methods that the application needs to share or make accessible over the Internet. You can access the Web service interfaces— called Web Service Description Language (WDSL)—via a standard URL. There are many free Web services, for weather forecasting, stock quotes, domain whois, language translators, and more. There are also community/reseller web services where you have to pay or join the community to consume the service. A typical example is the eBay developer program that allows you to build applications using eBay services, but you have to join to do so. You can read more at http://developer.ebay.com/developercenter/flex/toolkit/.

In the next example, I will invoke a simple, free web service just to show you how easy it is to consume it and get its response. With Flex, there are two ways to consume a web service: You can simply use the WebService component in MXML or AS classes; or you can use Flex Builder to auto-generate all the AS classes needed to use the WebService. Both ways are very easy to implement, and I suggest using the first one because it is easier to maintain and understand. However, when you need more powerful AS classes, you can use the Flex Builder option and auto-generate the classes.

■ **Note** The free web service we are going to use returns the public IP address of our machine. The WDSL URL is http://www.webservicex.net/geoipservice.asmx?WSDL.

If you put the WSDL URL into your browser, you should see an XML page describing all the WSDL definitions, as shown in Figure 8-18.

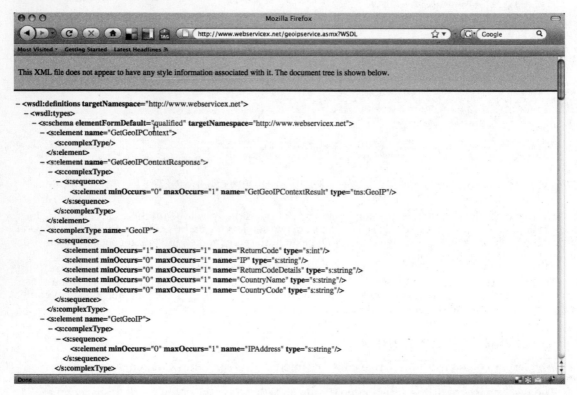

Figure 8-18. *Webservice WDSL definitions*

Reading the WSDL definitions can be difficult if you aren't familiar with the SOAP protocol, so Eclipse helps out by providing a tool that lets you browse the WSDL document and see the public methods.

Using Eclipse Web Services Explorer

To open the Eclipse Web Services Explorer, click on one of the icons shown in Figure 8-19, depending on which version of Eclipse you have installed. If you have Eclipse Galileo, you'll see the icon on the left. If you have an earlier version of Eclipse, you'll see the one on the right.

Figure 8-19. *Web Services Explorer icons in different versions of Eclipse.*

Then click on the WSDL page icon located at the top right of the new page opened, as shown in Figure 8-20.

Figure 8-20. *Using the Eclipse Web Services Explorer*

You should now see a TextInput box asking you to insert the WSDL URL (see Figure 8-21).

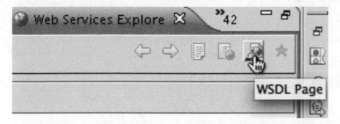

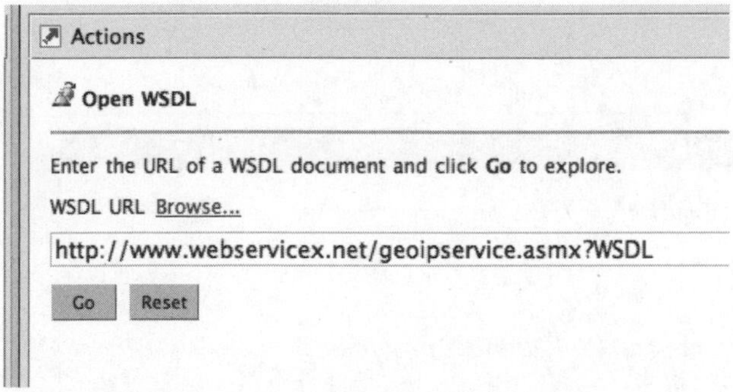

Figure 8-21. *Testing a WebService using the Eclipse Web Services Explorer*

Insert the URL http://www.webservicex.net/geoipservice.asmx?WSDL and click on GO. The Web Services Explorer will query the public service and retrieve all available services, as shown in Figure 8-22.

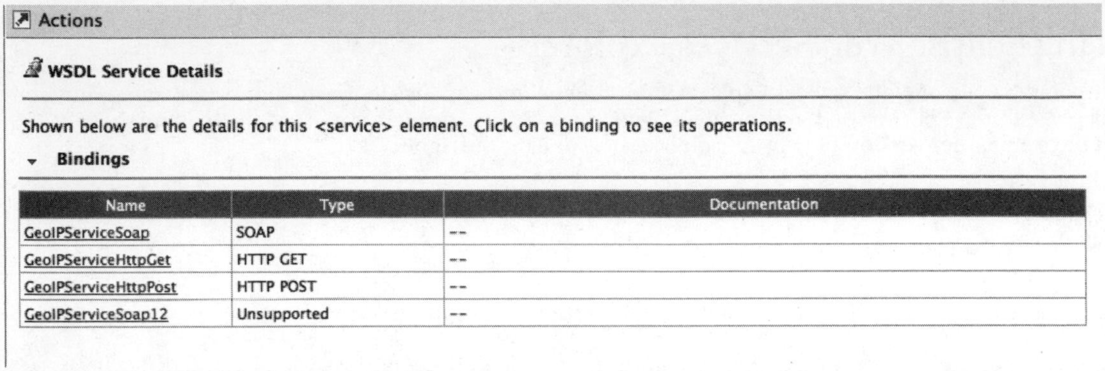

⌐ Actions

⚒ WSDL Service Details

Shown below are the details for this <service> element. Click on a binding to see its operations.

▾ **Bindings**

Name	Type	Documentation
GeoIPServiceSoap	SOAP	--
GeoIPServiceHttpGet	HTTP GET	--
GeoIPServiceHttpPost	HTTP POST	--
GeoIPServiceSoap12	Unsupported	--

Figure 8-22.Available services retrieved with the Eclipse Web Services Explorer

For our example, you have to choose the type SOAP by clicking on the corresponding hyperlink. This will display two operations (methods) with their descriptions (see Figure 8-23).

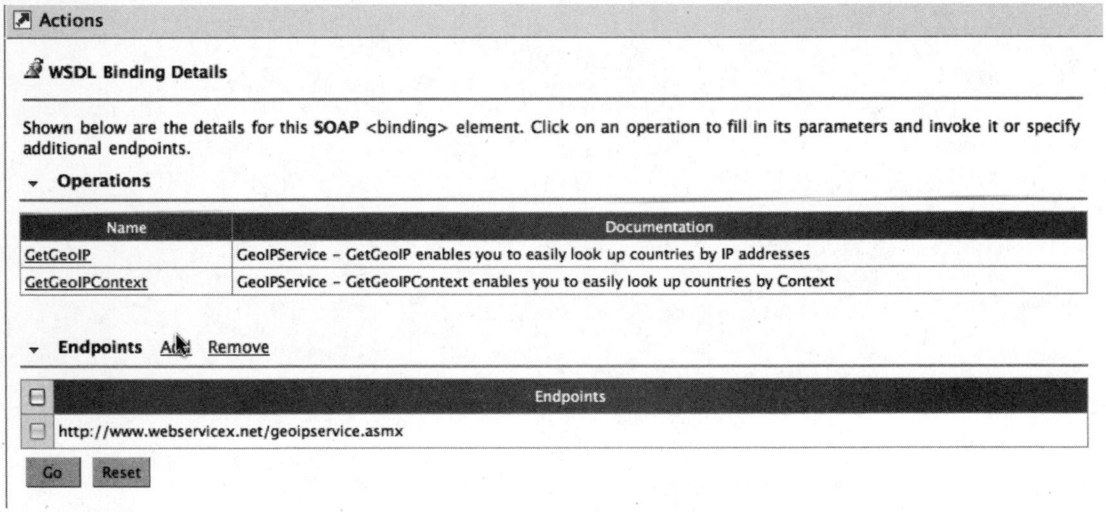

⌐ Actions

⚒ WSDL Binding Details

Shown below are the details for this **SOAP** <binding> element. Click on an operation to fill in its parameters and invoke it or specify additional endpoints.

▾ **Operations**

Name	Documentation
GetGeoIP	GeoIPService – GetGeoIP enables you to easily look up countries by IP addresses
GetGeoIPContext	GeoIPService – GetGeoIPContext enables you to easily look up countries by Context

▾ **Endpoints** Add Remove

☐	Endpoints
☐	http://www.webservicex.net/geoipservice.asmx

Go Reset

Figure 8-23. The two operations that GeoIpServiceSoap WebServices provides

You can look up countries by IP addresses using GetGeoIP, or by context using GetGeoIPContext. We will use the second operation GetGeoIPContext in our example.

Using the WebService Component

In this example, I will use the WebService component in MXML. The goal is to show the public IP address of my computer on the screen. To do this, I create a private variable called ip and bind it to a Label component:

```
<mx:Label text="My IP is:" />
<mx:Label text="{ip}" />
```

(As with the previous example, I will provide the full listing later in the chapter.) Next I create an instance of the WebService component and pass it the WSDL URL, the operation I want to use, and the handlers to handle the result or the fault of the operation:

```
<mx:WebService
        id="myService"
        wsdl="http://www.webservicex.net/geoipservice.asmx?WSDL">
        <mx:operation name="GetGeoIPContext" resultFormat="object"
            fault="{Alert.show(event.fault.faultString)}"
            result="getGeoIPContextHandler(event)"/>
</mx:WebService>
```

Here is the complete code:

```
<?xml version="1.0" encoding="utf-8"?>
<mx:Application xmlns:mx="http://www.adobe.com/2006/mxml"
                            layout="horizontal"
                            verticalAlign="middle"
                            horizontalAlign="center"
                            creationComplete="init()">

    <mx:Label text="My IP is:" />
    <mx:Label text="{ip}" />

    <mx:WebService id="myService"
                                        wsdl=↵
"http://www.webservicex.net/geoipservice.asmx?WSDL">
                            <mx:operation name="GetGeoIPContext"
resultFormat="object"
                                                        fault=↵
"{Alert.show(event.fault.faultString)}"
                                                        result=↵
"getGeoIPContextHandler(event)"/>
                </mx:WebService>
            <mx:Script>
        <![CDATA[
            import mx.controls.Alert;
            import mx.rpc.events.ResultEvent;
```

```
        [Bindable]
        private var ip : String;

        public function init() : void {
                myService.GetGeoIPContext.send();
        }

        public function getGeoIPContextHandler(event : ResultEvent) : void{
                ip = event.result.IP;
        }
    ]]>
        </mx:Script>
</mx:Application>
```

When I run the code, it will obtain my public IP address as shown in Figure 8-24.

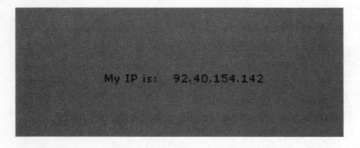

Figure 8-24. *The public IP address retrieved using the WebServices APIs*

Creating ActionScript Code to Consume a Web Service using Flex Builder

The other way to use the Web services is through Flex Builder. Let's create another application class called ASWebserviceTest.mxml. You know the routine: File ➤ New ➤ MXML Application. Then click on the menu bar and select Data ➤ Import Web Service (WSDL) as in Figure 8-25.

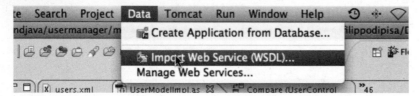

Figure 8-25. *The Eclipse "Import Web Service" wizard*

The Import Web Service wizard will prompt where you need to insert information. First, you have to confirm the project source folder, as shown in Figure 8-26.

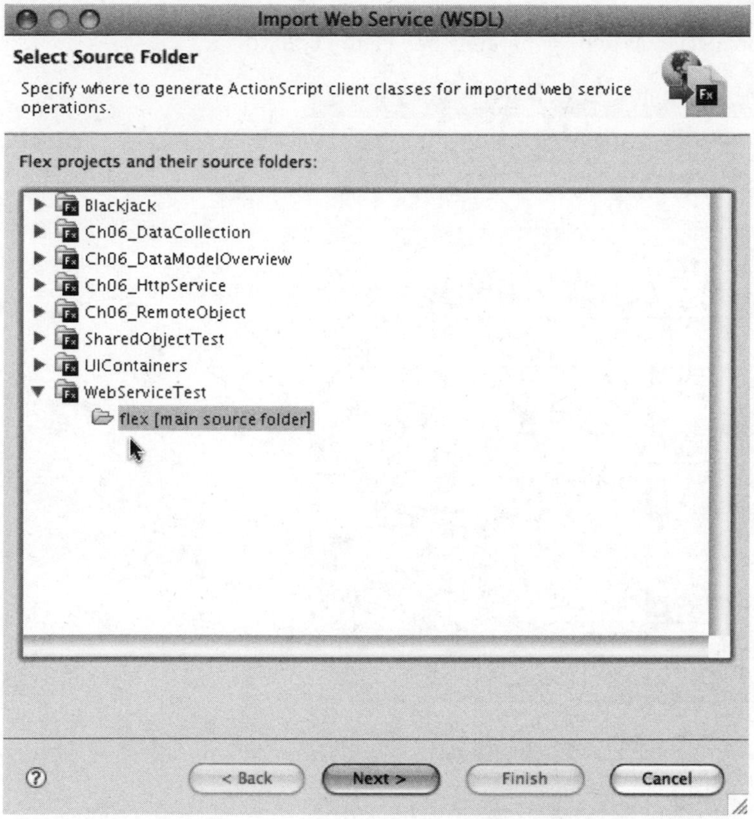

Figure 8-26. Setting the folder to store the classes generated by the WebService wizard

Next, you have to provide the WSDL URL as shown in Figure 8-27.

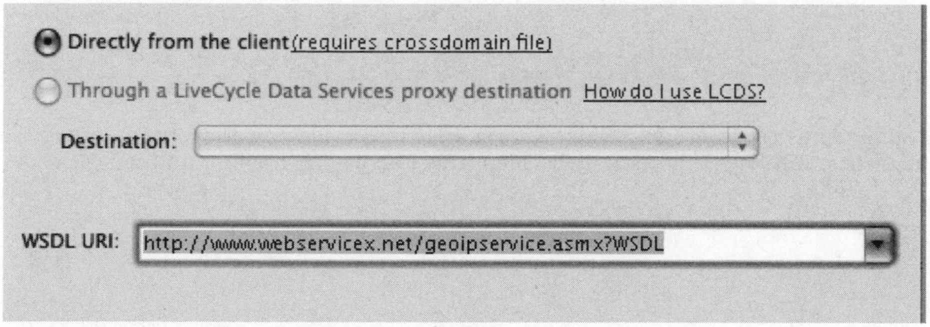

Figure 8-27. Setting the WSDL URI

Finally, you have to select the web service operations that you are interested in and give the package path and the Main class name for the AS classes to be generated (see Figure 8-28).

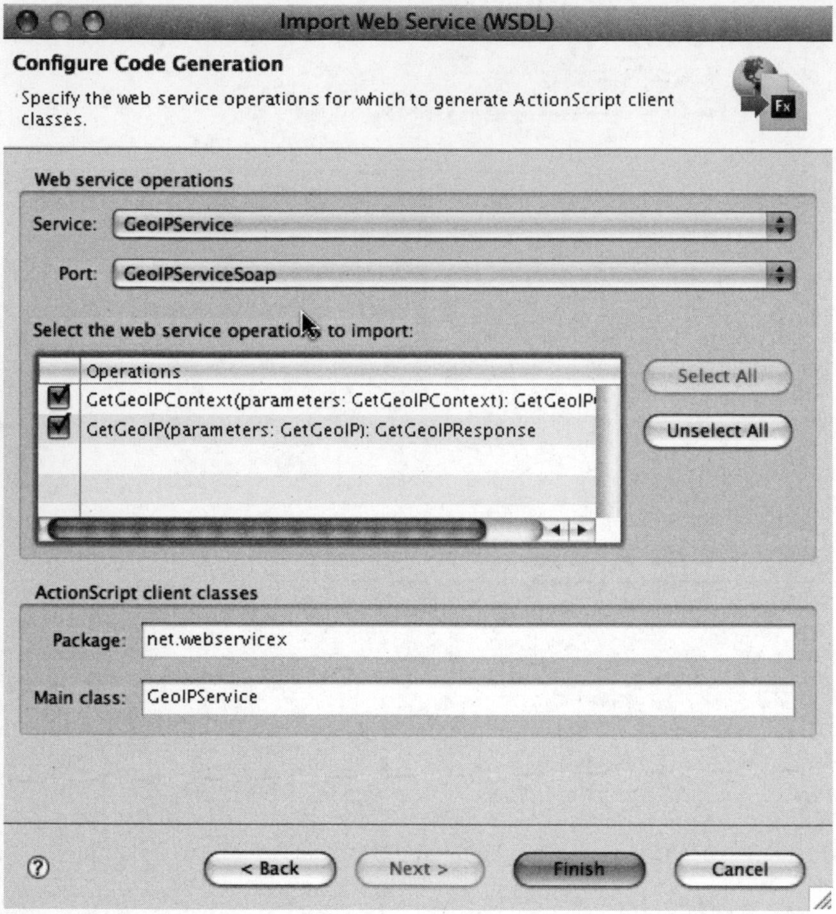

Figure 8-28. Selecting the operations to use in our classes

When you click on the Finish button, Flex Builder will generate all AS classes with instructions on how to use them. The instructions are in the Main class. Figure 8-29 shows instructions and sample code for GeoIPService.

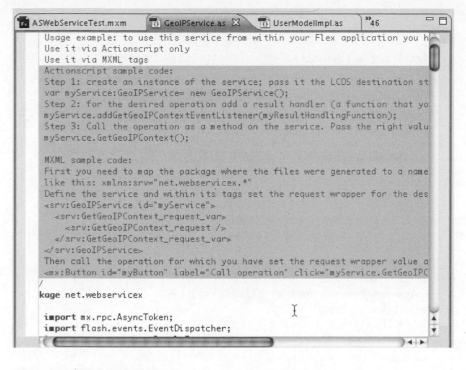

```
ASWebServiceTest.mxm    GeoIPService.as ✕    UserModelImpl.as   ⁷⁷46

Usage example: to use this service from within your Flex application you h
Use it via Actionscript only
Use it via MXML tags
Actionscript sample code:
Step 1: create an instance of the service; pass it the LCDS destination st
var myService:GeoIPService= new GeoIPService();
Step 2: for the desired operation add a result handler (a function that yo
myService.addGetGeoIPContextEventListener(myResultHandlingFunction);
Step 3: Call the operation as a method on the service. Pass the right valu
myService.GetGeoIPContext();

MXML sample code:
First you need to map the package where the files were generated to a name
like this: xmlns:srv="net.webservicex.*"
Define the service and within its tags set the request wrapper for the des
<srv:GeoIPService id="myService">
  <srv:GetGeoIPContext_request_var>
    <srv:GetGeoIPContext_request />
  </srv:GetGeoIPContext_request_var>
</srv:GeoIPService>
Then call the operation for which you have set the request wrapper value a
<mx:Button id="myButton" label="Call operation" click="myService.GetGeoIPC
/
kage net.webservicex

import mx.rpc.AsyncToken;
import flash.events.EventDispatcher;
```

Figure 8-29. Instructions for using auto-generated classes

Our goal now is exactly the same as in the previous example: we want to print our public IP address to the screen. The code will be very similar to the previous code, except that we will use the AS classes generated instead of the WebService component:

```
var myService:GeoIPService= new GeoIPService();
 myService.addgetGeoIPContextEventListener(myResultHandlingFunction);
 myService.getGeoIPContext();
```

We create an instance of the auto-generated Main class, GeoIPService, and then add an Event listener for handling the result. The rest of the code is the same as in the previous example. We simply assign the result to the ip variable that is bound to the Label component:

```
<?xml version="1.0" encoding="utf-8"?>
<mx:Application xmlns:mx="http://www.adobe.com/2006/mxml"
                    layout="horizontal"
                    verticalAlign="middle"
                    horizontalAlign="center"
                    creationComplete="init()">

    <mx:Label text="My IP is:" />
    <mx:Label text="{ip}" />
```

```
<mx:Script>
        <![CDATA[
                import net.webservicex.GetGeoIPContextResultEvent;
                import net.webservicex.GeoIP;
                import net.webservicex.GeoIPService;

                [Bindable]
                private var ip : String;

                 public function init() : void{

                        var myService:GeoIPService= new GeoIPService();

        myService.addgetGeoIPContextEventListener(myResultHandlingFunction);
                        myService.getGeoIPContext();

                }

                public function myResultHandlingFunction↵
(event:GetGeoIPContextResultEvent):void{
                        ip = event.result.IP;
                }

        ]]>
    </mx:Script>


</mx:Application>
```

Both ways are fine and easy to use. I prefer to use the first approach, instantiating the WebService component in AS rather than in MXML. The auto-generated classes solution is nice, even if the auto-generated code is not in the same style of your application. In the next section, I will show how to store data directly on the client machine.

Storing Data on the Local Machine

Flex provides a SharedObject class to store data on the hard drive of the user's machine. This solution is not suitable for our needs because the data is stored only on the user's local machine, not shared over the network/Internet. We could have used this solution in our previous example, but if we tried to see the application from another machine, we would get different results. Also, you can save only a defined amount on a user's local machine, depending on the FlashPlayer settings. For example, if the user configured his FlashPlayer to store just 10 KB, you can save a maximum of 10 KB and no more.

The shared object becomes useful when you have to store custom application settings or data on the client. It works like a browser cookie. Each application owns its shared objects and can access them only if they are running in the same domain. This is different from a cookie's shared object as it doesn't expire by default and is limited to a size of 100 KB compared to the much smaller browser cookie size of 4 KB.

■ **Note** If you use Flash Media Server, you can also store the shared object on the server for other clients to retrieve.

The next example will use the SharedObject class to store a shared object to the user's local machine in order to see the dates and how many times the user used the application. To show how the SharedObejct works, I have added a button that calls a function to delete the shared object from the local machine. To test it, refresh the browser repeatedly and you will see the date and the visit counter changing.

For the example, I created a Label component to which I bind the variable lastVisitMessage, and a Button that handles the function to delete the shared object from the user's local machine:

```
<mx:Label text="{lastVisitMessage}"/>
<mx:Button label="Delete Shared Object" click="deleteSharedObject()"/>
```

The variable lastVisitMessage will be set when the application has loaded, then the application will call the setSharedObject methods that create or update the shared object on the local machine:

```
private function setSharedObjet():void {
      sharedObject.data.lastVisitDate = new Date();
      sharedObject.data.counter = (getSharedObjet().counter ==
null)?1:getSharedObjet().counter + 1;
      sharedObject.flush();
}
```

Here is the complete code:

```
<?xml version="1.0"?>
<mx:Application xmlns:mx="http://www.adobe.com/2006/mxml"
                           creationComplete="init()">

  <mx:Label text="{lastVisitMessage}"/>
  <mx:Button label="Delete Shared Objed" click="deleteSharedObject()"/>

  <mx:Script>
        <![CDATA[

              public var sharedObject:SharedObject;

              [Bindable]
              public var lastVisitMessage:String;

              public function init():void {
                  sharedObject = SharedObject.getLocal("sharedObjectTest");
                  if (sharedObject.data.lastVisitDate==null) {
                      lastVisitMessage = "This is the first time that you⏎
 use this application."
```

```
                    } else {
                        lastVisitMessage = "This is the " + getSharedObjet().counter
+↵
" time that you used this application. Your last visit was on  " +
                            getSharedObjet().lastVisitDate;
                    }
                    setSharedObjet();
                }

            private function getSharedObjet():Object {
                return sharedObject.data;
            }

            private function setSharedObjet():void {
                sharedObject.data.lastVisitDate = new Date();
                sharedObject.data.counter = (getSharedObjet().counter ==↵
 null)?1:getSharedObjet().counter + 1;
                sharedObject.flush();
            }

            private function deleteSharedObjet():void {
                sharedObject.clear();
            }

        ]]>
    </mx:Script>
</mx:Application>
```

On refreshing your browser, you should see the counter and the date keep changing, as in Figure 8-30.

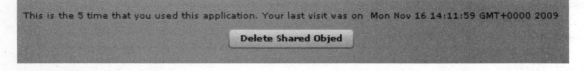

Figure 8-30. Storing a "cookie" on the local machine through the Flex ShareObject APIs

Summary

In this chapter I showed you the most important ways to structure the data on the client and to access data on a remote server. First, I showed you how to bind AS data collection to AS DataGrid components and how to create a real time search into the collection using filters. Next, I created a Java application that provided a list of users through servlets. The Flex client retrieved the XML using the HTTPService component. Finally, I showed you how you can use the Flex RemoteObject component.

In the next chapter I will introduce BlazeDS, the Java server that provides complete control over our Java application server —for instance, by allowing us to exchange objects between AS and Java and to push messages in real time.

CHAPTER 9

BlazeDS

In the previous chapter, I introduced the Flex `RemoteObject` component, but I didn't show you the complete process of how to build the server's application in order to allow the Flex client to use the Java native objects and services.

In this chapter, I introduce the BlazeDS server, a Java EE application that is useful in providing a set of services that allows you to connect multiple clients to a server-side application. Usually, a client is a Flex or an AIR application, which also supports JavaScript and Ajax combined with Flex, or as a stand-alone application. The examples will demonstrate how to use the Flex remoting services to retrieve and send data to a Java POJO web application, and how to use the Flex messaging services to update data in real time. We will implement a chat application where the two clients will exchange messages and display them in real time in a TextArea component.

Flex BlazeDS Architecture

As illustrated in Figure 9-1, a BlazeDS application consists of a client—typically developed using Flex, AIR, or Ajax—and a Java EE web application that contains the BlazeDS server. The BlazeDS server allows you to connect to a BlazeDS destination using the `RemoteObject`, `HTTPService`, or `WebService` Flex component.

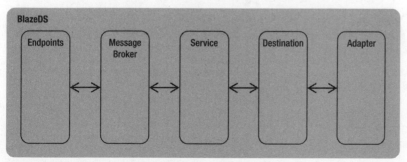

Figure 9-1. Flex BlazeDS architecture diagram

The Flex client makes requests over channels and routes them to *endpoints*. The request is then routed from the endpoints to a chain of Java objects, starting from the `MessageBrokerServlet` and ending at the adapter object, which is responsible for invoking the method on an object and returning the result. The endpoint extracts the message from the request, passes it to the message broker, and dispatches the message to a preconfigured destination. The destination is a kind of instance of the server-side services that you want to expose to the Flex client.

You could define all services and their destinations in the `flex-services.xml` file, but it is better to keep them in another file, such as `flex-remoting.xml`, and include this in `flex-services.xml` using the XML element `<service-include />`, as follows:

```
<services-config>
    <services>
        <service-include file-path="flex-remoting.xml"/>
    </services>
...

</services-config>
```

Adapters are responsible for contacting the back-end system and fulfilling the request. BlazeDS comes with a rich set of adapters, and you can also implement your own custom adapter if necessary to meet your needs.

Table 9-1 maps the Flex services to their corresponding BlazeDS destinations and adapters.

Table 9-1. *Flex Services and Their Corresponding BlazeDS Destinations and Adapters*

Flex Component	BlazeDS Destination	Adapter	Configuration File
HTTPService	HTTPProxyService	HTTPProxyAdapter	flex-proxy.xml
WebService	HTTPProxyService	SOAPAdapter	flex-proxy.xml
RemoteObject	RemotingService	JavaAdapter	flex-remoting.xml
Producer/Consumer	MessageService	ActionScriptAdapter/ JMSAdapter	flex-messaging.xml

Listing 9-1 shows an example of the `flex-remoting.xml` file with the `RemotingService` class and the Java adapter definition.

Listing 9-1. *Complete flex-remoting.xml File*

```
<?xml version="1.0" encoding="UTF-8"?>
<service id="remoting-service-@@messaging.id"
        class="flex.messaging.services.RemotingService">
    <adapters>
        <adapter-definition id="java-object"
```

```
class="flex.messaging.services.remoting.adapters.JavaAdapter"
                            default="true"/>
    </adapters>
    <default-channels>
        <channel ref="channel-amf"/>
    </default-channels>
</service>
```

In the next section, I will show you how to configure BlazeDS within a Java EE application using Maven.

Configuring BlazeDS

In order to use the BlazeDS services in your Java EE application, you need to take the following steps:

- Add the BlazeDS JAR files and dependencies to your WEB-INF/lib folder.

- Edit the BlazeDS configuration files in the WEB-INF/flex folder.

- Add the MessageBrokerServlet mapping and a session listener to the WEB-INF/web.xml file.

The BlazeDS JAR files and dependencies have already been published in the central Maven repository, so you don't need to download and install them in your local repository. To add the BlazeDS JAR files to your class path, include the dependencies shown in Listing 9-2 in your POM file.

Listing 9-2. Maven BlazeDS Dependencies

```
<dependency>
        <groupId>com.adobe.BlazeDS</groupId>
        <artifactId>BlazeDS-common</artifactId>
        <version>3.0</version>
</dependency>
<dependency>
        <groupId>com.adobe.BlazeDS</groupId>
        <artifactId>BlazeDS-core</artifactId>
        <version>3.0</version>
</dependency>
<dependency>
        <groupId>com.adobe.BlazeDS</groupId>
        <artifactId>BlazeDS-remoting</artifactId>
        <version>3.0</version>
</dependency>
```

■ **Note** There are Maven archetypes that automatically create the BlazeDS directory structure and POM configuration. In the next chapter, we will use an archetype that I have created to build a Flex-Spring-BlazeDS-

Hibernate project that will produce everything that you need in order to develop and run a project that uses this set of technologies.

Then you need to create a folder called `flex` in your `WEB-INF` directory. In your `WEB-INF/flex` folder, create the two basic BlazeDS configuration files:

- `flex-services.xml`-the configuration file where you define all elements needed to set up the connection, such as channels and other services configuration files. Listing 9-3 shows this file.

- `flex-remoting.xml`-the configuration file where you define the remote services classes and adapters to use with our connection. Listing 9-4 shows this file.

■ **Note** The standard code of both files typically comes with the default BlazeDS installation and/or with Maven archetypes. However, I'm demonstrating how to create them manually, so you are not totally dependent on automated tasks.

Listing 9-3. *BlazeDS flex-services.xml Configuration File*

```
<?xml version="1.0" encoding="UTF-8"?>
<services-config>
    <services>
        <service-include file-path="flex-remoting.xml"/>
    </services>

    <channels>
        <channel-definition id="channel-amf"
                            class="mx.messaging.channels.AMFChannel">
            <endpoint
                    url="http://{server.name}:{server.port}/↵
{context.root}/messagebroker/amf"
                    class="flex.messaging.endpoints.AMFEndpoint"/>
            <properties>
                <polling-enabled>false</polling-enabled>
            </properties>
        </channel-definition>
    </channels>

    <logging>
        <target class="flex.messaging.log.ConsoleTarget"
                level="Error">
            <properties>
```

```
            <prefix>[BlazeDS]</prefix>
            <includeDate>true</includeDate>
            <includeTime>false</includeTime>
            <includeLevel>true</includeLevel>
            <includeCategory>true</includeCategory>
        </properties>
        <filters>
            <pattern>Endpoint.*</pattern>
            <pattern>Service.*</pattern>
            <pattern>Message.*</pattern>
            <pattern>DataService.*</pattern>
            <pattern>Configuration</pattern>
        </filters>
    </target>
</logging>


<system>
    <redeploy>
        <enabled>true</enabled>
        <watch-interval>20</watch-interval>
        <watch-file>
            {context.root}/WEB-INF/flex/flex-services.xml
        </watch-file>
        <watch-file>
            {context.root}/WEB-INF/flex/flex-remoting.xml
        </watch-file>
        <watch-file>
            {context.root}/WEB-INF/flex/flex-messages.xml
        </watch-file>
        <touch-file>{context.root}/WEB-INF/web.xml</touch-file>
    </redeploy>
</system>
</services-config>
```

Listing 9-4. *BlazeDS flex-remoting.xml Configuration File*

```
<?xml version="1.0" encoding="UTF-8"?>
<service id="remoting-service-@@messaging.id"
        class="flex.messaging.services.RemotingService">
<adapters>
        <adapter-definition id="java-object"

class="flex.messaging.services.remoting.adapters.JavaAdapter"
                            default="true"/>
</adapters>
<default-channels>
        <channel ref="channel-amf"/>
```

```
    </default-channels>
</service>
```

In the flex-services.xml file, you first include the flex-remoting.xml file, and then define the channels that you are going to use in your connection.

In the flex-remoting.xml file, you define the RemotingService class, which informs a service adapter of the method to invoke in a service. In other words, when a remote destination gets a request, the RemotingService will invoke the defined adapter that is responsible for invoking methods and returning the result. Each destination has an adapter.

The channels elements can contain a set of channels for different goals. In this example, only one channel is defined, but you could have many other channels with different scopes. In the "Using Messaging Services" section later in this chapter, you will see how to set another channel in order to poll messages in real time between different clients. This means that you can update an object on a client, and the change will be dispatched to all other connected clients. The typical example of this is a chat application, which is the example presented in this chapter, but you could also use it for an application in which all clients need to see up-to-date data in real time, such as a poker game or a trading and stock information application.

The last step is to add the MessageBrokerServlet to your web.xml file, as shown in Listing 9-5. This basically starts all services and endpoints, and it is loaded by the standard class loader.

Listing 9-5. Complete web.xml File

```
<!DOCTYPE web-app PUBLIC
 "-//Sun Microsystems, Inc.//DTD Web Application 2.3//EN"
 "http://java.sun.com/dtd/web-app_2_3.dtd" >

<web-app>
        <display-name>Archetype Created Web Application</display-name>
        <context-param>
                <param-name>flex.class.path</param-name>
                <param-value>/WEB-INF/flex/hotfixes</param-value>
        </context-param>

        <servlet>
                <servlet-name>MessageBrokerServlet</servlet-name>
                <servlet-class>
                        flex.messaging.MessageBrokerServlet
                </servlet-class>
                <init-param>
                        <param-name>services.configuration.file</param-name>
                        <param-value>/WEB-INF/flex/flex-services.xml</param-value>
                </init-param>
                <init-param>
                        <param-name>flex.write.path</param-name>
                        <param-value>/WEB-INF/flex</param-value>
                </init-param>
                <load-on-startup>1</load-on-startup>
        </servlet>
```

```
    <servlet-mapping>
            <servlet-name>MessageBrokerServlet</servlet-name>
            <url-pattern>/messagebroker/*</url-pattern>
    </servlet-mapping>

    <welcome-file-list>
            <welcome-file>index.jsp</welcome-file>
    </welcome-file-list>
</web-app>
```

Once you have created the service configuration files, added the `MessageBrokerServlet` to the `web.xml` configuration file, and added all BlazeDS dependencies to your POM file, your application is ready to provide remoting services to your Flex client.

In the next section, you will implement the BlazeDS server in your user manager application. Then you will create Java classes that will expose the methods needed by the Flex client to retrieve all users stored in your `users.xml` file and to add new ones.

Using Remoting Services

The remoting service allows your Flex application to exchange ActionScript (AS) and Java objects in their native type in binary format. This means that you can pass the Java `User` object to the Flex client and have the same `User` object with all its properties translated in AS.

In order to use the remoting service, you need to configure at least a destination in the `flex-remoting.xml` file, where both the `RemotingService` class and the Java adapter are defined. The destination can be a single class, a bean, or even an object in a container and provided through a factory class. (In the next chapter, you will see how to use a Spring factory class to expose beans to the Flex client.) Here is an example of a destination using a simple Java class:

```
<destination id="userService">
    <properties>
        <source>com.apress.usermanager.service.UserServiceImpl</source>
    </properties>
</destination>
```

On the Flex client side, you use the `RemoteObject` component to connect to the remoting service destinations. In this example, you can access all public methods and properties of the `UserServiceImpl` Java class using the Flex `RemoteObject` component, as follows:

```
var service : RemoteObject = new RemoteObject("userService");
service.getUsers();
service.addEventListener("fault", handleFault);
service.addEventListener("result", handleResult);
```

You call the method `getUsers()`, which is defined into the `UserServiceImpl.java` class, and return a list of users, as follows:

```
public List<User> getUsers()
```

The Java method returns a List type of User that BlazeDS converts into an AS ArrayCollection in order to work with the Flex client that made the request.

Although BlazeDS and Flex provide functionality to serialize between AS and Java objects, you can use custom serialization by implementing the IExternalizable interface on your AS class and the interface Externalizable on your Java class, as shown in Listings 9-6 and 9-7. In these interfaces, you need to implement the methods readExternal and writeExternal on both Java and AS classes. Within these two methods, you can decide which properties and which types you want to serialize between AS and Java. This example serializes all properties as a String. In other cases, you might use another data type such as output.writeFloat(…), or you could decide to not serialize a property because you don't find it useful.

Listing 9-6. *Example of Using Custom Serialization in AS (User.as)*

```
[RemoteClass(alias="com.apress.usermanager.model.externalizable.User")]
public class User implements IExternalizable {
        public var commonName:String;
        public var lastName:String;

public function readExternal(input:IDataInput):void {
                        commonName = input.readObject() as String;
 lastName = input.readObject();
}

        public function writeExternal(output:IDataOutput):void {
                output.writeObject(commonName);
                        output.writeObject(lastName);
        }
}
```

Listing 9-7. *Example of Using Custom Serialization in Java (User.java)*

```
public class User implements Externalizable {
          public String commonName;
          public String lastName;

        public void readExternal(ObjectInput in) throws IOException,⏎
ClassNotFoundException {
                        commonName = (String)in.readObject();
                     lastName = (String)in.readObject();
        }

        public void writeExternal(ObjectOutput output) throws IOException {
            output.writeObject(commonName);
                        output.writeObject(lastName);
        }
}
```

■ **Note** Remember that you can also use BlazeDS with the HTTPService and WebService Flex components. Table 9-1 shows the BlazeDS destinations and adapters in order to use both components. Practically speaking, you can consume a WebService passing it through the BlazeDS server that proxies and fulfills the request.

Now you will implement the RemotingService on your user manager example application on both the Java and Flex sides.

Creating a Flex Java POJO BlazeDS Application

In the previous chapter, you created a Java web application that exposed two servlets to the Flex client in order to retrieve a list of users stored in an XML file, and allowed them to add new users to the XML. In this example, you will implement the BlazeDS server with the goal of exposing the new UserServiceImpl class to the Flex client, using the RemoteObject component to connect to the server.

The new classes will implement the Data Access Object (DAO) pattern explained in Chapter 5, as illustrated in Figure 9-2.

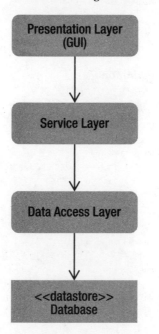

Figure 9-2. DAO pattern diagram

As explained earlier in the chapter, to use the BlazeDS server, you need to add all BlazeDS dependencies into your POM file, as shown earlier in Listing 9-2.

Then create a folder called `flex` in your `WEB-INF` directory. Within that folder, create the BlazeDS `flex-remoting.xml` and `flex-services.xml` configuration files. Figure 9-3 shows the directory structure, and Listings 9-8 and 9-9 show the contents of the configuration files.

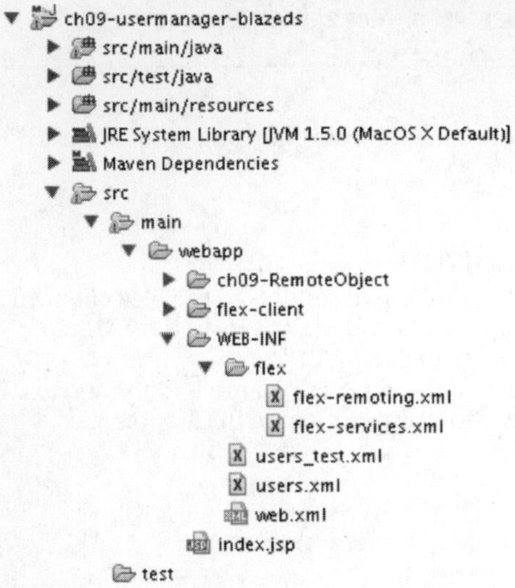

```
▼ 🗂 ch09-usermanager-blazeds
   ▶ 🗀 src/main/java
   ▶ 🗀 src/test/java
   ▶ 🗀 src/main/resources
   ▶ 🖳 JRE System Library [JVM 1.5.0 (MacOS X Default)]
   ▶ 🖳 Maven Dependencies
   ▼ 🗁 src
      ▼ 🗁 main
         ▼ 🗀 webapp
            ▶ 🗀 ch09-RemoteObject
            ▶ 🗀 flex-client
            ▼ 🗀 WEB-INF
               ▼ 🗀 flex
                     Ⓧ flex-remoting.xml
                     Ⓧ flex-services.xml
                  Ⓧ users_test.xml
                  Ⓧ users.xml
                  🖳 web.xml
            🖳 index.jsp
      🗀 test
```

Figure 9-3. Structure of the WEB-INF/flex folder containing the BlazeDS configuration files

Listing 9-8. Complete Code for the flex-remoting.xml BlazeDS Configuration File

```xml
<?xml version="1.0" encoding="UTF-8"?>
<service id="remoting-service-@@messaging.id"
         class="flex.messaging.services.RemotingService">
    <adapters>
        <adapter-definition id="java-object"

class="flex.messaging.services.remoting.adapters.JavaAdapter"
                            default="true"/>

    </adapters>

    <default-channels>
        <channel ref="channel-amf"/>
    </default-channels>

    <destination id="userService">
        <properties>
            <source>com.apress.usermanager.service.UserServiceImpl</source>
        </properties>
    </destination>
</service>
```

Listing 9-9. Complete Code for the flex-services.xml BlazeDS Configuration File

```xml
<?xml version="1.0" encoding="UTF-8"?>
<services-config>
    <services>
        <service-include file-path="flex-remoting.xml"/>
    </services>

    <channels>
        <channel-definition id="channel-amf"
                            class="mx.messaging.channels.AMFChannel">
            <endpoint
                    url="http://{server.name}:{server.port}/↵
{context.root}/messagebroker/amf"
                    class="flex.messaging.endpoints.AMFEndpoint"/>
            <properties>
                <polling-enabled>false</polling-enabled>
            </properties>
        </channel-definition>
    </channels>

    <logging>
        <target class="flex.messaging.log.ConsoleTarget"
                level="Error">
            <properties>
                <prefix>[BlazeDS]</prefix>
                <includeDate>true</includeDate>
                <includeTime>false</includeTime>
                <includeLevel>true</includeLevel>
                <includeCategory>true</includeCategory>
            </properties>
            <filters>
                <pattern>Endpoint.*</pattern>
                <pattern>Service.*</pattern>
                <pattern>Message.*</pattern>
                <pattern>DataService.*</pattern>
                <pattern>Configuration</pattern>
            </filters>
        </target>
    </logging>

    <system>
        <redeploy>
            <enabled>true</enabled>
            <watch-interval>20</watch-interval>
            <watch-file>
                {context.root}/WEB-INF/flex/flex-services.xml
```

```
        </watch-file>
        <watch-file>
            {context.root}/WEB-INF/flex/flex-remoting.xml
        </watch-file>
        <touch-file>{context.root}/WEB-INF/web.xml</touch-file>
      </redeploy>
   </system>
</services-config>
```

Once the two BlazeDS configuration files have been created, update the web.xml file by adding the MessageBrokerServlet and its mapping, as shown in Listing 9-10.

Listing 9-10. *Complete Code for the webapp web.xml Configuration File*

```
<!DOCTYPE web-app PUBLIC
 "-//Sun Microsystems, Inc.//DTD Web Application 2.3//EN"
 "http://java.sun.com/dtd/web-app_2_3.dtd" >

<web-app>
      <display-name>Archetype Created Web Application</display-name>
      <context-param>
            <param-name>flex.class.path</param-name>
            <param-value>/WEB-INF/flex/hotfixes</param-value>
      </context-param>

      <servlet>
            <servlet-name>MessageBrokerServlet</servlet-name>
            <servlet-class>
                  flex.messaging.MessageBrokerServlet
            </servlet-class>
            <init-param>
                  <param-name>services.configuration.file</param-name>
                  <param-value>/WEB-INF/flex/flex-services.xml</param-value>
            </init-param>
            <init-param>
                  <param-name>flex.write.path</param-name>
                  <param-value>/WEB-INF/flex</param-value>
            </init-param>
            <load-on-startup>1</load-on-startup>
      </servlet>
      <servlet-mapping>
            <servlet-name>MessageBrokerServlet</servlet-name>
            <url-pattern>/messagebroker/*</url-pattern>
      </servlet-mapping>

      <welcome-file-list>
            <welcome-file>index.jsp</welcome-file>
```

```
      </welcome-file-list>

</web-app>
```

As you can see, the `web.xml` file no longer contains the two servlets `GetUsers` and `AddUsers`, because now you are going to implement the `UserServiceImpl` class that exposes the `addUser()` and `getUsers()` methods to the Flex client, as shown in Figure 9-4.

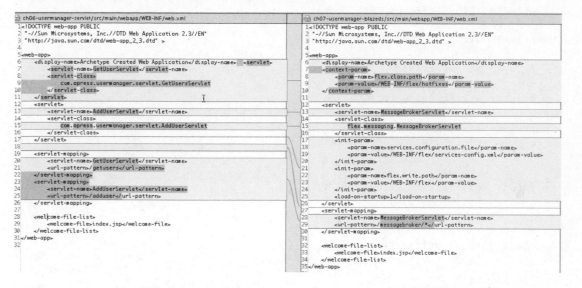

Figure 9-4. *Comparison between the web.xml file used in the previous example and the new web.xml that uses the remoting service*

Creating the Server Data Model

Creating the data model is quite easy, because at the end of the day, you just need the `User` entity. Before creating the entity, you need to create the data model package within your source folder, as shown in Figure 9-5.

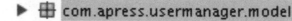

Figure 9-5. *Data model package*

Within the package `com.apress.usermanager.model`, create the `User` class, as shown in Figure 9-6. Listing 9-11 shows the code for `User.java` file.

Listing 9-11. *Complete Code for the Java User Entity*

```
package com.apress.usermanager.model;
```

```java
public class User {

    private String uid;

    private String username;

    private String commonName;

    private String lastName;

    private String email;

    private String password;

    public String getUid() {
        return uid;
    }

    public void setUid(String uid) {
        this.uid = uid;
    }

    public String getUsername() {
        return username;
    }

    public void setUsername(String username) {
        this.username = username;
    }

    public String getCommonName() {
        return commonName;
    }

    public void setCommonName(String commonName) {
        this.commonName = commonName;
    }

    public String getLastName() {
        return lastName;
    }

    public void setLastName(String lastName) {
        this.lastName = lastName;
    }
```

```java
    public String getEmail() {
        return email;
    }

    public void setEmail(String email) {
        this.email = email;
    }

    public String getPassword() {
        return password;
    }

    public void setPassword(String password) {
        this.password = password;
    }

}
```

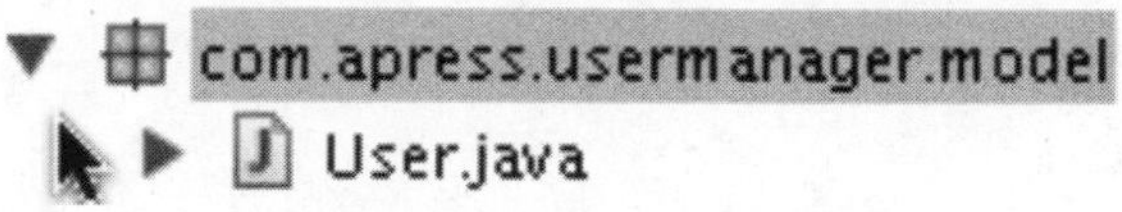

▼ ⊞ **com.apress.usermanager.model**
  ▶ ▶ 🇯 User.java

Figure 9-6. Data model package and User entity

Next, you will create the DAO layer.

Creating the DAO Layer

The DAO layer of the user manager example application consists of the UserDao interface, implemented by the UserDaoImpl class, which will deal directly with the XML file to retrieve and add users. Using the UserDao interface, you will be able to keep the same interface data type, even if you change the underlying DAO. For example, in Chapter 10, you will implement the same UserDao interface in your Hibernate DAO, so you won't need to adapt any classes that refer to the UserDao data types.

To keep the application scalable and tidy, you will create two packages, as shown in Figure 9-7:

- The com.apress.usermanager.dao package will store all interfaces of the DAO layer.

- The com.apress.usermanager.dao.xml package will store all DAO implementation classes dealing with XML.

Organizing the application in this way will allow you to easily implement other DAOs without affecting existing DAOs. For example, in Chapter 10, you will create a package called com.apress.usermanager.dao.hibernate, where you will store all your Hibernate implementation classes.

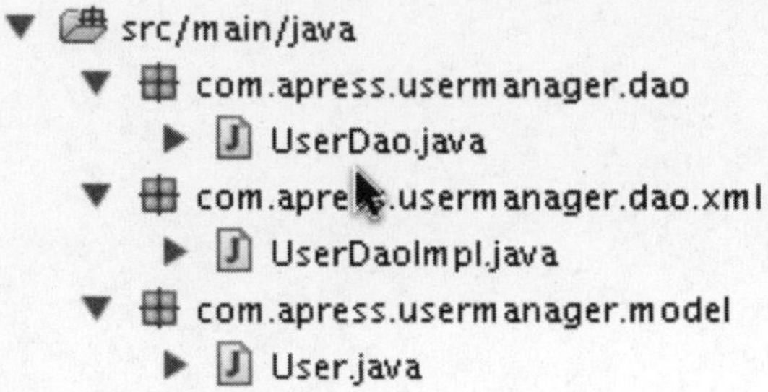

▼ 🗁 src/main/java
    ▼ ⊞ com.apress.usermanager.dao
        ▶ Ⓙ UserDao.java
    ▼ ⊞ com.apress.usermanager.dao.xml
        ▶ Ⓙ UserDaoImpl.java
    ▼ ⊞ com.apress.usermanager.model
        ▶ Ⓙ User.java

Figure 9-7. DAO packages

After you have created the two packages, create the UserDao interface and its implementation as shown in Listings 9-12 and 9-13.

Listing 9-12. Complete Code for the UserDao Interface

```java
package com.apress.usermanager.dao;

import java.io.IOException;
import java.util.List;
import com.apress.usermanager.model.User;

public interface UserDao {

        List<User> getUsers();

        List<User> addUser(User user) throws IOException;

        void removeUserByEmail(String email);

}
```

Listing 9-13. Complete Code for the UserDaoImpl Implementation Class

```java
package com.apress.usermanager.dao.xml;

import java.io.File;
import java.io.FileOutputStream;
import java.io.IOException;
import java.util.List;
import nu.xom.Attribute;
import nu.xom.Builder;
import nu.xom.Document;
import nu.xom.Element;
```

```java
import nu.xom.Elements;
import nu.xom.ParsingException;
import nu.xom.Serializer;
import nu.xom.ValidityException;
import com.apress.usermanager.dao.UserDao;
import com.apress.usermanager.model.User;


public class UserDaoImpl implements UserDao {

    protected File xmlFile;

    private String xmlFilePath;

    public UserDaoImpl(String filePath){
        xmlFilePath = filePath;
    }

    public List<User> getUsers(){
        return buildUserListFromXml();
    }

    public List<User> addUser(User user) throws IOException{
        try {
            Document doc = loadXml();
            Element root = doc.getRootElement();
            Element element        = xmlUserFactory(user);
            root.appendChild(element);
            saveOrUpdate(doc);
        } catch (ValidityException e) {
            e.printStackTrace();
        } catch (ParsingException e) {
            e.printStackTrace();
        }

        return getUsers();
    }

    public void removeUserByEmail(String email){
        List<User> users = getUsers();
        for(int i=0; i<users.size(); i++){
            if(users.get(i).getEmail().equals(email)){
                users.remove(i);
            }
        }
    buildXmlByList(users);
    }
```

```java
        private void buildXmlByList(List<User> users){
                Element root = new Element("users");
                Document doc = new Document(root);
                for(User user : users){
                        Element element              = xmlUserFactory(user);
                        root.appendChild(element);
                }
                try {
                        saveOrUpdate(doc);
                } catch (IOException e) {
                        e.printStackTrace();
                }
        }

        private List<User> buildUserListFromXml(){
                List<User> users = new java.util.ArrayList<User>();
                try {
                        Document doc = loadXml();
                        Elements elements = doc.getRootElement().getChildElements();

                    for(int i = 0; i<elements.size(); i++){
                            Element element = elements.get(i);
                            User user = new User();
                            for(int j=0; j<element.getAttributeCount(); j++){
                                    Attribute attribute = element.getAttribute(j);
                                    String attributeName =
attribute.getLocalName();

                                    if(attributeName == "commonname"){

        user.setCommonName(attribute.getValue());
                                    } else if(attributeName == "lastname"){

        user.setLastName(attribute.getValue());
                                    } else if(attributeName == "email"){
                                            user.setEmail(attribute.getValue());
                                    } else if(attributeName == "username"){

        user.setUsername(attribute.getValue());
                                    } else if(attributeName == "password"){

        user.setPassword(attribute.getValue());
                                    }
                            }
                            users.add(user);
                    }
                } catch (ValidityException e) {
```

```
                        e.printStackTrace();
            } catch (ParsingException e) {
                        e.printStackTrace();
            } catch (IOException e) {
                        e.printStackTrace();
            }
            return users;
    }

    private Element xmlUserFactory(User user){
            Element element              = new Element("user");
            Attribute commonName         = new Attribute("commonname",↵
user.getCommonName());
            Attribute lastName           = new Attribute("lastname", ↵
user.getLastName());
            Attribute email              = new Attribute("email",↵
user.getEmail());
            Attribute username           = new Attribute("username",↵
user.getUsername());
            Attribute password           = new Attribute("password",↵
user.getPassword());
            element.addAttribute(commonName);
            element.addAttribute(lastName);
            element.addAttribute(email);
            element.addAttribute(username);
            element.addAttribute(password);
            return element;
    }

    private void saveOrUpdate (Document doc) throws IOException {
        FileOutputStream fos = new FileOutputStream(xmlFile);
        Serializer output = new Serializer(fos, "ISO-8859-1");
        output.setIndent(2);
        output.write(doc);
    }

    private Document loadXml() throws ValidityException, ParsingException,
IOException{
            Builder builder = new Builder();
            xmlFile = new File("src/main/webapp/WEB-INF/"+xmlFilePath);
            return builder.build(xmlFile);
    }
}
```

The job of the UserDaoImpl implementation class is to create a list of User types from the XML file, which contains all user XML elements, and to add or remove new user XML elements to the file. For example, when you call the public method List<User> getUsers(), you first load all users from the

XML file, then create a collection of users, populating a Java list of type User List<User> with the elements retrieved from the XML file.

Next, you will create a JUnit test class to test all public methods in your DAO layer. If the tests pass, you can then continue with the example by creating the service layer.

Creating a Test Case Using JUnit

You should create a test class for at least each service or DAO class of your application. The UserDaoImpl test class must test all public methods and their results. With this class, you want to see if the method getUsers() returns a list containing all XML elements and if the method addUser() really adds a new element to the XML.

■ **Note** If you are new to Java, you may not be familiar with JUnit, which is a framework to write and run repeatable tests. Creating test classes allows you to keep your code under control by testing all of your application's code. If a test fails, it means that something has changed or that something is wrong. You will find it much easier to identify the problem.

You will use an XML test file containing four known users and use assertions to check if the getUsers() method is returning a List whose size equals 4, as follows:

```
public void testGetUsers(){
        List<User> users = userDao.getUsers();
        assertNotNull(users);
        assertEquals(4, users.size());
}
```

Before creating the test classes, you need to create the packages in which to store them. First, within the src directory, create a test directory to contain all test packages and resources. Then create a directory called java for storing your test classes (src/test/java). Next add src/test/jave as a source directory to the project properties. Finally, create the com.apress.usermanager.dao.xml test package within the src/test/java source folder.

Also, in your src/main/WEB-INF/ folder, create the user_tests.xml file containing the four test users, as shown in Listing 9-14.

Listing 9-14. Complete XML Code for the users_test.xml File

```
<?xml version="1.0" encoding="ISO-8859-1"?>
<users>
  <user commonname="John" lastname="Steuard" email="j.steward@apress.com"↵
 username="john22" password="342uiy"/>
  <user commonname="Richard" lastname="Mal" email="r.mal@apress.com"↵
 username="richard3" password="54jfjei"/>
  <user commonname="Maria" lastname="Seal" email="m.seal@apress.com"↵
 username="maria" password="323nncx"/>
```

```
<user commonname="Roger" lastname="Wisky" email="r.wisky@apress.com"↩
 username="roger" password="998reh"/>
</users>
```

Finally, create the `UserDaoTest.java` class within the package you just created, as shown in Figure 9-8.

Figure 9-8. *UserDaoTest.java and its package*

In order to create a JUnit test class, you need to extend the `junit.framework.TestCase`:

```
public class UserDaoTest extends TestCase {
…
}
```

To create a JUnit test class using Eclipse, select File ➤ New ➤ JUnit Test Case, as shown in Figure 9-9.

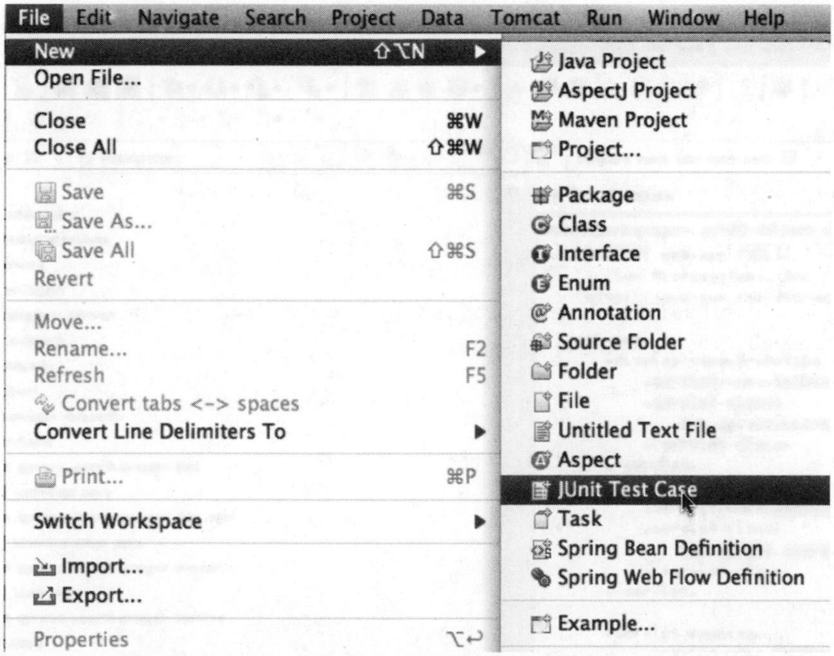

Figure 9-9. *Creating a new JUnit test case in Eclipse*

This test case will contain a setUp() method that will be executed before the other test methods to set up the entire test environment that you need to run the other tests. Then you will have the two test methods testGetUsers() and testAddUser(). Within the setUp() method is code to remove the new user recently added with the testAddUser() method, so your XML list always shows four users.

■ **Note** JUnit 3.8 requires you to add the word test at the beginning of the method that you want to test. With JUnit 4 and later, you can use annotation like @Test.

Listing 9-15 shows the complete code for the DAO test case.

Listing 9-15. Complete Code for the UserDaoTestCase Class

```
package com.apress.usermanager.dao.xml;

import java.io.IOException;
import java.util.List;
import com.apress.usermanager.dao.xml.UserDaoImpl;
import com.apress.usermanager.model.User;

import junit.framework.TestCase;

public class UserDaoTestCase extends TestCase {

        private UserDaoImpl userDao;

        private final String EMAIL_ADDED_USER = "dustin.robert@apress.com";

        protected void setUp() throws Exception {
                super.setUp();
                userDao = new UserDaoImpl("users_test.xml");
                userDao.removeUserByEmail(EMAIL_ADDED_USER);
        }

        public void testGetUsers(){
                List<User> users = userDao.getUsers();
                assertNotNull(users);
                assertEquals(4, users.size());
        }

        public void testAddUser(){
                List<User> users = null;
                User user = new User();
                user.setCommonName("Dustin");
```

```
            user.setLastName("Robert");
            user.setEmail(EMAIL_ADDED_USER);
            user.setUsername("dustin34");
            user.setPassword("43jh8978");
            try {
                    users = userDao.addUser(user);
            } catch (IOException e) {
                    e.printStackTrace();
            }
              assertEquals(5, users.size());
        }

}
```

The method testGetUsers() checks that the list is not null and is equal to 4. The method testAddUser() tries to add a new user to the XML, and then checks that the new list returned is equal to 5.

To run the test, right-click the test case, choose Run As, and then select JUnit Test, as shown in Figure 9-10.

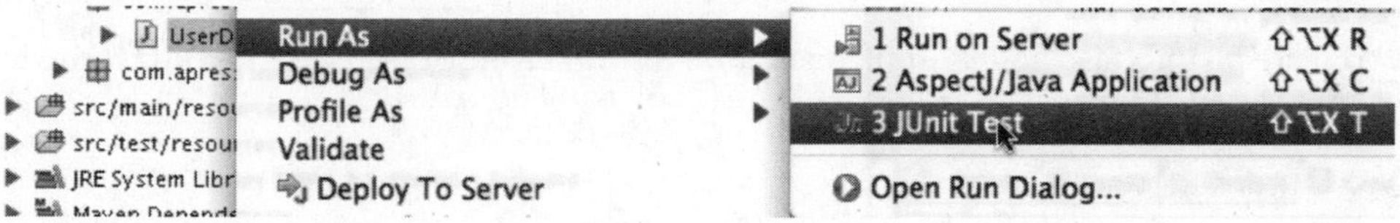

Figure 9-10. Running a JUnit test within Eclipse

If the tests ran without errors, you will see green checks next to them on the JUnit tab, as shown in Figure 9-11.

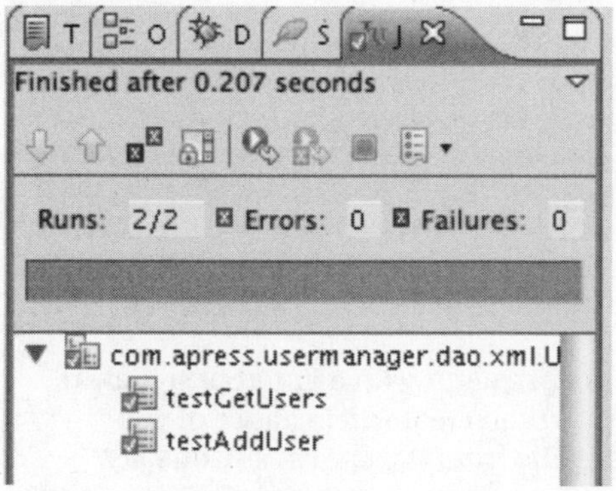

Figure 9-11. Eclipse JUnit tab showing all successful tests

Now that you've tested that your DAO layer is working properly, you can implement the service layer.

Creating the Service Layer

Finally, we have arrived at the service layer, which has all the services that you want to use with your Flex client. In this example application, creating the service layer will be very easy. Basically, it will just encapsulate the DAO public methods and nothing else:

```
public List<User> getUsers(){
        return userDao.getUsers();
}
```

However, keep in mind that a service layer usually does a lot more. For example, you could have a method addUser() that uses the DAO to store the user in the XML file or in a database, and then use the email services to send a confirmation email to the added user, as follows:

```
public  void addUser(User user) throws IOException{
        userDao.addUser(user);
        emailService.sendEmail(user);
}
```

You will also create an interface and its implementation for this layer. Unlike with the DAO layer, for the service layer, you will use one package for both files, as shown in Figure 9-12.

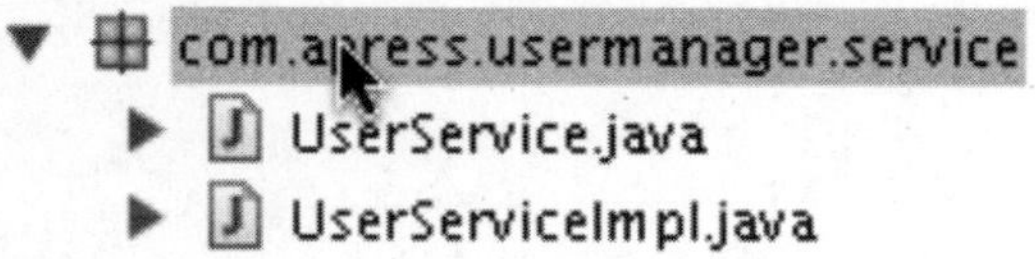

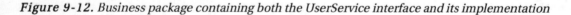

▼ ⊞ com.apress.usermanager.service
  ▶ 🗾 UserService.java
  ▶ 🗾 UserServiceImpl.java

Figure 9-12. *Business package containing both the UserService interface and its implementation*

The UserServiceImpl implementation will instantiate the UserDaoImpl class in the body of its constructor:

```
public UserServiceImpl(){
        userDao = new UserDaoImpl("users.xml");
}
```

This way, you ensure that every time you create an instance of the UserServiceImpl class, you will create an instance of the UserDao data type.

However, to keep the code scalable, you will create another constructor with a different signature that accepts as an argument a UserDao type object. That means you can create an instance of your UserServiceImpl by passing a userDao that uses a different XML file from the users.xml one, as follows:

```
public UserServiceImpl(UserDao userDao){
        setUserDao(userDao);
}
```

In Chapter 10, you will see how to use the Spring IoC container to inject all of your beans and let them be managed by the container. Using Spring, you can inject the UserDao to the container and then refer its instance to UserServiceImpl or other beans.

Listings 9-16 and 9-17 show the code for the interface and its implementation for the service layer.

Listing 9-16. *Complete Code for the UserService Interface*

```
package com.apress.usermanager.service;

import java.io.IOException;
import java.util.List;
import com.apress.usermanager.model.User;

public interface UserService {

        List<User> getUsers();

        List<User> addUser(User user) throws IOException;

}
```

Listing 9-17. *Complete Code for the UserServiceImpl Class*

```
package com.apress.usermanager.service;

import java.io.IOException;
import java.util.List;
import com.apress.usermanager.dao.UserDao;
import com.apress.usermanager.dao.xml.UserDaoImpl;
 import com.apress.usermanager.model.User;

 public class UserServiceImpl implements UserService {

        private UserDao userDao;
        public UserServiceImpl(){
                userDao = new UserDaoImpl("users.xml");
        }

        public UserServiceImpl(UserDao userDao){
                setUserDao(userDao);
        }

        public List<User> getUsers(){
                return userDao.getUsers();
        }
```

```
        public List addUser(User user) throws IOException{
                return userDao.addUser(user);
        }

        public void setUserDao(UserDao userDao) {
                this.userDao = userDao;
        }
}
```

Recall that when you created the `flex-remoting.xml` BlazeDS configuration file (Listing 9-8), you added a service destination referring to the `UserServiceImpl` class you just created:

```
<destination id="userService">
    <properties>
        <source>com.apress.usermanager.service.UserServiceImpl</source>
    </properties>
</destination>
```

Clearly, you can add all destinations that are needed, but for our little example, this will suffice.

Before running and testing the server, let's create a folder that contains the Flex SWF and HTML compiled file. Call the folder `flex-client`, as shown in Figure 9-13, and within it, store the `WEB-INF` root.

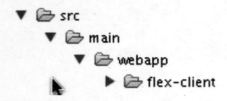

Figure 9-13. *The flex-client folder will contain all SWF and HTML compiled files.*

Now you are ready to run your application.

Configuring Eclipse to Run and Debug a Maven Application

You can run your server from the command line using the Maven command `mvn jetty:run`. Alternatively, you can run the server using just Eclipse, which is also useful when you want to debug your application.

The Maven Eclipse plug-in comes with a set of commands to build, clean, and install a Maven Java application, as shown in Figure 9-14.

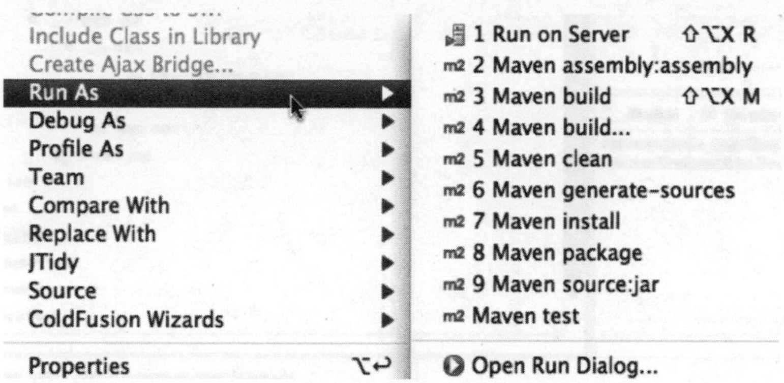

Include Class in Library
Create Ajax Bridge...

Run As ▶
Debug As ▶
Profile As ▶
Team ▶
Compare With ▶
Replace With ▶
JTidy ▶
Source ▶
ColdFusion Wizards ▶

Properties ⌥↵

▪ 1 Run on Server ⇧⌥X R
m² 2 Maven assembly:assembly
m² 3 Maven build ⇧⌥X M
m² 4 Maven build...
m² 5 Maven clean
m² 6 Maven generate-sources
m² 7 Maven install
m² 8 Maven package
m² 9 Maven source:jar
m² Maven test

▶ Open Run Dialog...

Figure 9-14. Eclipse set of Maven predefined commands

Unfortunately, it does not include a predefined command to run and debug a Jetty web application, so you need to configure it, as follows:

1. Open the Run dialog box by clicking the arrow next to the bug icon and selecting Open Run Dialog, as shown in Figure 9-15.

Ju 1 UserDaoTest
Fx 2 Chat
🗐 3 ch07-usermanager-blazeds
Ju 4 UserServiceTest
Fx 5 RemoteObjectTest
Fx 6 SharedObjectTest
Fx 7 ASWebServiceTest
Fx 8 HttpServiceTest
Fx 9 DataCollectionTest
Fx DataCollectionTest (1)

Run As ▶
▶ Open Run Dialog...
Organize Favorites...

Figure 9-15. Opening the Eclipse Java Run dialog box

2. In the launch configuration list, right-click the Maven Build application icon and choose New, as shown in Figure 9-16.

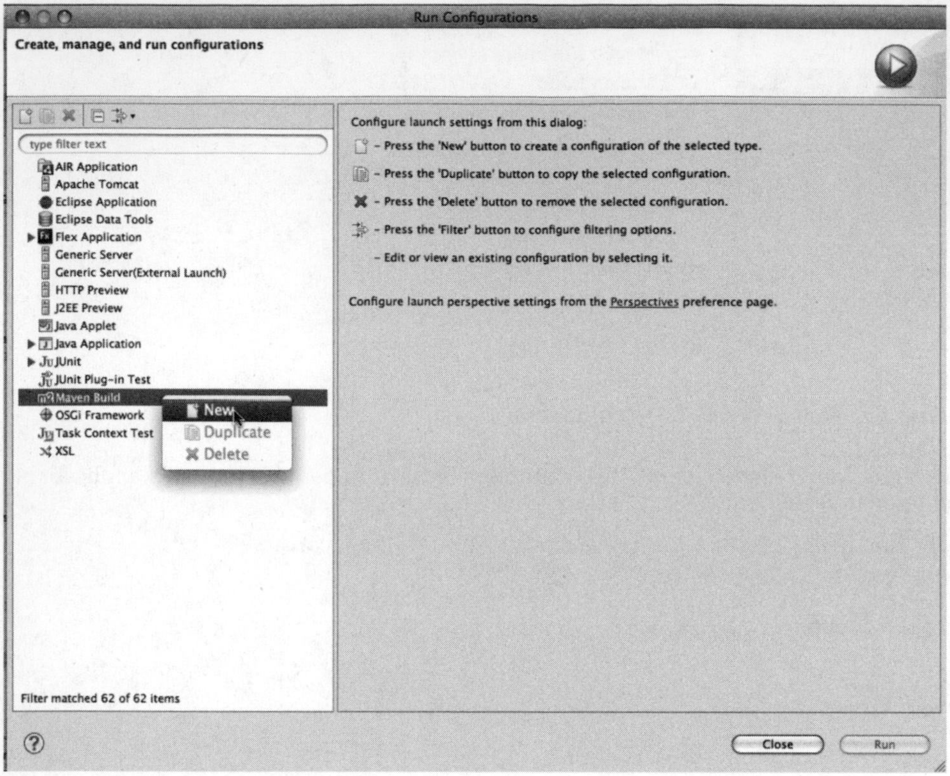

Figure 9-16. *Choosing to create a new configuration*

3. Specify the goals and the base directory of the project. The goal will be `jetty:run`, which will execute the Jetty Maven plug-in goal, as shown in Figure 9-17.

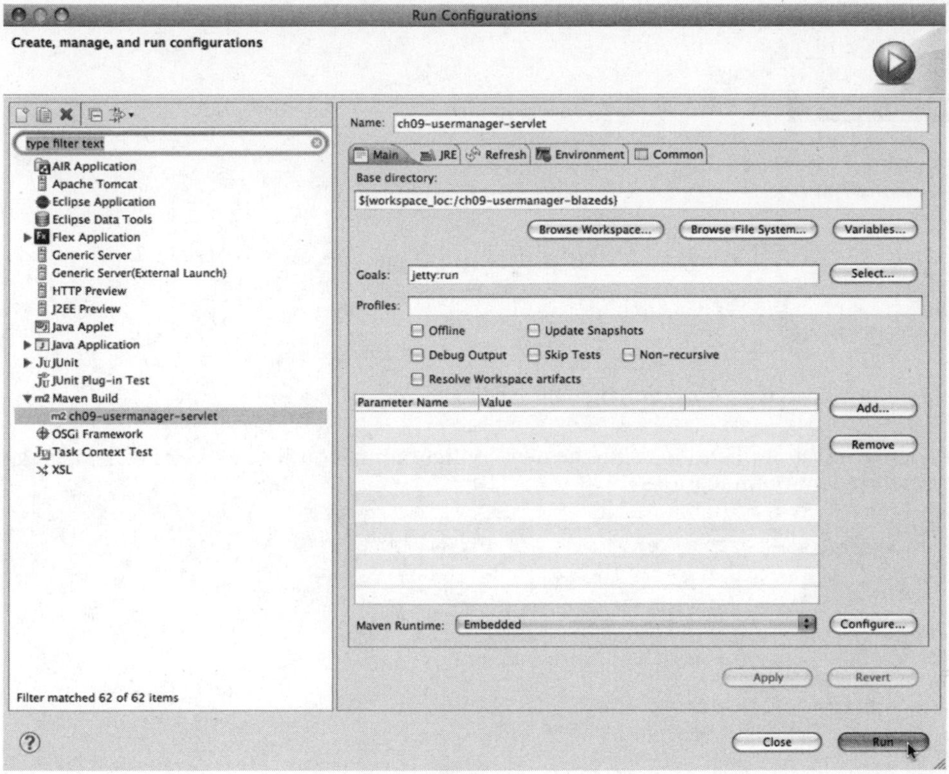

Figure 9-17. *Settings for the Maven Launcher*

　　4.　Click the Apply button to save the new configuration you just created.

Next you have to add to you POM file the maven-compiler-plug-in configured to use the version 1.5 of the Java SDK. Remember that each Maven plug-in must be defined within the `<plugins>` XML tag.

```
<plugin>
        <groupId>org.apache.maven.plugins</groupId>
        <artifactId>maven-compiler-plugin</artifactId>
        <configuration>
          <source>1.5</source>
          <target>1.5</target>
        </configuration>
</plugin>
```

Now you can click the Run button and use the configuration for both running and debugging your application, as shown in Figure 9-18.

Figure 9-18. *Debugging the application using the new configuration*

When you run or debug the application using the new configuration, you should see Maven logging in to the Eclipse console, as shown in Figure 9-19.

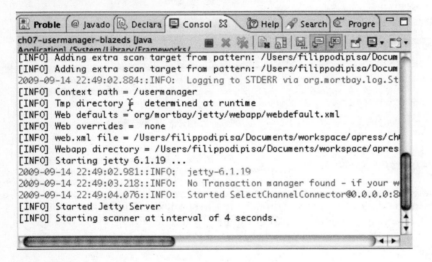

Figure 9-19. *Eclipse console showing the Maven project running with the Jetty plug-in*

Creating the Flex Client

The Flex client for this example will be the same as the one you created for the HTTPService example application in Chapter 8. The only differences will be the use of the RemoteObject component instead of HTTPService, and the mapping of the User entity with the Java User object. As explained in Chapter 6, you just need to replace the existing UserControlImpl code with the code provided in the "RemoteObject" section of that chapter, and then map the client entity with the remote server one using the RemoteClass metatag within the client entity:

```
[RemoteClass(alias="com.apress.usermanager.model.User")]
```

```
public class User{
}
```

The important change that was not covered in Chapter 8 is to configure your Flex project using a remote server. Usually, you can do this when you create a new Flex project by choosing the Java EE item within the Application Server Type combo box, and unchecking the "Use remote object access service" check box, as shown in Figure 9-20.

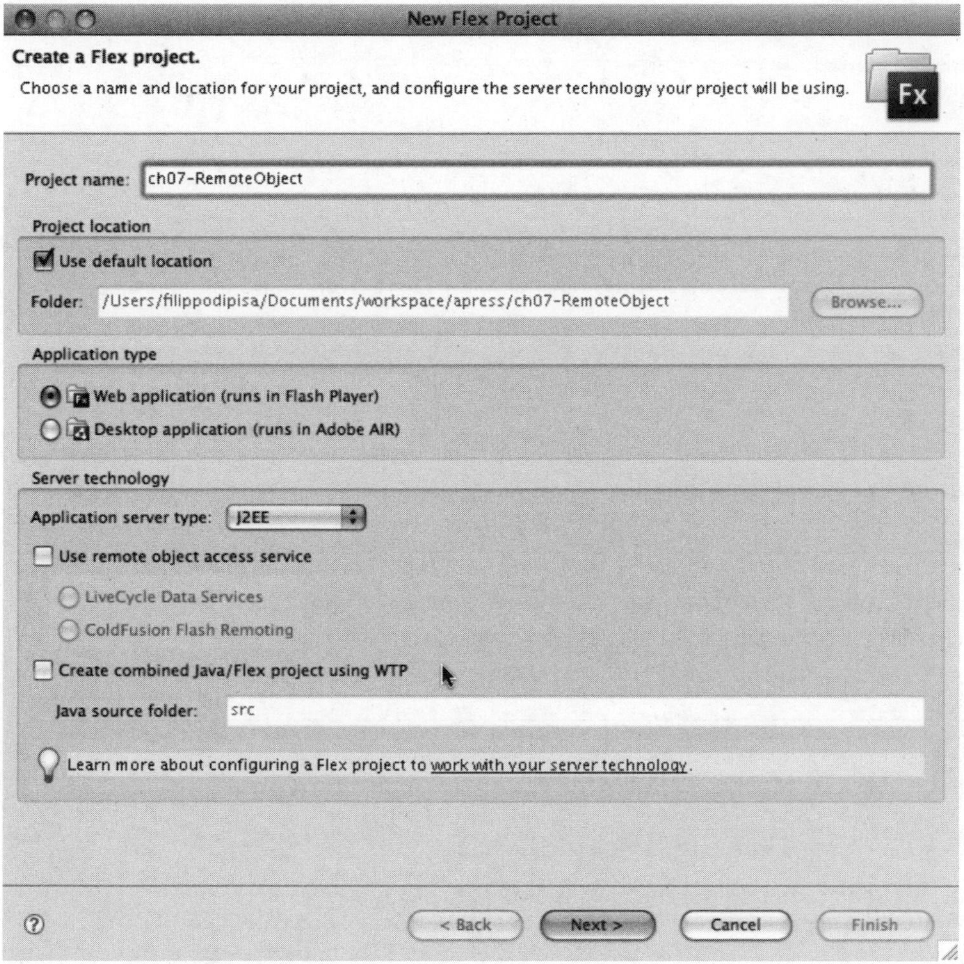

Figure 9-20. *New Flex Project dialog box with the server technology set to use Java EE as remote server*

In our scenario, you already have the Flex project, and when you created it, you didn't set a remote server. So when you view the project properties and select the Flex Server item, you are not allowed to set anything. So what can you do?

The solution is to edit the .flexProperties file located in the root of your project, as shown in Figure 9-21.

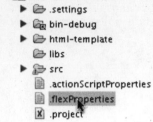

Figure 9-21. Edit the Flex project .flexProperties file to use a remote server

In order to be able to use remote server capabilities, you need to change the flexServerType value from 0 to 64, as shown in Figure 9-22. This setting will enable the Flex Server option in the project's Properties window.

```
Ch06_RemoteObject/.flexProperties                    Ch07_RemoteObject/.flexProperties
1 <?xml version="1.0" encoding="UTF-8"?>              1 <?xml version="1.0" encoding="UTF-8"?>
2 <flexProperties flexServerType="0" toolCompile="true" useServerFlexSDK="false" vers   2 <flexProperties flexServerType="64" serverContextRoot="/usermanager" serverRoot
3                                                     3
```

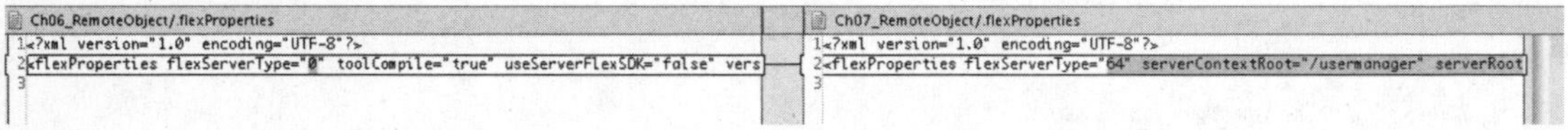

Figure 9-22. Changing the flexServerType value in the .flexProperties file

---

■ **Note** The Flex Server option in the project's Properties window presents the same options as the New Flex Project wizard. It contains the same settings that are available when you create a project using the remote service capabilities.

After editing the .flexProperties file, follow these steps to configure a remote server for the project:

1. In the project's Properties window, select Flex Server.

2. In the Flex Server window, provide the absolute path of your server webapp root folder, the application root URL, and the context root, as shown in Figure 9-23.

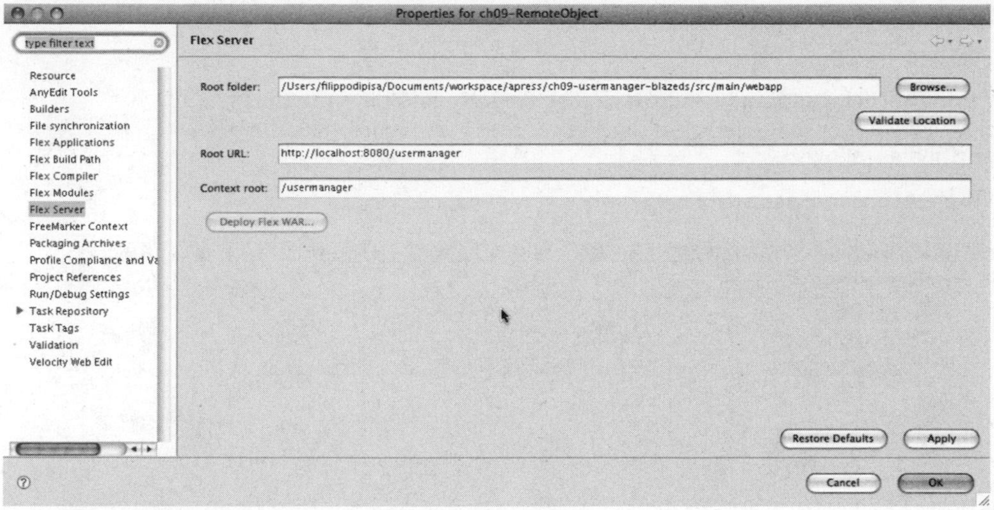

Figure 9-23. Flex remote server configuration settings

3. Click Apply.

4. Select the Flex compiler item from the list on the left.

5. Specify where the BlazeDS main services configuration file is located, in the form -services "{absolute path of you flex-services.xml}" -locale en_US. In Figure 9-24, this location is specified as follows:

```
-services "/Users/filippodipisa/Documents/workspace/apress/
ch09-usermanager-BlazeDS/src/main/webapp/WEB-INF/flex/
flex-services.xml" -locale en_US
```

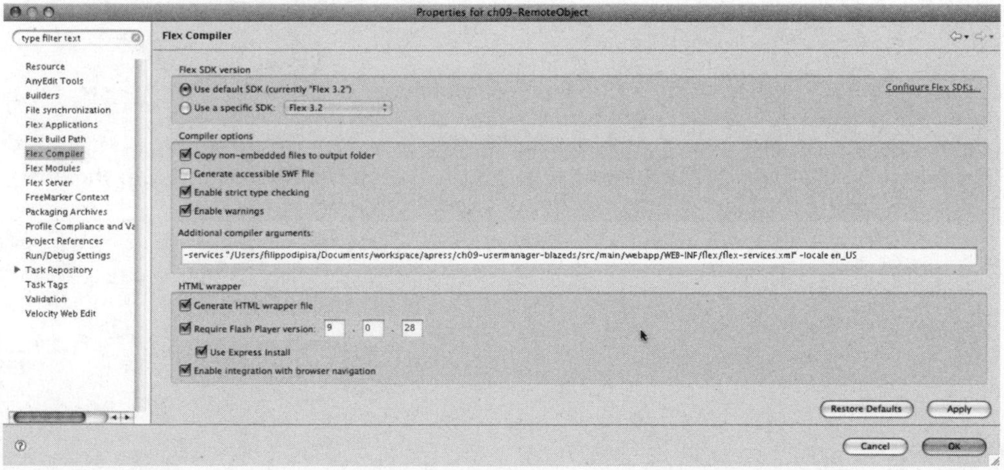

Figure 9-24. Flex compiler setting in order to use the remote server

6. Click Apply.

7. Select the Flex Build Path item.

8. Within the Flex Build Path window, change the output folder from the local folder `bin-debug` to the server folder `flex-client`. In Figure 9-25, this is specified as follows:

```
${DOCUMENTS}/ch09-usermanager-BlazeDS/src/main/webapp/flex-client
```

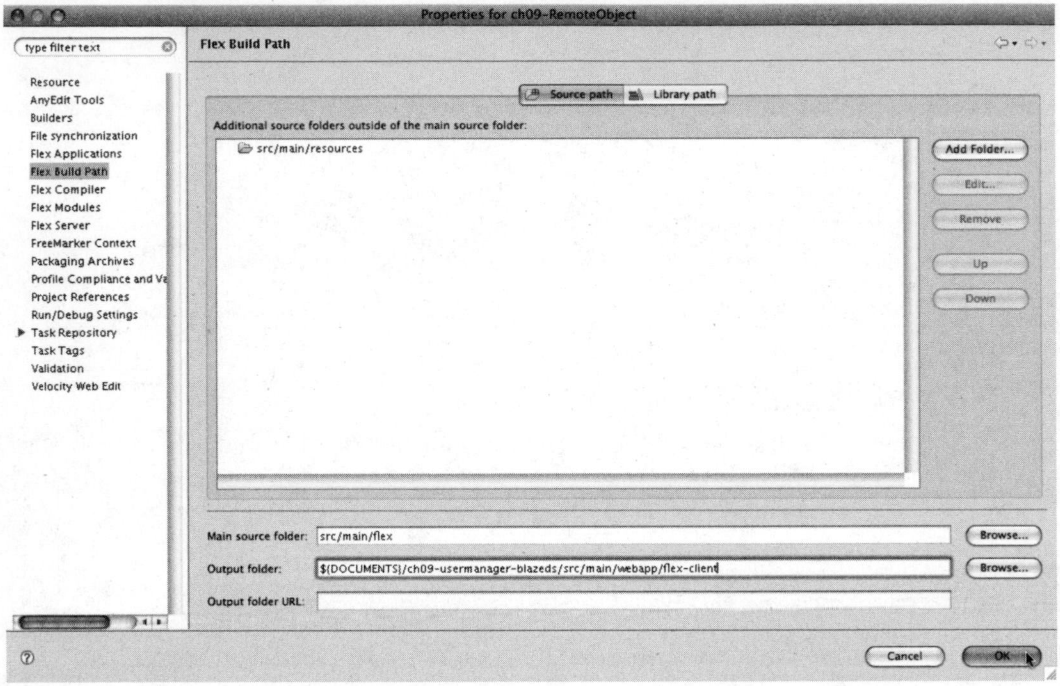

***Figure 9-25.** Flex Build Path window with remote server output folder configured*

Now you are ready to run and test the application. Be sure the server is running, and then change to the Flex perspective view, select your Flex application file, and run it as a Flex application. You should see the data grid listing all users, and be able to add new ones, as shown in Figure 9-26.

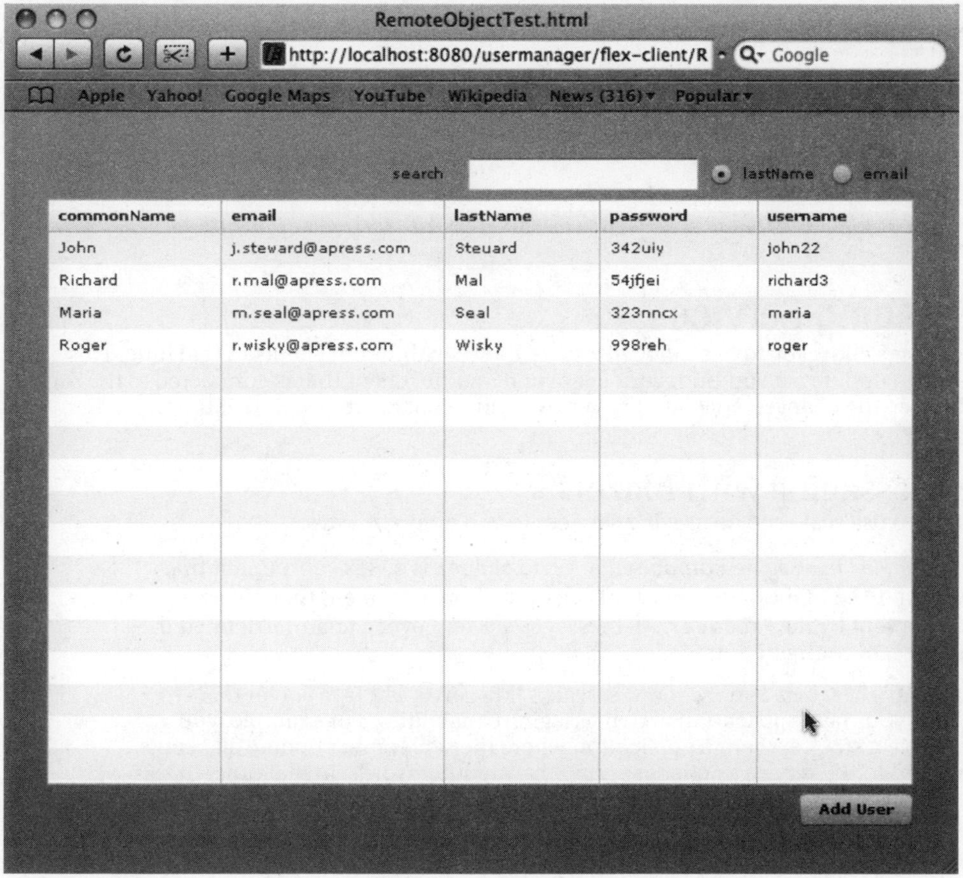

Figure 9-26. *Running your Flex application*

When you first start out, the configuration will seem annoying and long. But trust me, after you get used to it, the combination of these two technologies will improve your productivity, and it will open up new avenues for you, such as entertainment and marketing. This is because Flex is not just a user interface—it is also gaming, 3D, and much more.

When you are comfortable with all these new concepts, you can also use some of Maven's other plug-ins and dependencies, such as the Sonatype `flex-mojo` one, to build both the client and server at the same time. If you go for this solution, I suggest you always keep the Flex project separated from the Java project, and create a new Maven parent project that includes both. In that case, you can use Maven to run both projects in one go, but you will still have the two projects separated in order to use other Flex Builder capabilities, such as debugging or the Flex Web AIR pattern, which allows you to share the core of your Flex application with the web and desktop versions, as shown in Figure 9-27.

Figure 9-27. *A Flex application that is sharing its code with an AIR and web application*

Using Messaging Services

The messaging services allow you to exchange messages between different clients in real time. This means you are able to update data on both your client and another client that is connected to the same server, so that they see the changes, such as changes to a data set or an object, in real time.

Real-Time Messaging with BlazeDS

BlazeDS allows you to use real-time messaging services in two different ways:

- *Using the Flex messaging components:* mx.Producer is a Flex component that allows you to send messages. mx.Consumer is a Flex component that receives messages sent by the Producer. All messages are sent over a channel defined in your BlazeDS configuration file.

- *Using a Java Message Service (JMS) server:* A JMS server is a Java server that provides your Java application with messaging capabilities. For example, you could have a stock exchange application where the server must update all clients connected to the service as changes happen— in other words, in real time. In this case, the Java server is responsible for retrieving all data and then sending a message to all clients connected using a JMS server.

In the next section, I will show you how to implement a basic chat application using the Flex mx.Producer and mx.Consumer messaging components.

Creating a Simple Chat Application

Creating a basic chat application is a good way to understand how to use the Flex mx.Producer and mx.Consumer components to exchange real-time messages using the BlazeDS server. Although the example just exchanges simple text messages, you can apply the same implementation and configuration techniques to an application that exchanges more complex objects, such as data model entity objects.

In order to create the chat application example, you need to create a Maven project that contains the BlazeDS dependencies. Then you need to create the BlazeDS configuration files in order to configure the channels and adapters for working with real-time messages.

When you are happy with your server setup, you can create a simple Flex project using just MXML application classes containing the mx.Consumer and mx.Producer components, and TextArea and TextInput components, in order to send and receive messages.

Creating and Configuring the Maven BlazeDS Project

In the previous example, you created a BlazeDS application that was configured to work with the remoting services. To use the real-time messaging services, you just need to add a new configuration file, `flex-messages.xml`, in which you set the real-time message configuration. The new configuration file is imported into your main service configuration file, specifying the new services channel definition and endpoints. However, although it's not necessary, I think it is better (best practice) to create a new Maven project and add the BlazeDS Maven dependencies, plus the Jetty plug-in that allows you to start the application and test it, using your Flex client.

So let's create a new Maven project called ch09-chat-blazeds as we learnt in the chapter 8.

Then we have to configure the POM XML file with all dependencies and Maven plug-ins needed by the application such as the BlazeDS dependencies and the Jetty plug-in.

Listing 9-18 shows the complete code for this example's POM file.

Listing 9-18. Complete Code for the pom.xml File

```
<project xmlns="http://maven.apache.org/POM/4.0.0"
        xmlns:xsi="http://www.w3.org/2001/XMLSchema-instance"
        xsi:schemaLocation="http://maven.apache.org/POM/4.0.0
http://maven.apache.org/maven-v4_0_0.xsd">
        <modelVersion>4.0.0</modelVersion>
        <groupId>com.apress</groupId>
        <artifactId>ch09-chat-blazeds</artifactId>
        <packaging>war</packaging>
        <version>0.0.1-SNAPSHOT</version>
        <name>ch09-chat-blazeds Maven Webapp</name>
        <url>http://maven.apache.org</url>
        <dependencies>
                <dependency>
                        <groupId>junit</groupId>
                        <artifactId>junit</artifactId>
                        <version>3.8.1</version>
                         <scope>test</scope>
                </dependency>
                <dependency>
                        <groupId>javax.servlet</groupId>
                        <artifactId>servlet-api</artifactId>
                        <version>2.5</version>
                        <scope>provided</scope>
                </dependency>

                <dependency>
                  <groupId>com.adobe.blazeds</groupId>
                  <artifactId>blazeds-common</artifactId>
                  <version>3.0</version>
                </dependency>
                <dependency>
                   <groupId>com.adobe.blazeds</groupId>
```

```
        <artifactId>blazeds-core</artifactId>
        <version>3.0</version>
</dependency>
<dependency>
        <groupId>com.adobe.blazeds</groupId>
        <artifactId>blazeds-remoting</artifactId>
        <version>3.0</version>
</dependency>

</dependencies>
<build>
        <finalName>ch09-chat-blazeds</finalName>
        <plugins>
                <plugin>
                    <groupId>org.mortbay.jetty</groupId>
                    <artifactId>maven-jetty-plugin</artifactId>
                    <version>6.1.19</version>
                    <configuration>
                            <contextPath>/chat</contextPath>
                            <scanIntervalSeconds>4</scanIntervalSeconds>
                            <scanTargetPatterns>
                                    <scanTargetPattern>
                                            <directory>
                                                    src/main/webapp/WEB-INF
                                            </directory>
                                            <excludes>

<exclude>**/*.jsp</exclude>

                                            </excludes>
                                            <includes>

<include>**/*.properties</include>

<include>**/*.xml</include>
                                            </includes>
                                    </scanTargetPattern>
                            </scanTargetPatterns>
                    </configuration>
                </plugin>

        </plugins>

</build>
</project>
```

Next, create a folder called flex to hold your BlazeDS configuration files.

In the new flex-messages.xml file, add all the XML definitions to tell BlazeDS to use the flex.messaging.services.messaging.adapters.ActionScriptAdapter and the channel called channel-polling-amf.

Then add some new XML definitions in the flex-services.xml file, to tell the BlazeDS server the channel for real-time messages, its endpoints, and some properties, such the message polling interval time, as shown in Listing 9-19 with the channel-polling-amf definition.

Listing 9-19. *Real-Time Messaging XML Definitions in the flex-services.xml File*

```
<?xml version="1.0" encoding="UTF-8"?>
<services-config>
    <services>
        <service-include file-path="flex-remoting.xml" />
        <service-include file-path="flex-messages.xml" />
    </services>

    <channels>
        <channel-definition id="channel-amf"
            class="mx.messaging.channels.AMFChannel">
            <endpoint

url="http://{server.name}:{server.port}/{context.root}/messagebroker/amf"
                class="flex.messaging.endpoints.AMFEndpoint" />
            <properties>
                <polling-enabled>false</polling-enabled>
            </properties>
        </channel-definition>
        <channel-definition id="channel-polling-amf"
            class="mx.messaging.channels.AMFChannel">
            <endpoint

url="http://{server.name}:{server.port}/{context.root}/messagebroker/
amfpolling"
                class="flex.messaging.endpoints.AMFEndpoint" />
            <properties>
                <polling-enabled>true</polling-enabled>
                <polling-interval-seconds>4</polling-interval-seconds>
            </properties>
        </channel-definition>

    </channels>

    <logging>
        <target class="flex.messaging.log.ConsoleTarget"
            level="Error">
            <properties>
                <prefix>[BlazeDS]</prefix>
```

```
                        <includeDate>true</includeDate>
                        <includeTime>false</includeTime>
                        <includeLevel>true</includeLevel>
                        <includeCategory>true</includeCategory>
                </properties>
                <filters>
                        <pattern>Endpoint.*</pattern>
                        <pattern>Service.*</pattern>
                        <pattern>Message.*</pattern>
                        <pattern>DataService.*</pattern>
                        <pattern>Configuration</pattern>
                </filters>
        </target>
    </logging>

    <system>
        <redeploy>
                <enabled>true</enabled>
                <watch-interval>20</watch-interval>
                <watch-file>
                        {context.root}/WEB-INF/flex/flex-services.xml
                </watch-file>
                <watch-file>
                        {context.root}/WEB-INF/flex/flex-config.xml
                </watch-file>
                 <watch-file>
                     {context.root}/WEB-INF/flex/flex-messages-config.xml
                 </watch-file>
                 <touch-file>{context.root}/WEB INF/web.xml</touch-file>
        </redeploy>
    </system>
</services-config>
```

As you can see at the listing above, in the flex-services.xml configuration file I import also the flex-remoting.xml configuration file.

```
<services>
        <service-include file-path="flex-remoting.xml" />
        <service-include file-path="flex-messages.xml" />
</services>
```

This file is not used by our chat example, but I decided to keep also the remoting services configuration file to show you how to configure multiple services in a BlazeDS application. Figure 9-28 shows the configuration files in the flex folder.

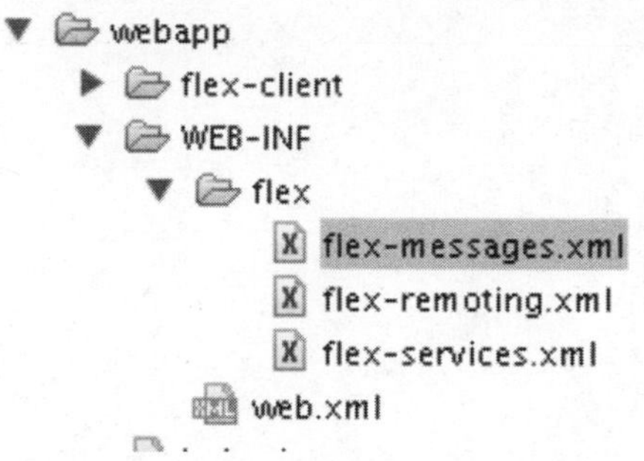

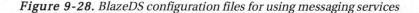

▼ 🗀 webapp
   ▶ 🗀 flex-client
   ▼ 🗀 WEB-INF
      ▼ 🗀 flex
         🅧 flex-messages.xml
         🅧 flex-remoting.xml
         🅧 flex-services.xml
      📄 web.xml

Figure 9-28. BlazeDS configuration files for using messaging services

The last step is to add a destination to configure the flex-messages.xml defining the default channel referring to the channel-polling-amf and adding a destination that will be shared by the AS `Producer` and `Consumer` objects.

Below the full listing for the flex-messages.xml file:

```xml
<?xml version="1.0" encoding="UTF-8"?>

<service        id="message-service-apt"
                    class="flex.messaging.services.MessageService">

    <adapters>
        <adapter-definition id="actionscript"

    class="flex.messaging.services.messaging.adapters.ActionScriptAdapter"
                                        default="true"/>
    </adapters>

    <default-channels>
        <channel ref="channel-polling-amf"/>
    </default-channels>

    <destination id="chat-application">
        <properties>
            <network>
                <session-timeout>
                    0
                </session-timeout>
                <throttle-inbound policy="ERROR" max-frequency="50"/>
                <throttle-outbound policy="REPLACE" max-frequency="500"/>
```

```
        </network>
        <server>
            <max-cache-size>
                1000
            </max-cache-size>
            <message-time-to-live>
                0
            </message-time-to-live>
            <durable>
                true
            </durable>
        </server>
    </properties>
</destination>
</service>
```

If you have configured everything correctly, you should be able to start the application by using the command mvn jetty:run.

Creating the Flex Project

The next step is to create a Flex project using the remote services setting and following the standard directory structure I've explained in the previous chapters.

In the remote service example, you changed the existing Flex project from a standard configuration to a project using the remote service. Now you must create a new Flex project using the remote service from the start. The server configuration process is exactly the same, but rather than using the Flex Properties window to set the server configuration details, now you will be prompted with the same options in the New Flex Project wizard, as follows:

1. In the first window, give your project a name and choose the J2EE application server type, as shown in Figure 9-29; then click Next.

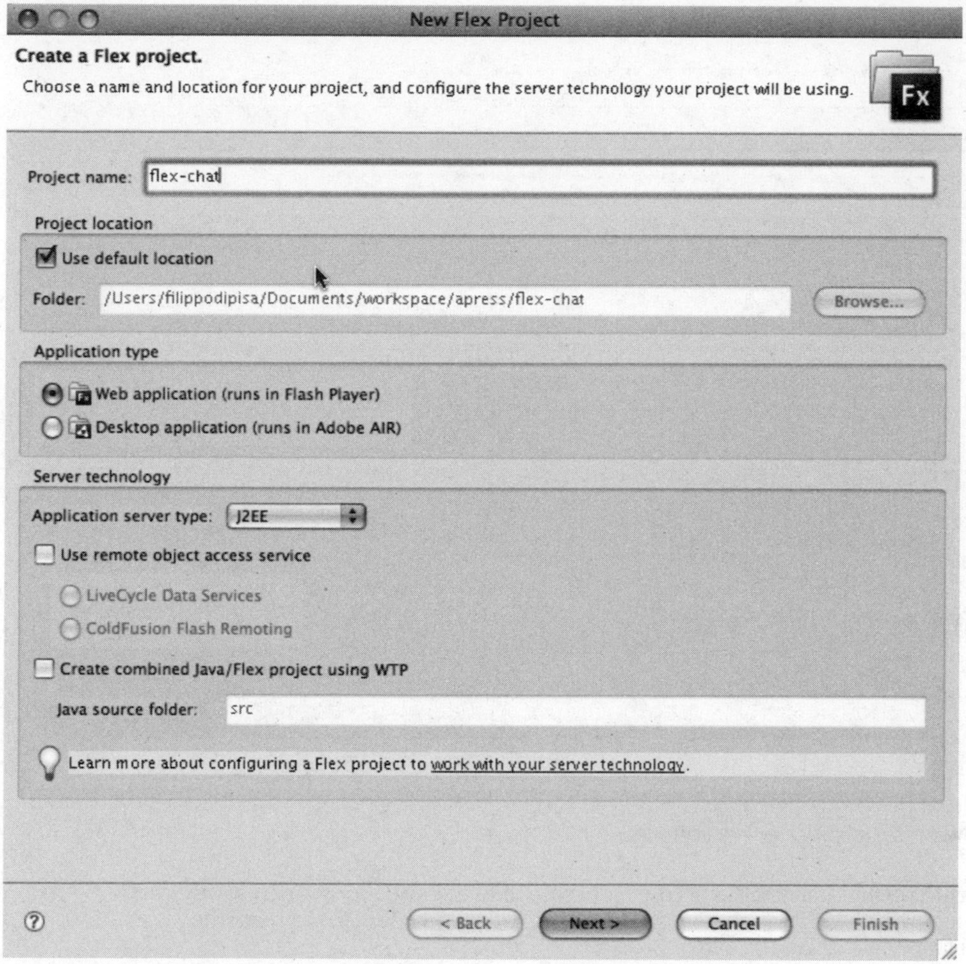

Figure 9-29. Creating a new Flex project using Java EE as a remote server

2. Set the server root URL and the server project absolute path URL, and configure the output folder to the `webapp/flex-client` server path, as shown in Figure 9-30. Then click Next.

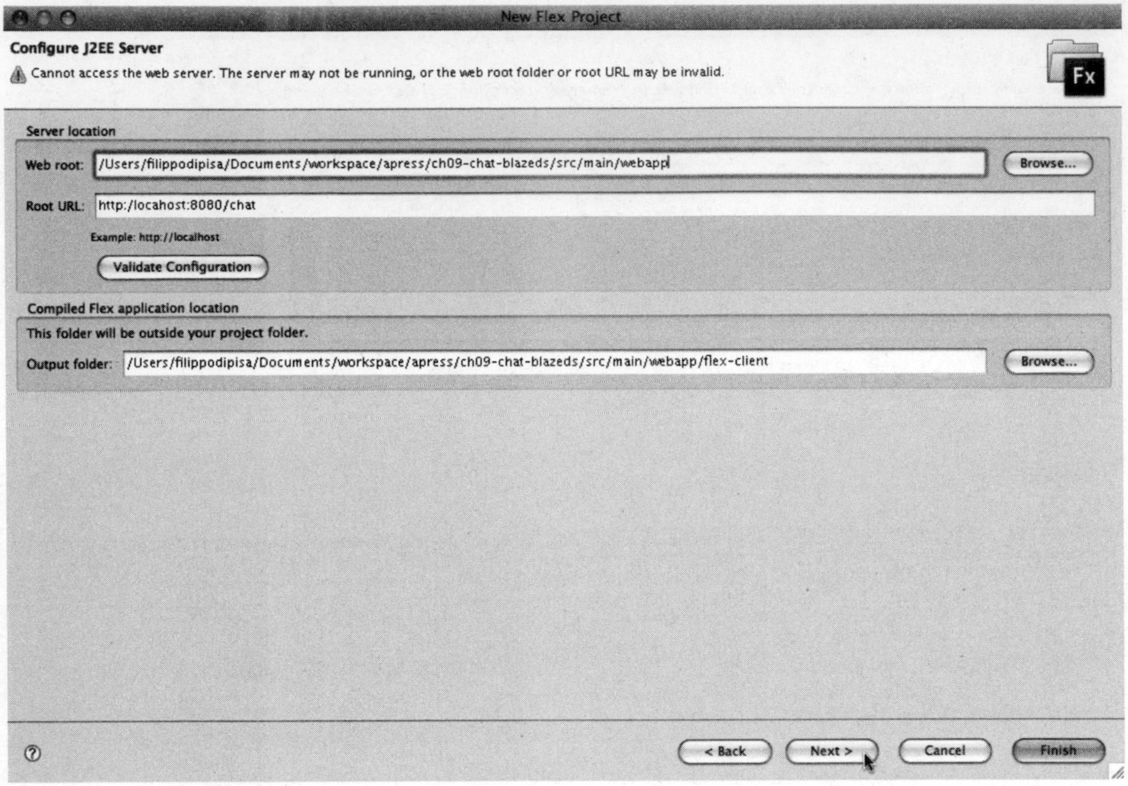

Figure 9-30. New Flex project server settings

3. Set the src/main/flex folder as the main source folder and src/main/resources as resources folders, as shown in Figure 9-31. Then click Finish to create the project.

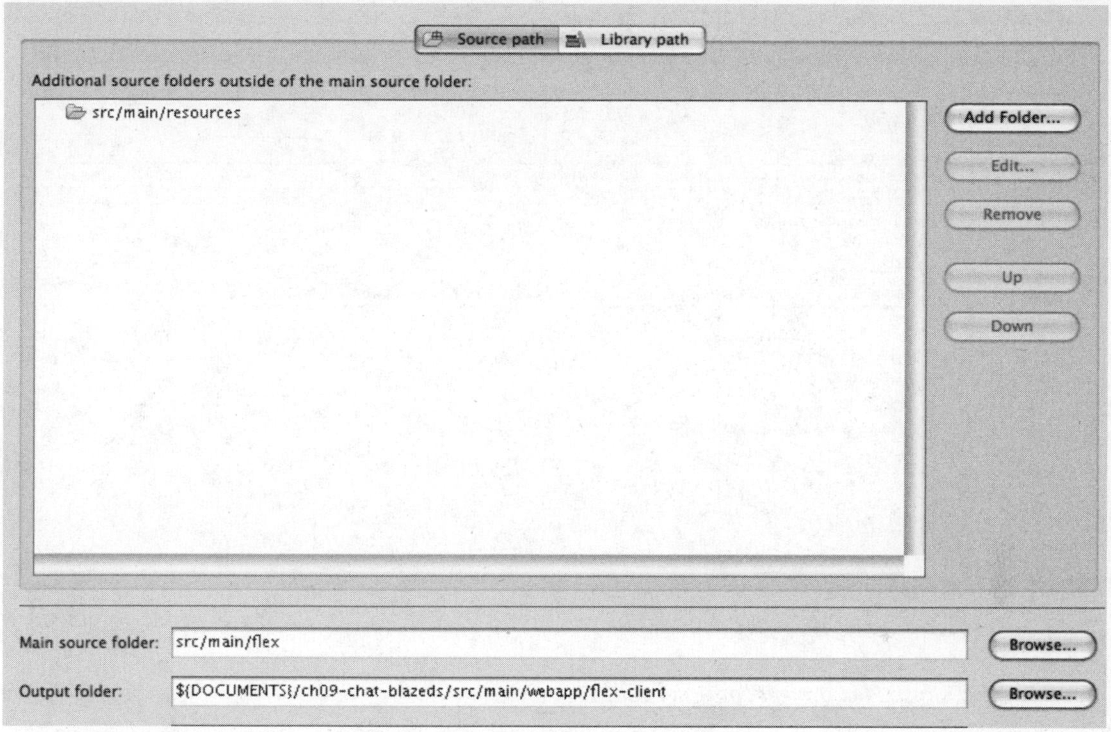

Figure 9-31. Eclipse Flex project path settings

Finally, open the project's Properties window, select Flex Compiler, and set the location of the BlazeDS services XML file (`flex-services.xml`). In Figure 9-32, this is specified as follows:

```
-services "/Users/filippodipisa/Documents/workspace/apress/
ch09-chat-blazeds/src/main/webapp/WEB-INF/flex/
flex-services.xml" -locale en_US
```

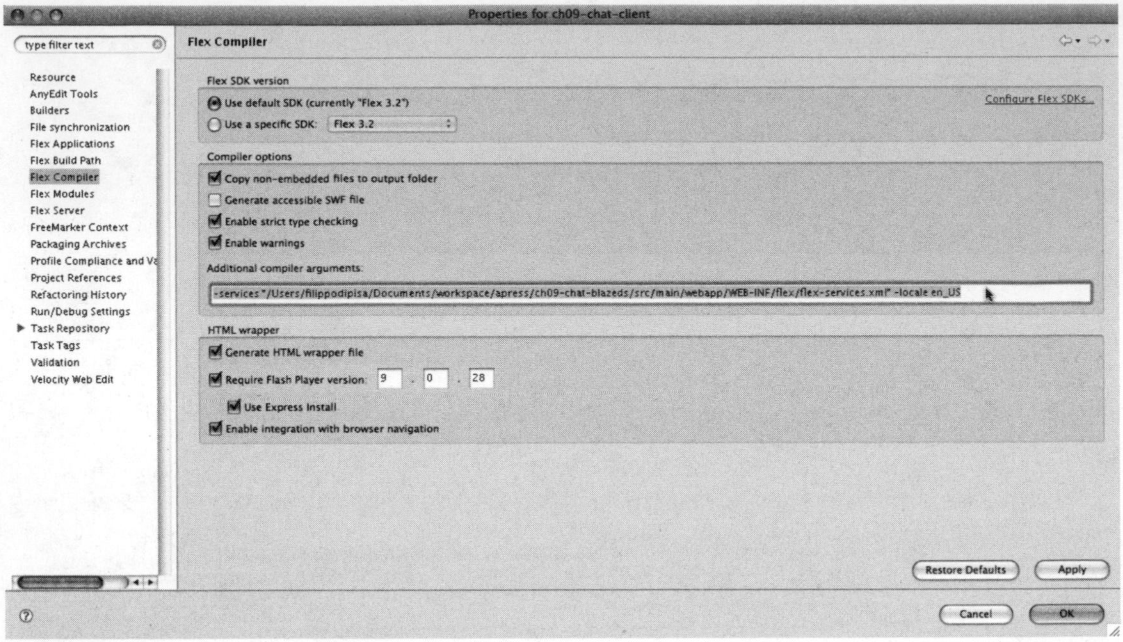

Figure 9-32. *Eclipse Flex project compiler settings*

Creating the Flex Code for Real-Time Messaging

With your server and project configured, you can now write some Flex code in order to exchange messages.

Start by editing the default Flex application file and adding a read-only TextArea component. This will log all messages exchanged by all the connected users. Then add an editable TextInput component, which allows users to write their messages and send them.

```
<mx:VBox width="100%" height="100%">
      <mx:TextArea id="messagesBoard" width="100%" height="80%"/>
      <mx:TextInput id="messageInput" width="100%" height="100" enter="send()" />
</mx:VBox>
```

The TextInput component will be listening for an enter event, which means it will dispatch the event to the send() function when the user presses the Enter key on the keyboard.

```
<mx:TextInput id="messageInput" width="100%" height="100" enter="send()" />
```

Within the send() function body, institute an asynchronous message using the Flex BlazeDS mx.messaging.messages.AsyncMessage class. This object contains all the properties needed from the Producer and the Consumer components in order to send and accept messages.

```
private function send():void{
```

```
        var message:IMessage = new AsyncMessage();
        message.headers = new Array();
        message.headers["sender"] = USERNAME;
        message.headers["recepient"] = USERNAME;
        message.body.userId = USERNAME;
        message.body.chatMessage = messageInput.text;
        producer.send(message);
        messageInput.text = "";
}
```

The AsyncMessage class APIs allow you to store the header and the body of the message in the object. In this example, the message header will contain an associative array with the same username that applies for both sender and recipient. To keep this application simple and easy to follow, I have used only one username for both sender and receiver. This means that each client will be able to exchange messages without any filters or security between the connected users. If you need filtering or security, you will need to create a message receiver filter to distribute all the messages, following your application logic and to meet its requirements.

Once you have set the headers and the body of your AsyncMessage, you need to pass it to the Producer, in order for it to be sent. In this sample class, the Producer is a private variable that you have set in the init() method on the application creationComplete event. The init() method is used to initialize the Producer, the Consumer, and the ChannelSet objects.

```
private function init():void{

        var channelSet : ChannelSet = new ChannelSet();
        var amfChannel : AMFChannel = new AMFChannel();
        amfChannel.url="http://localhost:8080/chat/messagebroker/amfpolling";
        channelSet.addChannel(amfChannel);

        producer = new Producer();
        producer.destination="chat-application";
        producer.channelSet = channelSet;

        consumer = new Consumer();
        consumer.destination="chat-application";
        consumer.channelSet=channelSet;

        consumer.addEventListener(MessageEvent.MESSAGE,messageHandler);
                                consumer.subscribe();
}
```

The Consumer listens for the event of type MessageEvent. When it is dispatched, it is passed to the messageHandler function as defined in the listener. The messageHandler function checks if the header of the message is set to recipient=filippo (filippo is the static username that I am using for both sender and receiver). If the condition is satisfied, it will bind the message body with the message board TextArea component.

```
private function messageHandler(event:MessageEvent):void {
```

```
        var message : IMessage = IMessage(event.message);
    if(message.headers["recepient"] == USERNAME){
        if(message.body.chatMessage != ""){
            messagesBoard.htmlText += message.body.userId + ": " +↵
message.body.chatMessage + "\n";
        }
    }
}
```

Listing 9-20 shows the complete listing for the Chat.mxml application component.

Listing 9-20. *Complete Code for ther Chat.mxml Application Component*

```xml
<?xml version="1.0" encoding="utf-8"?>
<mx:Application xmlns:mx="http://www.adobe.com/2006/mxml"
                            layout="horizontal"
                            creationComplete="init()"
                            horizontalAlign="center"
                            verticalAlign="middle">

        <mx:VBox width="100%" height="100%">
            <mx:TextArea id="messagesBoard" width="100%" height="80%"/>
            <mx:TextInput id="messageInput" width="100%" height="100"↵
enter="send()" />
        </mx:VBox>


    <mx:Script>
        <![CDATA[
            import mx.messaging.Consumer;
            import mx.messaging.ChannelSet;
            import mx.messaging.Producer;
            import mx.messaging.events.MessageAckEvent;
            import mx.messaging.events.MessageEvent;
            import mx.messaging.channels.AMFChannel;
            import mx.utils.ArrayUtil;
            import mx.collections.ArrayCollection;
            import mx.messaging.messages.AsyncMessage;
            import mx.messaging.messages.IMessage;

            private const USERNAME : String = "filippo";

            private var producer : Producer;

            private var consumer : Consumer;
```

```
            private function init():void{

                    var channelSet : ChannelSet = new ChannelSet();
                    var amfChannel : AMFChannel = new AMFChannel();

    amfChannel.url="http://localhost:8080/chat/messagebroker/amfpolling";
                    channelSet.addChannel(amfChannel);

                    producer = new Producer();
                    producer.destination="chat-application";
                    producer.channelSet = channelSet;

                    consumer = new Consumer();
                    consumer.destination="chat-application";
                    consumer.channelSet=channelSet;

    consumer.addEventListener(MessageEvent.MESSAGE,messageHandler);
                    consumer.subscribe();
            }

            private function send():void{
                    var message:IMessage = new AsyncMessage();
                    message.headers = new Array();
                    message.headers["sender"] = USERNAME;
                    message.headers["recepient"] = USERNAME;
                    message.body.userId = USERNAME;
                    message.body.chatMessage = messageInput.text;
                    producer.send(message);
                    messageInput.text = "";
            }

            private function messageHandler(event:MessageEvent):void {
                    var message : IMessage = IMessage(event.message);
                    if(message.headers["recepient"] == USERNAME){
                            if(message.body.chatMessage != ""){
                                    messagesBoard.htmlText +=↵
    message.body.userId + ": " + message.body.chatMessage + "\n";
                            }
                    }
            }

        ]]>
    </mx:Script>

</mx:Application>
```

In order to test the message exchange, run the `Chat.mxml` component as a Flex application twice so you have two clients opened. Then type a message in one of the clients and press the Enter key to send the message. You should see its text appear in the other client, as shown in Figure 9-33.

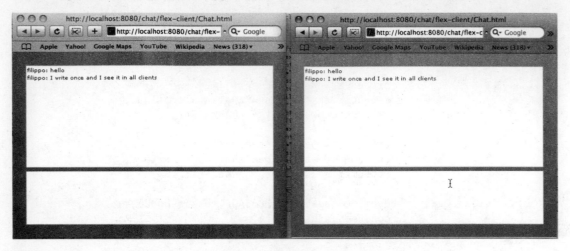

Figure 9-33. *The two chat clients opened to see the real-time exchange of messages*

You can improve this chat application by adding a user list, and the logic that allows the exchange of messages (which is only between users that are set into the user list).

Summary

This chapter introduced the BlazeDS server. You saw how to retrieve and send data to a Java application, and how easy it is to exchange real-time messages between different clients using the BlazeDS server.

Real-time messaging is very important in enterprise RIA development, so I suggest that you take the time to properly master all the concepts in this chapter. This kind of functionality has a large perceived worth to an application, whether or not it is used by the clients, so it can help you with development deadlines and "manager management."

Try to apply the same model to other kinds of applications that exchange more complex objects. You want your code to be standardized and extendable as much as possible, so you don't need to rework your code. If the logic is the same and the models are the same, any changes will require less of your time.

In the next chapter, you will see how to combine all the technologies that you have learned about up to this point and create a Maven, Spring, Hibernate, Flex application.

■■■

CHAPTER 10

Using Flex, Spring, and Hibernate Together

In the previous chapters I introduced you to Spring, Hibernate, Flex, and BlazeDS. Finally, in this chapter, I will show you how to put all that you've learned together to build the usermanager application using all the technologies covered in this book. Here's what you need to know or understand before starting:

- Set-up of the Eclipse IDE and other development tools

- Maven archetypes, Maven Jetty plug-in, and Maven dependencies

- The IOC container and the Spring framework concepts

- The ORM and Hibernate frameworks

- Annotations

- Flex

- BlazeDS

- The Flex RemoteObject and HTTPService components

If you're not sure of any of these technologies, you'll have to do some further work; otherwise, you may have difficulty following the steps in this chapter. If you are comfortable with your knowledge, however, let's start to write our first Flex-Spring-Hibernate-Maven application.

The Flex-Spring-Hibernate Maven Archetype

To create the usermanager project, this time we will use the Maven archetype functionalities; in particular, we will use the flex-spring-hibernate archetype I created to set up Maven projects using Flex, Spring, BlazeDS, and Hibernate. This archetype creates all the configuration files and downloads all the dependencies and plug-ins needed. Before we start coding, however, let's take a look at how the archetype works, and how to install it.

The idea of an archetype is to serve as a sort of template for a project, and I created this one to include everything we need for the Flex-Spring-Hibernate project. Below I explain how I created the archetype and what I added to it.

First, I configured the POM file with all of the Spring, BlazeDS, Hibernate, and MySQL dependencies, and I also added other useful dependencies such as the XOM libraries for processing XML with Java, as well as Velocity, the most used Java-based template engine. Velocity is useful in our scenario for creating e-mail or HTML views templates. Next I added all Maven plug-ins relevant to our development. The most important plug-in is the Jetty one; it's the servlet container used to run and test the application. Then I created all application trees for both the Java code and configuration files. The directory structure follows the standard Maven organization, so we have the /src/main and /src/tests folders. In the main folder there are subfolders organized by category:

- main

  - docs–where we will store the documentation;

  - java–where we will store the code; the java folder contains subfolders that are the MVC and DAO pattern default packages that will be created;

    - business–the package where we will create and store all our services classes, such as the UserService interface and it implementation;

    - dao–the package containing all DAO interfaces and their implementations; there's also a subfolder called hibernate that contains an abstract class called BaseHibernateDao where I abstracted the most used and useful methods to query the persisted objects. BaseHibernateDao implements the GenericDao interface, which is also in the dao folder;

    - mail–the package where we store all mail-related classes; this package comes with a class called MailSenderImpl that extends the JavaMailSenderImpl class by adding the from property; we will use this class to send all application e-mails;

    - model–the package where we will store all of the data model's classes; it contains the User and Authority entities. I added them because most applications must deal with security, and that typically involves users and authorities;

    - support–the package where we store all support classes; in this package I created a default StaticImporter class to import sample XML data into our database. This class is very useful for populating the database with sample data;

    - utils–the package where we will store all utility classes; it comes with the SpringUtils class that contains a useful method to get a bean from the container;

  - resources—where the main configuration files are stored, including most of those needed by Spring, Hibernate, Velocity and the other frameworks we are going to use in our application:

    - applicationContext-dao.xml—a Spring configuration file where I define the application DAOs, datasources, and Hibernate session factories;

    - applicationContext-resources.xml—a Spring configuration file where I define the resources settings, such as all properties files.

    - default-data.xml—an XML file containing the application database data samples. By default, this file contains the data for populating the database tables called users and authorities;

    - defaultEmailTemplate.vm—a Velocity template for e-mail. You can add as many Velocity templates as you want. The templates are empty to start;

- `flex-services.xml`—the BlazeDS service configuration file where I define the channels we are going to use to exchange messages between Flex and Java;

- `hibernate.cfg.xml`—the Hibernate configuration file where we have to put all our mapping classes. By default, the file comes with the `User` and `Authorities` entities mapped;

- `jdbc.properties`—contains all settings for the JDBC connection configuration. By default, it comes with the MySQL database configuration;

- `log4j.properties`—contains all parameters for the log4j configuration. Apache log4j is a framework for logging services;

- `mail.properties`—holds all properties relating to e-mail services. By default, the file comes with the `mailSender.host` set to `localhost` and the `mailSender.from` set to `test@yourDomain.net`;

- `velocity.properties`—stores all Velocity template properties; I added two commented properties to show you how to use it;

- uml–contains all UML files and comes with a file called `App.vpp`. This files works with the Eclipse-based UML IDE called Visual Enterprise Architect, that I use for creating UML diagrams;

- webapp–contains the web application. All contents of this folder will be placed in the root of your WAR file. It holds the flex-client and the WEB-INF subfolders;

  - flex-client–stores all Flex-related SWF and HTML files, all of which are Web-browsable;

  - WEB-INF–contains the application `web.xml` and the BlazeDS configuration files. These files can't be access directly from the web;

    - jsp–contains all jsp files, which are usually needed in a flex-java application;

    - `applicationContext.xml`–the main Spring configuration file where we define all our beans;

    - `flex-servlet.xml`–the spring-flex message broker configuration where I define the default channels and the remoting services;

    - `crossdomain.xml`–the file needed by Flash Player to allow communication between different Flex applications on different domains. Without this file, an external Flex/Flash application is not allowed to communicate with your application. Comes with the restriction to allow the Flex/Flash application only on the `localhost` domain;

    - `security.xml`–contains all the application security settings. Comes with basic Spring-security settings.

    - `web.xml`–contains all XML definitions to tell the servlet container how to deploy the web application. I added the definitions needed by Spring, Spring-security, and BlazeDS;

  - test–contains all resources and files related to the test environments. By default, it contains the subfolders *java* and *resources*;

- java –where we create the test packages. By default, it's empty;

- resources–where we create and store test-related resources files. By default, it is empty;

- pom.xml–the XML representation of the Maven project. I added all Spring, BlazeDS, Hibernate, and MySQL dependencies, as well as other useful plug-ins.

The preceding application structure will be used for each Maven project created using my archetype. Just for your knowledge, in the archetype source, there is also an archetype.xml file where I define all the directories and files I want to re-create when a new project is started.

```
<archetype>
  <id>flex-spring-hibernate</id>
  <sources>
    <source>src/main/java/dao/hibernate/BaseHibernateDao.java</source>
    <source>src/main/java/dao/GenericDao.java</source>
    <source>src/main/java/mail/MailSenderImpl.java</source>
    <source>src/main/java/model/Authority.java</source>
    <source>src/main/java/model/User.java</source>
    <source>src/main/java/support/StaticDataImporter.java</source>
    <source>src/main/java/utils/SpringContextUtils.java</source>
  </sources>
  <resources>
    <resource>src/main/resources/applicationContext-dao.xml</resource>
    <resource>src/main/resources/applicationContext-resources.xml</resource>
    <resource>src/main/resources/default-data.xml</resource>
    <resource>src/main/resources/defaultEmailTemplate.vm</resource>
    <resource>src/main/resources/flex-services.xml</resource>
    <resource>src/main/resources/hibernate.cfg.xml</resource>
    <resource>src/main/resources/jdbc.properties</resource>
    <resource>src/main/resources/log4j.properties</resource>
    <resource>src/main/resources/mail.properties</resource>
    <resource>src/main/resources/velocity.properties</resource>
    <resource>src/main/docs/Flex-Client-Configuration.txt</resource>
    <resource>src/main/sql/shema.sql</resource>
    <resource>src/main/uml/App.vpp</resource>
    <resource>src/main/webapp/WEB-INF/jsp/403.jsp</resource>
    <resource>src/main/webapp/WEB-INF/jsp/404.jsp</resource>
    <resource>src/main/webapp/WEB-INF/jsp/error.jsp</resource>
    <resource>src/main/webapp/WEB-INF/jsp/index.jsp</resource>
    <resource>src/main/webapp/WEB-INF/applicationContext.xml</resource>
    <resource>src/main/webapp/WEB-INF/crossdomain.xml</resource>
```

```
    <resource>src/main/webapp/WEB-INF/flex-servlet.xml</resource>
    <resource>src/main/webapp/WEB-INF/security.xml</resource>
    <resource>src/main/webapp/WEB-INF/web.xml</resource>
  </resources>
  <testSources>
      <source>src/test/java/dao/BaseSpringTestCase.java</source>
    <source>src/test/java/dao/ConfigLocator.java</source>
  </testSources>
</archetype>
```

Then, in the root of the archetype, there is another XML file called `archetype-catalog.xml` where I defined the archetype name, version, and group. Finally, there is the archetype POM file needed to build the archetype JAR file. Look back at Chapter 3 for how to create and build a Maven archetype.

■ **Note** Both archetype.xml and archetype-catalog.xml are only for archetype configuration; you won't see them when you create a project using the archetype.

Now let's start to set up the new usermanager Maven project using the flex-spring-hibernate archetype.

Using the Flex-Spring-Hibernate Archetype

As mentioned previously, I created a specific archetype that includes all libraries needed by Java, Hibernate, Spring, and Flex to enable communication with each other, through BlazeDS.

I called the archetype flex-spring-hibernate and I published it to my online repository. In order to use it, you have to configure your Maven Eclipse plug-in to use my online repository. This is very easy. Open the Eclipse preferences, expand the Maven item, and select the archetype item as shown in Figure 10-1.

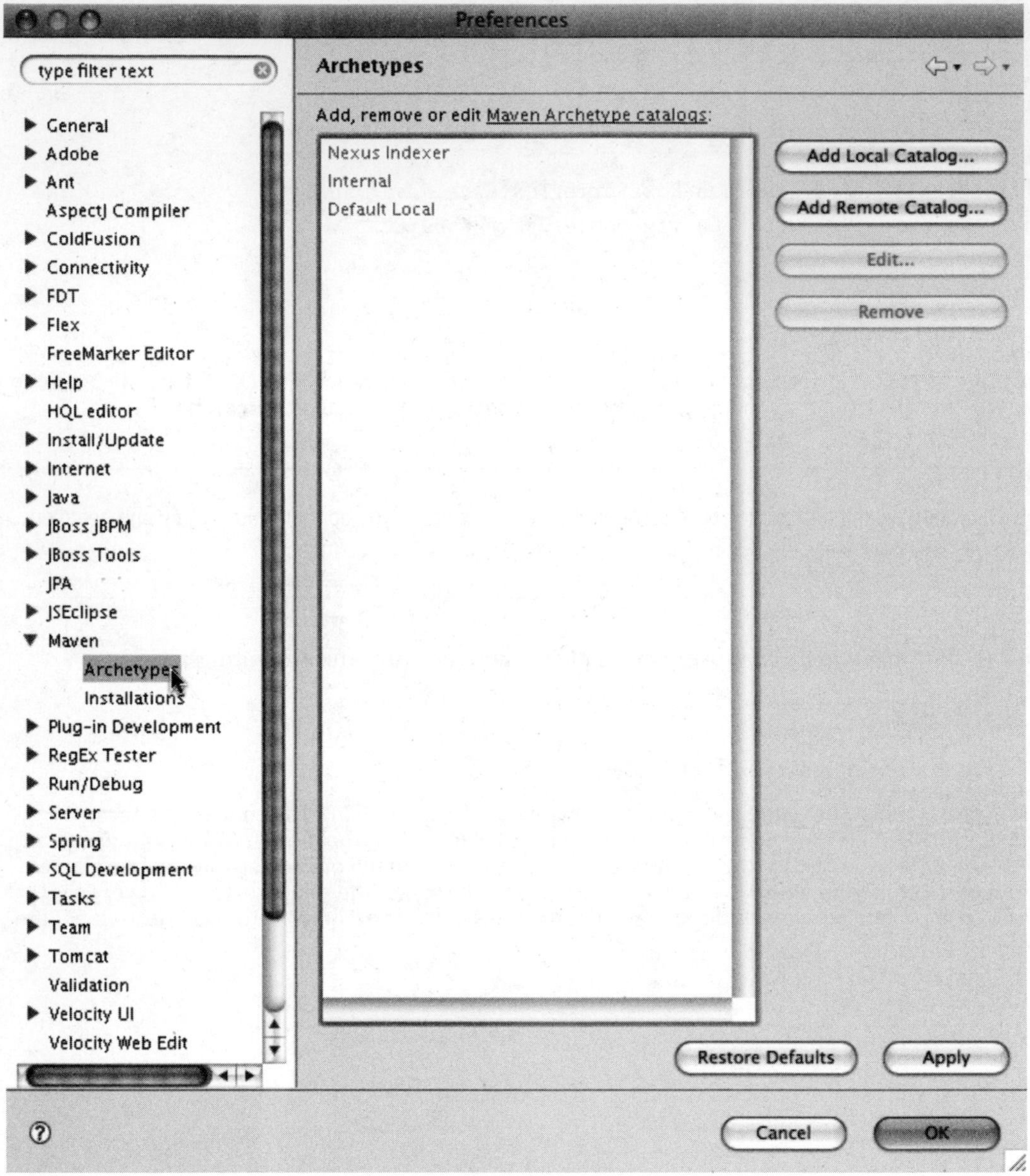

Figure 10-1. *Configuring the archetype catalogs*

Then click on the button labeled Add remote catalog and, as shown in Figure 10-2, enter the URL `http://filippodipisa.artifactoryonline.com/filippodipisa/libs-releases-local`. This is the URL where I deployed the archetype.

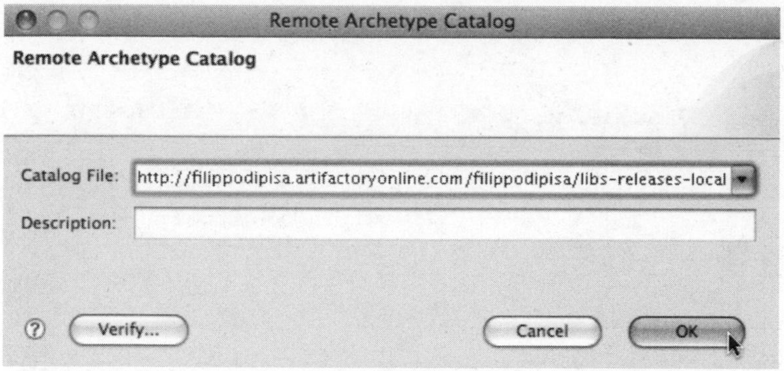

Figure 10-2. The URL of the online respository holding the archtype

You can leave the Description empty and click OK. Click on the button labeled Apply, and then you can close the window and start a new Maven project using the flex-spring-hibernate archetype.

To do that, open your Eclipse installation and choose File > New Maven Project. On the Select Archetype screen, set the Catalog to Default Local and you will see the archetype as in Figure 10-3.

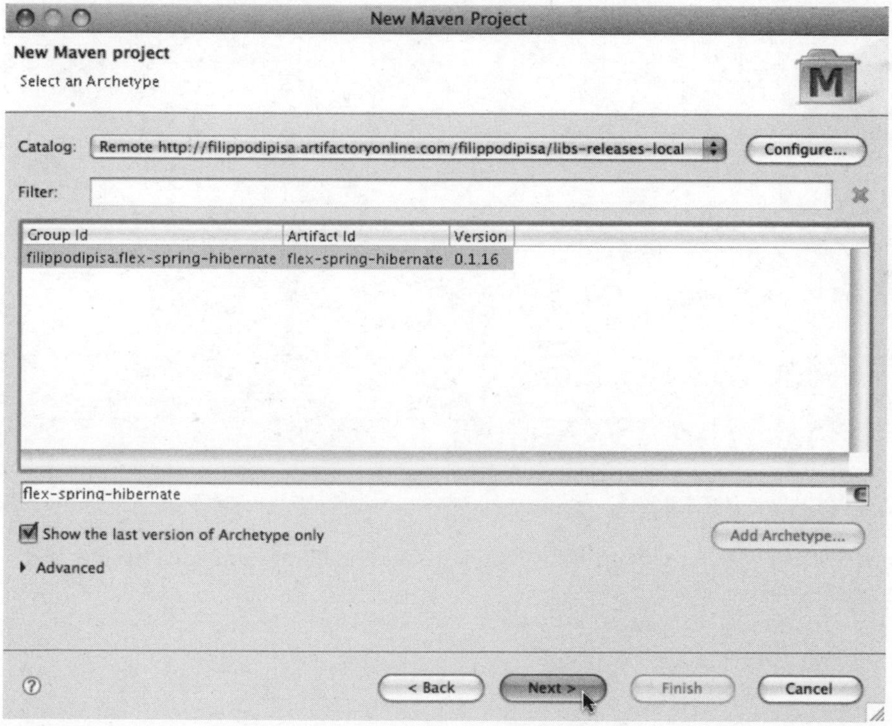

Figure 10-3. Starting a new Maven project using the flex-spring-hibernate archetype

Then insert the groupid, artifactid, version and the default package of your project and click Finish, as shown in Figure 10-4.

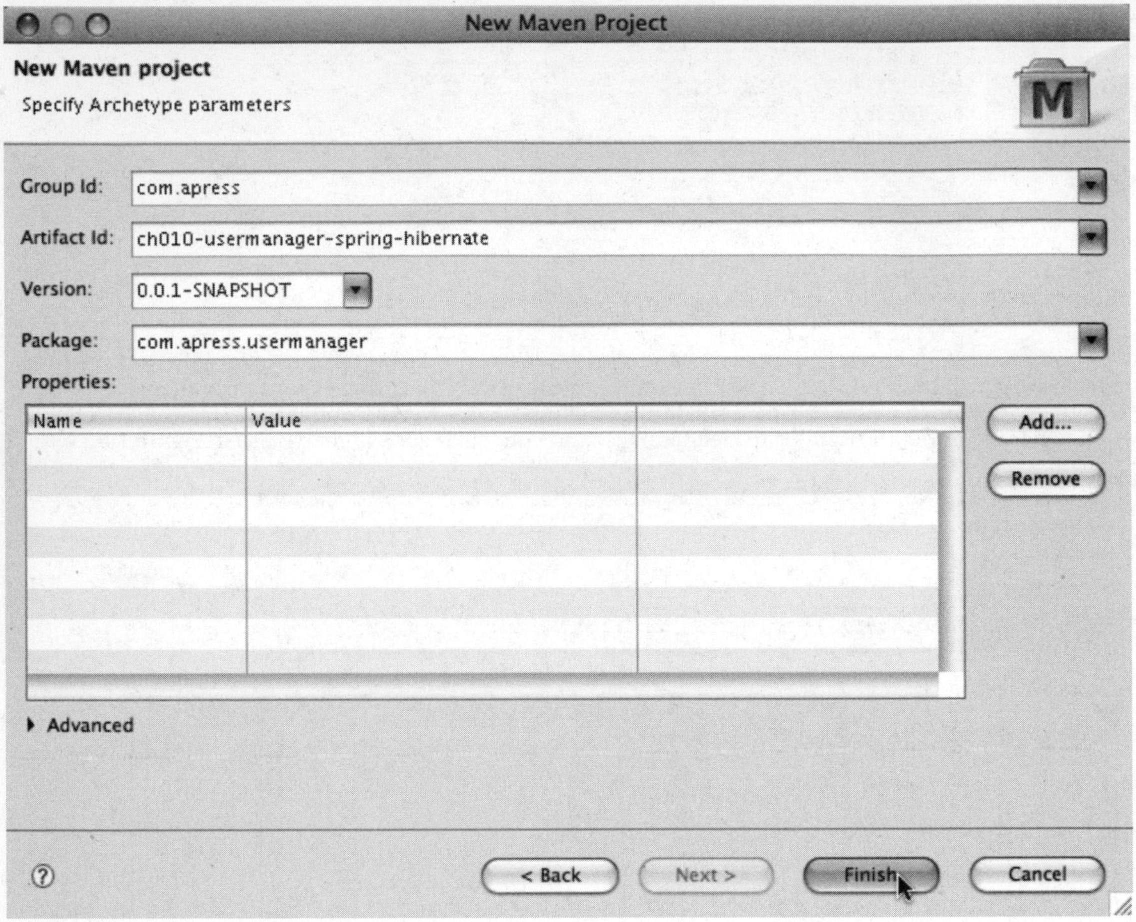

Figure 10-4. Specifying archetype parameters

As Figure 10-5 shows, Maven will create a project with all the files and libraries needed to start and develop a Flex-Spring-Hibernate project.

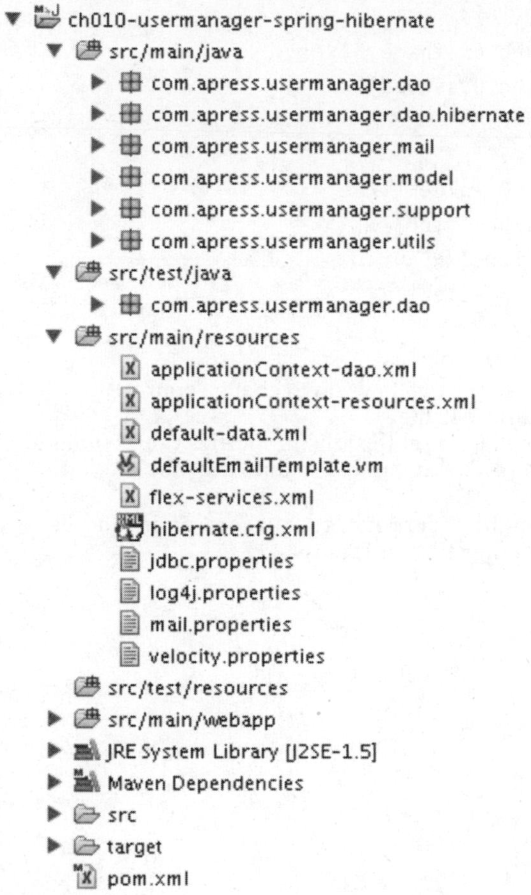

- ▼ 📂 ch010-usermanager-spring-hibernate
  - ▼ 📁 src/main/java
    - ▶ ⊞ com.apress.usermanager.dao
    - ▶ ⊞ com.apress.usermanager.dao.hibernate
    - ▶ ⊞ com.apress.usermanager.mail
    - ▶ ⊞ com.apress.usermanager.model
    - ▶ ⊞ com.apress.usermanager.support
    - ▶ ⊞ com.apress.usermanager.utils
  - ▼ 📁 src/test/java
    - ▶ ⊞ com.apress.usermanager.dao
  - ▼ 📁 src/main/resources
    - 🅧 applicationContext-dao.xml
    - 🅧 applicationContext-resources.xml
    - 🅧 default-data.xml
    - 📄 defaultEmailTemplate.vm
    - 🅧 flex-services.xml
    - 📄 hibernate.cfg.xml
    - 📄 jdbc.properties
    - 📄 log4j.properties
    - 📄 mail.properties
    - 📄 velocity.properties
  - 📁 src/test/resources
  - ▶ 📁 src/main/webapp
  - ▶ 🗄 JRE System Library [J2SE-1.5]
  - ▶ 🗄 Maven Dependencies
  - ▶ 📂 src
  - ▶ 📂 target
    - 🅧 pom.xml

Figure 10-5. *The project's files*

Configuring the Application

Before we start writing the business logic, we can start to get familiar with the project, configuring all XML and properties configuration files. First, we have to provide the application with a datasource that will be used by Hibernate to map the database tables with the Java persisted objects.

The datasource has been already set up by the archetype in the file called `applicationContext-resources.xml` located into `/src/main/resources/`. If you open this file, you'll notice a bean with `id=dataSource` as follows:

```
<bean id="dataSource" class="org.apache.commons.dbcp.BasicDataSource"
    destroy-method="close">
    <property name="driverClassName" value="${jdbc.driverClassName}"/>
```

```
        <property name="url" value="${jdbc.url}"/>
        <property name="username" value="${jdbc.username}"/>
        <property name="password" value="${jdbc.password}"/>
        <property name="maxActive" value="100"/>
        <property name="maxWait" value="1000"/>
        <property name="poolPreparedStatements" value="true"/>
        <property name="defaultAutoCommit" value="true"/>
        <property name="testOnBorrow" value="true"/>
        <property name="validationQuery" value="select 1=1"/>
</bean>
```

This bean uses properties set in the jdbc.properties file to allow you to change your JDBC properties without having to touch the bean configuration XML file.

To make your life easier and keep everything in one place, I set the jdbc.properties values into the POM configuration file; when we compile, Maven will replace the variable set into the jdbc.properties file with the ones set into the POM file.

So, let's open jdbc.properties, which is located in the /src/main/resources/ path. This file contains all the parameters needed to set up the JDBC connection, as follows:

```
jdbc.driverClassName=${jdbc.driverClassName}
jdbc.url=${jdbc.url}
jdbc.username=${jdbc.username}
jdbc.password=${jdbc.password}

hibernate.dialect=${hibernate.dialect}

# Needed by Hibernate3 Maven Plugin defined in pom.xml
hibernate.connection.username=${jdbc.username}
hibernate.connection.password=${jdbc.password}
hibernate.connection.url=${jdbc.url}
hibernate.connection.driver_class=${jdbc.driverClassName}
```

By default, the archetype sets the name of the database to the name given to the artifactId in the project wizard. To properly configure the JDBC connection, let's change the name of the database from ch10-usermanager-spring-hibernate to apress_usermanager, and let's change the username and password to the real username and password of your MySQL installation. In my case, these are apress and 123456, respectively.

To make these changes, open the POM file and change the JDBC values as the following:

```
<jdbc.url><![CDATA[jdbc\:mysql\://localhost\:3306/apress_usermanager?createDatabaseIf
NotExist=true&amp;useUnicode=true&amp;characterEncoding=utf-
8&amp;enableQueryTimeouts=false]]></jdbc.url>
<jdbc.username>user</jdbc.username>
<jdbc.password>pass</jdbc.password>
```

The last step for our configuration is to set the value for the `contextPath` property in the Maven Jetty plug-in defined in our POM file. By default, the archetype uses the `archetypeId` set through the project wizard; you need to change this from `/ch10-usermanager-spring-hibernate` to `/usermanager` as follows:

```
<plugin>
        <groupId>org.mortbay.jetty</groupId>
        <artifactId>maven-jetty-plugin</artifactId>
        <version>6.1.19</version>
        <configuration>
        <contextPath>/usermanager</contextPath>
        ...
```

That's it; your application configuration is done. As you can see, the archetype saved a lot of time by automatically setting up all resources and configuration files needed to develop a Flex-Spring-Hibernate project.

If you browse the files and folders created by the archetype, you will see that they are exactly the same as the ones explained in the archetype overview in the previous section.

we could start to write the code for our application now, but as I explained at the beginning of this book, I think that creating UML diagrams before coding makes us more productive. Many developers don't use UML at all because they think it's faster to write code directly. Probably, with a simple application like our usermanager example, we could carry on without creating diagrams. But when you have to deal with complex enterprise applications, UML becomes a must.

Planning the Application with UML

UML planning is one of the most important parts of application development. Some UML IDEs, such as Visual Paradigm, can even generate all the Java classes directly from the UML class diagram, so you can keep your classes synchronized with the UML diagram. This means if you add code or new classes to the project, the UML diagrams will be updated, and vice versa. In the next sections I will show you the entire architecture of both server and UI using the UML diagrams and some mock code. When that's done, we will start writing code using the UML diagrams as our guide.

The Data Model UML Diagrams

We start from the application data model. The usermanager application will contain users and authorities. Thanks to the archetype, if you open the `com.apress.usermanager.model` package, you should already have the two entities created by default.

■ **Note** If you are using Visual Paradigm for creating UML, you can use the instant reverse functionality that will create the base class diagram from the classes generated by the archetype.

However, the User entity is not complete for our needs, so let's design both classes as in the UML class diagram in Figure 10-6.

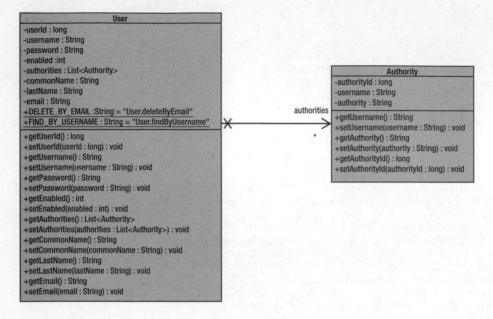

Figure 10-6. *Modeling the User and Authority classes*

As you can see, we added some new properties to the default User entity, including commonName, lastName, and so on. We also added two constants that we'll use to define the two NamedQueries as follows:

```
@NamedQueries( {
  @NamedQuery(name = User.DELETE_BY_EMAIL,
            query = "delete from User u where u.email = :email"),
  @NamedQuery(name = User.FIND_BY_USERNAME,
            query = "from User u where u.username = :username")
})
```

If you don't remember what NamedQueries are, please take a look in Chapter 5.

When you are happy with the data model diagrams, you can start to write the UML diagrams for the DAOs layer. Note that the full listing of User.java is featured later in this chapter.

The DAOs UML Diagrams

The archetype already created the package com.apress.usermanager.dao containing the interface GenericDao, as well as com.apress.usermanager.dao.hibernate, which contains the abstract class called BaseHibernateDao that extends the Spring class HibernateSupport and implements the GenericDao interface.

I decided to add these classes to the archetype to avoid duplicate code. For example, you could have an application with two DAOs, one to deal with users (UserDao), and a second to deal with groups (GroupDao). Without using the architecture shown in Figure 10-7, you could have methods such as findById and save them in both DAOs. My archetype helps by offering a generic interface, and this abstract implementation provides a pattern that allows you to reuse all common methods in the entire application.

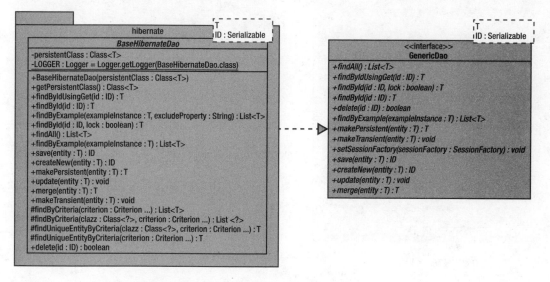

Figure 10-7. *The archetype Hibernate generic DAO classes*

In our scenario, we will need to create just the UserDao interface and its implementation for now. The archetype again saves us time. Indeed, by having the UserDao interface extend the GenericDao interface, we can inherit all methods such as save and update that are already implemented in the BaseHibernateDao abstract class. Even if you are a beginner, you can start to save, merge, and retrieve objects without knowing the Hibernate syntax.

So let's create our DAOs UML diagram to visualize our needs. As you can see in Figure 10-8, we created the `UserDao` interface, extending the `GenericDao` interface. Then we created the `UserDao` implementation class (`UserDaoImpl`), which extends the generic abstract class `BaseHibernateDao`.

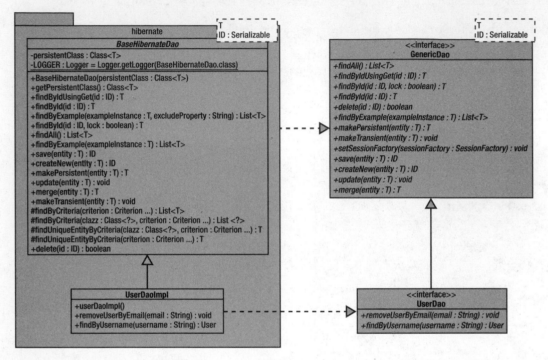

Figure 10-8. *Modeling the DAOs*

With this pattern, we can use all implemented methods in the `BaseHibernateDao` abstract class. In other words, as you can see in the `UserDao` interface, we have to write just two methods that are not included in `BaseHibernateDao`. The methods are `removeUserByEmail` and `findByUsername`. When we want to save a user into the database, we will use the method called `merge`, inherited by the `GenericDao` interface and implemented in the `BaseHibernateDao` class.

At this stage we have completed our DAOs and data model UML architecture. Now that we know how to manage our application data, we have to architect the service layer that will work directly with the Flex client.

The Service Layer UML Diagram

In our scenario, the service layer will include just one interface/class pair. Our UI is composed of a grid containing all of the users, from which we can add, edit, and delete users. To do that, we have to provide the Flex client with the user service layer containing the methods to add, edit, and delete users.

The service layer will be composed of the `UserService` interface and its implementation as shown in the UML class diagram in Figure 10-9.

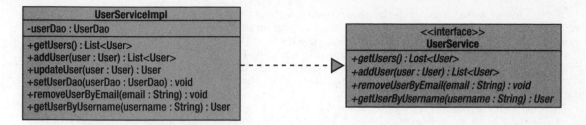

Figure 10-9. *Modeling the service layer*

As Figure 10-9 shows, in the `UserServiceImpl` implementation class, there is a setter method not defined in its interface. This method, called `setUserDao,` is needed by Spring to inject the `userDao` bean instantiated into the container.

Now our UML design is almost done. We have created the service layer that uses the DAO layer to deal with the persisted objects. The last step is to architect application security.

Architecting Application Security

At this stage, everyone can see, modify, and even delete all users and their details. This is very insecure, so we have to implement something so that only administrators can see, edit, and delete a user. The non-administrator users will be able to see and edit only their own details. Because our UI is developed in Flex, we have to implement something that is able to authenticate and return authenticated user roles to our Flex UI application.

My archetype includes a basic Spring security configuration. Open the file `security.xml` located into the `/src/main/webapp/WEB-INF/` folder. In this file I configured the Spring security authentication provider to use a database via JDBC:

```
<authentication-provider>
    <jdbc-user-service data-source-ref="dataSource"/>
</authentication-provider>
```

By default, I have protected all URLs, except the `/messagebroker` and the `/flex-client/` URLs. Within the `flex-client` folder, we will store all our Flex-related SWF and HTML files (basically, our UI). The `/messagebroker` URL is the servlet to exchange real-time messages between Flex and Java.

```
<http auto-config="true" session-fixation-protection="none" >
    <intercept-url pattern="/messagebroker/**"
access="IS_AUTHENTICATED_ANONYMOUSLY" />
    <intercept-url pattern="/flex-client/**" access="IS_AUTHENTICATED_ANONYMOUSLY"
/>
    <intercept-url pattern="/**" access="ROLE_USER" />
</http>
```

As this listing shows, by default the /messagebroker and the /flex-client folder are accessible recursively (all files and subfolders) by everyone. All the other folders and files beside these are accessible only by the authenticated users having the ROLE_USER role.

Configuring security between Flex and Spring is very easy. Essentially, the archetype has already configured everything to allow the Flex client to send the login to the channel. If the login is successful, it will get back an event containing an array of the authorities. Then it stores all authorities in our Flex data model. Quite cool, isn't it?

Just for your knowledge, if you open the flex-servlet.xml file, you will see a tag <flex:secured /> defined within the message broker definition. When this tag is present, the Flex authentication request will be routed to the Spring AuthenticationManager.

Injecting the Spring Beans

Now that we created all of our puzzle pieces, we have to inject them and their references into the IoC container. So, to see if our puzzle is complete, let's create the last UML diagram to visualize all of the Spring beans that will be instantiated in the IoC container. First we have to inject the Hibernate session factory, the datasource, the property configurer, and the static importer beans to allow our application to use a database, to load the properties stored in the external properties file defined in the property configurer bean, and to populate the database with the default data contained in an external XML file set to the static importer bean (see Figure 10-10).

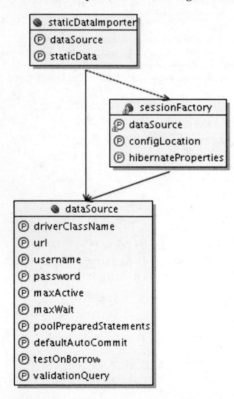

Figure 10-10. *Injecting the Hibernate session factory, the datasource, property configurer, and static importer beans*

Secondly, we have to instantiate the user service and its related DAOs in the Spring IOC container (Figure 10-11).

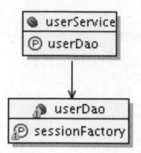

Figure 10-11. Instantiating userService

Now we've completed diagramming the server application. The Flex client is pretty similar to the examples in the previous chapter. Basically, we could copy and make just few changes to the previous `RemoteObject` example, to make it work with the new server that uses Spring and Hibernate. However, it's useful to create the UML architecture for the GUI as well.

Flex Client GUI Architecture

Our GUI is composed of a main view containing the users grid, the user form, and the login form views. Different views are shown depending on the `workFlowState` value stored in the data model. The default value of the `workFlowState` is set to show the login form view. If the user authentication is successful, the `workFlowState` value will be set to the users grid view, and so on.

The `workFlowState` value is stored in the application model, which will keep all views up to date when the value changes. First, our GUI data model must have the `User` entity mapped to the Java `User` entity (see Figure 10-12).

User
+userId : String
+username : String
+commonName : String
+lastName : String
+email : String
+password : String
+enabled : int
+User()

Figure 10-12. Mapping the User entity

The AS User entity will have the same properties as the Java User entity. Then we create the UserModel interface and its implementation where we'll define the workFlowState property and other important application properties needed by the other layers (Figure 10-13).

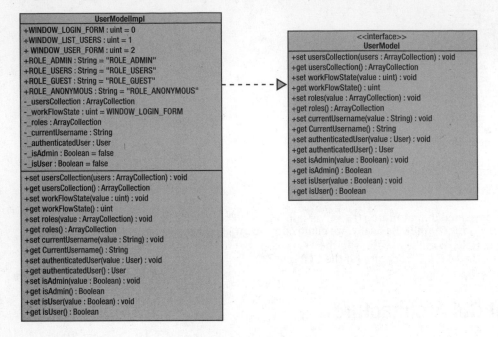

Figure 10-13. *The* UserModel *interface and its implementation*

As you can see from the UML class diagram in Figure 10-13, I have created static constants indicating the name of the visible view to use with the workFlowState property. Then I created the static constants that define the application roles allowed. The other public properties realized by the interface are to store the authenticated user roles and to set whether the user is an administrator.

The GUI views will communicate with the server data model through the GUI application controller. In the controller we define the methods to retrieve and update data from the Java server services. Our GUI controller will be very simple and it will be consist only of the UserControl interface and its implementation as the UML class diagram in Figure 10-14 shows.

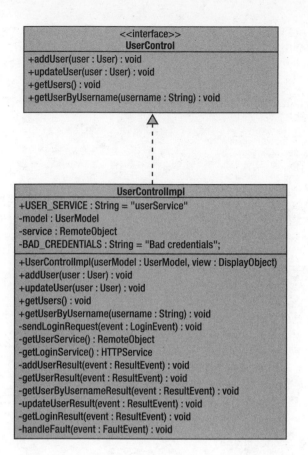

Figure 10-14. *The* UserControl *interface and its implementation*

In the UserControlImpl implementation class, we will implement all UserDao interface methods and then create the private methods needed to deal with the Java application. Within the UserControlImpl constructor, we will set the model and view objects that are required to make the controller work.

The last piece of our MVC pattern is the architecture of the views. According to the constants set in our GUI model, we will have three views:

- login form (corresponds to the static constant WINDOW_LOGIN_FORM)

- users list (corresponds to the static constant WINDOW_LIST_USERS)

- user form (corresponds to the static constant WINDOW_USER_FORM)

The login form will be the default view, because the user can see the users list or the user form only if she is authenticated. The authenticated users that have the ROLE_USERS role will be able to see and edit just their own details; the users authenticated with the ROLE_ADMIN role will be set as administrators and will be able to see the users list and edit details for all users. The administrators will be able to add new users as well.

Codingwise, all our views will be MXML classes to keep the code more readable for the designers. The login form MXML class will be a composite custom component extending the Flex HBOS container to contain a Flex Panel container and a Flex Form containing Flex username and password controls. The user form view will extend the Flex Form container and will contain all form controls needed to edit and view user details.

Figure 10-15 shows the UML class diagram for both the LoginForm and UserForm classes:

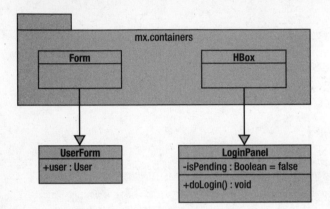

Figure 10-15. *The* LoginForm *and* UserForm *classes*

The UserForm will have a public bindable property of type User to set the user to the form. Each form component will be bound with the related user property as in the following example:

```
<mx:FormItem label="Common name">
  <mx:TextInput id="commonName" text="{user.commonName}"
                change="{user.commonName = commonName.text}"/>
</mx:FormItem>
```

The users list view will be just an extension to the Flex Grid control with the user columns already added. To provide a more interactive UI, we will also create a special TextInput control that will filter the users collection by the value inserted.

Figure 10-16 shows the UML class diagram for both the UserGrid and CollectionTextInputFilter classes.

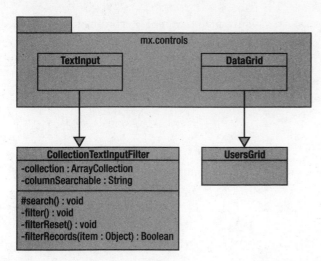

Figure 10-16. *The* UserGrid *and* CollectionTextInputFilter *classes*

The CollectionTextInputFilter component requires a collection and the name of the collection column where to apply the filter. When the TextInput value changes, we will trigger the protected method called search that will call the filter functions.

In the next section we will create the code for all the UML diagram classes. Visual Paradigm (the UML IDE I used to create the diagrams for the entire book), lets me generate all classes, interfaces, and other objects from the UML class diagrams for both Java and ActionScript. It doesn't create the MXML classes, however, and you will need to create them manually.

Let's start now to write the code for the flex-spring-hibernate-blazeds-maven application.

Develop the Flex-Java-Spring-Hibernate Application

In the previous sections we created the usermanager project using the Flex-Spring-Hibernate Maven archetype. Then we modified the Spring configuration files created by the archetype for our needs. Finally, we architected both the server code and the GUI using UML. With a good UML IDE like Visual Paradigm you could generate all Java and AS classes directly from the UML diagrams—avoiding having to create each one manually. However, this time, we are going to create every single class and package manually according to the UML class diagrams.

Because I have already explained the entire application architecture, in this section I will focus more on the code syntax and algorithms. I will follow the same sequence used in the architecture, replacing the UML diagrams with the code.

Coding the Domain Objects

As already explained, when we created the domain objects UML the archetype created the default User and Authority entities. We only have to modify the default User and Authority entities to adapt them to our application needs, such as adding some properties and the Hibernate annotations as we defined in the UML class diagram in Figure 10-6.

To do that, open the class User located in com.apress.usermanager.model. According to the UML class diagram, we have to add to the User entity the following properties not added by the archetype:

```
private String commonName;
```

```
private String lastName;
```

```
private String email;
```

Next we have to annotate each new User class property that we want to map to the database using the @Column annotation:

```
@Column(name="common_name")
private String commonName;
```

```
@Column(name="last_name")
private String lastName;
```

```
@Column(name="email",unique=true, nullable=false )
private String email;
```

Here we are telling Hibernate to map the User Java property called commonName to the users database table column called common_name, and so on. For the property email, we use additional annotation attributes to tell Hibernate and the database that the value of this column must be unique and not null. This means we can't have two or more users with the same e-mail.

Finally, our UML tells us to add two public static constants that we will use to define the name of the embedded named queries:

```
public static final String DELETE_BY_EMAIL = "User.deleteByEmail";
```

```
public static final String FIND_BY_USERNAME = "User.findByUsername";
```

This gives us two named queries called DELETE_BY_EMAIL and FIND_BY_USERNAME. In Chapter 5 I explained how to create named queries using the annotations @NamedQueries and @NamedQuery. Remember that a named query can be defined by setting the aforementioned annotations just under the @Table annotation, like this:

```
@Entity
@Table(name = "users")
@NamedQueries( { @NamedQuery(name = User.DELETE_BY_EMAIL, query = "delete from User
u where u.email = :email"),
@NamedQuery(name = User.FIND_BY_USERNAME, query = "from User u where u.username =
:username") })
```

```
public class User {
...
```

Here's an example of how we use a named query in our DAO:

```
public void removeUserByEmail(String email) {
        Query query = getSession().getNamedQuery(User.DELETE_BY_EMAIL)
          .setString("email", email);
        query.executeUpdate();
}
```

After amending the User entity, our work is complete for the domain objects. Indeed, the two entities should already be mapped within the Hibernate configuration file called hibernate.cfg.xml located into the /src/main/resources/ folder.

Listing 10-1 and Listing 10-2 show the complete code for both entities User and Authority, and their XML mapping definition for the hibernate.cfg.xml configuration file shown in Listing 10-3.

Listing 10-1. User.java

```
package com.apress.usermanager.model;

import java.util.List;
import javax.persistence.CascadeType;
import javax.persistence.Column;
import javax.persistence.Entity;
import javax.persistence.FetchType;
import javax.persistence.GeneratedValue;
import javax.persistence.Id;
import javax.persistence.JoinColumn;
import javax.persistence.NamedQueries;
import javax.persistence.NamedQuery;
import javax.persistence.OneToMany;
import javax.persistence.Table;
import static javax.persistence.GenerationType.IDENTITY;

@Entity
@Table(name = "users")
@NamedQueries( { @NamedQuery(name = User.DELETE_BY_EMAIL, query = "delete from User
u where u.email = :email"),
```

```java
@NamedQuery(name = User.FIND_BY_USERNAME, query = "from User u where u.username =
:username") })

public class User {

        @Id
        @Column(name="user_id",unique=true, nullable=false )
        @GeneratedValue( strategy = IDENTITY )
        private long userId;

        @Column(unique=true, nullable=false )
        private String username;

        @Column
        private String password;

        @Column
        private int enabled;

        @OneToMany(cascade = CascadeType.ALL, fetch = FetchType.EAGER)
        @JoinColumn(name = "user_id")
        private List<Authority> authorities;

        @Column(name="common_name")
        private String commonName;

        @Column(name="last_name")
        private String lastName;

        @Column(name="email",unique=true )
        private String email;

        public static final String DELETE_BY_EMAIL = "User.deleteByEmail";

        public static final String FIND_BY_USERNAME = "User.findByUsername";

        public long getUserId() {
                return userId;
        }
```

```java
public void setUserId(long userId) {
        this.userId = userId;
}

public String getUsername() {
        return username;
}

public void setUsername(String username) {
        this.username = username;
}

public String getPassword() {
        return password;
}

public void setPassword(String password) {
        this.password = password;
}

public int getEnabled() {
        return enabled;
}

public void setEnabled(int enabled) {
        this.enabled = enabled;
}

public List<Authority> getAuthorities() {
        return authorities;
}

public void setAuthorities(List<Authority> authorities) {
        this.authorities = authorities;
}

public String getCommonName() {
        return commonName;
}
```

```java
        public void setCommonName(String commonName) {
                this.commonName = commonName;
        }

        public String getLastName() {
                return lastName;
        }

        public void setLastName(String lastName) {
                this.lastName = lastName;
        }

        public String getEmail() {
                return email;
        }

        public void setEmail(String email) {
                this.email = email;
        }
}
```

Listing 10-2. Authority.java

```java
package com.apress.usermanager.model;

import javax.persistence.Column;
import javax.persistence.Entity;
import javax.persistence.Id;
import javax.persistence.Table;

@Entity
@Table(name = "authorities")
public class Authority {

        @Id
        @Column(name="authority_id")
        private long authorityId;

        @Column
```

```java
        private String username;

        @Column
        private String authority;

        public String getUsername() {
                return username;
        }

        public void setUsername(String username) {
                this.username = username;
        }

        public String getAuthority() {
                return authority;
        }

        public void setAuthority(String authority) {
                this.authority = authority;
        }

        public long getAuthorityId() {
                return authorityId;
        }

        public void setAuthorityId(long authorityId) {
                this.authorityId = authorityId;
        }
}
```

Listing 10-3. *hibernate.cfg.xml*

```xml
<?xml version="1.0" encoding="utf-8"?>

<!DOCTYPE hibernate-configuration PUBLIC
"-//Hibernate/Hibernate Configuration DTD 3.0//EN"
"http://hibernate.sourceforge.net/hibernate-configuration-3.0.dtd">
<hibernate-configuration>
    <session-factory name="sessionFactory">
```

```
        <mapping class="com.apress.usermanager.model.User" />
        <mapping class="com.apress.usermanager.model.Authority" />
    </session-factory>
</hibernate-configuration>
```

In order to test the new code, delete any previously created database called `apress_usermanager` from your MySQL database system and run the command:

```
mvn jetty:run
```

Now refresh your MySQL database explorer and if you have configured everything well, you will see the new `apress_usermanager` database with the `users` and `authorities` tables containing the new columns added into the Java entity classes (see Figure 10-17).

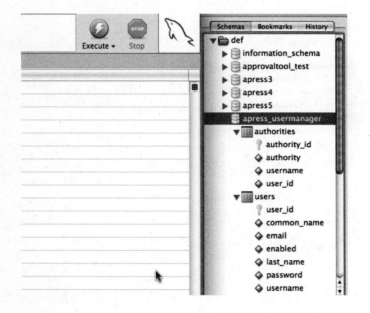

Figure 10-17. *The* new `apress_usermanager` *database*

Now we can begin to write the code for the application DAOs.

Coding the Hibernate DAO objects

Comparing our DAOs UML in Figure 10-8 with the default classes already created by the archetype in `com.apress.usermanager.dao`, you can see that in order to complete the UML requirements, we have to write just a few lines of code. As explained earlier, by using the generic DAO pattern created by the archetype, we can inherit all of the useful methods to handle operations, such as to `save`, `update`, and `retrieve` data from persisted objects.

The UML tells us that we need to add two more methods not included in the `GenericDao` interface created by the archetype. Indeed, our application needs to provide our DAO with one method to remove users by e-mail, and one method to retrieve a user by username. Both methods are not implemented in the `GenericDao` interface. So let's create the `UserDao` interface extending the `GenericDao` one to inherit its methods that we are going to use for saving and updating a user.

Here is the listing for the `UserDao` interface:

```
package com.apress.usermanager.dao;

import com.apress.usermanager.model.User;

public interface UserDao extends GenericDao<User, Long> {

        void removeUserByEmail(String email);

        User findByUsername(String username);
}
```

Once the `UserDao` interface has been created, we have to create its implementation; because the implementation will use Hibernate, we will create the `UserDao` implementation class, called `UserDaoImpl`, in the `com.apress.usermanager.dao.hibernate` package.

Following the UML class diagram, the `UserDaoImpl` class must extend the `BaseHibernateDao` class and implement the `UserDao` interface as follows:

```
package com.apress.usermanager.dao.hibernate;

import com.apress.usermanager.dao.UserDao;
import com.apress.usermanager.model.User;
import org.hibernate.Query;

public class UserDaoImpl extends BaseHibernateDao<User, Long> implements UserDao {

        public UserDaoImpl() {
                super(User.class);
        }

        public void removeUserByEmail(String email) {
                Query query = getSession().getNamedQuery(User.DELETE_BY_EMAIL)
        .setString("email", email);
                query.executeUpdate();
        }
```

```
        public User findByUsername(String username) {
                return (User)getSession().getNamedQuery(User.FIND_BY_USERNAME)
        .setString("username", username).uniqueResult();
        }

}
```

As you can see, to extend the BaseHibernateDao class you just have to write the code for the two new methods realized by implementing the UserDao interface. For both methods, we will use the named queries defined in our User entity class. That's it.

Before starting to code the service layer, it would be good to create a test class to test the two new just-implemented methods.

Create a Test Case

In order to create a test class able to work with Spring and Hibernate, you have to set up a test environment to load all the configuration files and inject all the beans into the Spring IOC container. Luckily, the archetype has already created the ConfigLocator and the BaseSpringTestCase classes in the package com.apress.usermanager.dao stored into the /src/test/java folder. The ConfigLocator object provides the methods to set and get the configuration files needed by our tests.

Below is the code for the ConfigLocator class:

```
package com.apress.usermanager.dao;

public class ConfigLocator {

        private static final long serialVersionUID = 1l;

    private String[] locations;

    public ConfigLocator() {
            locations = new String[] {
                            "classpath:/applicationContext-resources.xml",
                            "classpath:/applicationContext-dao.xml",
                            "/WEB-INF/applicationContext.xml",
                                "/WEB-INF/security.xml"
            };
    }

    public void setLocations(String[] locations) {
            this.locations = locations;
    }
```

```
    public String[] getLocations() {
        return locations;
    }
}
```

The `BaseSpringTestCase` class extends the Spring
`AbstractDependencyInjectionSpringContextTests` class, overriding the `getConfigLocation`
method to use the configuration files set in the `ConfigLocator` class. Here is the code for the
`BaseSpringTestCase` class:

```
package com.apress.usermanager.dao;

import org.apache.commons.logging.Log;
import org.apache.commons.logging.LogFactory;
import org.springframework.test.AbstractDependencyInjectionSpringContextTests;

public abstract class BaseSpringTestCase extends
                AbstractDependencyInjectionSpringContextTests {
    /**
     * Log variable for all child classes. Uses LogFactory.getLog(getClass())
     * from Commons Logging
     */
    protected final Log log = LogFactory.getLog(getClass());

    /**
     * Sets AutowireMode to AUTOWIRE_BY_NAME and configures all context files
     * needed to tests DAOs.
     *
     * @return String array of Spring context files.
     */
    @Override
    protected String[] getConfigLocations() {
        setAutowireMode(AUTOWIRE_BY_TYPE);
        // to have a single place to add configLocations, even if more than
        // one
        // BaseTestCase class is present
        return new ConfigLocator().getLocations();
    }
}
```

In order to create our `UserDaoTest` test class, we have to extend the `BaseSpringTestCase` abstract class and add the setter property of type `UserDao` to inject the `userDao` bean instantiated in the Spring IoC container. Then we have to create the beans needed by our test class; we can define them in the `/WEB-INF/applicationContext.xml` configuration file loaded by the `BaseSpringTestCase` class, as follows:

```
<bean id="userDao" class="com.apress.usermanager.dao.hibernate.UserDaoImpl">
        <property name="sessionFactory" ref="sessionFactory" />
</bean>

<bean id="userService" class="com.apress.usermanager.service.UserServiceImpl">
        <property name="userDao" ref="userDao" />
</bean>
```

As you can see, we created in the IoC container an instance of the `UserDaoImpl` class where we inject the `sessionFactory` bean created earlier in the application. Then we created an instance of the `UserServiceImpl` class, injecting the `userDao` bean instantiated into the IoC container.

Once we are happy with our Spring `applicationContext.xml` configuration file, we have to create the test DAO package called `com.apress.usermanager.dao` within the `/src/test/java` folder. We will keep all our test packages and classes in the `/src/main/test` folder.

Our test class aim is to assert that all the `UserDaoImpl` implementation class public methods work properly. Remember that in order to create a test method, you have to start the method with the word `test` or set the annotation `@Test` just above the method itself. All methods beginning with `test` or annotated with `@Test` will be executed as JUnit tests.

Here is the full listing of our `UserDao` test class:

```
package com.apress.usermanager.dao;

import java.util.List;
import com.apress.usermanager.model.User;
import com.apress.usermanager.dao.BaseSpringTestCase;

public class UserDaoTest extends BaseSpringTestCase {

        private UserDao userDao;

        private final String EMAIL_ADDED_USER = "dustin.robert@apress.com";

        private final String USERNAME = "dustin34";

        public void testGetUsers(){
                userDao.removeUserByEmail(EMAIL_ADDED_USER);
```

```java
        List<User> users = userDao.findAll();
        assertNotNull(users);
        assertEquals(4, users.size());
    }

    public void testAddUser(){
        List<User> users = null;
        User user = new User();
        user.setCommonName("Dustin");
        user.setLastName("Robert");
        user.setEmail(EMAIL_ADDED_USER);
        user.setUsername(USERNAME);
        user.setPassword("43jh8978");
        userDao.merge(user);
        users = userDao.findAll();
        assertEquals(5, users.size());
    }

    public void testGetUserByUsername(){
        User user = userDao.findByUsername(USERNAME);
        assertNotNull(user);
        assertEquals(user.getUsername(), USERNAME);
    }

    public void testRemoveUserByEmail(String email){
        userDao.removeUserByEmail(email);
        List<User> users = userDao.findAll();
        assertNotNull(users);
        assertEquals(4, users.size());
        User user = userDao.findByUsername(USERNAME);
        assertNull(user);
    }

    public void setUserDao(UserDao userDao) {
        this.userDao = userDao;
    }

}
```

The `UserDaoTest` test class is quite easy to understand. The first method called `testGetUsers` first removes, if it exists, the user we are going to use for our tests. Second, it uses the `userDao` injected bean to retrieve all users added by default to the database.

Because we know that there are four default users, we can use a JUnit assert expression to compare the expected result with the one retrieved from the database. With `testAddUser`, we create a `User` object and then use the DAO to save it into the database. Here we are using the `merge` method that is implemented in the `GenericDao`. With the `testGetUserByUsername` method, we assert that the user retrieved by username is the same user we are using for our testing. Finally, with the `testRemoveUserByEmail` method, we test if the DAO's `remove` API works. To do that, first we remove the user and then we retrieve all users stored in the database; the result must be equal to 4, the number of the default users.

Using unit tests will help you develop stable applications and save a lot of time. Unit tests can sometimes seem annoying and you may think you don't need them, but get used to testing every single class or component.

If all tests pass, it means our DAO is working as we want, so we can start to write the service layer.

Coding the Service layer

Following the UML, you can see that the service layer is more or less a wrapper for the DAO. If you think you could have used the DAO directly, you are wrong. Using a service layer allows us to encapsulate different DAOs and other classes into our service layer. For example, in our scenario, our service layer includes a method called `addUser` that will basically encapsulate the `UserDao merge` and `findAll` functions, in order to return an up-to-date users list after you add a new user. In the future, you could encapsulate the e-mail service layer within the same method body, in order to send a confirmation e-mail once a user has been added.

■ **Note** As we did for the `UserDao`, we will create the `UserService` test class as well.

Listing 10-4 show the full code for the `UserService` interface; Listing 10-5 shows its `UserServiceImpl` implementation; and Listing 10-6 shows the `UserServiceTest` test class. Before creating the classes, you have to create the package `com.apress.usermanager.service` where you will store both the interface and implementation class. To store the unit test class, create the package `com.apress.usermanager.service` in the `/src/test/java` test folder.

Listing 10-4. UserService interface

```
package com.apress.usermanager.service;

import java.util.List;
import com.apress.usermanager.model.User;

public interface UserService {
```

```
    List<User> getUsers();

    List<User> addUser(User user);

    void removeUserByEmail(String email);

    User getUserByUsername(String username);

    void doLogout();


}
```

Listing 10-5. *UserServiceImpl implementation class*

```
package com.apress.usermanager.service;

import java.util.List;
import org.springframework.security.context.SecurityContextHolder;
import com.apress.usermanager.dao.UserDao;
import com.apress.usermanager.model.User;
import flex.messaging.FlexContext;

public class UserServiceImpl implements UserService {

        private UserDao userDao;


        public List<User> getUsers(){
                return userDao.findAll();
        }

        public List<User> addUser(User user){
                userDao.merge(user);
                return getUsers();
        }

        public User updateUser(User user){
                return (User)userDao.merge(user);
        }
```

```
        public void setUserDao(UserDao userDao) {
                this.userDao = userDao;
        }

        public void removeUserByEmail(String email) {
                this.userDao.removeUserByEmail(email);
        }

        public User getUserByUsername(String username) {
                return userDao.findByUsername(username);
        }

    public void doLogout() {
                String username = "unknown";
                try {
                        username =
SecurityContextHolder.getContext().getAuthentication().getName();
                        FlexContext.setUserPrincipal(null);
                        FlexContext.getHttpRequest().getSession().invalidate();
                        FlexContext.getFlexSession().invalidate();
                        SecurityContextHolder.clearContext();
                } catch (RuntimeException e) {
                        //dosomething like logging
                }
        }

}
```

Listing 10-6. *UserServiceTest test class*

```
package com.apress.usermanager.service;

import java.util.List;

import com.apress.usermanager.dao.BaseSpringTestCase;
import com.apress.usermanager.model.User;
import com.apress.usermanager.service.UserService;


public class UserServiceTest extends BaseSpringTestCase {
```

```java
    private UserService userService;

    private final String EMAIL_ADDED_USER = "dustin.robert@apress.com";

    private final String USERNAME = "dustin34";


    public void testGetUsers(){
            userService.removeUserByEmail(EMAIL_ADDED_USER);
            List<User> users = userService.getUsers();
            assertNotNull(users);
            assertEquals(4, users.size());
    }

    public void testAddUser(){
            List<User> users = null;
            User user = new User();
            user.setCommonName("Dustin");
            user.setLastName("Robert");
            user.setEmail(EMAIL_ADDED_USER);
            user.setUsername(USERNAME);
            user.setPassword("43jh8978");
            users = userService.addUser(user);
            assertEquals(5, users.size());
    }

    public void testGetUserByUsername(){
            User user = userService.getUserByUsername(USERNAME);
            assertNotNull(user);
            assertEquals(user.getUsername(), USERNAME);
    }

    public void testRemoveUserByEmail(String email){
            userService.removeUserByEmail(email);
            List<User> users = userService.getUsers();
            assertNotNull(users);
            assertEquals(4, users.size());
            User user = userService.getUserByUsername(USERNAME);
            assertNull(user);
    }
```

```
public void setUserService(UserService userService) {
        this.userService = userService;
    }

}
```

Now we are ready to configure BlazeDS in order to expose to the Flex GUI the Spring bean called userService that contains the APIs that allow the Flex GUI to retrieve, edit, and add users.

Export Spring Services to BlazeDS

The last milestone of our application on the server side is to configure BlazeDS to allow the Flex GUI to use the userService bean and its methods. The archetype already created all the configuration that BlazeDS needs. The only thing you have to do is to define a remote destination using the XML definition `<flex:remoting-destination />`.

To do that, open the **flex-servlet.xml** file and add a remoting destination for the userService bean as follows:

```
<flex:remoting-destination ref="userService" />
```

By setting a remoting destination, we will be able to use the Spring userService APIs within our Flex GUI using the RemoteObject component as follows:

```
public function updateUser(user:User) : void{
        var service : RemoteObject = new RemoteObject("userService");
        service.addEventListener("fault", handleFault);
        service.addEventListener("result", updateUserResult);
        service.updateUser(user);
}
```

In this example I created a Flex updateUser function that calls the userService bean remote updateUser function in order to update a User from Flex to Java. Very easy, no?

At the end of the day, thanks to the archetype, we have to add just one or more destinations for the beans we want to use within Flex.

```
<flex:remoting-destination ref="bean1" />

<flex:remoting-destination ref="bean2" />

<flex:remoting-destination ref="bean[n]" />
```

Now, the server side of our application is done. You can try to build it using the command `mvn install` in a terminal window on Mac, or in a command prompt on Windows, or you can use the Eclipse Maven plug-in and select the Maven Install command as explained in previous chapters.

Give Jetty a try as well, using the command `mvn jetty:run`. Otherwise configure your Eclipse Maven plug-in as explained in Chapter 9.

Finally it is time to alter the Flex GUI created for the Chapter 9 example in order to use it with the new Spring-Hibernate server.

Coding the Flex GUI application

In the previous chapter I created a Flex GUI that used the `RemoteObject` component to deal with the BlazeDS destination that exposed the `com.apress.usermanager.service.UserServiceImpl` implementation class to Flex.

```
<destination id="userService">
        <properties>
            <source>com.apress.usermanager.service.UserServiceImpl</source>
        </properties>
</destination>
```

Now we'll use the Spring-Flex libraries to expose the `userService` bean to the Flex GUI

```
<flex:remoting-destination ref="userService" />
```

As you can see, the destination id is exactly the same, so that the Flex GUI doesn't know that the server underlying the layers has changed and it will work as before.

However, because we want to be tidy and elegant, we will create a copy of the previous chapter's Flex GUI and set it up to be used with the new Spring-Hibernate server.

■ **Note** If you want to directly use the Chapter 9 example, you have to reconfigure the Flex Remote properties.

First copy the `ch09-RemoteObject` and then paste it in the same location. Eclipse will show the Copy Project window asking for the new name for the project copied. Rename the `ch09-RemoteObject` to `ch010-RemoteObject`, as Figure 10-18 shows.

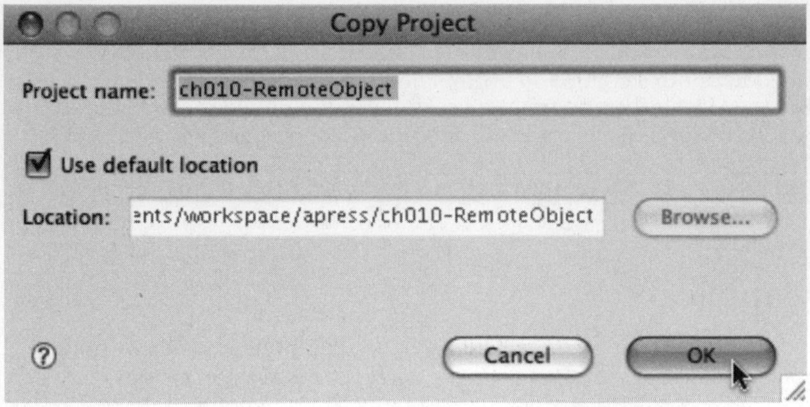

Figure 10-18. Copying the ch09-RemoteObject project to the ch010-RemoteObject one.

Next, open the project properties and set the output folder to the new Spring-Hibernate server's
/src/main/webapp/flex-client folder, as shown in Figure 10-19. Every time you build the Flex
project, all files generated by the Flex compiler will be stored into this directory.

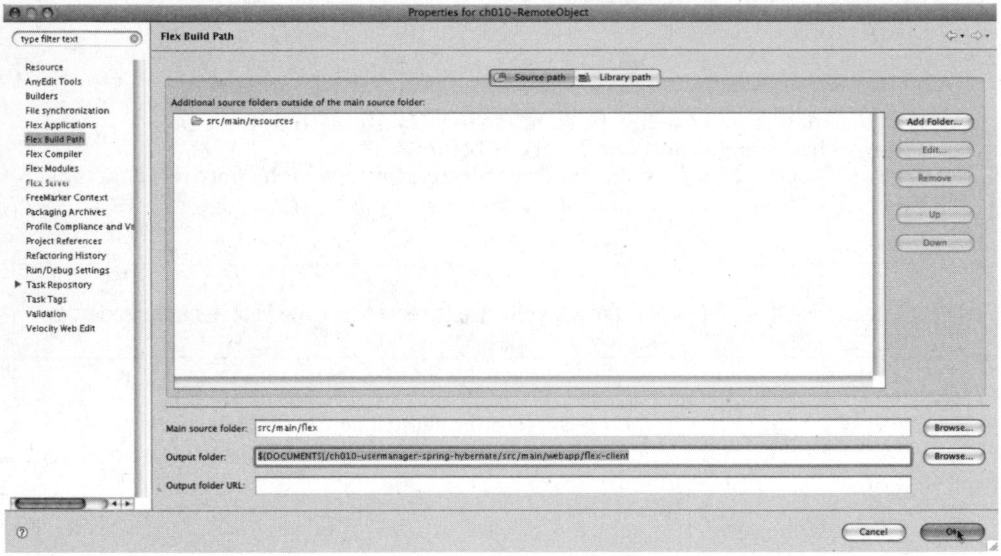

Figure 10-19. Setting the output folder

Now you have to select the Flex Server properties and change the Root folder path in order to use
the new ch10-usermanager-spring-hibernate project (see Figure 10-20).

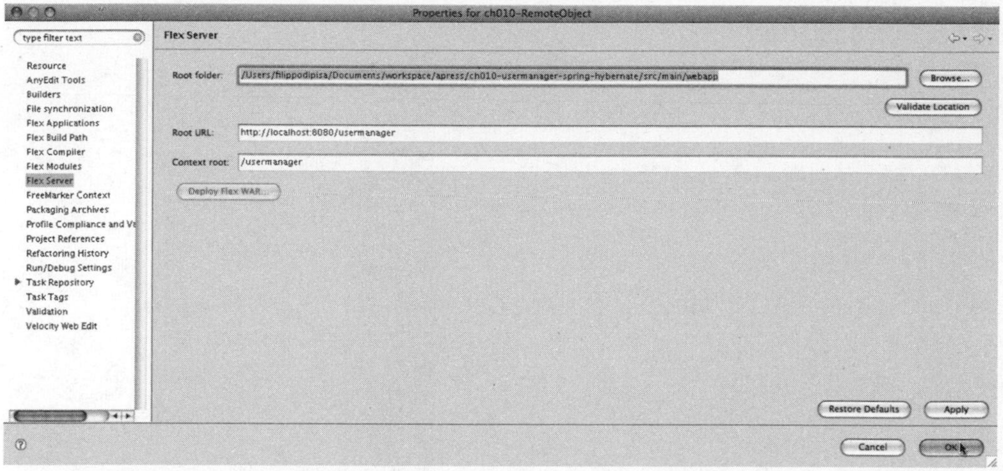

Figure 10-20. Changing the Root folder path

Finally, in the Flex Compiler, you need to change the path of the `flex-services.xml` BlazeDS services configuration file in order to use the file in the new project (see Figure 10-21).

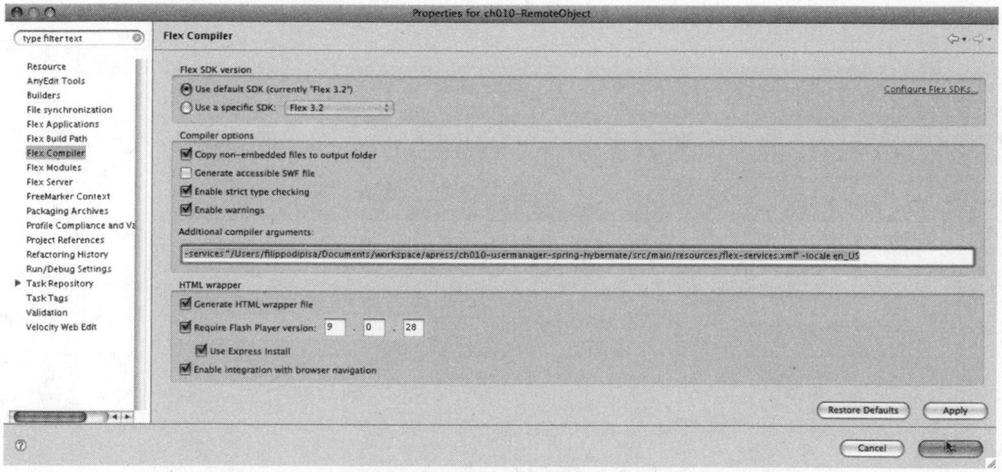

Figure 10-21. Changing the BlazeDS services configuration file

That's it. The GUI is now ready to work with the new server-side application. Before running the GUI, clean it using Project Clean on the Flex Builder top menu bar, then build it using Project Build.

When you run the Flex GUI, you should see the Users grid containing the default users added into the database, as shown in Figure 10-22.

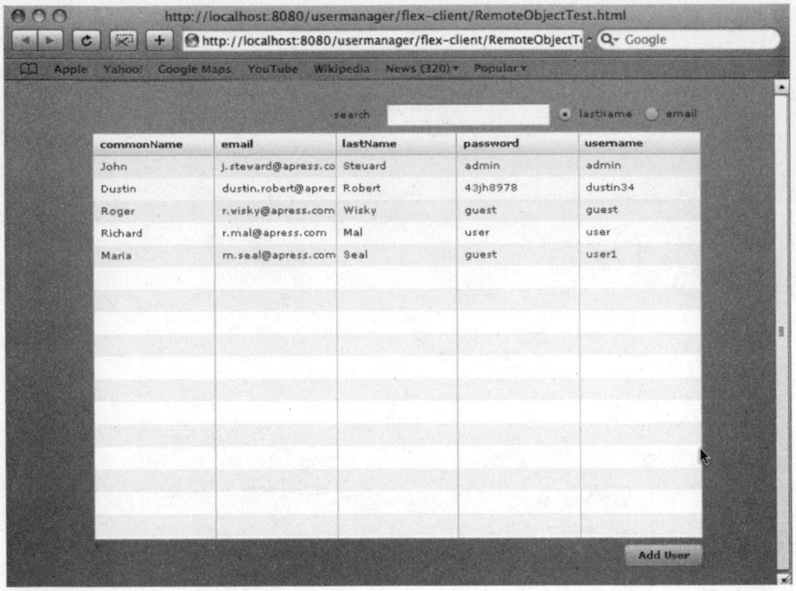

Figure 10-22. *The Users grid*

The last test is to click on the Add User button and, when a screen like the one in Figure 10-23 appears, try to add a user.

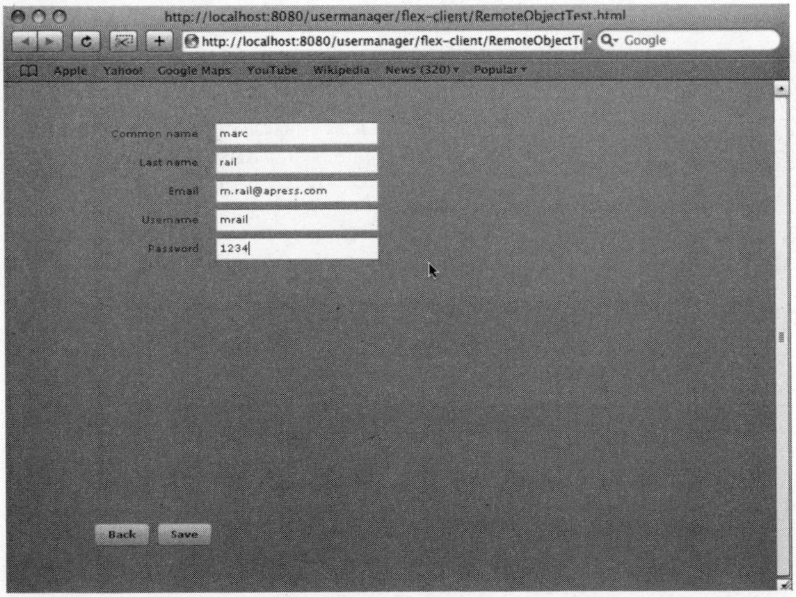

Figure 10-23. *Adding a new user*

Now go back to the grid and you will see that the new user has been added (Figure 10-24).

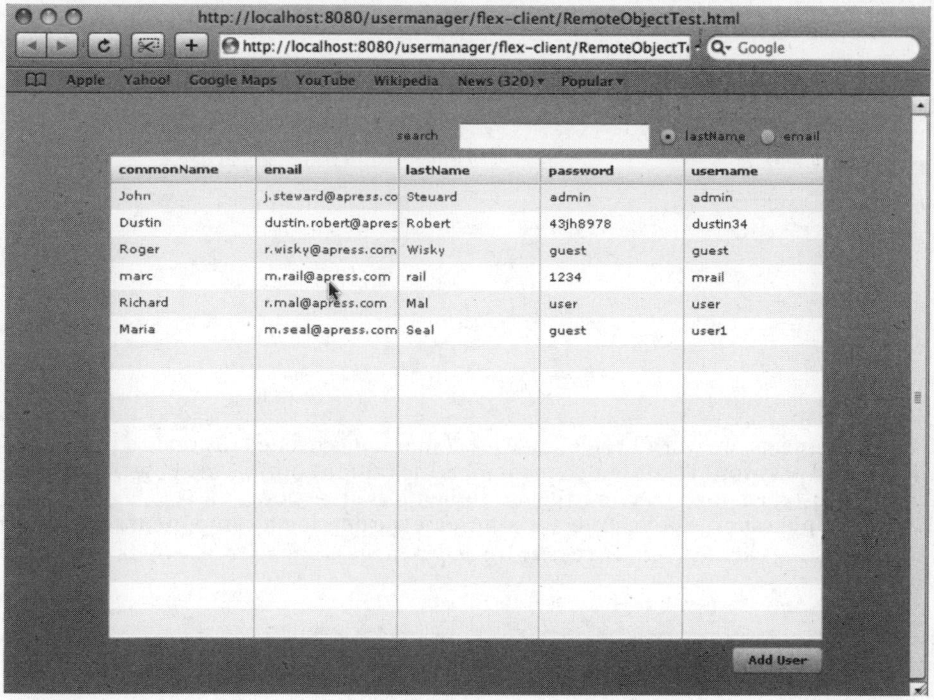

Figure 10-24. *The new user has been added*

At the moment everybody can see everything. All users can add new users and see the entire users list. But we need to protect the application by setting permissions on the views level. We will have a set of users with access to everything, and another set with access to only their details and nothing else.

Luckily, the archetype already comes with the Spring-security basic configuration. Essentially, when I created the archetype, I configured it with all Spring-security dependencies, and I added the `security.xml` configuration file into the `/src/main/webapp/WEB-INF` folder. The `security.xml` file contains the basic Spring-security XML definitions to protect the application using URL patterns and HTTP.

Since the server is ready to provide the security, we can concentrate on the Flex GUI.

Add a Login Form to Flex

In order to secure the Flex GUI, the first thing to do is to create the login form (from this point we will be referring to it as LoginPanel), following the UML created in the previous sections of this chapter, as you can see in Figure 10-15, the Flex LoginPanel is a composite component based on the `HBox` layout container. As with the other view classes, we will use MXML for the login component, to make it easier to design and maintain.

Remember, to extend a class using MXML, you have to start the class using the base class XML namespace. Because the login form MXML composite component is based on the `HBox` layout container, we have to start the MXML class with the `HBox` XML element as follows:

```
<?xml version="1.0" encoding="utf-8"?>
<mx:HBox
        xmlns:mx="http://www.adobe.com/2006/mxml"
        minWidth="400" minHeight="250"
        horizontalScrollPolicy="off" verticalScrollPolicy="off"
        horizontalAlign="center"
        verticalAlign="middle"
        >


        ...


</mx:HBox>
```

Within the HBox XML elements, we will add all of the Flex components needed to create a panel containing the username and password TextInput controls, plus the Button controls to allow the user to insert his login details and post them to the server to get an authenticated session.

In accordance with the application architecture, we will create the new login component called LoginPanel.mxml in the existing package com.apress.flexandjava.usermanager.view, as shown in Figure 10-25.

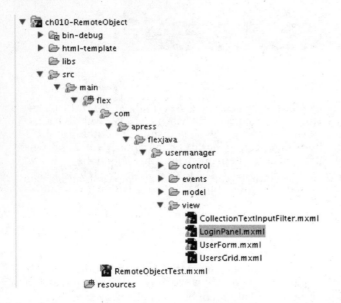

Figure 10-25. Showing the new Flex LoginPanel composite component just created.

Next we'll use the Flex Builder design tools to add all of the components, dragging them from the components explorer into the LoginPanel design area (see Figure 10-26).

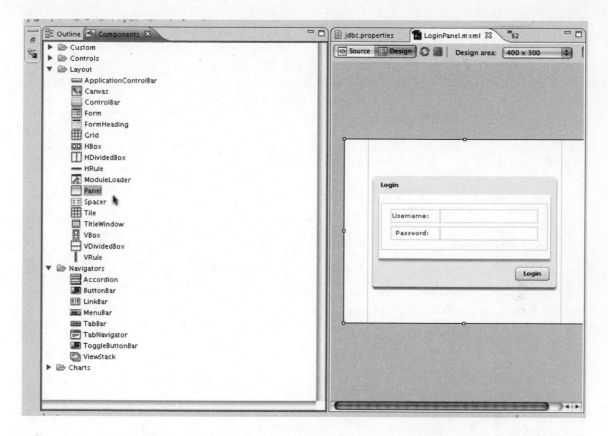

Figure 10-26. *Showing the Flex Builder components explorer and the LoginPanel in design area view mode*

To set the `Panel` title, id, and the `TextInput` and `Button` labels and ids, you can use the Flex Builder properties explorer as shown in Figure 10-27, or you can switch back to the source view to manually add the component properties.

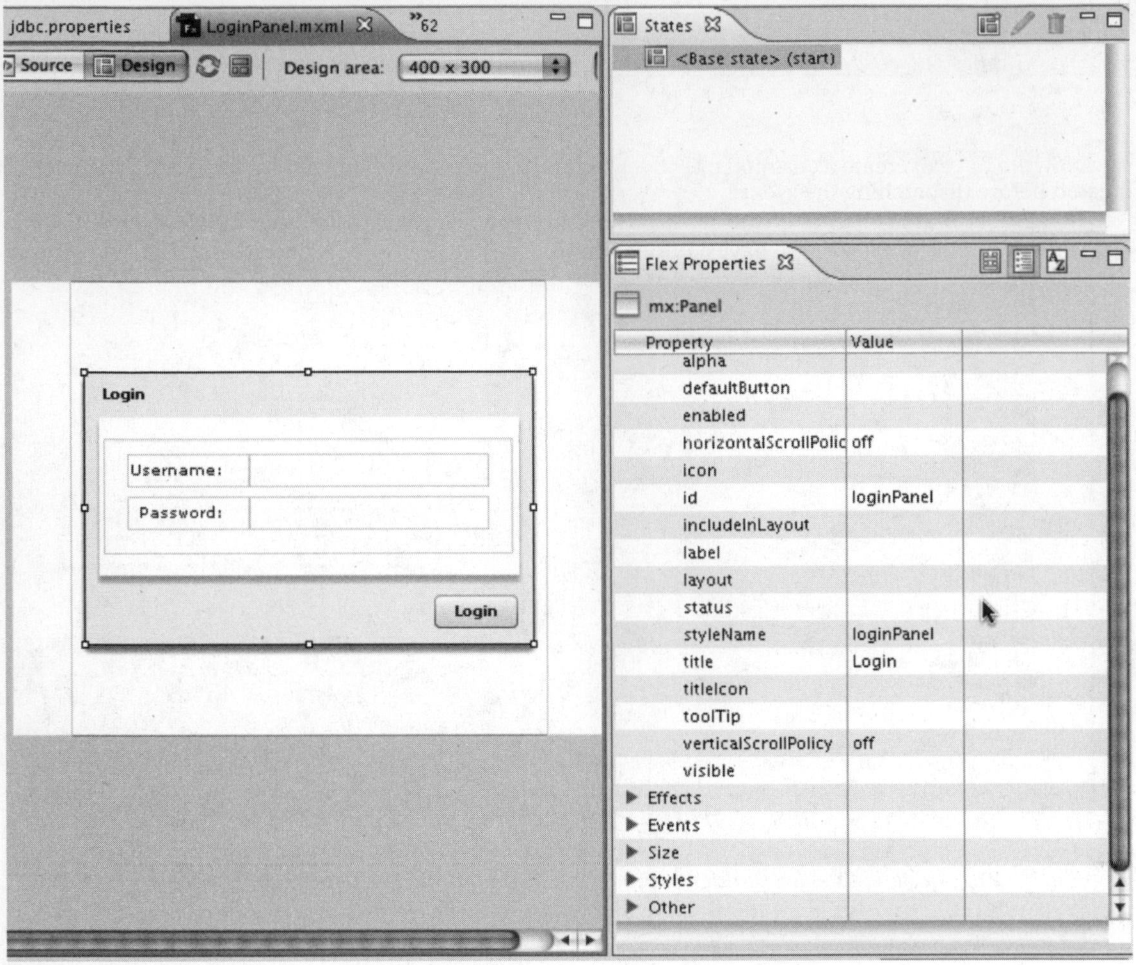

Figure 10-27. Showing the Flex Builder Flex Properties Explorer

Finally, we have to write the doLogin() method that will be executed when the login button is clicked. The doLogin() method will create a User entity containing the username and password inserted into the respective TextInput controls, and will dispatch a custom event called LoginEvent containing the just-created User entity.

```
public function doLogin() : void {
        var user : User = new User();
        user.username = username.text;
        user.password = password.text;
        var event : LoginEvent = new LoginEvent( user );
```

```
        dispatchEvent(event);
        isPending = true;
    }
```

Now we have to create a custom `LoginEvent` class in order to store a reference to the `User` entity created before dispatching the event.

Remember that in order to create an AS custom event, you have to extend the `flash.events.Event` class; in our scenario, we will also have a public property called `user` of type `User` that is needed to set the User entity reference in the custom event instance as follows:

```
public class LoginEvent extends Event
{
        public static const LOGIN_EVENT : String = "loginEvent";

        public var user : User;

        public function LoginEvent(u:User){
                super(LOGIN_EVENT, true);
                user = u;
        }

}
```

We will create our custom event in a package that doesn't exist yet—`com.apress.flexandjava.usermanager.events`—so first let's create the folder `events` within the `com/apress/flexandjava/usermanager` folder. Then we can create the `LoginEvent` AS class:

```
package com.apress.flexjava.usermanager.events
{
        import com.apress.flexjava.usermanager.model.User;

        import flash.events.Event;

        public class LoginEvent extends Event
        {
                public static const LOGIN_EVENT : String = "loginEvent";

                public var user : User;

                public function LoginEvent(u:User){
                        super(LOGIN_EVENT, true);
```

```
                        user = u;
            }


    }
}
```

At this point, when you click on the form login button, the `LoginEvent` is dispatched, but there are no objects listening for it, so nothing really happens. Now we need to post the username and password to the server in order to process the authentication. To do that we have to:

- Add to the controller the code necessary to create the view that contains the `LoginPanel` container

- Listen for the `LoginEvent` custom event

- Execute the call to the server using the `HTTPService` component when the `LoginEvent` is caught.

When you create an instance of the `LoginEvent` custom event, you set the event attribute `bubbles` equal to `true`. Because we dispatch the event from within the `LoginPanel` class, we can't set the listener for this event in our `UserControlImpl` controller, where we have defined the service to call the server authentication process, because both the `LoginPanel` and `UserControlImpl` objects don't have references to each other. By setting the custom event `bubble` property to `true,` we ensure that the `Event` is bubbled up through the direct ancestor that is our main view containing the `LoginPanel` component.

To call the service methods added to our controller, we have to create a reference to the main view in the controller itself, so that we can add the event listener to the view directly within the controller.

```
public function UserControlImpl(userModel : UserModel, view : DisplayObject){
        model = userModel;
        service = getUserService();
        view.addEventListener(LoginEvent.LOGIN_EVENT, sendLoginRequest);
}
```

Unfortunately, in Chapter 9's usermanager example we didn't have any view reference in the controller, so we have to make some changes to both the `UserControlImpl` and the Application `RemoteObjectTest` classes.

This listing shows in bold the changes that we have to make to the Flex Application file (mine is called `RemoteObjectTest.mxml`):

```
public function init():void{
            model = new UserModelImpl();
            control = new UserControlImpl(model, this);
    }
```

This listing shows in bold the changes that we have to make to the userControlImpl implementation class:

```
public function UserControlImpl(userModel : UserModel, view : DisplayObject){
        model = userModel;
        service = getUserService();
        view.addEventListener(LoginEvent.LOGIN_EVENT, sendLoginRequest);
}
```

As you can see, the changes are very few. We added the view argument of type DisplayObject into the UserControlImpl constructor and changed its instantiation by adding the view instance (this). By doing this, we make the view listen for the LoginEvent and execute the call to the server (sendLoginRequest) when the LoginEvent is dispatched.

Now we have to add the remote service component in order to post the username and password to our server application and get back the user roles. To do this, first we have to define the channel we are going to use to communicate to the server, then we have to send the username and password to the server to get the authentication.

To define a channel, we simply add a few lines of code to the getUserService() method:

```
  private function getUserService() : RemoteObject {
                var service : RemoteObject = new RemoteObject(USER_SERVICE);
                var cs:ChannelSet = new ChannelSet();
                var amfChannel:Channel = new AMFChannel("my-amf",
                "/usermanager/messagebroker/amf");
                cs.addChannel(amfChannel);
                service.channelSet = cs;
                service.addEventListener("fault", handleFault);
                return service;
    }
```

As you can see, I added a ChannelSet containing the AmfChannel. Then I set the ChannelSet to our service.

Now we have to create the sendLoginRequest method that is triggered when the LoginEvent event is dispatched. The sendLoginRequest function will retrieve the service instance and will use its channelSet login API to send the username and password to the server. Then it will handle the result or the fault event within the AsyncResponder added to the token.

```
var token : AsyncToken = service.channelSet.login(event.user.username,
event.user.password);
token.addResponder(new AsyncResponder(getLoginResult, handleFault));
model.currentUsername = event.user.username;
```

Next we have to implement the service result handler to get the `authorities` array returned by the server and set it in the Flex GUI model; then we need to change the `workFlowState` model property, to set the screen that the user is allowed to see, depending on the authorities set in the `ResultEvent` object returned by the server.

```
private function getLoginResult(event:ResultEvent, token:Object = null):void{
    model.roles = new ArrayCollection(event.result.authorities);
    if (event.result.authorities.indexOf(UserModelImpl.ROLE_ADMIN) >= 0) {
        model.workFlowState = UserModelImpl.WINDOW_LIST_USERS;
        model.isAdmin = true;
        getUsers();
    } else if (event.result.authorities.indexOf(UserModelImpl.ROLE_USERS) >= 0) {
        model.isUser = true;
        model.workFlowState = UserModelImpl.WINDOW_USER_FORM;
        getUserByUsername(model.currentUsername);
    } else {
        Alert.show(BAD_CREDENTIALS);
    }
}
```

As this listing shows, first we set the authorities in the model, then we set the view depending on the roles found into the array retuned by the server. To do that, we have to add the `WINDOW_LOGIN_FORM` public static constant to our `UserImplModel` model, and change the default value of the `workFlowState` property from `WINDOW_LIST_USERS` to `WINDOW_LOGIN_FORM`. This means that when we load the application, the default screen will be the login form, not the users list anymore.

So we add the following to the model:

```
public static const WINDOW_LOGIN_FORM : uint = 2;
```

Next, we change from:

```
public var workFlowState : uint = WINDOW_LIST_USERS
```

to:

```
public var workFlowState : uint = WINDOW_LOGIN_FORM;
```

Finally, we add the roles of type `ArrayCollection` into our model as follows:

```
public var roles : ArrayCollection
```

That's it. Here's the complete code of the entire Login GUI process:

UserControl.as

```
package com.apress.flexjava.usermanager.control
{
        import com.apress.flexjava.usermanager.model.User;

        public interface UserControl
        {
                function addUser(user:User) : void;

                function updateUser(user:User) : void;

                function getUsers() : void;

                function getUserByUsername(username:String) : void;
        }
}
```

UserControlImpl.as

```
package com.apress.flexjava.usermanager.control
{
        import com.apress.flexjava.usermanager.events.LoginEvent;
        import com.apress.flexjava.usermanager.model.User;
        import com.apress.flexjava.usermanager.model.UserModel;
        import com.apress.flexjava.usermanager.model.UserModelImpl;

        import flash.display.DisplayObject;

        import mx.collections.ArrayCollection;
        import mx.controls.Alert;
        import mx.messaging.Channel;
        import mx.messaging.ChannelSet;
        import mx.messaging.channels.AMFChannel;
        import mx.rpc.AsyncResponder;
        import mx.rpc.AsyncToken;
        import mx.rpc.events.FaultEvent;
        import mx.rpc.events.ResultEvent;
        import mx.rpc.remoting.RemoteObject;

        public class UserControlImpl implements UserControl
        {
```

```
            private var model : UserModel;

            private var service   : RemoteObject;

            public static const USER_SERVICE : String = "userService";

            private const BAD_CREDENTIALS : String = "Bad credentials";

            public function UserControlImpl(userModel : UserModel, view :
DisplayObject){
                    model = userModel;
                    service = getUserService();
                    view.addEventListener(LoginEvent.LOGIN_EVENT,
sendLoginRequest);
                    service.doLogout();
            }

            public function addUser(user:User) : void{
                    service.addEventListener("result", addUserResult);
                    service.addUser(user);
            }

            public function updateUser(user:User) : void{
                    service.addEventListener("result", updateUserResult);
                    service.updateUser(user);
            }

            public function getUsers() : void{
                    service.addEventListener("result", getUsersResult);
                    service.getUsers();
            }

            public function getUserByUsername(username:String) : void{
                    service.addEventListener("result",
getUserByUsernameResult);
                    service.getUserByUsername(username);
            }

            private function sendLoginRequest(event:LoginEvent) : void{
```

```
                            var token : AsyncToken =
service.channelSet.login(event.user.username, event.user.password);
                        token.addResponder(new AsyncResponder(getLoginResult,
handleFault));
                        model.currentUsername = event.user.username;
                }

                private function getUserService() : RemoteObject {
                        var service : RemoteObject = new
RemoteObject(USER_SERVICE);
                        var cs:ChannelSet = new ChannelSet();
                var customChannel:Channel = new AMFChannel("my-amf",
"/usermanager/messagebroker/amf");
                cs.addChannel(customChannel);
                service.channelSet = cs;
                        service.addEventListener("fault", handleFault);
                        return service;
                }


                private function addUserResult(event:ResultEvent):void{
                        model.usersCollection = event.result as ArrayCollection;
                }

                private function getUsersResult(event:ResultEvent):void{
                        model.usersCollection = event.result as ArrayCollection;
                }

                private function getUserByUsernameResult(event:ResultEvent):void{
                        model.authenticatedUser = event.result as User;
                }

                private function updateUserResult(event:ResultEvent):void{
                        model.authenticatedUser = event.result as User;
                        Alert.show("User updated");
                }

                private function getLoginResult(event:ResultEvent, token:Object =
null):void{
                        model.roles = new
ArrayCollection(event.result.authorities);
```

```
                            if
(event.result.authorities.indexOf(UserModelImpl.ROLE_ADMIN) >= 0) {
                                model.workFlowState -
UserModelImpl.WINDOW_LIST_USERS;
                                model.isAdmin = true;
                                getUsers();
                        } else if
(event.result.authorities.indexOf(UserModelImpl.ROLE_USERS) >= 0) {
                                model.isUser = true;
                                model.workFlowState =
UserModelImpl.WINDOW_USER_FORM;
                                getUserByUsername(model.currentUsername);
                        } else {
                                Alert.show(BAD_CREDENTIALS);
                        }
                }

                private function handleFault(event:FaultEvent, token:Object =
null):void{
                        Alert.show(event.fault.message);
                }


        }
}
```

LoginEvent.as

```
package com.apress.flexjava.usermanager.events
{
        import com.apress.flexjava.usermanager.model.User;

        import flash.events.Event;

        public class LoginEvent extends Event
        {
                public static const LOGIN_EVENT : String = "loginEvent";

                public var user : User;

                public function LoginEvent(u:User){
```

```
                        super(LOGIN_EVENT, true);
                        user = u;
            }


        }
}
```

UserModel.as

```
package com.apress.flexjava.usermanager.model
{
        import flash.events.IEventDispatcher;

        import mx.collections.ArrayCollection;

        [Bindable]
        public interface UserModel extends IEventDispatcher
        {
                function set usersCollection(users : ArrayCollection) : void;

        function get usersCollection() : ArrayCollection;

        function set workFlowState(value : uint) : void;

        function get workFlowState() : uint;

        function set roles(value : ArrayCollection) : void;

        function get roles() : ArrayCollection;

        function set currentUsername(value : String) : void;

        function get currentUsername() : String;

        function set authenticatedUser(value : User) : void;

        function get authenticatedUser() : User;

        function set isAdmin(value : Boolean) : void;
```

```
        function get isAdmin() : Boolean;

        function set isUser(value : Boolean) : void;

        function get isUser() : Boolean;




    }
}
```

UserModelImpl.as

```
package com.apress.flexjava.usermanager.model
{
        import flash.events.EventDispatcher;

        import mx.collections.ArrayCollection;

        [Bindable]
        public class UserModelImpl extends EventDispatcher implements UserModel
        {
                private var _usersCollection : ArrayCollection;

                private var _workFlowState : uint = WINDOW_LOGIN_FORM;

                private var _roles : ArrayCollection;

                private var _currentUsername : String;

                private var _authenticatedUser : User;

                        private var _isAdmin : Boolean = false;

                        public var _isUser : Boolean = false;

                        public function set usersCollection(value :
ArrayCollection) : void{
                                _usersCollection = value;
                        }
```

```
public function get usersCollection() : ArrayCollection{
        return _usersCollection;
}

public function set workFlowState(value : uint) : void{
        _workFlowState = value;
}

public function get workFlowState() : uint{
        return _workFlowState;
}

public function set roles(value : ArrayCollection) : void{
        _roles = value;
}

public function get roles() : ArrayCollection{
        return _roles;
}

public function set currentUsername(value : String) : void{
        _currentUsername = value;
}

public function get currentUsername() : String{
        return _currentUsername;
}

public function set authenticatedUser(value : User) : void{
        _authenticatedUser = value;
}

public function get authenticatedUser() : User{
        return _authenticatedUser;
}

public function set isAdmin(value : Boolean) : void{
        _isAdmin = value;
}
```

```
                        public function get isAdmin() : Boolean{
                              return _isAdmin;
                        }

                        public function set isUser(value : Boolean) : void{
                              _isUser = value;
                        }

                        public function get isUser() : Boolean{
                              return _isUser;
                        }

                        public static const WINDOW_LIST_USERS : uint = 1;

                        public static const WINDOW_USER_FORM : uint = 2;

                        public static const WINDOW_LOGIN_FORM : uint = 0;

                        public static const ROLE_ADMIN : String = "ROLE_ADMIN";

                        public static const ROLE_USERS : String = "ROLE_USERS";

                        public static const ROLE_GUEST : String = "ROLE_GUEST";

                        public static const ROLE_ANONYMOUS : String =
"ROLE_ANONYMOUS";

              }
}
```

LoginPanel.mxml

```
<?xml version="1.0" encoding="utf-8"?>
<mx:HBox
        xmlns:mx="http://www.adobe.com/2006/mxml"
        minWidth="400" minHeight="250"
        horizontalScrollPolicy="off" verticalScrollPolicy="off"
        horizontalAlign="center"
        verticalAlign="middle"
        >
```

```
<mx:Spacer height="100%" width="100%"/>
<mx:Panel
        id="loginPanel"
        title="Login"
        width="300" height="180"
        horizontalScrollPolicy="off" verticalScrollPolicy="off"
        horizontalAlign="center"
        verticalAlign="middle"
        styleName="loginPanel"
        >
                <mx:Form id="loginForm" styleName="loginForm" paddingTop="10">
                        <mx:FormItem label="Username: ">
                                                <mx:TextInput id="username"
enter="doLogin()"/>
                        </mx:FormItem>

                        <mx:FormItem label="Password: ">
                                                <mx:TextInput id="password"
displayAsPassword="true" enter="doLogin()"/>
                        </mx:FormItem>

                </mx:Form>
                <mx:ControlBar horizontalAlign="right">
                                        <mx:Button label="Login" enabled="{ !isPending }"
click="doLogin()" />
                </mx:ControlBar>
</mx:Panel>
<mx:Spacer height="100%" width="100%"/>

<mx:Script>
                <![CDATA[
                        import com.apress.flexjava.usermanager.model.User;
                        import com.apress.flexjava.usermanager.events.LoginEvent;

                        private var isPending : Boolean = false;

                        public function doLogin() : void {
                                        var user : User = new User();
                                        user.username = username.text;
```

```
                                       user.password = password.text;
                                       var event : LoginEvent = new LoginEvent(
user );

                                       dispatchEvent(event);
                                       isPending = true;

                       }

               ]]>
               </mx:Script>
</mx:HBox>
```

RemoteObjectTest.mxml

```
<?xml version="1.0" encoding="utf-8"?>
<mx:Application xmlns:mx="http://www.adobe.com/2006/mxml"
                               xmlns:view="com.apress.flexjava.usermanager.view.*"
                               layout="horizontal"
                               creationComplete="init()"
                               horizontalAlign="center"
                               verticalAlign="middle">
     <mx:ViewStack id="viewStack" selectedIndex="{model.workFlowState}">
             <view:LoginPanel />
             <mx:Panel  horizontalAlign="right" paddingTop="10">
                    <mx:HBox>
                            <mx:FormItem label="search">
                                     <view:CollectionTextInputFilter
tabIndex="1"

               collection="{model.usersCollection}"

               columnSearchable="{columnNameToSearch}" />
                                    </mx:FormItem>
                                    <mx:RadioButtonGroup id="searchMethodGroup"
itemClick="handleSearchMethod(event)"/>
                            <mx:RadioButton tabEnabled="true" tabIndex="2"
label="lastName" selected="true" groupName="searchMethodGroup"/>
                            <mx:RadioButton tabEnabled="true" tabIndex="3"
label="email" groupName="searchMethodGroup" />
                            </mx:HBox>
                        <view:UsersGrid dataProvider="{model.usersCollection}"
width="100%" height="100%" />
```

```
                    <mx:ControlBar width="100%">
                            <mx:Button label="Add User"
click="{model.workFlowState = UserModelImpl.WINDOW_USER_FORM}" />
                    </mx:ControlBar>
              </mx:Panel>
              <mx:Panel  horizontalAlign="center" verticalAlign="middle">
                       <view:UserForm id="userForm"
user="{model.authenticatedUser}" />
                       <mx:ControlBar width="100%">
                            <mx:Button label="Back" click="{model.workFlowState
= UserModelImpl.WINDOW_LIST_USERS}" visible="{model.isAdmin}" />
                            <mx:Button label="Save"
click="{control.addUser(userForm.user);model.workFlowState =
UserModelImpl.WINDOW_LIST_USERS}" visible="{model.isAdmin}" />
                            <mx:Button label="Update"
click="{control.updateUser(userForm.user);}" visible="{model.isUser}" />
                       </mx:ControlBar>
              </mx:Panel>
       </mx:ViewStack>
       <mx:Script>
              <![CDATA[
                     import
com.apress.flexjava.usermanager.control.UserControlImpl;
                     import com.apress.flexjava.usermanager.control.UserControl;
                     import com.apress.flexjava.usermanager.model.UserModel;
                     import mx.events.ItemClickEvent;
                     import mx.collections.ArrayCollection;
                     import com.apress.flexjava.usermanager.model.User;
                     import com.apress.flexjava.usermanager.model.UserModelImpl;

                     [Bindable]
                     private var columnNameToSearch : String = "lastName";

                     [Bindable]
                     private var model : UserModel;

                     [Bindable]
                     private var control : UserControl;

                     public function init():void{
                     model = new UserModelImpl();
```

413

```
                        control = new UserControlImpl(model,this);
                        }

                        private function
                        handleSearchMethod(event:ItemClickEvent):void {
                        columnNameToSearch = event.currentTarget.selectedValue as
                        String;
                        }
                ]]>
        </mx:Script>
</mx:Application>
```

Now you can run the server, compile the Flex GUI, and try to login as administrator and then as a user to see the differences.

Summary

In this chapter we saw how to create a Flex-Spring-Hibernate project using the Flex-Spring-Hibernate Maven archetype. The archetype created the entire project directory structure containing all of the Spring, Hibernate, and BlazeDS configuration and properties files. It also added all packages usually needed for this kind of application using the MVC and DAO patterns. The archetype also configured the security using http Spring security and the database as the authentication provider.

On the Flex GUI side, we copied the Chapter 9 RemoteObject example, making a few changes to implement security, such as the login form and permissions on the different views of the application itself.

With this example, I tried to cover the most important aspects of Flex-Spring-Hibernate-Maven development. You can reuse the same archetype to start you own project, and you'll see how your developer productivity will quickly increase.

Java and Flex let you create amazing applications using proper object-oriented languages and the latest software engineering, making you not just a better developer but also a better software engineer.

Index

■ G

■H

■I

■J

You Need the Companion eBook

Your purchase of this book entitles you to buy the companion PDF-version eBook for only $10. Take the weightless companion with you anywhere.

We believe this Apress title will prove so indispensable that you'll want to carry it with you everywhere, which is why we are offering the companion eBook (in PDF format) for $10 to customers who purchase this book now. Convenient and fully searchable, the PDF version of any content-rich, page-heavy Apress book makes a valuable addition to your programming library. You can easily find and copy code—or perform examples by quickly toggling between instructions and the application. Even simultaneously tackling a donut, diet soda, and complex code becomes simplified with hands-free eBooks!

Once you purchase your book, getting the $10 companion eBook is simple:

❶ Visit **www.apress.com/promo/tendollars/**.

❷ Complete a basic registration form to receive a randomly generated question about this title.

❸ Answer the question correctly in 60 seconds, and you will receive a promotional code to redeem for the $10.00 eBook.

Apress®
THE EXPERT'S VOICE™

233 Spring Street, New York, NY 10013

Offer valid through 4/10.